The Temptress Voyages

The Temptress Voyages

Single-handed Passage

Temptress Returns

EDWARD ALLCARD

Lodestar Books

Single-handed Passage
first published 1950 by Putnam & Co. Ltd.
Temptress Returns
first published 1952 by Putnam & Co. Ltd.

This combined edition published 2022 by
Lodestar Books
71 Boveney Road, London, SE23 3NL, United Kingdom

lodestarbooks.com

A CIP catalogue record for this book
is available from the British Library

ISBN 978-1-907206-57-3

Typeset by Lodestar Books in Adobe Jenson Pro

Printed in the UK by CPI Books

All papers used by Lodestar Books
are sourced responsibly

MIX
Paper from
responsible sources
FSC® C171272

Publisher's Note

Our sole source for the photos in this book has been to scan from copies of the first editions, and this can result in poor image quality, in the form of an overlaid screen pattern. Unfortunately this cannot economically be detected before the book is printed. Please excuse any examples which have occurred.

CONTENTS

Temptress Drawings

Single-handed Passage
9

Temptress Returns
167

Beaufort Scale of Wind Force

Glossary

Temptress Lines

PARTICULARS

LOA	34ft 6in
LWL	31ft 6in
Beam	10ft 4in
Draft	6ft 8in
Displacement	14 tons
Weight of iron keel	3.64 tons

FEET

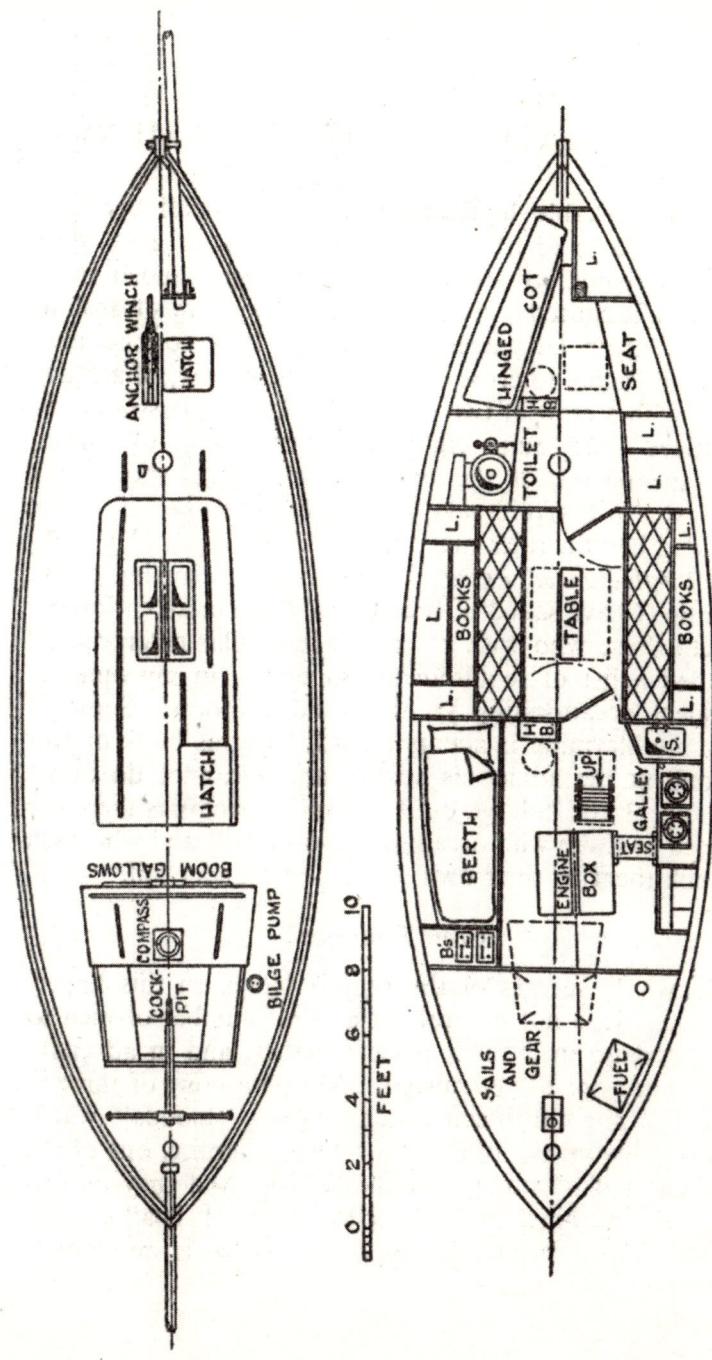

Temptress — Deck Plan and Accommodation Plan
Water tanks, twenty-five gallons each, are under the saloon berths

Single-handed Passage

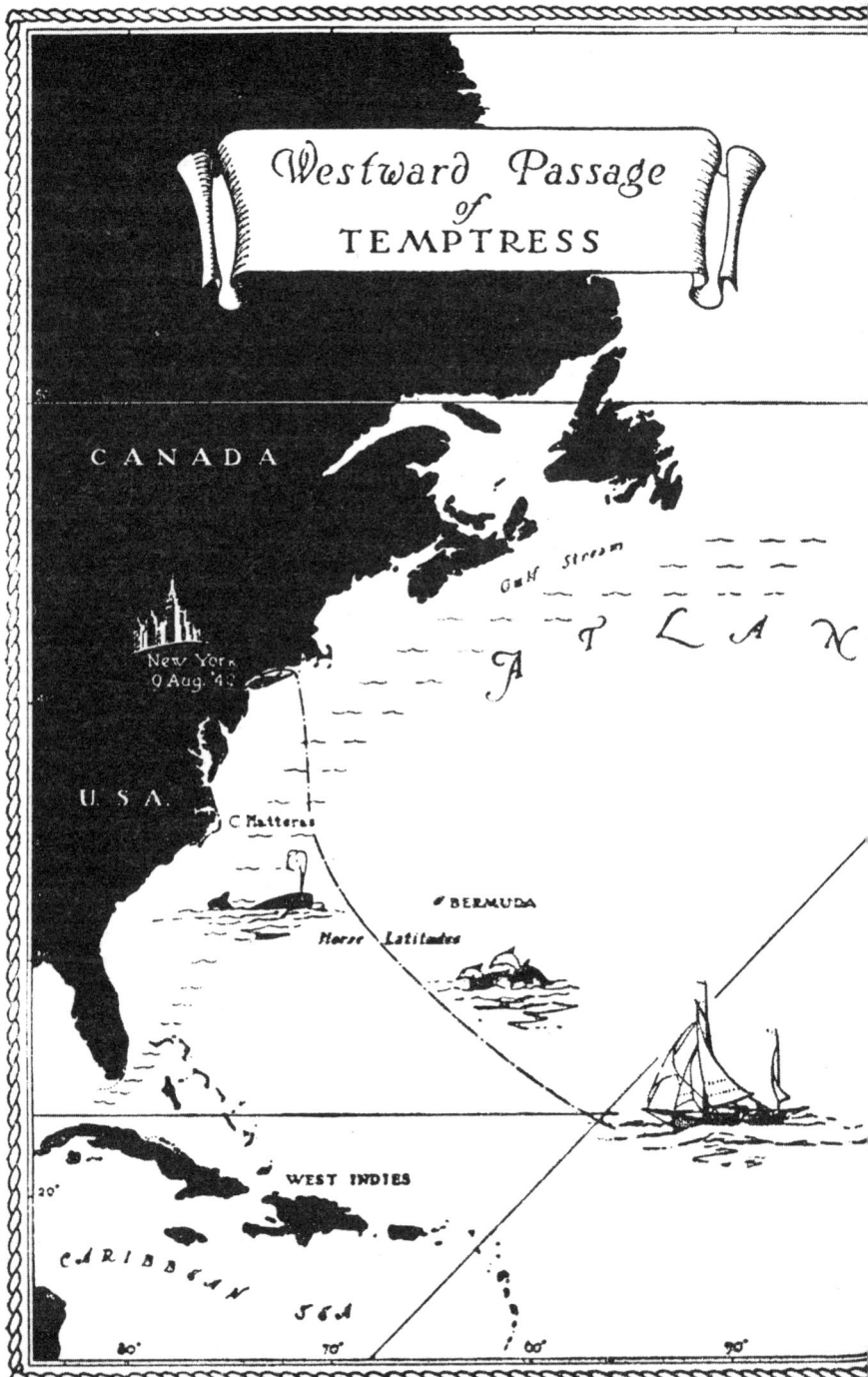

Westward Passage
of
TEMPTRESS

CANADA

Gulf Stream

ATLAN

New York
9 Aug. '49

U.S.A.

C. Hatteras

BERMUDA

Horse Latitudes

WEST INDIES

20°

CARIBBEAN

SEA

80°   70°   60°   90°

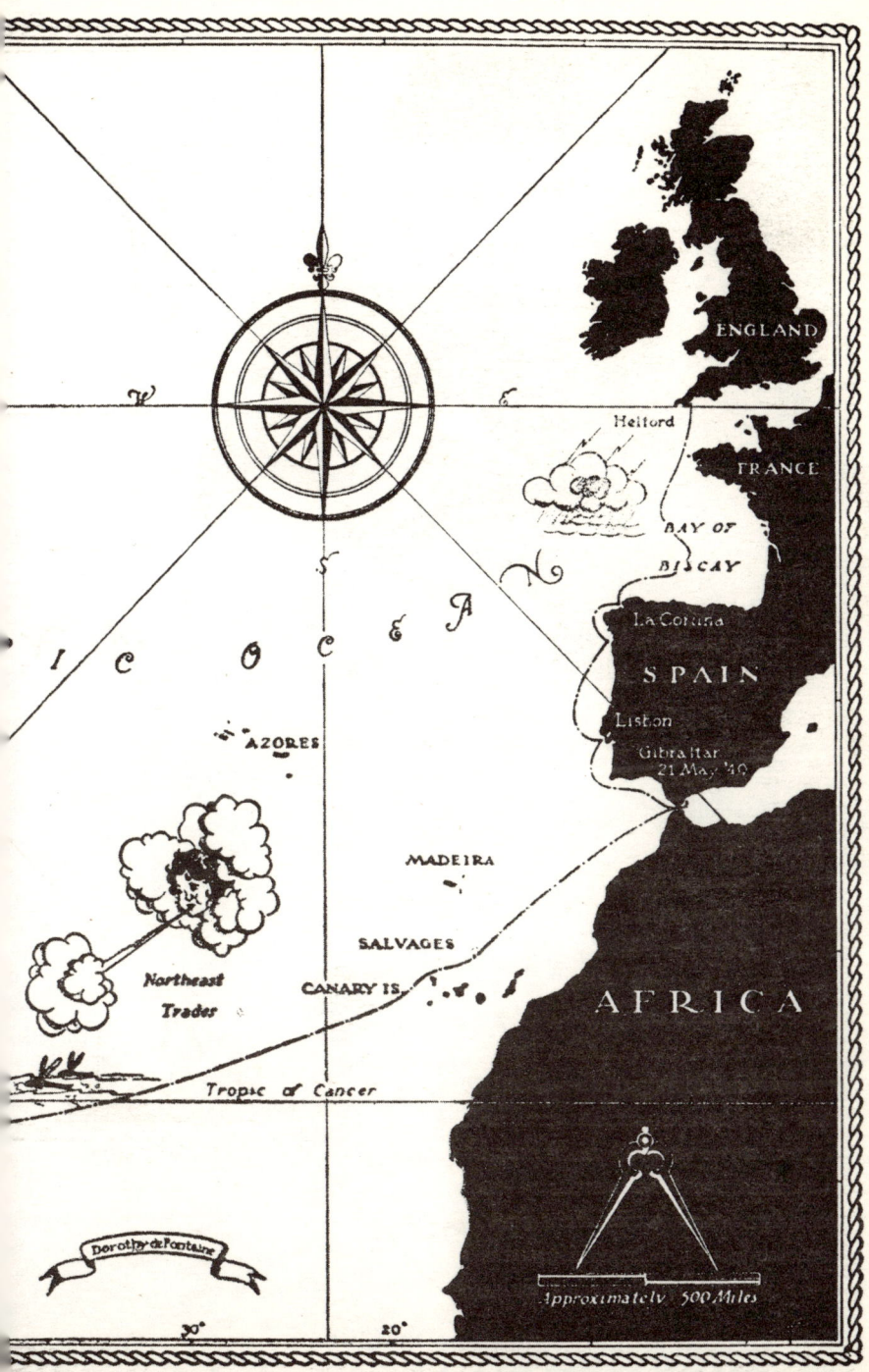

ENGLAND

Helford

FRANCE

BAY OF
BISCAY

La Coruña

SPAIN

Lisbon

Gibraltar
21 May '49

AZORES

MADEIRA

SALVAGES

Northeast
Trades

CANARY IS.

AFRICA

Tropic of Cancer

N A T L A N T I C   O C E A N

Dorothy de Fontaine

Approximately 500 Miles

30°   20°

I

ENGLAND

The evening of August 27th, 1948, was cold, and so muffled up was I with oilskins and a towel round my neck that it was with some effort that I twisted round in the cockpit to gaze astern. The once friendly land of Cornwall was already but a thin grey line, and was dropping fast as *Temptress* lurched over the waves sent tumbling down the Channel before an easterly breeze. It was my departure from England.

Settling myself more comfortably at the kicking tiller I sighed and said out loud, 'Well, I'm off once more, and will not turn back this time.' Not that I was feeling particularly brave, nor had I yet gained confidence in the boat. Indeed, she had only become mine a few months previously, and this was her first season afloat for ten years. Perhaps it was a bit foolhardy setting off direct for Gibraltar, but it was comforting to know that the French port of Brest could be used as a bolt hole for the next two days if anything alarming happened. At least the boat had had a shakedown cruise up Channel from Dartmouth to the Solent and back to Falmouth and Helford before setting forth on the ocean.

Morale had not been improved by the failure of my first attempt to reach Gibraltar the previous winter in the twenty-ton cutter *Content*. Setting forth from Penzance at the end of November, I had waltzed into a series of biting gales. Various gear had carried away, including the metal tiller jaws. This had left me with no means of steering for two and a half days, until repairs could be effected, during which time the loose rudder had worked open a seam in the lower part of the transom and water had poured in. Preferring to risk losing the yacht on a lee shore rather than foundering at sea, course had been set to return to England in a gale of wind with bad visibility. After a total of eight days at sea, the iron-bound coast had been picked up shockingly close, but I managed to scramble into some sort of shelter and anchor near Newlyn, too exhausted to enter harbour, and with the boat rolling ominously with tons of water in the bilges. I had had just enough strength to pump out before collapsing on my bunk.

Repairs had taken some time in Penzance. Then finally, in January, a friend and I bounced round the Lizard at night, over a terrific swell, with the rigging lit up by the eerie blue light of St. Elmo's Fire. After stops at Falmouth and Plymouth I found myself at Dartmouth, where I was fated to come across my present boat, *Temptress*. She was smaller than *Content* and was really far better suited for the single-hander.

And now here I was, with *Temptress* throbbing with life as the wake twirled out astern. All the troubles of the shore were over. No more lists. No more exasperating delays caused by others. No, there would be no turning back again. I had another look round the horizon. The curtain of night had begun to fall. The only sign of land was a faint fan of light reflected in the clouds from the last lighthouse in my country. To the north three black silhouettes pin-pointed with light showed where three trawlers were plying their trade. To the south there was nothing foreign to the sea, just the sharp line of the horizon and a multitude of jet-black clouds low in the heavens.

I secured the tiller line and stood up to stamp my feet. Eight bells and all's well on the first night at sea. There was just enough light to read the log. Reaching for the logbook in the forward cockpit locker, I wrote, 'Log 24. Wind E., Force 3.10/10ths cloud.' My pencil remained poised over the 'Remarks' column, but the jerking of my fishing line prevented any redundant words, and there was no time lost in hauling in a fine mackerel. What perfect timing for dinner! Thus prompted I immediately lowered the reaching staysail which I had carried all day, and hoisted the working one, which was backed to heave her to, and I thankfully left the windy deck to cook the fish over the Primus stove.

Things looked very snug in the cabin after the chill above, and I felt satisfied with my floating home. *Temptress* seemed perfect for the arduous duties that she would be asked to perform, and she was well worth all the financial difficulties that had been experienced when she had become mine. What a relief it had been when *Content* had been sold. For not only had I a better boat for the job, but was also in pocket, and therefore I had been able to buy a new mainsail and do various alterations to make *Temptress* safer for ocean travel. There were still many things to be done before the great Atlantic itself could be tackled, but these would have to wait until Gibraltar.

This is a suitable opportunity to describe *Temptress*. She is old enough, having been built in 1910 on the banks of the river Fal, above the famous port of Falmouth, at Calenick. She has a slightly rounded bow and pretty canoe stern, while a deepish forefoot and long straight keel make for steadiness on the helm. They built well in those days. Planking is of one-inch-thick pitch pine, copper fastened on grown oak frames, and my pride and joy are her scrubbed teak decks, 1½ inches thick.

Her lengths are 34 feet over-all by 29 feet on the waterline. Her beam of 10 feet with 6-foot draught, allied with ample freeboard, give a little ship which for her size is remarkably stiff, able, and dry.

She is rigged as a yawl, with gaff mainsail and marconi mizzen, and following the English practice, she carries two headsails, the jib set flying on the bowsprit but with roller furling gear, and the forestaysail, sliding up and down the forestay on permanent hanks. My only light-weather sail is a huge reaching staysail which is hoisted on the working sail halyards after clipping it to the forestay. Although the mainsail was new, all the other sails were of doubtful age, but I counted on them to carry me to Gibraltar. The staysail looked reasonable, but the various jibs seemed to be in somewhat shaky condition. The mainsail was of almost too heavy canvas, hand sewn throughout by Harris of Appledore, and it could be expected to stand up to any weather that the hull could. I do not like messing about shifting to storm trysail in a gale of wind, and consider that a trysail should merely be used as a spare mainsail if the big sail is damaged or unbent for some reason. Roller reefing was fitted and promised to be a great trouble saver. Most of the rigging was installed in the standard manner and not specially adapted to single-handed sailing. There had been no time to clean up the somewhat haphazard leads of the running rigging; in fact it could not be said that the boat was properly fitted out. There had scarcely been time to make the hull seaworthy and install the gear. Even the actual launch had been alarming, for two of us had been unable to keep her afloat, and had beached her just in time to save the engine and generator from being submerged. There had been much shaking of heads among the locals, many of whom never expected to see me again—they may still be right.

The little engine was in first-class order, as it had been overhauled the previous winter. It was a seven-horsepower petrol/paraffin engine which could propel the boat at four knots in still water, and it had a large generator driven off the flywheel to charge a heavy-duty battery of twelve volts.

Another job which had been done just before *Temptress* became mine was the renewal of keel bolts. The iron keel, which weighs about four tons, was therefore not likely to part company with the boat—always an alarming possibility. But there were many other things that could happen to a thirty-eight-year-old boat that had been on shore for ten years, and I was not looking forward to any gales.

The accommodation on board is surprising. Right aft there is the small self-bailing cockpit with the handy ready-use locker at the fore end. There is a narrow bridge deck across the ship between the low doghouse and the main cabin top, so there is no direct access below from the cockpit. The main hatch leads down to the after compartment, which has the galley to starboard with its two Primus stoves in gimbals, and my bunk opposite. Forward of this is the saloon, with a settee on each side, lockers behind, and shelves above for books. There is a bulkhead and door at each end of the saloon, and forward is a long fo'c'sle containing a hinged cot, a pump W.C. which is partitioned off and is used as a sail locker at sea, and innumerable lockers where provisions are stowed. There is standing headroom aft of the fo'c'sle.

Fresh water is carried in two galvanised tanks under the settees, each tank holding twenty-five gallons. Using loose containers, sixty-two gallons in all can be carried, which is enough for one hundred and twenty days. The stainless-steel sink in the galley has two pumps, one for fresh water from the tanks, and one which leads direct from the sea. Needless to say, salt water is used whenever possible, but that is no hardship now there are on the market really good sea-water soaps which can be whipped up into a soft lather even in salt water.

The engine is encased in a mahogany box abaft the ladder leading down from the main hatch, and is so installed that the sides of the box are portable, making for very easy access. There are two fuel tanks, and, with loose containers, there is a capacity of twenty-four gallons, enough for a range of about two hundred and fifty miles. The tank holding the petrol is at deck level inside the cockpit doghouse, which considerably reduces risk of fire.

A patent folding propeller is situated on the starboard quarter, and thus the area of the rudder is not reduced by the usual aperture, which makes for good manoeuvrability. Often with quick action of the helm, I have averted a premature gybe, which otherwise might not have been possible.

In spite of my fears, there seemed to be a good chance of crossing the Bay of Biscay before the next batch of bad weather came on. The barometer was high and steady, and the radio gave no indication of a change from 'fine with easterly winds.'

On that first night at sea, after my supper of fresh mackerel, I took the helm until one o'clock in the morning, when the wind lightened and a fine rain began to fall. The night was as black as the inside of a cow. No lights had been seen for three hours, which showed we were in a deserted part of the 'Approaches.' A chance for rest.

The paraffin navigation lights had already been lit, but before going below I switched on a powerful all-round electric lantern, and after a good look round I retired to my bunk out of the cold and wet, leaving the boat hove to and kicking about unsteadily in the short swell.

2

FAIR WINDS...

The morning of the second day was the sort which makes one feel how wonderful it is to have been born in this complicated world. The whole atmosphere seemed to have been washed clean by the night's rain and dew, and there was a sparkling freshness in the air which matched to perfection the fair scene of soft blue sky and reflected glory of the sea.

A good night's rest and mackerel fishcakes for breakfast further encouraged this feeling. It was with a light heart and a hum in my throat that I let the staysail draw, as the bowsprit swung round to the correct course of south-south-west. The bow wave began its chuckle as the log, after being stilled through the early hours, again resumed its lazy rotation. The boat continued her unsteady way towards the golden climes.

I would have been better employed in setting the reaching staysail than in sitting hunched up over the helm with my thoughts busy on the pleasure of the seascape and my position on the chart. But my mood suddenly changed to action as I felt a sharp nip on the inside of my thigh. I straightened up, giving an explosive 'Damn'—a search proved the worst. I had evidently picked up a flea at Helford on my last dash ashore to a telephone booth, when I had phoned Falmouth to tell the crew of *Content*, who were also bound for Gibraltar, that I was off. I just could not find the confounded animal, and it was to give me intense annoyance in the days to come.

The history of the day gradually unfolded. My first noon sight agreed closely to the dead-reckoning position. The log completed its first rotation. The odd steamer came and went. In the afternoon the wind, after faltering for some time, eased away, backing to the north-east, and the gear, losing the control of bellying canvas, began its harsh tune of rattling blocks, snatching spars, and kicking rudder.

An evening breeze calmed the jarring gear as a red sun set in a school of bulbous clouds. Two hours later the loom of the shore lights of France could plainly be seen. There could be no sleep for me that night, for we were approaching one of the busiest highways of the world. The sighing wind pushed *Temptress* along, with the mast swaying sublimely against the background of the starry firmament. At midnight the direct light of Ushant beckoned across the black water, but its bearing altered painfully as the sands of night ran lethargically through the glass of time.

By dawn, after seventeen hours at the tiller, and safe in the knowledge that ships could avoid me, I hove to and moved stiffly below. I kicked off my sea boots and attempted to beat some life into my chilled feet before rolling fully dressed into my bunk. A deep sigh of pleasure escaped me as warmth slowly crept into my frigid limbs and I sank into the new-found luxury of sleep.

Ignorance is bliss. Just how much of those three hours of sleep was in dense fog I could not know. In fact, it seemed bright enough when I awoke, with even the suggestion of sunlight filtering through the portholes. But the groans of sirens made me uneasy, and I scrambled out to see thick fog-banks which were now on the point of being dispersed by the strengthening sun. I felt a sense of guilt at some neglect of duty—sleeping soundly in dawn mist only a few miles off Ushant.

While the stove hissed busily away under the kettle I turned on the radio to listen to the shipping forecast, which stated: 'Anticyclone situated south of British Isles. Biscay... light to moderate variable winds. Good visibility.' Sure enough, the mist was soon eaten up, so that by eight o'clock the Isles of Ushant were clearly visible. After a hearty breakfast I pumped out the bilges and picked up course to the south-west, the boat heeling to a rippling breeze still from the east.

The morn throbbed with activity and interest. The land, the queue of ships of all shapes and sizes, the action on *Temptress* in setting light-weather canvas, the passing of a basking shark, and the live movement of the boat itself provided a stirring kaleidoscope. Even the wind fitted into the variegated picture, for its force rose and fell continually, while shifting a point or two around the cardinal East, and this kept me busy trimming sail.

By the afternoon we were in the Bay of Biscay in amazingly smooth water, as France now acted as a bulwark against the varletry of waves coming from the east; however, there was now an immense swell setting in from the west, too big to affect a small boat but denoting some gale far away.

Shipping grew denser, providing a sense of company, for although I did not actually feel lonely, I had not been at sea long enough to acclimatise myself to the sudden change. My track lay inside the shipping lane, so when the wind veered towards the south-east, making it possible for the boat to sail herself, I snatched another few hours of sleep, coming on deck again just in time to see a most wonderful sunset, breath-taking in its magnitude, and in which the whole sky took part. Though it looked fine enough and the barometer remained steady, there was that colossal swell to remind one of bad weather.

Thus the whole of the second night was spent in slipping quietly through the darkness, under working canvas, peacefully asleep, to the accompaniment of a steady chuckle at the bow. The hours slid gracefully by till the grey of dawn hardened the familiar outlines, and, lo, it was daylight once more and possible to roll into my welcome bunk and surrender to sleep.

After a fitful slumber I was awakened by the rise of temperature as the sun poured down its rays, and by the singing through the hull of the ship's propeller. Blinking sleep out of my eyes I stuck my head out of the hatch to see a steamer coming up astern. She was riding high, water pouring out of her scuppers as the deck was being hosed down. She wallowed past close to port, and men lining her bulwarks waved flutteringly in Continental fashion. Her propeller thumped round like a gigantic egg whisk. There was one solitary man leaning on the rail right aft above the name *Sainte Mere Eglise*. He made no sign, but for a long time after, this black dot of a man could be seen as if magnified in the distance.

Although course was at right angles to the light south-east wind, *Temptress* merely nibbled at the miles, and my time was spent peeling potatoes, cooking, and watching various ships through the binoculars. It was pleasant enough in the hot sun but we were getting nowhere, and there was the feeling that this was a fattening up for some bad weather. There was still the big swell, and on the radio I had picked up a gale warning for North Ireland, far enough away at the moment, but the secondary depressions which would follow it would probably affect the Bay and produce head winds into the bargain.

Course was altered to work out farther to the westward, and by the afternoon an occasional vessel was seen to the east. The most picturesque sight of the day was a large yawl, presumably a French fisherman, although in the light wind he was under power only, with no headsails set. He passed about six miles away, sharply silhouetted against the grey haze which circled the horizon.

The next ship, very smart-looking with white topsides over green boot-top, came racing up astern. I thought, 'This is a good chance to signal Lloyds.' My father had already arranged that Lloyds would advise him whenever I was reported. I plugged in my Aldis signalling lamp and started to attack as he came into close range—but without the slightest effect. He foamed by and showed me his ample stern marked *Heferite Alexandria*, and was soon two miles away. Then, just as I had consigned him and his wash to the devil, I was surprised to see him give a sharp turn and head straight for me, then proceed to hurtle by at about seventeen knots, damned close, with an officer screaming something at me through a megaphone from the bridge. I rushed to close the hatches as a wall of water burst on the topsides, then shook my head and waved him away. He gave another sweeping turn back to his course and was soon hull down. What a lash-up!

The wind lightened further and veered to the south, and later petered out altogether, leaving an oily calm, with the gear slatting about cruelly in the swell. The sky, which had been clear all day, became scratched with mare's tails soaring up in extravagant arabesques from the westward, while the boat lay stagnant in the hole she had made for herself in the morning sea. Lord! What progress! Fourth day out and only sixty miles from Ushant. Cape Finisterre was still three hundred and twenty miles away, and the radio was beginning to mention the possibility of south-west winds. To ease the strain on the gear, the headsails were lowered and mainsheet pinned right in.

The sunset veiled by cirrus was like a most delicate painting. The immense glassy swells gave grotesque reflections, twisting up the clouds and distorting the sun until it had been swallowed in the lower cloud strata suspended above the wavering horizon. Twilight endured to its limit before planets and stars shyly twinkled forth and darkness took over from the radiance of day.

Such was the prologue to the most magical night I have ever experienced. To make some progress, before midnight the engine was started, and the stem cut through the smooth sheets of water, while a luminous golden wake sparkled out astern. The reflection of the stars and absence of horizon completely nullified sense of balance or relative positions of sea and sky. *Temptress* appeared to be gliding through space itself among the falling stars and meteors which were continually crossing the firmament. Every now and again mysterious lights blazed at varying depths, while no less than four huge islands of phosphorescent light appeared ahead and floated by as the bow wave clove into and murdered a million and more reflections on the glassy surface.

At two o'clock in the morning, when it was obvious that we were well outside the steamer track, the fuel was turned off. The engine seemed to run an age before all was silence, and another age before the way was off the ship and she remained floating among the stars, while I sought such a mundane necessity as sleep.

3

...AND FOUL

The dawn of the last day of August met me red and cold on my early morning survey. There was still no wind and it was pleasant to creep back into my warmed blankets, where I lay luxuriously dozing until fully awakened by the foreign ripple of wavelets along the waterline. The new breeze was, as I had feared, from the southwest. Thus after being four days on the port tack, *Temptress* had quietly put herself about.

After my good sleep I felt very fit, especially after preparing a hearty breakfast, and I was put into an exceptionally good humour first by the smooth operation of my insides (it is extraordinary how interested one gets in one's stomach at sea), and second by the successful swatting of an athletic fly which had been annoying me for some days. It only needed the despatching of that confounded flea in order for me to have complete mental harmony.

It was a change to see the log rotating as the boat chopped along to the south, close-hauled on a wind which hardened and veered as the day unfolded. The shipping forecast spoke of a gale to the north of Ireland, and north-west winds for Biscay, which seemed right enough, as the huge swell had gradually changed direction to that quarter. *Temptress* was already on the edge of the deep sounding line and it was almost certain that we would get clear of north Biscay without experiencing a gale. By nightfall the occasional steamer was seen to the west, as the track had been re-crossed during the day. Later it suddenly came on thick, and the wind began to hum in the rigging. It appeared that my 'yachting' was over.

As rain started to beat a tattoo on my oilskins I hove to, rolled down the equivalent of one reef in the mainsail, and went below to cook my dinner of fishcakes from a mackerel captured on the spinner during the day. The barometer was anxiously consulted, but it heartened me by its steadiness, showing that the gale up north was not coming any nearer.

During a restless night the sea attacked us from varying directions as the wind veered, and a yellow dawn showed an unnecessarily knobbled ocean, with wind from the north-west. I made haste to trim the sails and get cracking at an impressive pace on the correct course, with the log humming round at a speed not previously achieved. Everything seemed set for a great day's run. It was indeed an exciting morning, for it was a continual 'Sail O!' as one after the other French tunnymen were sighted creaming along under full sail, thereby shaming me into unrolling to full mainsail myself. The fourth one approached from dead ahead and came rushing past close to port, enabling me to get an impressive photograph, while exchanging courtesies of the sea.

Having backed the staysail to let her jog along by herself while lunch was being eaten, I regained the helm to find that the wind threatened to ease away. Sure enough, in two hours it did, with swell increased, leaving horrible conditions. The gear, of course, started to crash about, and the snatch of the mainsheet transferring its thrust to the gaff jaws bent the mast like a bow in an alarming fashion. The mainmast was obviously too thin for the job, and it continued to give me increasing anxiety as it wobbled and switched aloft.

In spite of the exasperating conditions a reasonably accurate sight was obtained and fix plotted on chart. We were over 2590 fathoms from the earth beneath and 160 miles from Estaca Point, the nearest bit of Spain.

The evening brought respite from the jerking and wrenching of gear as the swell lengthened and a new draught from the west steadied the ship.

A small coaster approached from the south-west, and her crew gave me a cheery wave. Just then I heard a buzzing in the sky and was surprised to see an aeroplane high overhead. Below the western horizon it was a common sight to see wisps of smoke, which at once gave my position and showed that we were clear of the main steamer track. Thus I could look forward to a better rest in the coming night.

The sky was almost clear as the sun dropped towards the horizon. Then a tiny cloud crossing the scarlet orb produced the curious effect of a mouth which gave a realistic leer before the spinning world tipped the horizon up and blotted them both from view.

The quiet night nevertheless held an air of expectancy which the falling barometer did nothing to dispel. There was also that huge swell, which was ominous in its constancy and magnitude. It was true, I tried to tell myself, that we were in the south of the Bay and there had been a good sunset, but it was with some uneasiness that I gave my final look round before turning in for a fitful sleep.

Thursday, September 2nd, is a day I will not easily forget. It started for me at 0655 with a shipping forecast which made me thoughtful… 'Gale warning. Severe locally. Including W. Channel. Depression west of Ireland heading E.S.E.'

The bare details of the weather conditions written in the logbook show nothing of the heavy oppressiveness of the atmosphere nor of the gently smouldering hate that seemed to be pregnant in the black clouds covering the sky. The swell was gigantic but merely ruffled by a light and undecided breeze from the south-west.

The best thing to do was to get as far south as possible before the storm affected my area, so, close-hauled on the starboard tack, I steered my craft over the hills and valleys of the sea. It was during one of my apprehensive looks around the horizon that I thought I saw a tiny splash of white astern. It vanished, then—yes—there it was again. An hour later my binoculars momentarily picked out the white hull and sails of what was undoubtedly a sailing yacht overhauling me. It was very cheering to have company. Later there was more, for a steam fishing boat was sighted to the west. He altered course and came towards me, looking like an immense marine spider, with rows of long tunny rods sprouting out of each side. He ran close. Spanish! My first contact.

All this time the wind was imperceptibly hardening, and the bow wave, which had started with a gentle cough, grew a flowing moustache as speed increased, until at noon it had all the commotion of a bone in its teeth. A new sea was by then scurrying over the top of the giant swells; even so, sail was not reduced, and under all plain canvas I drove her relentlessly south through the stampede of white horses and whirling spray.

In the early afternoon I pulled the staysail to weather and went below for a cold lunch. The barometer had fallen another tenth and jerked down further after a slight tap from the nail of my index finger. 'Well, it can miss me yet.' But things became worse up top, and I rolled down two turns of the boom before taking the helm and letting the staysail draw. The other yacht, to my surprise, had gone about and was standing off to the west. Half an hour later two more turns were taken in the main, but still the wind mounted and the sea did nothing to lag behind.

At five-thirty the weather really started to take its gloves off. A shocking combination of steep breaking seas and a mounting swell were being whipped up by a strong wind, throwing more and more dirt over the weather side, and the exceptional lurches would send solid water cascading along the lee deck. More sail reduction was necessary. The boat was once more hove to, the jib completely rolled up by the Wykeham Martin furling gear, and the mainsail was rolled down as far as it would go, so that the gaff jaws were only about six feet above the gooseneck of the boom. Then again to the helm and on we fled, away from the growing storm.

It was not till seven o'clock that I gave up all pretence that the depression would pass to the north. Never have I seen such obvious signs of an imminent gale. The former black clouds had merged into a uniform grey pall from horizon to horizon, through which a hazy sun with evil halo foretold the worst. The sea was rough and growing every moment, with crests beginning to claw threateningly down the advancing fronts of the waves. In the rigging the wind was tuning up like a band of performers ready for the curtain.

The last preparation was a wet and beastly job on the foredeck— the job of reefing the staysail and lashing the clew to the weather shrouds. No more could be done. I made my way aft on hands and knees, not in itself a posture calculated to improve morale, and dropped below. It was up to *Temptress* to look after herself, hove to as she was under close-reefed main and reefed staysail.

A Biscay gale warning came through on the French radio. There was no escape. As darkness fell it seemed very lonely out there, and a tightening feeling seized the pit of my stomach. It was still warm and dry below, but as I braced myself on the galley seat and meditatively stirred some thickening porridge with a wooden spoon, unsettling thoughts kept repeating themselves in my head. The boat was untested and not ready for a gale... she was thirty-eight years old and had not been afloat for ten years... were the fastenings all right?... would a plank spring?... would she spew her caulking? And so it went. At each heavy lurch I whispered, 'Damn.' Still the note of the wind shrilled higher, and still the barometer fell.

By midnight the battle was fully on, with wind screaming in the rigging and driving capstan bars of rain through the wall of darkness. The logbook has a bare statement: 'Wind gale force. Rain. Very rough.' I rolled into my bunk, not expecting to sleep, but fatigue had its due, and the minutes that seemed like hours when awake were more than offset by the odd hours of oblivion. Then the night was over.

I turned out at 0655 and could just hear the shipping forecast above the roar of the wind. 'North-west gale for Biscay.' There was no reason to doubt it. I hesitated to go on deck at first, then slid back the hatch enough for head and shoulders. The sight was stupendous and exceptionally impressive from that vantage point of sea level. It was blowing great guns, and a gigantic sea was piling Ossa on Pelion. When she was on the crests of the waves, the whole boat vibrated with the force of the wind, and then did a sickening plunge into the trough before being wrenched upwards like a lift, ready to be assaulted by the following mountains. The odd avalanche bursting on the topsides did not encourage me to remain long in admiring the pretty view, and the hatch was soon closed.

Although the galley was up to windward it was not difficult to boil some water for Bovril and then make the inevitable breakfast bowl of porridge, into which I gave unenthusiastic digs with the spoon.

The day dragged on as I lay in my bunk, unable to sleep any more, with nothing to do except wait... wait... wait... The barometer steadied during the morning, then tended to rise. Just after noon the mass of cloud began to break up until, looking out of a port, it was possible to see a square of blue, enough, indeed, to patch a Dutchman's trousers, which foretold correctly the complete clearing of the sky.

With the sun out and lighting up the dazzling white crests, the great Atlantic storm waves were appalling in their size. The wind shifted to north-west and at once built up a new set of seas. The afternoon conditions showed a further deterioration, with wind, sea, and motion worse. At nightfall there was no sign of improvement, and I could only hope that the gear would stand up. The very thought of having to do anything complicated on deck in the raging darkness was enough to scare one. After a feeble dinner I could do nothing except retire again to my bunk and allow the minutes to pass with desperate slowness. Thank heaven I was not sea-sick.

During the night I still could not sleep, nor could I stop myself from repeatedly looking at my watch. Several times I thought the confounded thing had stopped. The minute hand crept lethargically round, and the hour hand—oh, Lord! And nothing to listen to except that devilish wind screaming over the vessel. The only relief was when a freak sea broke at an inauspicious moment. There would be a moment's silence in the whoosh of tortured waves, a hiss of approaching water, a crash like gunfire as the liquid wall hurled the boat before it to leeward, a momentary silence—and then the roar of water pouring green over the entire vessel. I would stiffen in my bunk with my heart beating faster, then relax when the characteristic gurgle of water running through the scuppers heralded the end of *that* incident. Halfway through these delightful little experiences, which took place about once an hour, infuriating jets of water would squirt at me through the chinks in the hatch. Gradually the blankets became soaked, and the resulting stink did nothing to offset the foul atmosphere below. Somehow the night passed, but still the relentless wind howled out of the north-west and those monstrous waves swept disdainfully by. Jammed in the corner of the saloon, I twisted the switch of the radio and listened eagerly for the shipping forecast. Surely they would promise respite from this everlasting wind. The voice of the announcer came through. '... centre of the depression has reached the North Sea but has altered course to the *South*...' That was not much help. The almost unbearable monotony continued.

During the lurches to leeward, bilge water started to surge up the ship's side and bound back over the cabin flooring. A job to do! Judging a suitable moment, I opened the hatch, scrambled out to the cockpit, and rigged the bilge pump on the coaming. This was no mean pump. To begin with, the diameter of the barrel was four and a quarter inches, so one could put one's hand down to clear the bottom valve should it become fouled. But then it never did foul, for I had made several major modifications at Dartmouth, where it had first been a failure. These modifications surely would have shocked the original designer. It had been converted into 'the perfect pump' for the cost of fourpence! The whole of the natty brass bottom-valve assembly had been ruthlessly torn out with hammer, cold chisel, and hacksaw, and replaced with a block of wood with an adequate hole in it covered by an oiled leather flap, thus making it into a pump so powerful that it once brought up a nut and bolt! A child could use it, shifting half a gallon at each stroke, and on that stormy day it was no labour to pump out the twenty-five gallons of water in the bilges.

While pumping I kept a wary eye on the seas, and was able to reach safety below before one of the breaking giants smothered the vessel.

Then more waiting. Would that damned wind never cease?

In the late afternoon there was a bit of excitement. The boat gave a queer sort of twist, immediately followed by the flogging of canvas up forward. It seemed to be only a second before I was out of my bunk and on the foredeck, hanging on precariously to the bitts. The roller line of the jib had broken, the sail had set itself tearing the clew out and was in immediate peril of flogging itself into shreds. Muttering thanks for the English practice of having a bowsprit traveller, I let go the outhaul, cast off the halyards, and managed to get the somewhat ancient bit of muslin aboard without a single tear, and to lash it, a sodden mass, to the inboard end of the bowsprit. I just had time for an unseemly scramble aft and slammed the hatch over my head as a perfect sow of a sea swept the staggering yacht from end to end, tipping her over so far that it seemed impossible that things could stay in place below. But all was well. Later I paid another visit to the deck to clear the bilges before the third night of the gale commenced.

Darkness fell. The lack of exercise and the wretched waiting for things to change had put me in a state of mental and physical stagnation. With ill humour I rolled into my bunk, the only place one could stay with safety. It seemed an age since we had been properly making way. It was actually fifty-five hours. Conditions might have been worse, but by then I was past appreciating anything. However, the boat was standing up pretty well, probably better than I, and, of course, there was the comforting thought of ample searoom. So yet one more night of monotony and fitful dozing was on stage, and it was not made any more pleasant by the Helford flea, which had still escaped capture and was the cause of much bad language and exasperating but fruitless searches.

At midnight it seemed as bad as ever. The barometer, which had risen slightly the previous morning, had been steady for eleven hours, which agreed with the radio report that the storm centre was over Germany, thus keeping a uniform distance from me. Until the barometer rose, this thrice-damned wind would continue to afflict.

The first symptoms of a change came just after two o'clock in the morning. The shrill yelling of wind in the rigging dropped for a few seconds to a whistle before continuing with its nerve-wracking tune of destruction. Later there was another lull. The gale was beaten. It was wavering. Even in the squalls it seemed to lack that relentless power with which we had been assaulted for so long.

About an hour before the dawn I was rudely awakened from a doze by the terrific crash of tons of water pouring over the vessel. I sat up with wildly beating heart, sensing by the shattering noise that something had carried away on deck. However, a flashlight showed that binnacle and dinghy were still there. I stayed in the hatch for some time, letting the wind blow through my hair and breathing great gulps of clean sea air, for the foul atmosphere below could almost be bailed out with a bucket. There was still a strong breeze blowing; but one thing was certain—the gale was over. On sixty hours had it blown.

This was my ninth day at sea.

4

SPANISH WATERS

At eight o'clock on September 5th, there was merely a fresh breeze blowing, but still a filthy sea, the aftermath of the long-drawn-out gale. It needed a hot cup of coffee and some solid breakfast to snap me out of the mental and physical torpor brought on by my long period of inactivity.

Things were a mess on deck. The rigging screws of the topmast shrouds had slackened back, allowing the wires to dance about from the masthead. The main shrouds were all hanging in bights. The jib needed bolt rope restitching and a new clew. The starboard coaming of the cockpit had split for two feet. Most of the halyards and all sheet ends were trailing over the side. Everything was caked with salt. All the newly applied varnish had been completely washed off bowsprit and boomkin. In fact, there was a mess.

The first job was to clear the bilges of the odd twenty gallons therein, for she had undoubtedly started a leak somewhere. This was easy with my wonderful pump. The next job was to find out where I was, which was not so easy. Although the sky was overclouded the sun gave a veiled peep now and then, allowing me to take a chain of difficult sights, which agreed surprisingly well, considering the violent motion of the boat and the occasional glimpse of the horizon. A position was marked on the chart checking near enough with the somewhat vague dead reckoning kept during the gale. *Temptress* had done well in drifting to the south for only fifty miles. The intense mathematics of the morning was followed by a minor bout after the meridian altitude sight. The reeling cabin of a small yacht is not the best place for complicated calculations, but I felt pretty certain of my position.

A hearty lunch put me on the top of the world and gave me plenty of energy for repairing the jib with palm and needle, and generally unravelling the knitting on deck.

My big moment came when, with jib set, full staysail hoisted, and more mainsail unrolled, the ship was once more in sound and seamanlike condition. Sail was trimmed to make the boat bucket along on her course amongst the disorderly seas which, not controlled by sufficient wind, had fallen out of their uniform ranks. *Temptress* had been hove to for seventy-two hours. She had passed her test.

Two curlews appeared from the south to have a look at us, thus giving the first indication of the approach to land.

At dusk, cold rain set in from the west, encouraging me to heave to for a watch below. At midnight the sea had definitely eased. In a very much better frame of mind than that of the previous evenings, I rolled into my bunk with the pleasurable anticipation of making a landfall on the morrow.

Boom... boom... booooom. I had hardly collected my scrambled thoughts from a dream about watching two small ships coming into harbour, when again a siren blared. In an instant my head was out of the hatch; I was blinded by a blaze of lights alongside and met by concentrated yelling from an incredible number of Spaniards who lined the bulwarks of what was presumably a fishing boat stopped only a few yards away. I waved, then turned to go below, only to be attacked by a renewed outburst of shouting. Heavens knew what all the fuss was about; however, I climbed into the cockpit, let the staysail draw, put the helm up to sail clear, and made way towards the south for about half a mile. At that they seemed satisfied.

For some time after heaving to again, I gazed at their lights to see if they were going to approach me, then went below to cook a predawn breakfast. Although I had not worn oilskins or jersey on deck it had been quite warm, which convinced me that land would be seen not far off when daylight broke.

The overcast sky made it a very slow dawn, but as soon as it was decently light, it was with a twinge of excitement that I slid open the hatch. Then 'Land O,' I cried. There it was—Spain! A dark blue, uneven line set amidst black clouds, unidentifiable and possibly not

more than fifteen miles off. Several fishing boats were in sight, dancing about in the confused sea, while I did my best to drive the boat to
windward. After two hours the wind backed and freshened to Force
5, making the sea even more exasperating, and producing very wet
sailing indeed. All the time it was extremely black to west and north,
giving warning of the rain squalls which followed.

There was another excitement with one of the Spanish tunnymen, which made a slow circle round me. When he was close I
pointed and shouted, 'Punta Estaca? Punta Estaca?' I could not have
caused a greater commotion if I had dropped a bomb amongst them.
After a hesitation of uncomprehension the great light dawned, and
a thousand arms seemed to appear and gesticulate wildly in any
direction between west and south. At the same time there was an
indescribable bedlam of gratuitous advice. Evidently Estaca Point
had not yet been passed, but it was hardly what Norie would have
classed as a 'fix.'

A lot of things began to happen to the weather soon after midday. The wind, without any warning, dropped; so did torrential rain,
and in half an hour the sea was as flat as my singing. We must have
been in the centre of a miniature depression, for two hours later we
were bowling along under full sail before a beautiful fair wind from
the north-east, with decks rapidly drying off. Land around Estaca
Point was at last identified. I had made a perfect landfall.

The day was rounded off by a dark and forbidding evening with a
stormy-looking sunset. There could be no question of sleep because
of the number of craft about, but this turned out to be the start of
a wonderful night's sail. By midnight the wind had hauled round to
the east, and while we rushed along with a phosphorescent wake
streaming out astern I took repeated cross bearings from shore lights
winking in the darkness. In spite of the initial head wind and calm,
fifty-four miles had been made good, and still we kept going.

The wind continued to veer until the boat, running on the starboard gybe, was sailing more and more by the lee while being forced
northward of the true course. Instead of gybing I hauled in the
mainsheet, luffed up, wended ship, and left her hove to long enough
for me to make some hot coffee. By that time the wind was south-

east and had freshened to a really smart breeze, so when sheets were trimmed and course picked up to pass the finger of land, *Temptress*, under full sail, staggered off through the darkness like an express train, with a triumphant 'whoosh whoosh' as she sank deep into the troughs of the sharp beam sea.

The six o'clock dawn was wild and spectacular. The great Cape Ortegal was beginning to affect the steadiness of the wind, until an hour and a half later I was completely becalmed under its lee. Bathed in the early sun the rugged pink and mauve coast of Spain reared fantastically above me, while all round me the sea boiled with marine life. Fishes large and small were leaping out of the dark blue water, while birds above swooped down to snatch minor prey missed by the hunters below.

Beautiful as the scene was, I was getting nowhere, apart from being tired after twenty-four hours at the helm. The ocean currents which met there caused quite a jabble of water, making the boat dance, with spars and gear snatching and rattling about in an exceptionally irritating manner. The mainsail was lowered to save chafe, and I went below. After breakfast there was still no wind, but, the tide setting on shore, I decided to start the engine and motor out to sea a few miles to get some sleep. This was not to be, for a jet of water came out of the compression cocks. The engine was full of sea-water, from the bottom of the sump to the spark plugs. It must have entered through the exhaust pipe before the cock was turned off at the onset of the gale. Alarmed that the corrosion might permanently harm the engine, which probably would have to be stripped right down, I gave up the idea of carrying on direct for Gibraltar and planned to enter the nearest port, which I rather vaguely ascertained from the small scale chart to be Cedeira.

This is the start of a terrible confession. *I never managed to find Cedeira*, a fact it is hoped the reader will keep secret, for it was a shameful thing for someone of my assumed experience. My excuse is that one rocky headland is much like another, but, vast heaving…

Meanwhile the sun grew very hot, the currents were setting towards the rocks, and every now and again a breeze would set in from the open sea, prompting me to set the mainsail, but before the sails had been correctly trimmed it would die away. Three times I hoisted that confounded chunk of canvas, getting more and more angry, until at last to my great relief, the horizon to the north-west grew dark with ripples. Soon the creases were smoothed out of the sails, and the boat slipped along in blessed peace.

It was perfect, skimming sublimely past that wonderful coast in the glorious sunlight, and I was in a happy frame of mind when course was altered to round the point which was expected to mark the north side of the gap in the hedge leading to Cedeira. But horrors! The cliffs continued to stretch away into the mauve mist. Feverish examination of the chart did not help much, except to show that I might be anywhere within fifteen miles of it. Distances, too, were very deceptive in that visibility. An hour later an opening appeared and I sailed in past some unpleasant rocks, but it soon became obvious that it was getting too narrow and I gybed to pick my way out of the reefs to the safety of open water.

There was nothing to do except carry on down the coast till something happened. It was impossible to miss the entrance. Finally, in the late afternoon, a wide opening was made out ahead and it was just possible to distinguish the loom of land on the starboard bow. But surely, I thought, this was far too wide for Cedeira. Then it dawned on me like a ton of bricks that this was Coruña Bay, miles away to the south. Well, so much the better. Course was altered to cross the enormous bay towards La Coruña, which should be sheltered from the big Atlantic swell which rolled up astern, sending *Temptress* along in a series of rushes as she cut through the water before a falling breeze.

There was quite a fleet of white sails gliding round off the town, but outside them, with scarcely any steerage way, was a very shaky outfit evidently heading out to sea. I levelled my glasses at her and said out loud, 'Well, I'm damned,' recognising her at once as the *Our Girls*, which had been anchored near me in Helford River and which had set off three days before me. With a crew of three she had been able to keep going twenty-four hours every day and had missed the gale. This was just as well, what with her gaping topside seams, a match stick for a mast, and her twin engines, one of which had a vital part broken, while the other had had the propeller stolen by the simple method of sawing off the outboard part of the propeller shaft. With her extra sail area *Temptress* had no difficulty in sailing up to them, and after exchanging pleasantries I hardened in all sheets and lay close-hauled for the town quay, succeeding, to my surprise, in beating some of the local craft which had come out to escort me in. Though, it must be said, their helmsmanship was-not of the best.

The wind was blowing along the quay, on which an enormous crowd was standing. I approached at right angles, dropped the mainsail when still well clear, rolled up the jib, then at the last moment cast off the halyards of the staysail and luffed up alongside an ex-Fairmile B-class yacht which was flying the British ensign. No one came on deck in answer to my hail of '*Antonina*, ahoy', but the manoeuvre had been correctly judged, allowing me to leap aboard and moor my craft single-handed.

Hardly had I stowed the mizzen and cleared up on deck when a voice from the motor-yacht said, 'Hallo. Where have you come from?'

'Oh, Helford River, eleven days out.'

'Well, I'm damned! You must have been in that gale. They lost four tunnymen from here, you know. You must be tired. Come aboard for dinner.'

'Thanks very much.'

And I *was* tired, *and* hungry. For some reason I had not had a meal since breakfast, and had been almost continuously at the helm for over thirty-six hours.

I slept well that night.

5

SPAIN

It would have been easy to sleep the clock round that first night at La Coruña, but there was not the chance. A hail from Antonina, followed by the roar of her engines warming up, told that she was preparing to get under way for Vigo and the south.

Temptress was warped clear so that she lay alongside the quay itself, directly under the eyes of the crowd. This group of harbour bystanders forms one of the main features of the port, as far as yachtsmen are concerned. It has been stated: 'No work is done at La Coruña except by waiters.' Of course, this is one of those silly statements that so much annoy the locals, yet please the utterer. The rest of the population seems to be split into two sections, the part that sits drinking in the innumerable cafés, and the other part which stands on the quay, silently gazing down on any vessel moored there. This is not just a floating number of sightseers, but evidently a serious pastime.

One is tempted to imagine a typical gazer hurrying over his dress in the morning, rushing out of the house while pulling on his coat in case he should be late, then walking briskly down the quay to join the others already gathered there. By about nine o'clock there may be a hundred or more people who just stand, look, and hope for something to happen. Members of the *Antonina* outfit said they often felt a sense of guilt for putting on such a poor show; but the simplest thing was all that was required to amuse the crowd. For instance, if I should come on deck to empty the contents of the gash bucket over the side, a ripple of excitement would run through the multitude. And once when I pumped the bilges the crowd was literally standing six deep. Had I done anything extraordinary, like jumping up on deck wearing nothing but a wrist-watch and waving an empty gin bottle, they would surely have fainted with the thrill, and there would have been one almighty splash into the oily water. And that oil! But enough…

Before *Antonina* cast off, a couple of her crew came over to say good-bye, bringing with them a young Spanish lad, called Luis, whom they recommended me to take aboard. They said that for food, cigarettes, and a bed he had been a great help to them, and had proved (so they thought) scrupulously honest. They had found him very useful for looking after things if they were all ashore, as it was most unwise to leave a boat unattended. Even then they had lost their entire butter supply!

Luis came eagerly aboard. My Spanish grew quickly, and I did Luis well, feeding him better than my stores really allowed, giving him pocket money, cigarettes, and treating him as an equal. In fact, well enough, I thought, to prevent him deserting, tipping off the dock thieves as to my movements and where my valuables were kept, and organising the theft of my watch, fountain pen, and all the money I had on board. I turned in on that particular night in a blue frame of mind, but at the first peep of daylight I awoke with a flutter of apprehension as I saw the hatch above me wide open, whereas it had been closed the evening before. When the bare top of the engine case showed that all the clothes worn during the day, my naval rain-coat, and everything attainable from the hatch had been stolen, I was mentally sick and murderous at heart.

The clothes were old and did not matter so much. But the watch was a good one and my only means of navigation. It had cost twenty pounds in London, replacing a similar Omega which a bomb splinter had taken off my wrist during the war. I was fairly certain which of Luis' pals had pinched it, as he too had disappeared into the underworld. I told the fishermen that I would shoot him or put him in jail before leaving. From that time on a loaded revolver was always under my pillow, and had anyone come aboard during the night there would have been a nasty accident—a very nasty accident.

Luis made the mistake of revisiting the scene of his crime, but failed to keep hidden sufficiently and was nabbed by a fisherman, who brought him to me. I sent for the police and dragged him aboard. One can hit hard with the back of one's hand. He was handed over to the police a blubbering mess, only too eager to tell all about his elder partner. They got him within twenty-four hours, and, what is more, got my watch back. I consider myself lucky. The thief went to jail. He could consider himself lucky too.

Thieving from ships has been brought to a fine art in La Coruña. So beware, you mariners! This was the place where (so the story goes) a yachtsman was buying his own rope over the stern as another Spaniard was paying it out over the bows. Then there is the trick of securing to the bollards fine wires which are fastened to a ship's mooring lines, which are then stealthily cut as near to the ship as possible. When the vessel drifts off from the quay the remaining part of the moorings are cast off and dropped into the water where they sink to the bottom, from where they can be retrieved by means of the wires at a suitable opportunity.

Almost every boat that visits this outwardly beautiful town has its 'thief' story, and the sheer effrontery of these *hijos de perras* is only rivalled by that of the Indian who achieved fame by stealing a bed on which an Anglo-Indian colonel was sleeping.

Between the intervals of catching criminals and making fenders, which last no time against that abominable wall, jobs went ahead, such as sorting the engine, mending sails, and overhauling damage done by the gale. In spite of the amount of time wasted by many visits to the police, etc., in five days the boat was ready for sea. Two more days were allowed to pass, however, due to the unsuitable weather and the fact that I had developed an embarrassing complaint, no doubt brought on by the unaccustomed and highly seasoned Spanish food.

Interesting as my time had been, I was eager to get out to the safety of the open sea, to be able to sleep without the danger of being 'coshed,' and to be free from the attention of that wretched crowd. Luckily it had recently discovered a good counter attraction in the Italian square-rigged training ship *Amerigo Vespucci*, which was paying a short visit. The cheerfulness and seamanship of the Italian cadets in the boats was very impressive, and made me sorry that the British Admiralty could not consent to naval training in sail, surely the best body- and character-building sport in the world.

After *Antonina* had roared away on the first day, looking like the 'complete smuggler,' several yachts came and went. The *Viking* had been the cutter sighted in the Bay of Biscay, and we swapped lies about the gale. She was from Sweden initially, bound for South America. Instead, she set off back for Sweden, with the gift of some of my English charts, but still with no sextant aboard. On the fourth day a little steel schooner flying the Belgian flag and called *Ortac* tied up astern. They were a family concern which I was fated to meet again at sea off the south coast of Spain, and later in Tangier. Then there were three lads of different nationalities on a queer-looking motor-yacht from which they had sold the engines to buy a sailing vessel, then fitting out in the inner harbour. It looked a pretty slow business to me.

Incidentally, there was what appeared to be rather a nice yacht club almost opposite my berth, but if the members had the slightest interest in visiting foreign yachts they certainly did not show it. In fact, when I went along to the building after being there for a week, and asked a steward if he could show me where my two four-gallon water containers could be filled, he staggered me by saying that the president of the club was not there at that moment and that he would ask permission the following morning. In the end one of the lads off the motor-yacht filled them for me. This lack of hospitality from a local yacht club is very rare in Spain, and one usually hears enthusiastic accounts from visiting yachtsmen. This is especially so at Vigo, where they evidently put forth a special effort to please foreigners and make their stay as enjoyable as possible.

Naturally, all sorts of people came down to say Hallo, or rather, *Buenas dias*, ranging from the reporter of *El Ideal Gallego*, who took me out to lunch, to a little girl who could not have been more than seven years old, who came down at eleven o'clock at night and tried to persuade me to go with her to her 'house,' saying that as a boat *Temptress* was beautiful but could not be compared with Spanish *senoritas* (presumably for homework).

One interesting visitor was a naturalised American who was the brother of the so-called stowaway who left Spain in the motor fishing boat belonging to Dod Osborn on his unsuccessful attempt to cross the Atlantic. There were several stories circulating about Dod Osborn, originally of *Girl Pat* fame, but perhaps the less said the better, for I believe he is a bigger man than I.

As all my money had gone, I was reduced to selling tea and cigarettes to the local inhabitants in order to raise funds for fresh stores and a new sheath knife to replace the one lost with my clothes, now seemingly gone for good.

So it was on the morning of September 15th, exactly a quarter of an hour after the *Amerigo Vespucci* cast off, and after a week in port, that my revolver was unloaded, the engine started, and the first turns of the propeller drew *Temptress* away from the quay and the record crowd thereon. There was almost no wind in the harbour, but the cloud carry promised a fair wind outside.

After exchanging national courtesies with the military fort, we were soon plunging along into a head swell. By midday we were clear of the harbour and heading for Herminio Point under full sail, with a healthy breeze on the starboard beam. Ahead, already hull down, the *Amerigo Vespucci* showed a rectangle of grey canvas on the horizon, while overhead bulbous grey clouds covered the heavens as wind and sea increased below. It became oilskin weather and too much of a good thing. As the hours went by, first two turns, then two more, and then two more again were rolled up in the mainsail, while the boat fled its spectacular way through the rough water, and white-fanged crests were whipped up by half a gale. As the sky cleared, still the wind increased, until spume lifting from the turbulent surface denoted gale force. It was crazy sailing. We had done just forty miles in six hours when a steamer heading north altered course toward me. My ensign was still streaming as stiff as a board from the naked mizzenmast, and what with the weather being hardly ideal for small-boat sailing he probably expected trouble.

The ship came ploughing up the ocean dust, an impressive picture of ruthless power sedately pushing ten thousand tons of displacement casually up to windward. She came up to pass only a ship's length off, and the dark group of figures on the wings of the bridge separated out into individuals. Our aggregate speed was about twenty knots and we were soon overlapping. She was British, the *Register* of London. They gave a very hearty wave from the bridge, and when *Temptress* staggered along with decks awash, past her stern, above the whistling of the wind I heard a ragged cheer from the crew. Bless them all. It was very heartening. I waved furiously with my right hand, while keeping a careful eye on the waves hissing up astern, before turning back to the business on hand. It was blowing gale force out of a cloudless sky, and to reach the shelter of Camarinas Bay it would be necessary to gybe when past some outlying reefs, then weather the point on the south side of the entrance. Already light was failing. It was a delicate situation. If course were altered too soon, submerged rocks would rip the bottom open; if the alteration should be delayed, it would be impossible to weather the point, as there was too much wind and sea to beat to windward.

After a series of doubtful bearings the moment arrived. The gybe was hectic. The gale was brought on the port beam, and over the boat went, over... over... until topsides, bulwarks, then even the stanchions, log, and mainboom end were dragging through the water. Solid spray whirled up over the weather side to masthead height. The surface of the water was just a seething mass of white. My heart started to beat wildly with anxiety as to whether the point could be safely passed. I give a shiver now when thinking in retrospect of that wild sail in the dark, clawing desperately to windward of Punta de la Barca with its guardian rocks. If the wind had not given an occasional lull as the shelter of the north shore was reached, it could never have been done, but at last we were in the darkened bay and clear of the angry seas, with only a strong breeze blowing. It was a most exhilarating 'flog' up the bay until the lights of Camarinas were on the beam. I went forward to furl the jib, lower staysail, and then waited for her to come head to wind before dropping anchor in four fathoms. The slatting mainsail was lowered till, suddenly, all was peace. It had been a pretty adequate fifty-three-mile sail, finished off by that hair-raising scramble in the dark.

I was awakened by sunlight streaming through the portholes, but

wind still hummed shrilly in the rigging. During the night the anchor chain had rasped violently on the bobstay as the boat sheered
about from side to side. Doing that peculiar roll necessary to vacate
my bunk, I looked out of the hatch. What a wonderful sight was
unfolded before my eyes! The land, which had been but a black mass
in the darkness when sailing in, was now a colourful picture of dazzling beauty. Set in a deep blue cloudless sky, the bright early-morning sun was casting extravagant shadows on hillside and vale, while
beaches of golden sand contrasted to perfection the colours of the
steep lower slopes and the white-flecked blue of the jostling waters.
White houses of the town, set back from a tiny bay which formed
the fascinating harbour, actually enhanced Nature's picture. That
combination of sky, mountain, and sea left me without any doubt—I
was standing at Keats's 'magic casements opening on the foam,' and
Camarinas was the most beautiful bay I had ever seen.

Water had again got into the engine, so bad was the exhaust pipe lay-
out. It was obviously necessary to keep the valve always closed at sea.
The engine would be useless in an emergency, and this was one of
the reasons why *Temptress* stayed at anchor all that day, although the
moderate gale was fair. I did not feel like deliberately heading out to
sea with my whipping mast, and making port with a wind too strong
for one to tack can be a dangerous pastime. There were plenty of jobs
to do after the ship had been cleaned of the dirt from La Coruña,
and the day was well spent.

Two members of the Guardia Civil made a somewhat perilous
voyage out to see me, and we had as friendly a chat as my smattering
of Spanish allowed. One question took me a long time to understand.
It was made more difficult because one of the men, although he was
able to write the plural of a word, was unable to show it to me in the
dictionary since he did not know how to spell it in the singular. They
could not understand why I chose to anchor right out in the bay instead of in their harbour. My Spanish could not cope with telling
them that my experiences at the shore at La Coruña had sickened me
of the land, and that the clean sea air was only just beginning to sweep
away the stale disgust entailed by loss of faith in human nature.

There was a stirring sight in the afternoon. A sailing boat about ninety feet long appeared from the mouth of a small river which flowed into the bay on the other side, and which led to an inland town. Her decks were piled with logs to a height of seven feet, and as soon as she emerged from shelter to cross to Camariñas harbour she heeled over, gunwale flush with the water, while on the windward side waves dashed against the logs and washed across the foredeck. As the craft foamed along under a huge boomless mainsail, with a single man coping with a massive tiller controlled by tackles, it was amusing to see that the remainder of the crew, four of them, were playing cards under the lee of the cargo, seemingly oblivious of the stormy elements, and as though they were anchored in some quiet haven. It was only when they were actually in the harbour and head to wind that they left their game to let the sail come down with a run. The trader then coasted on for at least ten boat lengths while threading in and out of various craft, before coming alongside the unloading quay, as pretty as you please. It had been a first-class bit of seamanship.

Again, a little open boat shot out of the harbour under a rag of sail to cross the bay. With two men up to windward she bounced past me and tore along like a racing dinghy. Freeboard was nil. Before she reached the other side, I saw through my glasses that one man was furiously bailing.

There was not much doubt that the men of Camariñas would be pleasant to meet, but I had no desire to go ashore at that time, in case the actors should prove less beautiful than the stage.

As darkness fell the wind eased gradually away and the rising of the moon gave a magical quality to the scene. I stayed for an hour or more half out of the hatch, drinking in the sensations of the night, before the falling dew made me shiver and seek the warmth below.

The 'yate inglis' must have excited considerable comment in the town, and no doubt many an eye was turned towards us next morning as *Temptress* glided along their shore towards the open sea. I gave one last look back before the point cut off the bay from view. The sun was showing it up to perfection, and I left with a final memory of what is still to me a 'dream bay.'

Outside, the conditions were perfect for sailing. The wind was on the port quarter, slightly off shore. It freshened enough to make me roll up one reef in the main after Cape Toriñana, and we foamed along with a huge swell coming up dead astern. As Cape Finisterre was approached the wind died away till all my light canvas was hoisted. There was plenty of wind to be seen out to sea, but I wanted to close in with the Cape in order to send a message to Lloyds.

Helped by a slight current I worked my way in amongst some small boats fishing off the end of the famous Cape and out of the ocean swell, and started to attack the signalling tower with my Aldis lamp, which for the single-hander is much easier than code flags. I stabbed and stabbed away with no result whatsoever, until a window suddenly shot up and some flags jerkily rose into view. They were not easy to read in that lifeless air, but they were identified as DLK. While steering with that portion of my anatomy so apt for the purpose, I peeled rapidly through the code book. Ah... DLK. Here we are... 'You should signal by International Code of Flags.' Ouch! What a rap over the knuckles!

Then started a performance which must have kept them amused for weeks. To begin with, no proper stowage for my flags had at that time been organised, and soon there was a complete shambles on deck. They evidently had a very powerful telescope and my every movement must have been watched, for they would scarcely let me get the confounded flags hoisted off the deck before they would acknowledge! The sun grilled down and sweat was pouring off me as I sent up hoists asking them to report me 'all well.' After all my efforts they had a further pithy comment to make. They had not seen my national colours. I obliged them and cleared up the riotous mess of flags, but as I was carrying them below more flags on shore caught my eye. 'Heavens!' I groaned.

'What now?' PYU... More scuffling through the book. But it was all right, for they had only signalled 'Good voyage.' Further routing preceded the hoisting of 'Thank you.' Thank goodness that was over. I felt mortified, however, that my signalling had been somewhat landlubberly.

Weeks later I heard from my father that he had received a message from Lloyds stating that the yacht *Temptress* had been sighted off Finisterre, 'cruising pleasantly south.' Presumably they have humorists stationed at the Cape!

As the yawl lay motionless on the glassy sea, with sails hanging dejectedly, a little Spanish coaster slowed down alongside to offer me a pluck into Corcubion Inlet, but I was waiting for a breeze to carry me out to sea and so to Gibraltar.

Two hours later we had hardly moved, and there was only enough air to smooth out the wrinkles in the lightest of canvas. Out to sea the most amazing mirages appeared. One steamer had its own image suspended above it, the right way up, with smoke pouring from the funnel of the top one.

Even that tiny breeze petered out, till it was obvious that a glassy calm and fog would prevail at night. The engine was started at six o'clock, in order that the entrance to Muros Bay could be identified before darkness fell. One hour and a half later the setting sun provided a breath-taking picture. Mountains and shore were veiled in an unreal amethyst light, while to the west a grandiose sunset formed, crazy in its malformity. The sun itself, focal point of the creation, sank to the horizon haze as a distorted blood-red ball, while wild streaks of cirrus gathered into fantastic contours of purple and orange, and one great host of swept-up mares' tails was like a terrible fire. On wrenching my eyes away from this awe-inspiring kaleidoscope of nature I looked ahead and nearly jumped out of my skin, for over the bowsprit an enormous moon—and red—hung suspended over the silent mountains.

It will be a long time before I forget the serene beauty of that quiet moonlit night, as the little engine pushed us through the gap in the steep hills and up the deep inlet. At the head of the tiny bay in which Muros was built I distinguished myself by running gently aground, with the sand showing white under me in the moonlight. It was an easy matter getting off, however, by the simple expedient of putting the engine in astern, then standing myself on the outboard end of the bowsprit. This put her down by the head, thus reducing her draught sufficiently to float clear.

As the splash of the anchor and rattle of chain disturbed the silence, I said to myself, 'This is the last time I will anchor in Spain until Gibraltar.' For I had determined to wait for a breeze, then clear right out to sea beyond the wind-upsetting influence of the land.

6

PORTUGAL

Temptress silently drifted clear of the tiny bay before faint breaths from the north, leaving behind her the fascinating arched houses along the Muros quay. There was promise of wind, for it had been a red dawn and the barometer needle had waked from its immobility.

That second peaceful morning typified somehow a certain aspect of Spain. The hills, bathed in the increasing warmth of the sun, drowsily breathed an air of mañana, and the only sound to be heard was the inevitable roar of the lazy swell against the rocks on the far side of the bay.

Finally, to save the last of the ebb I had to kick *Temptress* clear of the land under engine, before the genuine northerly wind rippled over the water and the chuckle of the bow wave ceased to be drowned by the noise of machinery.

It was foggy. To the north, land was completely hidden in black, and to the south only occasional glimpses could be seen in a white haze. The sun was hot overhead, and as I peeled off my clothing a great capture was effected. Many and vain had been the meticulous searchings for that oft-cursed Helford flea. That day, however, it met its doom, after a stay of twenty-three days. A thumbnail vice caused its sticky end, and I was free at last from its exasperating presence.

Round about midday an interesting fleet of no less than five picturesque trading ketches sailed out of the mist, one of which ran close enough for me to get a good view and photograph. She had seen far better years, and with her patched sails and tarred hull had an air of extreme ripeness. The old man steering seemed half asleep, until we were alongside; then he waved violently towards the north-east. I shouted 'Muros,' but he still continued to wave and point, for some unknown reason…

The wind hardened into a fine beam wind, so that an hour before sunset all signs of land had disappeared, and steamers on the Finisterre route began to be sighted.

The sun, distorted by the haze, set like an egg-shaped ball of fire.

By midnight the log showed fifty-three miles for the day, and we were on the outside edge of the steamer track, but I sailed on for another two hours for safety's sake, before rolling down the equivalent of one reef and heaving to for food and sleep. The last lights of a vessel to be sighted had been very peculiar, as well as being outside the normal track. She passed about one mile away, and I logged her as a battleship. It was a mild night, but the dew was very heavy, with the rigging actually dripping as if it were raining.

The next day gave even better results, and *Temptress*, in spite of being hove to for nearly nine hours, reeled off seventy-seven miles under glorious conditions of sparkling sunshine and deep blue sea. No steamers were sighted, but a flock of stormy petrels bore me company, as well as a grey bird shaped like a sparrow, which attempted several times to alight on the rigging, before flying off, I fear, in the opposite direction to the land.

The wind piped up at sunset, so for dinner there was only time to dart below and grab a saucepan of cold porridge which was enjoyed on deck. Midnight marked the end of thirteen continuous hours at the helm, and the logbook states: '2400. Log 21. Heave to. Roll 4 turns. Wind N.4. Choppy. 9/10ths cloud. Plot position and turn in.'

It was blowing fresh in the morning, with the boat climbing up and over breaking seas, while the wind, still in the north, drummed energetically in the wire rigging. The night had produced such a varied category of new and extra noises that I had been guilty of failing to investigate a knocking. This cost me no less than the port navigation light, which had been battered to pieces by the lee runner block breaking clear of the shroud where it had been lashed.

In September the Portuguese Trades blow very erratically. After giving me a wonderful push in the morning they eased away at midday, until at four o'clock the wind was very light, leaving the boat jerking clumsily about and making hardly any progress.

Although the day was mostly cloudy, two accurate sights were obtained, giving a satisfactory intercept of two miles. My latitude was 40° 30', and position about ninety miles off shore. This was hardly a place where one would expect to see land birds, but within an hour of each other, two flew on board and proceeded to make themselves thoroughly at home. The first was of a yellow-grey plumage and was the size of a chaffinch. It landed on the deck in a state of complete exhaustion and promptly closed its eyes. The second was very different, being a very fit wagtail. The deck began to look like the bottom of a bird cage, with Ryvita crumbs scattered about and two bowls of water. The wagtail proved very tame, eating and drinking happily, and coming so close to me that I could almost stroke it. However, the first bird became more and more miserable and remained just a pathetic little bundle of feathers up against the cabin-top coaming, refusing all overtures of food.

Temptress rolled about after dark in the lifeless air, and I was in the act of turning down one reef for safety, in preparation for my night's sleep, when there was a sudden crack, a heavy splash and, wow, things began to happen! The main boom was being flung broad off, one side to the other, with shattering force, as the boat rolled heavily. The pin at the end of the boom had sheared off, and the Y-piece carrying both topping lifts and the mainsheet had dropped into the water. With great difficulty and at considerable risk, I finally captured the heavy spar with a line, and after some confusion the mainsail was lowered. It was an awkward job with no topping lift or boom gallows, and the whole time I was hindered by those confounded birds. Every step taken had to be checked by flashlight. What a horrible crackling sound a bird crushed on deck would make!

Nothing useful could have been done in the dark, so, lashing the boom securely, I left the boat under headsails and turned in. Everything had suddenly become very wrong. My mind raced with schemes and alternatives. Would a repair be possible?

The first thing I looked at in the morning was the latest bird situation. The grey bird was upside down—dead. Over the side with it. The wagtail, which had been so perky the day before, could hardly stand, presumably demoralised by seasickness, and he died later. Over the side with it. Yet a third bird put in an appearance, but he flew off again. I had done my best for them, but was glad to be free of the nuisance.

The day was overcast but very warm, with a light southerly air blowing over the swells. I examined the damage and decided that it would be possible to make a new bolt. It was a great stroke of luck that a bolt of the right thread was found in my things-that-might-be-useful-sometime box. After removing the whole casting from the end of the boom, I took it below to modify the new bolt with hacksaw, cold chisel, and rivetting hammer. The most exhausting job was rivetting the end over the hole in the Y-piece, and sweat poured down my naked body as I flogged away, not exactly helped by the systematic and heavy rolling of the vessel. By eleven o'clock the repaired fitting was on the boom and the sail hoisted. The gear was now as strong as new, which was a great relief to me. It was one example of the safety of the open sea. Had the fitting broken when close to the shore it might have caused the loss of the whole boat, and possibly myself into the bargain.

It was very pleasant letting the yacht sail herself close-hauled into the light headwind, after those man-killing hours at the helm the last few days, and by the afternoon the sea had smoothed itself out delightfully. There was plenty of time to prepare good meals, and to clean the ship above and below decks.

The wind brought up more clouds in the evening and freshened from the south-west, but by letting the boat chop along unattended, I ate a leisurely dinner below, then turned on the radio to hear—believe it or not—the strains of *Jolly Boating Weather*. It was.

Another day passed in similar fashion. The wind started in the south with the boat on the port tack, and the shift of wind at noon caused me to go about. Two more birds came to afflict me, a small yellow one hopping wearily around the deck, and a fat bird with a tiny head, which perched on the crosstrees, where it had the greatest difficulty in staying. Every half hour or so it was flung off as the boat pitched into a dirty little head sea, a sea which kept the speed down to one knot instead of three. How that bird kept up there as long as it did was a mystery, for the mast whipped fore and aft as indeed I myself noticed while re-reeving a new burgee halyard through the truck.

A good sunset and a heavy dew gave birth to a very quiet moonlit night, and I dared to let the boat cut through the hours of darkness under full sail. During the day I had had a fit of navigation mania, and was completely sure of my position, what with a morning position line, meridian altitude, afternoon longitude by chronometer, and a night position line from a planet.

Although enjoying myself, progress was hardly startling; my runs from Muros Bay had been 53, 77, 43, 45, 30, and the next day only 15 miles. In fact business got so slack that I started to do a little reading. Some of the time was spent in poring over the chart, making futile predictions as to where we were likely to be in so many days' time. In fine weather this is always a casual interest, but when things are unpleasant it occupies most of one's waking thoughts. The only vessel sighted was a peculiar fishing boat, presumably from Lisbon. This gave me a navigation check, as a bank of 200 fathoms is marked on the chart, whereas we had been over depths of 2000 fathoms and more.

Faint airs from the north raised my hopes in the evening after a calm spell, and prompted me to lower the mainsail and let *Temptress* roll gently to the south under headsails, while I slept below.

The coming of daylight dispelled any hope of a fair wind, and the weather remained true to the pattern of the last few days—a light south wind in the morning, with a veer and freshening after noon, making me perform my pre-prandial tack. Most of the sky remained overclouded, especially to the east, where land should have been visible, as it was reckoned to be only about thirty or thirty-five miles off.

A big swell from the south-west foretold a change, and sure enough, in the afternoon good progress was made under every stitch of muslin possible to hoist.

At six o'clock in the evening a very black cloud formed to windward, and I got the big reaching staysail off just before a sudden increase in wind and a shower of rain. Twenty minutes later I shouted, 'Land O.' It was my first sight of the Portuguese coast and the sixth day out of sight of land. It was a long way off, but checked with my assumed position, if that lump of grey was indeed the mountain on the north side of the bay leading to the river Tagus.

Land soon vanished again in the murk, and the weather became ominously black, with the wind freshening, backing to the south, and kicking up a steep sea, preventing any reasonable progress. This was the fourth day of head winds, and portents were bad. I had heard stories at La Coruña of the south-westerly gales that were experienced in winter off the Portuguese coast, so when the wind jumped to Force 5 and the barometer started to fall rapidly, my brave cracking to windward under full sail suddenly changed to a mood of extreme caution. My motto of 'Everything or Nothing' fitted my actions perfectly, for the mainsail was rolled up six turns, the jib and mizzen stowed, and the staysail pulled to weather, leaving *Temptress* hove to on the starboard tack in what was merely then a fresh breeze. She had not been pumped that week, so the famous bilge pump now transferred fifty gallons back to where it rightfully belonged.

It did blow up during the early part of the night, and several heavy rain squalls made me very glad of my reduced canvas. All I had to do was to take a rather perfunctory lookout. A solitary steamer crossed my bows, heading in the direction of where the Tagus and Lisbon should have been, according to my reckoning.

At four o'clock the following morning the wind, having exhausted itself after such a display of energy, dropped right away, leaving an absolute stink of a sea, which flung poor *Temptress* about like a cork, with the gear rattling and jarring in painful fashion.

It was just before the dawn that a light to the north-west was sighted flashing four every twenty seconds. I cursed when it could not be identified on the chart, but assumed it to be Cape de Roca, and repeated the famous last words, 'The chart's wrong.' As a matter of fact it was, and in daylight it was possible to fix my position with accuracy.

When the wind came away it was from the south-south-east, dead noser again for Cape St. Vincent. Disgusted at these unco-operative winds I decided to sail into the Tagus to see what Lisbon looked like, while waiting for a slant.

The coast was most interesting, and the land fell right away to the east in a great curve which was the shallow approach to the river. Having no decent scale chart of the entrance, I hung about in the unnaturally green water, taking the opportunity for a snack, until a coaster coming up from the south altered course confidently towards the land, and so we rattled after him in grand style, with the wind on the starboard beam and the ocean breakers nibbling at the stern. Using the first of the flood, I ran past the forts marking the Tagus proper and saw many sailing craft ahead of me scudding merrily through the dancing waters.

Then took place one of those amazing coincidences one reads about, for there, waiting for me hove to, was *Content*, my own last boat and the one in which I had made my first unsuccessful attempt to reach Gibraltar. We were soon sailing only four feet apart, her skipper and I excitedly shouting our news across the narrow strip of water. They were twelve days out of Vigo. It was with a mixture of pride and embarrassment that I told them that *Temptress* was only eight days out of Muros, for Muros was sixty miles to the north of Vigo and they had a crew of four!

Bearing away a trifle, to extricate my crosstrees from their rigging, I drew clear and headed for the north shore, where a clipper-bowed schooner flying the British ensign was anchored. I hailed him for advice, then shot past his stern. A few minutes later my own anchor thumped into Portuguese soil.

7

PORTUGUESE WATERS

It was nearly high water. Bubbles which had been busily scurrying by slackened their speed and began to dawdle lazily along the hull waterline, and as I finished the last bite of lunch a moving finger of a sunbeam traced an arc across the cabin table as *Temptress* slowly twisted in the changing tide.

It was hot work weighing anchor, but when it was lashed down securely on deck I sat for some minutes in the cockpit letting her drift towards the sea, with sails still stowed. There was not a breath of wind, and it was amusing to dwell on my secret visit to Portugal.

On my anchoring near the schooner *Mollyhawk* two days before, the Nicholsons had told me of the fathoms of red tape and delay before one was allowed to go ashore. Although I normally do my best to conform to the regulations, my stay was to have been only long enough to buy some bread, butter, and rice, so it had been decided to ignore the authorities and just row to the nearest beach, taking the tram into Lisbon to change the little Spanish money that was left. And this was what had been done, although I could not help smiling at the psychology used to fox the interested armed policeman who had come down the sandy beach while the dinghy was being hauled clear of the tide. Before he had had a chance to open his mouth I had asked him in poor Spanish whether it was safe to leave the oars in the boat. By the time we had made each other understood he had quite forgotten to question me on my business. 'Once a Portuguese, always a Portuguese,' or so the Spaniards say. The Portuguese say, 'Once a Spaniard, always a Spaniard,' so where are you?

By the time the entrance forts could be made out through the hazy fog, *Temptress* was ploughing through the water under power with mainsail aloft as we met the first of the ocean swells. A few minutes later my eyes narrowed as I peered into the mist to starboard at a white mass that at first looked like the bridge of a steamer. As the tide and engine swept me clear of a fogbank I saw a sight that made my heart beat above the normal. It was no ship that I had seen, but the top of a gigantic breaker. And there were many more, both to port and starboard. A huge swell from the north-west was rolling in from the Atlantic and was tripping up on the sandbanks flanking the unbuoyed channel. The tide pouring out of the Tagus built up these swells into awe-inspiring toppling breakers in which no vessel built would last more than a few minutes. The engine chose that inauspicious moment to keep me on tenterhooks by running erratically for a period before lapsing into silence, thus leaving me in a state of flux which the heavy booming of those monstrous masses of water did nothing to dispel. The engine started again after being switched on to petrol, but its uneasy running gave me anxious moments until those sandbanks were brought abaft the beam.

A liner of about 20,000 tons, travelling faster than the swells, came sweeping in from seaward aud passed only a few cables away, while many passengers lining the rail waved to me. Another vessel passed even closer, within a biscuit toss; it was a heavily laden coasting schooner which lumbered by under her thumping diesel towards the north with her sails sheeted in to cut down the rolling. The next vessel was yet smaller, being merely an open dory which held a single-handed gentleman unconcernedly rowing amongst the massive swells about seven miles offshore, presumably tending the fishing floats which were liberally dotted over that part of the ocean.

With the batteries nicely charged and Cape Espichel abeam, the engine, after running six hours, was stopped as day changed into a clear night. The entry in the log at 2230 is, 'Flapping along at 1 knot to S.W. Close-hauled on the starboard tack. Boat sailing herself with gear jarring. Several ships about. Retire to bunk fully dressed ready to keep regular lookout.'

It was just before two o'clock in the morning that the sound of a distant siren sent me once more to the deck. My worst fears were realised. Instead of a clear starlit night, a dense mantle of white mist had descended over the area, so thick that the powerful electric light lashed to the mizzen shrouds looked like an anaemic glow, while dark shadows of sails and rigging lay clear-cut on the wall of writhing vapour.

In almost every direction the muffled moan of sirens could be heard. It was an unhealthy spot. All the coastal shipping would be attempting a landfall at Cape Espichel and pushing blithely through the fog on their business, with scant concern for smaller fry.

After donning oilskins to keep out the cold, wet atmosphere I uneasily took the helm, adjusted the sheets to make the best speed possible, and diverged from the shore in a direction which should finally take me clear of the inner lane of shipping. In spite of my anxiety it was fascinating sailing at first, for there was little indication of being on water at all. There was enough wind on the beam to hold the boat steady, and all that could be seen were the black shadows cast on the fog, which by their static locations removed all sense of motion of the boat or any reality of the existing conditions.

After steering, and blowing my fog siren regularly for about half an hour, during which time no steamer had caused me serious alarm, I became conscious of one coming up from the south with a siren of deeper note. It was obviously outside the others. There was no doubt that he was coming up fast, and the unchanging bearing showed that a dangerous contretemps was quickly developing. On he came—a mile, a half a mile, a quarter of a mile, closer and closer, with his blaring siren answered each time by my manually operated pipsqueak. Still the fog pressed heavily on me, giving not the slightest chance of any avoiding action, in spite of my control of the vessel. I altered course to the west, estimated at right angles to his. Another blast, dead on the port beam. Intuition of disaster seized me as cold sweat ran down my face. I plied the foghorn in panic and despair. He stopped blowing, then noises of the juggernaut smote at me out of the impenetrable darkness. A rumble of machinery, a whine, a metallic clang— then, O God, a hiss of bow wave and he was on top of me. With mouth hanging open, and shaking with painful agitation, I leaped to the mizzen rigging and looked up with a crazy hope of jumping onto his anchor. For an instant a haze of light appeared seemingly right overhead, a man shouted, a sea threw *Temptress* further on her course, and a pulsating noisy mass seemed to hover for an age by the stern before the heavy thump, thump, thump of the propeller drew level and was past. I was saved.

Boooom went his siren again, but he was on the safe quarter, and I seized my own to send a triumphant blast through the night, before shaking my fist at him and continuing my interrupted trick at the helm.

Only a quarter of an hour later a few stars could be seen overhead. The shadows dispersed and suddenly we were clear of the coastal fog, while astern the groaning of sirens could still be heard as steamers continued to play their dangerous version of blind man's buff.

The bright early-morning sun mocked my fears of the night; although we were on the edge of the main steamer track, I pulled the staysail to weather and retired below to snatch a few hours' sleep, leaving the boat rising and falling in leisurely fashion over those vast swells, the speed of which the gentle wind was doing nothing to encourage.

Refreshed by three hours' sleep and fortified by a no mean bowl of porridge—my inevitable breakfast—I resumed the helm, finding that the wind had veered to slightly east of north. It had freshened to a fine sailing breeze which forthwith sent *Temptress* scudding away to the south-west under bulging canvas. It did not take long at that rate to cross the shipping lane, and by ten o'clock a steady procession of steamers on one of the busiest routes in the world could be seen astern. When the steamers themselves were too far off to be visible, dark spirals of smoke ascending from below the horizon clearly gave away their secret.

There was a more interesting sight at midday when I joyously cried, 'Sail O.' It was just a flash of white on the horizon way out on the starboard beam and only visible when we were both on top of a wave. But two hours passed before it was possible to identify with any degree of accuracy. He was then about three or four miles off and converging steadily. His snowy white canvas dubbed him a yacht, and after patient work with binoculars, which nearly caused a gybe, it was possible to see that he was a ketch or schooner under square sail, raffees, and some sort of topsail; but for all his high kites he was making nothing on *Temptress*, who was doing her best to race the seas under full sail.

The wind was picking up at every moment and steering required more and more attention, as breaking seas began to play a pick-a-back on top of the ocean swell.

It was not until seven hours after first sighting the yacht that it was possible to get a reliable glimpse. When he was only one mile away and preparing to cross my wake, he was suddenly thrown up to the top of an immense wave at the same time that I was on a crest. His whole outline was exposed. It was *Mollyhawk*, and she had had twenty-four hours' start of me! But what a beautiful sight she was! Her graceful sheerline swept up to the clipper bow half hidden by the white dust of her bow wave as she lifted easily over the crest in the natural manner only attainable by a sailing vessel. I had only just time to notice his fisherman topsail set abaft the raffees before we sank into our respective troughs, and so big were the seas that it was not even possible to see his mainmast head.

As *Temptress* staggered on under full sail, *Mollyhawk* crossed my stern to drop under my port quarter. I was longing to close with him for the thrill of running alongside, but a gybe would have been necessary and would probably have broken the straining mainmast. Any reduction of sail would have let him get ahead, so we drove on till dusk at maximum speed, with seas breaking violently astern. But it needs two men to race seventy-foot schooners in eleven-ton yachts, and when spindrift began to fly and steering became wild I had to stop that madness and do something about that over-powering press of canvas. Heaven knows what I would have done without roller reefing. As it was, I had to make several hair-raising journeys forward, leaving the helm temporarily lashed, while I wound my little handle by the mast. The speed dropped to five or six knots. There remained one more journey to roll up the jib, back the staysail, then jam the helm down as a wave roared underneath. After battering to windward for a number of lengths she slowed up at last, and, lo, was quietly hove to, needing no attention, in a position fifty miles away from the scene of entertainment during the previous night, and well outside all known steamer lanes. Of course, heaving to is a sheer waste of time, but I had to sleep and eat, and at that time had not learned the trick of lowering the mainsail and letting the boat chase through the night under headsails alone.

Mollyhawk had given me a great day of company and interest. When they met me at Gibraltar they said that my powerful white light had been visible for a long time as they sailed through the night, and they had wondered how I was faring. I was faring very well. After a respectable dinner I brought my log up to date, rolled into my bunk to leeward, and was soon lulled to sleep by the thrumming of the wind through the rigging.

In the morning it was blowing fresh as ever, with a rough tumbling sea. Wham! A hectic gybe, and we were skidding away to the south-south-east amongst the white horses glistening in the brilliant sun. But as the hours ticked by, wind decreased from fresh to moderate, and moderate to light, until in the afternoon it fell right away, veering to the east. Immediately there was hell to pay with the gear, which slammed, crashed, and rattled as the capricious *Temptress* played and bounced about in a manner which was not conducive to polite language.

The horizon distance was deceptive and upset my navigation sights, which just would not check, and altogether it was a somewhat exasperating day. In the evening I put a generous cross on the chart thirty-five miles west of Cape St. Vincent. Very soon it would be possible to alter course to the east and to head direct towards the Straits of Gibraltar.

As the sun's rays weakened, the odd puff from the north developed into a continuous draught, the sails gave up their fandango, and bubbles started their procession along the hull. *Temptress* picked up her skirts and waltzed her way in fine style, approximately in the direction of the Mediterranean.

A lump of white substance bobbed quickly past. It might have been ambergris worth a fortune; but who would waste a fair wind which money cannot buy? In any case there was beauty to watch in the west, for the red sun was setting strangely into the horizon fog.

That lovely night breeze was wasted anyway, for another fogbank wrapped its repellent arms round me, and not wishing to tempt fate further, I went about and hove to, drifting in the wrong direction, to be sure, but safe from being cut down. Many times during the night I put my head out of the hatch and listened for sirens; but there was nothing. Nothing but the slap of waves against the sides, the creak of gear, and the river of white vapour flowing eerily over the black waters.

Temptress still had that leak which had developed in Biscay, and in the morning bilge water had begun to squirt over the flooring aft. Thirty-five gallons of the Atlantic were pumped back to the proper side of the planking before the boat was gybed and sails trimmed to a fine north-east wind. During the morning there occurred one of those incidents which assume such exaggerated importance at the time, for a freighter of at least 10,000 tons came out of the haze astern, heading in an easterly direction. Easterly! So I was past the lowest point of Portugal. In the afternoon there was further confirmation that the sights, which I seemed to have been working out at the helm nearly all day, were correct, for there was a pronounced easterly swell. This swell, allied with the old friend from the north-west and the sea dished up by the existing wind, made the most extraordinary motion, holding back *Temptress* to five knots average speed as she rolled, bounded, and leaped along in a series of spectacular rushes.

Although the sun had had no difficulty in burning up the fog, heavy black clouds hung in the direction of land, and over and over again presumed land dissolved into nothingness.

Calculations told me that the light of St. Vincent should be visible when darkness fell, but a pin-point of light flashed its welcome soon after sunset, when the day could scarcely be said to have surrendered its place to night. The accuracy of celestial navigation had again been proved. Having checked my position by handbearing compass, course was altered to get myself firmly on the chart, as during the day we had been sailing precariously along the bottom edge and in danger of running off altogether.

The wind had done me proud and it had been a great day's run. It was not long after dark, however, that land began to affect the wind, and small fogbanks would roll over the Cape, blotting out the lights for an hour at a time and temporarily reducing visibility. Steamers were everywhere, and there was no predicting when they would alter course to take the turn. At 2245 the wind was suddenly cut off and the gear started to bash about in its inimitable manner.

By midnight, after two steamers had run very close and had been warned off by floodlighting the sails, which were then white, the motor was started and course set to approach the land and get clear of the traffic. In two hours, when we were north of the steamer tracks and in calm water, the engine was stopped and sails trimmed to a light easterly air. Just before dawn this wind freshened, bringing with it a considerable swell from the east. After nineteen hours at the helm, only interrupted by a break for lunch, I was very hungry, and took the opportunity of preparing a good dinner, or is it a breakfast at four o'clock in the morning? Daylight showed that we were four and a half miles from the cliffs, and, heaving her to, I dropped into an uneasy slumber of some hours before once more taking the helm.

Conditions had deteriorated. The big easterly swell was out of all proportion to the strength of wind, although that became quite fresh enough at midday and forced me to roll down six turns in the mainsail. An hour later there was hardly any wind again, and I made a tack close inshore right under the steep red cliffs, in a vain search for smoother water. Then another fitful squall swept along the coast, followed by more light airs, and all the time there was that wretched head sea which prevented any reasonable progress and made the mast flex violently at point of gaff thrust in a manner which threatened to snap it in half.

8

THE STRAITS

The big seas obviously denoted strong easterly winds in the Straits of Gibraltar, and I searched the chart to find if there was a suitable place to anchor. Portimao seemed the only chance, so after enduring several hours of no wind and heavy seas, I started the engine and managed to keep it going while setting a course towards the shallow bay and quieter water. The sky became overclouded after sunset, making it very dark as the entrance to Portimao River was approached. It was low water and too risky to attempt the entrance, so after taking repeated bearings, which were plotted as best as possible on the wholly inadequate chart, the anchor was let go in four fathoms at an estimated distance of three cables from the beach, on which the surf was breaking with an ominous roar. The tide swung the boat parallel to the shore but also to the swell, so that when the mainsail was lowered the most fiendish roll was built up. It was simply wicked. First one gunwale then the other dipped under water, as the mast described an arc in the sky fanned out by an included angle of ninety degrees.

It was an anxious night. At midnight the wind came away fresh again, but luckily obliquely offshore. The lights in the houses seemed very close, and that frightful roll prevented me from snatching sleep for more than a few minutes at a time. Then every so often a rasp on the bobstay, followed by a vicious jerk on the anchor chain, sent a jar through the boat, as a swell lifted us violently upward.

The first grey light and then the red dawn did nothing to show improvement in the amenities of the anchorage. The swell was bigger and was thundering on the hard sand, and was even doing its best to break to seawards of me. A vertical rock about forty feet high, which had been invisible in the darkness, was unpleasantly close, and I made preparations to extricate myself under sail in the light wind which was blowing along the shore. The boat was rolling far too heavily for the engine to run. It was a tricky manoeuvre, for the scend of the sea would have been sufficient to throw her on the beach. It was not easy hoisting the mainsail, but when it was done I watched my chance to break out the anchor and hoist the headsails as she paid off on the right tack. Slowly but surely she climbed the swells and edged gradually away from one of the most unpleasant anchorages it has been my lot to select.

There were many fishing boats anchored off the mouth of the river, evidently waiting for the tide, and I decided to follow them in, as progress under the prevailing conditions was practically impossible. After making two tacks, the ship was put about to close the others. Just then a mass of broken water to windward heralded a squall. There was scarcely time to roll up four turns on the boom before it hit. Half out of control, the boat raced towards the fishermen, amongst whom it was now madness to anchor; the helm was jammed down and we went about like a rater with flogging canvas and thumping blocks before being hove to on the port tack. In an instant, the wind had increased to half a gale and a steep sea was sending heavy bursts of spray over the foredeck. There was still far too much sail up, so taking all my clothes off and chucking them down the hatch to keep dry (much to the astonishment of a passing fisherman), I went forward, rolled up the equivalent to close reef in the mainsail, and furled the jib, getting many shower baths into the bargain. The Levanter had struck. It had developed all the symptoms specified in my manual—overcast sky, repeated rain squalls, bad visibility, and for me the double danger of steamers to the south, and, should the wind shift, a lee shore to the north.

I could only stay hove to and gradually drift clear of the land, taking pot luck with the steamers. In four hours the wind dropped under gale force and the clouds rolled back, but the sea remained so bad that it was a waste of time and energy trying to sail. In spite of bad temper, bad language, and fiendish motion, I managed to cook a slap-up lunch—two hot courses with vegetables and all the rest of it. But even this failed to improve my temper, and at dusk, when the wind dropped to Force 3, causing the boom to smash from side to side, with the whole ship shaking at every roll, the following entry appeared in the log: 'Damn and blast the weather. No progress. Bad position. A long cold night ahead. Feel tired and dispirited. Oh! for a quiet anchorage away from this blasphemous jabble.'

Before midnight it breezed up again, just enough to whip up the sea once more to unsatisfactory proportions. The night was spent in bobbing up and down the hatch watching steamers and checking my position when the shore lights became visible.

After being hove to for twenty-four hours, full sail was hoisted; with mainsheet pinned right in, no way was possible, and with sheets eased, the ten-foot-high swells jarred the gear excessively, with the mast bending like a bow. By the afternoon there was no wind at all. Becoming resigned to the wrenching of gear, I lay in my bunk reading Slocum's *Liberdade* voyage. A rushing noise made me look out and I had a start, for a vast stern of a steamer was only a few feet past the bowsprit. He must have passed damned close.

The glassy swell went down and down and down. The end of every hour showed a difference. When night came it could not have been more different from the previous, for it was one of those fantastic nights, as quiet as death, with *Temptress* lying so motionless that she might have been in harbour. In fact, at midnight I cast off all the main-shroud rigging screws, regreased them, and reset the rigging.

'Surely,' I thought, 'this calm must mean a change of weather.' For forty-eight hours Gibraltar, which was only one hundred and seventy-five miles away, had not been brought any nearer. It was my seventh day out from the river Tagus.

The morning was beautifully clear and sunny, with light airs from the north which slowly hardened into as lovely a little breeze as one could wish. *Temptress* slid through the deep blue water under every stitch of canvas available. A high, brown-tinted coastline could be seen on the port beam, but it had been decided to drop the land altogether and head south of the steamer track, and navigate by sextant. There was much too much activity where I was. No less than nine

vessels were in sight. A pretty trading ketch thumped by to windward, no doubt cursing the change of wind as much as I rejoiced.
The next visitor was a white-sailed schooner which I recognised as
Ortac, belonging to a Belgian who had spoken to me at La Coruña.
He was under 'Solent' rig—that is to say, foresail and engine, and evidently he was not feeling very sociable, as he passed at least two cables off. When he was well ahead he started messing about with his
mainsail, for the wind had backed and freshened so that *Temptress*
was overhauling him.

The wind picked up still further in the late afternoon, and fearing
for my large and ancient reaching staysail I had to take it in, although
it gave some pretty impressive flaps before it had been muzzled on
deck. The rest of the day was spent with the tiller in one hand and
a fly swatter in the other, as a plague of man-eating houseflies had
invaded the boat. Much slaughter was effected, and I got in some
excellent shots, both forehand and backhand.

As my course edged us away south, only the occasional steamer
or smoke could be seen to the north, but there was always something
interesting to watch. In the evening, while the boat was tearing along
before the quartering breeze, a school of porpoises which had been
gambolling near suddenly turned and rushed towards *Temptress*,
only to turn away at the very last moment. They were last seen leaping clear of the white horses astern, as if bent on getting the maximum enjoyment out of life.

The fine breeze held and was too good to waste. Before heaving
to for dinner I had rolled down four turns in the main. Then started a great night's sail, with boat creaming steadily along on a real
passage maker, with roaring bow wave and bursts of spray coming
over the weather quarter, while breaking crests glowed strangely in
the darkness. Just before three o'clock in the morning I must have
nodded over the helm, for a crash of the boom as it came over in a vicious gybe woke me thoroughly. The whole boom and mainsail were
pinned against the runner, and the boat lay over many degrees, far
off course, with solid water pursuing itself along the lee deck. Angry
at myself for being caught napping, I just forced the helm up without touching the mainsheet. The boom hesitated, lifted, then hur-

tled over the other side with a jolt that seemed to twist the boat out of shape. 'Take that, you b——,' I muttered, before peering into the compass to check the course. The mad rush was continued for half an hour before heaving to. My bunk was sought with mind almost free from the anxiety which is always present in some mental or physical form—namely steamers, steamers, steamers, an ever-growing hazard to the small-boat mariner, and one which radar and automatic pilots do nothing to allay.

The sun was high in the heavens and the temperature in the cabin mounting when I next looked out on deck. A delightful breeze from the north-west, a rippling sea flecked here and there with delicate white horses, and a wonderful soft sky merging into an horizon haze began for me a day which proved beyond doubt that we had reached the sapphires and diamonds of the south. It was one of those days that reward one a hundredfold for all the sacrifices, the gales, the adversities, and the hardships of a sailor's life. I will never forget that perfect day—those glorious plunges from under the bobstay, followed by drying, naked, in the hot sun, then the thrill of the afternoon when a small white streak shot out of the water, glided to the right, and vanished. My first flying fish. No, I will not forget… the friendly waves, the symmetry of sail, the magic of the sea.

The sun set at the end of that day like a great ball of fire which seemed to hover above the horizon before extinguishing itself in the ocean. Instead of heaving to as previously, I lowered the mainsail and let the boat steer herself under headsails alone, with helm lashed amidships. As I prepared dinner below she swayed along before the wind at one and a half knots. Thus ended a most happy day's run of fifty-two miles, bringing the African coast within sixty miles.

The blissful weather continued, and next day *Temptress* wafted along under full sail, scarcely needing any attention at the tiller, thus allowing me plenty of time for navigation. The path of a navigator is rarely smooth, and on that day not only did cloud and haze conceal the land, which should have been visible, but for some reason which I never found out, the meridian altitude gave a latitude thirty-eight miles south of the dead-reckoning position. So when I wasn't bathing, cooking and eating, my time was taken up by mathematics, until

I was satisfied that I knew where we were.

After the afternoon position line had been plotted it showed that the steamer track should not be far below the horizon, and sure enough, the glasses picked out a row of little black pillars of smoke to the north-east. Later in the evening a cloud seemed to stay at a queer angle. It remained motionless. Land! Land O! That never-ceasing thrill. And how much more so when it is a mysterious land like Africa, whose massive heights loom through a shifting heat haze, then vanish before one has time to take a bearing. At dusk the haze thinned, and veiled blue mountains could sometimes be glimpsed in a sector between south and south-east. At ten o'clock it was estimated that the light of the great Cape Spartel should be visible, and as nothing was apparent to my straining eyes from the cockpit, I optimistically climbed onto the foredeck. And there she flashed, 'one', 'two', 'three', 'four', providing another triumph for my battered old sextant.

Already to the north many lights of steamers could be seen, and there was no question of a night's rest. Nor should one be necessary before Gibraltar, which was but fifty-five miles away, and had I not heard about that grand tide that sweeps one through the Straits? There was also something about violent races which beset small craft, but ignorance was bliss, as none of these unpleasant phenomena were marked on my small scale chart.

Soon lights could be seen winking on the Spanish shore, which kept me busy with cross bearings. Then the wind took right off and from midnight to one o'clock I let the current do its best while I prepared hot food. The engine was started and run for two hours until a breeze came away from the south. Dawn came at seven. I was, of course, ready for daybreak and looking forward to seeing the two shores, but I was far from expecting such a spectacle as that dawn unfolded before my eyes. It was an incredible sight. So accustomed was I to objects close to the surface that the jagged mountains of Africa seemed to rear up to fantastic heights, and these were silhouetted as black masses against a crimson sky so violent in hue that it showed that no picture, however lurid, can be called 'impossible.'

Turning away stiffly, for dawns are cold anywhere, I bent down and craned under the boom to look ahead. Yes, there it was, the sentinel of the Straits, the massive Rock of Gibraltar, which had been my goal for—how long? I peeled through the logbook, which is always kept within easy reach of the helm. It had been six weeks to the day that *Temptress* had sailed from England.

Freighters of all shapes and sizes were thrusting their unpoetic way both east and west, but they could see me now, and I took the opportunity to invade the comparative warmth of below for a hot meal. Sitting on the lee settee with my feet up, and holding an empty coffee cup in my hands, I closed my smarting eyes. My head nodded forward... forward... forward... and I leaped up just in time, nearly having been guilty of sleeping on watch. And what a place to choose!

There was a storm brewing up above, and heavy black clouds had gathered over the Spanish coast. Meanwhile, the wind had changed to south-west, freshening the whole time. Gybing ship and lying a good full on the port tack, I sloshed my way over to the north side of the Straits to Tarifa Point, which was marked on my recent chart as a Lloyds Station. My code flags were hoisted and light flashed, but not a sign came from the supposed signal tower, even when I worked close inshore.

After wasting a provoking hour I flung the flags down the hatch, and my ill-humour after them, then started a ripsnorting sail to Gibraltar Bay. This was concluded with a stirring bout of rhythmic rolling in the midst of a tide rip. *Temptress* under full sail and going like a rocket, with half a gale of wind dead astern, averaged eight and a half knots from Tarifa.

After a bathe to freshen me up and a meal, so that I would not arrive in port either tired or hungry, I drew clear from the shelter of the weather side and rattled over to Gibraltar at a great rate before north-west squalls. Off the aircraft runway, with the fantastic Rock rearing high above, my sails came down one by one, and the anchor splashed over the side. It was half-past two in the afternoon of October 8th. My first lap was over.

9

GIBRALTAR

For many years the Rock of Gibraltar has been called the Key of the Mediterranean, and has been synonymous with strength and reliability, although since the development of modern war equipment it is no longer the impregnable fortress of times past.

My very first sight of the Rock, after dawn on the last day of my voyage from England, fascinated me, and the familiarity of a seven months' stay did nothing to take away my first impressions. During the whole of my sojourn right up to the last look as I sailed away into the Atlantic for America, that gaunt rugged lump of marble bred an air of tradition and superiority over the tin-pot mortals and petty gods scratching out their temporary existence below.

This is no place to give an account of the Rock's stirring history throughout the ages. It was, however, captured by the English and Dutch forces in 1704, and assigned to the British in 1713 at the close of the War of the Spanish Succession. In the last war Gibraltar proved invaluable for the assembly of convoys for Malta and elsewhere, and since the harbour was difficult to bomb the attempt was rarely made.

In peacetime, however, the town of Gibraltar is looked upon in a very different light, and it can be called now, somewhat impolitely, but without fear of much contradiction from its many visitors, not the Key, as in wartime, but the Personification of Constipated Bureaucracy. That is scarcely the fault of the Rock, but definitely the fault of a certain group which governs it. Unfortunately, this group appears to do everything possible to discourage yachtsmen, men who during the war filled three out of every four fighting posts in the

Royal Navy and who were hailed as 'Britain's hidden reserve.' Nowadays there is no place in the world in which the amateur sailor is so persecuted with redundant regulations. Heaven knows how many of these rules I wittingly or unwittingly broke during my stay. After I had been there over six months I found out that I should have had a Fishing Permit for practising spearing the small fish that swim in the harbour. And the number of times I had to make out a 'crew list' in triplicate…! In the end I was given so many passes and permits that I learned to chuck them overboard. This practice was never even noticed, which goes to prove their futility. However, the issuing of passes in the first place helped to satisfy that ever-growing host of officials in this modern world who do nothing much more than sit on their ample bottoms, scribbling on bits of paper, and doing no good to themselves or anybody else.

However, I enjoyed my stay, and learned to become fond of Gib. This is not difficult if one can avoid being strangled by the red tape, and if one can forget that it is the most law-abiding of places, having more police per head of population than anywhere else on the globe. One must remember, however, that the abundance of policemen makes jobs for the Gibs, and the abundance of regulations makes jobs for the policemen, and the abundance of yachtsmen makes jobs for the regulations, and the abundance of harbour makes it almost essential for yachtsmen to call there, especially in these days of 'financial areas.' Finance, still and all, does not seem to worry the inhabitants, what with their eleven millionaires and almost complete lack of taxes. Instead of taxes they have a Naval Dockyard where they undertake to do work on visiting ships (and yachts) at fantastic prices. Then there is the State lottery with a weekly draw of tickets costing ten shillings each, to which I regularly subscribed, with the success that one usually achieves in these matters.

As regards the dwellers in this teeming outpost, they can be classed into two compotatory entities: the Gibraltarians themselves (Gib. for the Gibs), and the floating population, consisting chiefly of members of the British armed forces. These conform (except for a few individualists) to the standard pattern of colonial cliques which seem to invite and be invited to chattering cocktail parties, while looking somewhat aghast at anyone who is not 'regularised.' This probably accounts for the fact that I was invited to fewer houses during my seven months' stay in Gibraltar than during my first seven days in America. On the other hand, great hospitality was shown to me by visiting yachts and ships of the Royal Navy. I am especially grateful to the officers of the cruiser *Cleopatra* and the destroyer *Volage*. Incidentally, Admirals seem to have a penchant towards single-handed mariners, and I could always count on a cheery wave from the Admiral, who was a rightly popular one. He did not, however, give me a new jib and green vegetables as was the lot of Captain Slocum at the time of his visit.

The Royal Gibraltar Yacht Club is a handy gathering place for visiting yachtsmen and naval officers, and I took advantage of the temporary membership facilities offered. During the so-called winter, which in climate is about equivalent to the English summer, the club is usually very quiet during the week, but on Saturday it is 'socially' correct to pay it a visit. At noon the club begins to fill up, until there are dozens of men and women who combine to make a noise like the parrot house of the zoo. The flocking is all to the good of the club, whose profits rise as do the number of elbows in the region of the bar.

I am indebted to the R.G.Y.C. for meeting Willie Piccone. It is difficult to see how the club, or Gibraltar itself for that matter, could be quite the same without his puckish grin and wagging finger. To me personally, he was tremendously helpful, for amongst other things he loaned me the use of what was known as 'Willie's Shed,' where previously he used to tune up his sailing boats, thereby becoming frightfully unpopular, as he proceeded to win nearly every available sailing cup.

To call the corrugated iron structure a shed is in itself an understatement. Outwardly, perhaps, there is nothing to show that it is different from any other shed, and one would not give it a second glance in passing. But when one opens the door and is confronted by a full depth screen on which is inscribed THE IRON CURTAIN, one realises that here is a workshop of unusual amenities, and there need be no surprise when a radio automatically goes on with the lights.

Assuming that one has come to work, one can then pass the bed, the gallery of beauties, the dart rack, the dart board, an automobile on blocks, a dinghy, and reach at last the workbench. In the meantime, it is as well to keep the eyes straight ahead, so as not to be beguiled into reading the various slogans on the walls or examining the peculiar objects hanging from the roof. The last item, but certainly not the least, is a large barrel marked oil. In this barrel is kept some of the best sherry in Gibraltar.

It was in this shed that I made my new mast. The famous mast! A book could be written about that sturdy stick. Of course, to get anything cheap it is essential to cut labour costs. Well? What spar has the least labour expended upon it? Obviously, a tree. Herein lay some difficulty, for I was not quite certain how to set about obtaining one, as this was to be my first tree. There were obviously no suitable trees growing in Spain or Morocco, and no spars of any sort over thirty feet long. Deck freight from England would not be expensive, so I sent off a letter to the one man in the south of England who could help me if anyone could, namely Bob Lovell of Vosper Limited. Immediately things began to happen. He managed to locate in Hampshire a group of trees reputed to be Corsican pine, which the Spaniards later called Portuguese pine. Telegrams began to flow between England and Gibraltar. 'A tree has been selected,' followed by 'Tree rejected.' Then I heard that another tree had been chosen, and the chips were flying. Then absolute silence. Hell! What was happening? It was getting near Christmas and freights sometimes took weeks, even months. A pessimistic letter arrived, only to be followed immediately by a wire. 'Spar shipped on board ship *Palomares*.'

After a few days a white ship stood in past the detached mole and docked at the far end of the harbour. I damned the expense of a taxi and was soon standing on the quay arranging with the stevedores to lift the rough octagonal stick off the deck and drop it into the water.

Had it been taken round to the shed by road, there would have been endless formalities to cope with, including an import licence to get it to the shed, and an export licence to get it to the boat, with a futile waste of everybody's time. To avoid these machinations we had great fun towing the fifty-foot piece, which weighed nearly half a ton, across the harbour in Piccone's comic little one-cat-power launch, and in weather quite unsuitable for such operations. Had the engine stopped, the tree would have mowed us down like a battering ram. When we landed safely at the quay nearest to the shed, we asked the policeman to give us a hand in lifting it ashore so as to keep him from asking awkward questions.

In the end we could not shut the doors, so were forced to cut off eighteen inches from the mast. As it happened, a lot more finally came off the length. In places it was going to be one inch and a half greater in diameter, and was working out so much heavier than the old one that I lopped it down to 41 feet 6 inches total length (it has a bury of 6 feet 6 inches), and its greatest diameter came out at 7⅞ inches.

For weeks I hacked away with a peculiar hand-adze of Spanish design, then followed with over two thousand strokes of the plane. I think Willie was somewhat appalled at the amount of mess made in his shed, for he is tidy by nature; however, I could not help those tremendous piles of shavings, the destruction of which he accomplished early in the morning, by burning them at the back. One day the fire brigade turned out in full force, but it was all right— 'it was only Allcard's mast.' After that everybody I met seemed to ask after its progress.

Finishing that white stick was a delight—a brisk sandpapering, a caress with the hand, a slight cut here and there to take out any bumps, a glass of that so-excellent sherry, another smoothing with fine sandpaper, and the job was done.

Before putting on the fittings, the mast was soaked in linseed oil, and about a gallon and a half of the oil was absorbed. It was a good mast. Except for two bolts at the hounds plates and at the masthead sheave, there were no holes drilled through the stick, as all the fittings were of the clamped variety. After ordering longer wire runner backstays which were to lead from opposite the jib halyard (the Dockyard first made them of the wrong type of wire, then eighteen inches too short), I had all the servings of the main shrouds and these new runners made of leather, the only material that lasts in serious cruising. The normal type of serving invariably chafes through, and the 'Irish pennants' jam up an important block at moments of stress.

The job of stepping the new mast was left to the last; it was not until April 4th that the doors of the shed were flung wide open and the squeaking of trolley wheels and the blocking of traffic heralded the mast's first journey along the road to the dockyard crane, *Temptress*, and America!

Time seemed to be slipping by very fast. Originally I had aimed at leaving Gibraltar during April, so as to arrive on the other side before the hurricane season started. But working alone, so much time was wasted in shopping and preparing meals, and up to the New Year I had not started working on the boat, as all my time was taken up by writing.

At Christmas I had taken an interesting holiday by going to Seville by coach. The port of Seville—surprisingly large, considering that it lies fifty miles up river—is the place where Magellan had fitted out his ships, and one of them, the little *Vittoria*, received the everlasting distinction of being the very first ship to sail round the world.

My various visits to Spain helped me to pick up Spanish, and after the New Year I took regular lessons from a Spaniard who is known to the British as 'Loose Morals,' not because of any tendency to devote himself unduly to the opposite sex, but solely because of his name—Luis Morales. These lessons, allied with my conversations with a certain dancer at the Arizona Night Club and much listening to the radio, gave me a satisfactory command of the language, an advantage which I found extremely useful since it enabled me to get all sorts of jobs done in Spain at a quarter of the price demanded at Gibraltar.

The biggest job was having the boat hauled out to have the bottom cleaned off and repainted with antifouling. I had great fun at the same time. The mast had not yet been stepped, so I went under engine across to the Spanish port of Algeciras. There was a big swell that day coming from the Mediterranean, and it was a relief when I reached shelter round the end of the mole. Clear of the noise of the breakers, it was then possible to hear sustained shouting in the direction of the slipway. As I moored to the buoy off the slip, the cause became clear. There were about twenty Spaniards launching an open fishing boat by hand, encouraging themselves with outbursts of intense shouting.

As my dinghy grated onto the shingle, one Spaniard broke away from the job at hand and ran towards me thrusting a quarter-full bottle of brandy into my hands. No doubt twenty mouths had already had a pull at that same neck, but I immediately put it to my own lips, tipping it well back, then showed signs of great pleasure accompanied by '*muchas gracias*'. It was a case of true hospitality straight from the heart.

The Spanish workmen were a delight to work with, and very thorough. I remember wandering off one time while seven of them were scrubbing the bottom ready for painting, and they would not leave the job until I had been recalled. They had then craned forward, while I was examining both sides, anxiously awaiting my pronouncement as to whether the bottom was considered clean. When I had said '*Muy bueno*', their faces broke into smiles, and they danced off to their lunch like a happy band of children.

I found that the sternpost had been attacked by the gribble ship worm, picked up in the Torpedo Camber of Gibraltar, but nothing more could be done than thrust as much anti-fouling as possible over the area, which, however, did not dry out enough to do much good. Nevertheless, I reckoned that not too much damage would develop on the Atlantic crossing to prevent me from sailing back to England in the autumn, should I be unable to make enough dollars to stay throughout the winter.

In the Camber, happily, there does not seem to be any sign of the much-feared teredo worm, which, needing only a pin hole to enter, burrows back and forth along the grain of the wood, never breaking into a previous passage and in the meantime growing steadily. The record worm to be found is reputed to have been six feet long and one and a half inches in diameter. The gribble is a much less alarming marine isopod crustacean. It can only penetrate up to a quarter of an inch, although, of course, the wood eventually breaks away and allows it to have another meal off the exposed timber. The gribble nearly ruined my dinghy, which I had foolishly left afloat, and which had paint rubbed off the bottom. I saved it just in time by coating the affected areas with a kind of creosote, cementing over the holes, and thoroughly repainting.

The bill I received for slipping *Temptress*, applying paint, putting a graving piece in the deadwood aft where it was going rotten, repairing ironwork on the sternpost, and launching came to only seven pounds. This gives some idea of how cheap it is to have work done on a boat in Spain. Since there is a shortage of material, however, it is necessary to supply one's own paint, especially antifouling. I used International Paint's Kobe Green, which is a terrible price but is probably the best antifouling on the market. I have not heard of any paint that will prevent goose barnacles from sticking to the bottom, and in accounts of warm water cruises there is nearly always some mention of these pests retarding progress. They do not affect the timber, so unless one is racing, there is little harm in them.

Temptress's clean bottom gave an increase of half a knot, as I found out on my return to Gibraltar, the last trip I was to do under power with no mast or sails on board, a type of rig that always causes me a twinge of anxiety in spite of the reliability of the engine. I have lost count of the number of times *Temptress* made that occasionally stormy crossing to Spain. Algeciras with its yacht club is a very pleasant town and port, being further outside the tourist area than is La Linea, which is nearest Gibraltar. On one trip we had no less than a party of fourteen aboard, most of my guests being from the wardroom of the cruiser *Cleopatra*. As a matter of fact, that party got rather out of hand... It was half-past five in the morning when we broke innumerable port regulations to regain the safety of the Torpedo Camber.

CONCLUSIONS

As is usual when fitting out a boat, nothing seems to get done for weeks, and then suddenly the results of one's labours fall into place like the end of a jigsaw puzzle. Thus it was with me. At the beginning of April the boat looked like a dirty derelict, but after three weeks she became a smart, seaworthy vessel out for her first sail in the Straits of Gibraltar, stretching her new headsails, of flax and hand-sewn throughout, especially made for me by Ratsey. Initially I had written to Chris Ratsey and told him that I wanted the sort of jib that would stand up to being hoisted on one side of the Atlantic and lowered on the other.

I like a moderate-sized jib that can be left up in all weathers. The single-hander has better things to do than mess about changing jibs. The forestay sail is permanently hanked to the forestay, which comes down to the stemhead, and has one deep reef in it with two cringles at the reef to facilitate the reduction of sail and allow for an extra line to be used instead of the sheets when hove to in a gale.

The mainsail and mizzen had been new when I had left England, and I merely had to modify the mainsail to suit roller reefing better, then treat the two sails to save them from being rotted by the sun or being attacked by mildew when stowed wet. There are many brands of canvas-protecting solutions on the market, nearly all of them good for preventing mildew, but there is one that I think ideal for the long-distance cruiser. It also prevents chafe, since it always remains slightly greasy. This solution, which I have used now on my last three boats, is called Kanvo, made by D. S. Weston & Company, of Glasgow. Although one can get this stuff in white I bought the red, which tanned the sails russet brown, a very pleasing colour which, further-more, does not show the dirt.

It was at the end of April that I began to get abreast of the 'list' business, and started to cross off more items to be done than I would add. This list-making is one of the notorious features of getting ready for sea. To begin with, the sheet appears neat and orderly. One makes a list of perhaps ten or twenty jobs that must be done before one sets sail; as soon as these major jobs are tackled, complications arise and positively breed more items, till one actually finds that one does a job before adding it to the list, then crosses it off immediate-ly, in order to persuade oneself that at least some progress is being made.

Various diversions were going on while the work was forging ahead, the chief being the life on the waterfront, which varied con-tinually as yachts came and went. There were few permanents. The *Our Girls* had safely arrived from La Coruña, and lay neglected in the corner of the basin with seams gaping to such an extent that a copy of the *Times* could have been pushed through. Another of the permanents was the stately schooner *Kalkara*, belonging to a rugged individualist named Commander Greer, who, ably backed up by his wife, steadfastly refused to conform to the usual social life of the Ser-vice, and spent most of his time fitting out. His spare time was spent doing his naval duties at the Dockyard as a doctor. He was also very helpful to us in the Camber, and all of us at one time or another went to him with our various ills and complaints. Commander Greer is a man who likes tall masts, a tall dog, but a short wife. His bull mastiff puppy already stood about a yard high. It was fairly well-behaved if you overlook a rather distressing habit of biting through the centre of the mainsheet. The yacht was designed by the Commander, acting under the advice of Captain Illingworth, the hull being built in the creek at Malta, after which *Kalkara* was named. She had had to en-dure several showers of bomb splinters during the war. After the war, by a strange coincidence, both the yacht and the Greers were found at Gibraltar. This friendly pair were almost unique amongst the cou-ples in the yachts in the fact that they were married. Which reminds me of the serious reply of an old Scotsman to a comment of mine, when he was showing me round a large yacht on the Firth of Clyde: 'D'ye no' ken? Immorality' (he pronounced it eemorality) 'is the verra backbone o' yachtin.'

The most impressive yacht in the harbour was Captain Cunning-ham-Reid's *Pious Puffin II*, which was reputed to have been built since the war at a cost of fifty thousand pounds. Although steel-built in Holland on the lines of a Dutchman, she had a two-foot-deep keel instead of the normal leeboards.

Nearly all the yachts that arrived in Gibraltar were supposed to be bound across the Atlantic, but only a very small percentage were finally successful. By the time I had left, only one sailing boat had reached the other side, namely my old friend *Mollyhawk*, which arrived at the West Indies.

Gibraltar. One may smile sadly. The Port of Lost Hopes. Failure was usually due to the incompatibility of crew. That was my least worry. Albeit on two separate occasions I did nearly acquire a crew. Although I arrived at Gibraltar with the full intention of sailing across the Atlantic single-handed, and still held this intention one month before I left, two alternative schemes cropped up in the meantime.

The first was like a romantic story in a magazine. One is apt to think that these things just do not happen. I mean, what does a young bachelor do when a strikingly pretty, starry-eyed and sun-burned blonde, aged somewhere in the middle twenties, comes aboard and asks him to sail her to Cape Town? Well, that is exactly what happened to me. Her name was Jackie. Furthermore, she had sailing experience, as she had voyaged to Gibraltar in a yawl from England.

What difficulties there are to overcome in sailing the oceans alone! How one's life's ambitions are in danger of being chucked away by some chance encounter! I did not agree to take her, but my mind was in a turmoil. I am convinced that she had no ulterior motive, and wanted only to get to South Africa, but she must have been either too innocent or too dumb to see that we would have probably finished up by being spliced. Undoubtedly I should have fallen in love with her, and, after all, there would have been no male competition on the voyage. I was weakening as the days went by, as I thought, 'It will give me the chance to visit Tristan da Cunha. And what a wonderful run back it would be in the south-east trade winds. And what fun it would be teaching her...' Then, with no warning, she had gone. I received a letter from her explaining that the shipping agent had called her up to tell her that there was a ship leaving for Africa within the hour, and did she want a passage? Well, she had been three months in Gibraltar, and I was not a sure bet, so off she went. I gave a big sigh of relief, then another sigh. Did you regret your decision, Jackie? I know that during my long hours at the helm in the Atlantic I let my mind rove amongst dreams of the adventures we might have had... and pondered whether it was good or bad that the ship *Campanella* happened to call in at that moment of our lives.

The other project was to that one as chalk is to cheese. One of the boats that the Port of Lost Hopes had collected was an ancient converted Brixham trawler called *Gold Seal*. She had arrived with four men and two girls on board, and was bound round the world. It astonished me that they had managed to get her venerable bottom as far as Gibraltar. Then there was that bit of sheerstrake, the main topside strength plank, which one could push in quite easily with one's hand. I cannot say either that I thought her crew ideal. In fact, one was tempted to inquire, what were the other three thousand, nine hundred and ninety-four applicants like? For the owner said that he had received four thousand replies to his advertisement for a crew! One of them, however, was my good friend, a burly ex-tank-corps major of my own age, nicknamed (for some obscure reason) Pluto. He was anxious to leave the vessel, as he saw no further chance of either getting his money back or getting any nearer to New Zealand. One Saturday at the yacht club, when we were sitting outside in the hot sun chatting over a glass of beer, Pluto said, 'I'm damned if I know what to do. It's more difficult to get to New Zealand from here than from England. What do you suggest?'

Half jokingly, I replied, 'What would you say if I offered to take you, provided you paid all expenses and fitted out the boat for a single-handed passage back?'

'Why, I would jump at it. You're not serious, are you?'

'Sure, I'll run you out there.'

So he moved aboard *Temptress*—that is, after getting permission from the authorities. Believe it or not, a yachtsman is so persecuted at Gibraltar that he cannot even sleep on another yacht without special permission. Even then I had to give Pluto a written pass for him to go ashore, and, of course, once more I had to write out a crew list in triplicate.

Things went smoothly with us, but after three weeks' work on board, Pluto said that he must make a quick visit to England in order to settle up his affairs. Armed with a list of things to buy there, he left on the plane. I never saw him again. He wrote asking me to forward his kit, and it transpired that he had taken up fruit farming instead.

The problems of the lone sailor again seemed simple. It was to be neither South Africa nor New Zealand, but, once more—'New York, or bust!'

As the date of my departure drew near and could be fixed within a day or so, weather permitting, I was increasingly eager to be off, although I had a slight twinge of awe at what was being attempted. Every day's delay brought me nearer to the worst months of the hurricane season.

In the first week of May the famous list had shrunk to almost nothing. The last major job (and one of the most important) was the making of a permanent gallows. Except for small items, *Temptress* was ready for sea. There were several store items that were unobtainable where we were, and as I wished to see something of Morocco I set off for Tangier with a friend who wanted a lift there. As is usual in the Straits, the wind was light easterly at the start, then proceeded to breeze up rapidly, and there was ample opportunity to try out the modified roller-reefing gear. We battered through various tide rips, going like an express train, making a sensational time to Tangier Bay, where the wind was up to gale force. It blew so fresh, in fact, that we did not immediately risk making the harbour, which is very exposed, but anchored under the lee of the land until the wind eased in the evening.

Tangier harbour and roadstead was full of the most interesting craft, from large steamships down the range to trading schooners, yachts, smugglers, and small bumboats. As it happened, there was rather a slump in the contraband trade at that time, especially as a few days before a boat had been caught off the French coast, and two friends of mine had been thrown into jail.

A lot has been said to the detriment of Tangier, but not being there long enough to see the seamy side, I found it by far the most fascinating place it has been my lot to visit, and it was my first introduction to the Arab world. I fully believe that provided one was, of course, reasonably covered, one could walk down the streets wearing absolutely any garment, however extraordinary, and not a soul would look round.

After two days of strong east winds I set off back for Gibraltar, and on the way got caught in a vicious electric storm on the Spanish coast, which forced me to reef right down and lower the staysail, before running back to Tangier to save pulling my new sails completely out of shape. I again anchored among the heterogeneous craft. *Gold Seal* had moved there, and another ex-Brixham trawler called *Renown* sailed in. I had last seen her in Cardiff Docks. There was one peculiar motor ship, called *Sokta*, which appeared to be an emigrant vessel, and every time it blew hard, which it did every day, she dragged her anchor, much to the alarm of the boats in her lee.

On the evening of the fourth day the wind did not drop at fall of darkness, and there followed an anxious night for all. *Temptress* plunged violently, with the chain rasping hard on the bobstay as she sheered from side to side. It blew hard all the next day, with the spindrift lifting off the surface, and I made no attempt to go ashore, but spent the day finishing off work on the rigging, in spite of the hectic motion.

The exasperating wind at last died down, and clouds coming up from the south-west heralded a change.

Before dawn *Temptress* was under way before a westerly wind, and made the forty-mile run to Gibraltar at an average speed of five knots.

There was now nothing more to do but store up the boat and go. The pattern of my departure unfolded. On Sunday, May 15th, there was a great clearance of my outstanding correspondence, and on Monday I worked out the final list of stores with the ship chandler, Rodriguez & Son, and went backwards and forwards to the town for extra items.

On Tuesday there was more shopping and the ferrying of stores across the Camber by dinghy. An extraordinary sight! One hundred days' stores aboard an eight-foot boat!

Boxes, tins, sacks, cartons, jars, and even paper bags cluttered the ship from end to end, temporarily swamping the saloon, the fo'c'sle, and the engine. Before turning in that night I had to remove a pile of stuff from my bunk.

On Wednesday, repeated journeys in the dinghy laden with fresh water cans enabled me to fill up the two main tanks of twenty-five gallons each and all the loose containers with sufficient water for one hundred and twenty days at sea.

All this time the wind stayed in the west, but at any moment it might have turned back to the prevailing quarter of the east. By Thursday the wind had blown from the west for five consecutive days. Splendid! All the more reason to suppose that there would not be foul winds later. That was my last day ashore. One more visit to the shops for fresh food, the collection of a Bill of Health, two more items, then my pencil zigzagged back and forth across the last entry on my last list. Except for stowage on board, I was ready. Seized with a frantic urge to get away from the shore, I almost ran back to the boat. Only a few people knew of my imminent departure, and miraculously, by a simple subterfuge, the news had been kept from the reporters. I decided to finish my preparations for sea at anchor out in the bay, free of all possible disturbances. I started the engine, the lines were cast off, the engine put in astern, a last shove from a boat hook kept *Temptress* off as she worked herself clear, and my last link with the shore was severed—at least for the rest of the summer, and possibly for all time. Only the final reckoning would prevent me from reaching the other side of the Atlantic.

I had been in and out of the Torpedo Camber many times, but this time held a powerful air of finality, and I could not help chuckling out loud with happiness as I looked back. On every deck people were standing. I felt a sense of friendliness flowing between us. Final waves. Diminishing shouts of 'Good luck.' Then it was suddenly gone. They were gone, now only past acquaintances. I turned away and pointed the bowsprit towards the future.

The west wind had dropped. *Temptress* ploughed through water like glass. As I rounded the corner of the mole leading to the open anchorage, a slight ripple over the surface spread towards us and fanned my cheek. The new wind. Wind from the east. Thus I knew that the gods favoured my venture.

I had hardly anchored when Cecil White rowed over from his motor-yacht *Fenella*, inviting me to dinner. This was very welcome, as my galley situation was one of confusion. What was even more welcome, he presented me with three bottles of medicine—Scotch medicine, in bottles which usually come wrapped in straw.

II

FIRST WEEK

Saturday, May 21st, 1949.—My knife stayed poised for an instant, then cut cleanly through the loose end of a new whipping. The last job. *Temptress* was ready for sea. Below decks everything was well-stowed and lashed down fit for the worst weather. Above decks she was all shipshape to the best of my ability and the depth of my pocketbook.

Overhead the sun shone brightly out of a blue sky that faded in all directions into a circle of haze, while a perfect fair wind which had been gathering in strength all the morning swept easily round the almost vertical north-east face of the Rock.

Clank clank clank clank… clank clank clank clank… the pawl of the windlass seemed to say, 'We're off, we're off… we're off, we're off…' I plied the lever faster, faster, only too eager to go, without the slightest qualm about the staggering distances to be sailed. With the chain up and down, the anchor appeared reluctant to leave Gibraltar sand, and I had to exert my full effort to break it out. Immediately it drew clear, the boat, under bare poles, paid off, allowing me plenty of time to lash the anchor firmly on deck, for I did not expect it to go down again until it hit American soil.

Then up went the mainsail, with me dragging on both halyards at once; the jib was broken out, sheets eased, and with the helm up the boat paid off, gathered speed quickly, and skidded off downwind. By the time we were at the entrance of the Admiralty harbour, *Temptress* was under full sail, all halyards neatly coiled, and ensign rippling in the breeze from the mizzen truck. It was a stirring day of departure. I swept through the entrance and headed close-hauled for the yacht club house, where I could see a large crowd gathered. A squall descended from the Rock, making the boat heel to her gunwale and show a considerable expanse of her green-painted bottom to the assembled party.

Running as close as I dared to the lighters off the club, I dipped my ensign. They did not seem quite ready for it, as there was some delay before the reply. Then their flag fluttered down, but just as I was about to hoist my own again, a vicious squall attacked us from starboard and the boom slammed over in an unexpected gybe, taking the ensign halyard with it. By a fluke I managed to grab and clear it so as to hoist the ensign to its proper position. How mortifying it would have been to have left with ensign flapping out to leeward at half-mast!

Temptress made short work of the distance to the south entrance, running swiftly before the shifting puffs of wind, as a mouse tries to avoid the sharp cuffs of a cat. Sailing inside the harbour can be very treacherous in a wind from the Levant, and on occasion I have seen whole surface areas whipped into liquid confusion, so that it is impossible to distinguish between wind and water. But on that day the squalls were not that bad. As the gaping mouth of the harbour walls dropped astern there were only mild puffs which kept me busy trimming sail as the two winds coming round each end of the Rock struggled for mastery.

It was not long before we picked up the true wind from the Mediterranean, and the bellying mainsail drove the hull forward in the forty-mile race against the current, a race to get clear of the Straits before dark and before the almost inevitable evening calm could overtake and leave me becalmed in the midst of the steamers.

Over towards the Spanish coast, between me and Algeciras, a large three-masted schooner was being towed clear of the unreliable head winds of the Bay. By the time I was off Carnero Point the fishing boat cast off his tow about a mile astern of me, and the schooner began to pile on sail. With her foresail, mainsail, mizzen, three headsails, three jib-headed topsails, and finally a huge squaresail set on the foremast, she presented a wonderful picture in the brilliant sun as she prepared to tack downwind by heading over to the African coast, which now could be seen looming through the blue haze.

The east wind remained true to form, increasing steadily as Tarifa Point became clearer. It was grand sailing weather. At the end of one hour after leaving the Bay, I rolled up two turns in the mainsail without altering course or touching the mainsheet or, for that matter, the peak halyard. I cannot extol the virtues of roller reefing more. The standard method of reefing would have turned that simple operation into a wet and messy struggle in that sea, apart from the waste of time involved.

As Tarifa Point came abeam, the wind was blowing on moderate gale force. With two more turns in the boom *Temptress* was cracking along at her maximum speed, and she made short work of the rather alarming patches of seething breakers which marked the various tide rips. Already way ahead, the schooner had gybed and was evidently heading up the Spanish coast towards Cadiz.

Progress was even better than I had reckoned on, and only six hours from Gibraltar, Malabata Point was already abeam and the tall square houses of Tangier could plainly be seen glistening in the sinking sun.

Before reaching the yellow lighthouse of the great Cape Spartel, the boat was sailing so well that we overtook and passed a fisherman under power, but I resisted the temptation of offering him a tow.

When the Cape was abeam and the great Atlantic was spread before me, I suddenly realised the enormity of the job at hand. Only once before had the voyage been done non-stop from the Mediterranean to New York by the long southern route, and that was twenty-six years ago by Alain Gerbault, who had taken one hundred and one days. But I had told my friends in Gibraltar and written elsewhere that I expected to take eighty days, for I had stronger sails and gear, and expected to choose a more practical route than he did, especially in the region of Bermuda, which he passed to the north-east.

The distance from Gibraltar to New York as taken by power vessels is not much over three thousand miles, but by the Trade Wind route for the sailing vessel one has to go south-westwards past the Canaries and as far south as about 22°N latitude before swinging north-westwards between the West Indies and Bermuda and thence to New York, thus getting three benefits: the trade winds, the north equatorial current, and the Gulf Stream off the American coast. This distance involves sailing not far short of five thousand miles. The route I had selected would be about three hundred miles longer than Gerbault's, but quicker. In my book rack there was a school atlas for Atlantic data, and I had been given various charts of the American coast which would come in handy when making a landfall. I had not wasted any money in buying any charts of the Canaries, Cape Verde Islands, the West Indies, or even Bermuda, so confident was I that if I made port at all it would be New York.

Off Spartel my thoughts were on the future but my actions were for the present, for I set to zero and streamed the log, and altered course to west-south-west.

Seven miles more were sailed into the ocean before the sun set as a red molten ball and the cooling land killed the strong winds of the day. The last minutes of daylight were used to lower the mainsail, and as the boat steered herself towards the west under headsails alone, I slipped below, feeling very pleased with the afternoon's run of forty-three miles against the current. Already my face was smarting from the sun and wind, the first stage of toughening myself for the long hours that would have to be spent steering in the fierce heat of the tropics.

After putting the clocks back two hours to conform with Greenwich Mean Time, I poured myself a gin and lime, then stood, head out of the hatch, gazing out across the sea. What a shattering change had come into my life! What would the weather do? Had not the voyage started just too well? 'But,' I thought, 'there is no practical reason why the crossing should not be successful.' As I let the drink run smoothly over my tongue and down my throat, while listening to the Spanish music wafting up from the cabin, it was felt that there were many worse off than this person.

After a fitful sleep of a very few hours I got up soon after dawn and surveyed the scene with somewhat jaundiced eye, in spite of the fair morning. After a steady breeze all night, the wind had fallen light from the east-north-east, allowing the boat to roll around in the various swells. No land was visible; in fact, it was quite possible that no land would be seen now till landfall on the other side.

A hot breakfast put new life into me and by eight-thirty full sail was hoisted to a new breeze from the north, no doubt the first puffs of the Portuguese Trades, which should now be in full swing on the western coast. The morning was spent floundering along pleasantly enough under a hot sun, and it was good to note that the snatching of the mainsheet had very much less bending effect on the new mast.

It was not pleasant long. At midday, after a brief calm spell, a rising wind came away from the north-west, and within the hour the forehatch had to be closed against the beam sea being built up over the ocean swell. By rolling down two turns in the main and backing the staysail, it was possible to leave the helm lashed while the boat travelled fast enough with the wind on the beam.

By dusk *Temptress* was being hammered up and down violently by big breaking seas, and everything seemed set for a dirty night. The staysail was reefed and more turns taken in the boom before the all-round white light was lit and the boat left to find her own way amongst the waves.

Five o'clock in the morning is a poor time to get up, even under ideal conditions, but during a cold grey dawn in a small boat with a rough sea, and after a night of little sleep when one is already feeling a bit seedy, the cup of enjoyment is not filled to overflowing. The steep sea was just forward of the beam, making the boat heartlessly lively. It took a hot drink and several hours at the helm to make me feel fit again. The afternoon found us plunging along at four and a half knots in a lumpy sea, and although the clouds had broken up, allowing the sun to shed its warmth, it was cold enough for a jersey and windguard.

The fourth day showed no improvement in the weather, but it was distinguished by giving me my first sight of a pilot fish which had taken up position by the stem. The sun made a feeble effort to break through at noon, making it possible to take a meridian altitude which was shown later to have been quite inaccurate. Meanwhile, throughout the whole day the wind ponderously veered in a very impressive manner, until in the evening it was blowing really fresh from the north-north-east, driving before it big cross seas which started to flood the decks. Above, a blanket of dark clouds cast a complete shadow over the turmoil below.

It was no longer possible for the boat to steer herself with the mainsail up, before a wind so far aft, so at dusk the big sail was rolled right down till the gaff jaws were only a few feet above the gooseneck on the boom, making it comparatively easy to lower altogether. The new boom gallows proved a great success; it was not long before the mainsail was securely stowed, and the boat continued on her course under headsails alone, with the tiller left unlashed.

Down below, sitting on the galley seat and preparing a bowl of porridge, listening to the whistle of wind while bracing myself against the sickening rolls and lurches, I felt tired, dirty, and unkempt, but I had made my choice. Let the wind howl mournfully through the rigging. Let the black seas sweep the hull from end to end and back again. It could do nothing to shake my determination or to turn me for an instant from the search for the unknown adventures ahead.

After a restless night during which it was not easy to prevent myself from being thrown out of the bunk, so bad was the rolling, I got up to find perfectly vile conditions. It was cold. Black and grey clouds scudding low over the water covered the sky, while rough seas and big came charging down on the starboard quarter in a manner which one would expect in the English Channel and not in the thirties of latitude.

Temptress was still on course under headsails and had already reeled off thirty miles on her own and was coping so successfully, except for the frightful rolling and lurching, that I left her to it and attempted to do a little reading. A friend had given me some 'thrillers,' and to my amazement it was found that they scared me! After losing myself in the book I had difficulty switching my mind back to the extraordinary conditions of the moment. That night I had nightmares, which decided me to put this type of book aside until I was mentally acclimatised to my new way of life. Later on in the voyage these books did not affect me and were read, sometimes at the helm, before being consigned to the deep.

The day passed and another night, as the boat with decks awash corkscrewed her way to the south-west before the steep seas piled up by half a gale of wind. Fine rain was being driven over the waters at dawn of the sixth day, and I was getting anxious about my position—chasing madly on with islands and unmarked reefs under my lee. I hoped my course was leading me between the Salvage Islands, with their neighbouring reefs, and the Canaries, but I was uncertain just what the Canary Current was doing to me. Ralph Stock in his *Dreamship* was very nearly wrecked in those waters when a current had refused to follow the arrows on the chart.

Although it was overclouded at noon, two and a half hours later the sun showed itself for a few instants, and I made a dive for the sextant, managing to get a reasonable sight for a position line which, allied with the vague dead reckoning, allowed me to put a cross on the chart about two hundred miles off the Canaries.

The weather remained unutterably vile, and before the day was out the wind touched gale force. Every now and again a big sea would sluice over the quarter. *Temptress* did not seem to mind the weather, and continued to knock off seventy miles or so a day under the headsails, without even the helm lashed.

Another night was upon me. It always seemed to be. As darkness fell there was always that twinge of anxiety. There was the danger of steamers, sailing coasters and fishermen, and that gnawing doubt of the whereabouts of land. As I was scrambling six eggs and a chopped onion for supper, the boat gave a spectacular lurch, immediately followed by the roar of solid water over the decks, and through the chinks in the hatch a part of the ocean squirted right into the saucepan and down my neck. Damn the weather! I shouted curses at the unheeding elements. Before turning in I donned oilskins and pumped fifteen gallons of bilge water over the side.

By midnight the wind had eased slightly to Force 5 Beaufort Scale, but the sea did not improve and was so big that the barometer was pumping up and down in uncanny fashion as the boat tossed about in the waves. However, in spite of the extravagant motion I had quite a good sleep, having become mentally tough enough to stay seven hours in my bunk without giving any lookout.

In the morning there were signs of a change. The wind had backed to the north, and the clouds began to break up, letting the sun through for a series of sights which made me pretty certain of my longitude. The sun was out at noon but was so high in the heavens (over 80° angle) that it was very difficult to point the sextant at the right bearing, especially as the boat was rolling abominably. So my latitude was still uncertain, and it could not be obtained accurately by plotting morning and afternoon position lines as is possible in more northern latitudes, since the bearing of the sun was either in the east or the west except around midday.

Occasionally a series of immense waves came along, and at unexpected intervals one would spill over the quarter and souse the whole deck, making it unwise to open the hatch except for an instant. Thus the atmosphere down below became very foul—almost bad enough to shovel out.

For the last few days there had been two pilot fish darting along at the lee side of the stem, but when I went forward to examine the headsail sheets I saw that they had deserted me, either in disgust at the poor rate of progress, or because they had found proper business with a shark, for their profession is to test all food before their master deigns to eat. An Irishman will tell you that the pilot fish follows the shark in advance. It is said that on occasion it will actually take refuge inside the shark's mouth, but subsequent investigation and study of these elasmobranch fishes did not give me any evidence to support the theory.

The barometer was rising, and what with less wind and resultant sea, and a fair amount of sun, the day could be said to have been the least unpleasant of the trip. In fact, by the evening the wind was down to a mere healthy sailing breeze, but in the smoother water the boat still maintained her three knots. She could have done with the mainsail up, had it not been so late in the day to start such antics single-handed. During the day several ships had been sighted, and each one brought on an orgy of futile speculation as to where bound.

A heavy dew added to the many other signs of coming good weather, and it was in a better frame of mind that I turned into a bunk which was itself steadier than of late.

Thus ended my first week at sea. If it had been enjoyable, I cannot say in all honesty that I had noticed it.

12

LAND SIGHTED

Saturday, May 28th, was the first day of reasonable sailing conditions since leaving Gibraltar. The calmer sea prompted more organised meals, with a properly laid table and use of plates, knives, and forks (just like other people). I had a good wash, brushed and combed my hair, and generally the standard of living went up several points. Gone forever were the eating out of saucepans, the stacking of dirty plates, and the ill-prepared food. It always takes a little time to find one's feet in a new type of life, and I felt that I had now shaken down into sea routine.

It was calm enough to have all the hatches open, and it was a great relief to have clean fresh air eddying through the boat. There was promise that the thin clouds would roll back for a noon sight. As I did not want too much speed until I was certain of my position, it was enough to hoist the mizzen and ease the head sheets, which immediately made her pick up a knot, although it was now necessary to steer. *Temptress* had steered herself under headsails for nearly four days without any attention whatsoever.

A morning position line and a noon altitude gave me a fix at a point forty miles to the north-east of Allegranza, an outlying islet off the north of the island of Lanzarote, so I altered course to west, which was expected to carry me between the Salvage reefs and the whole group of the Canaries.

Before starting to prepare lunch I decided on a gin to celebrate the onset of good weather. It was the only bottle on board and was over half full, but when I opened it the smell seemed so foreign to the sparkling fresh air without that my mind was changed. The open hatch was near. I did not even bother to look out to see the splash.

After a spell of bad weather it is always one of the rites to explore the food locker for something special. It wasn't necessary to broach tinned food, and a fine Spanish omelette was the result of my labours, the special part of it being the mashed potatoes. You might well say, 'What's special about potatoes?' That's just it. Potatoes, for the single-hander, act as a morale gauge, for one who can find the time and energy to peel and otherwise prepare them is obviously in a happy frame of mind. A fresh fruit salad followed the omelette, and coffee followed the salad. I felt like a good sleep, but there is no peace for the wicked, and enough energy was summoned to hoist the mainsail. With the sail up it was like putting the boat into high gear, and she was soon flying along through the dancing blue waters with the fine breeze precisely on the starboard beam.

One snag about sailing in the tropics is that the nights are long all the year round, so sunset came at eight o'clock that evening. The wind, of course, inconveniently freshened, making *Temptress* roar along in tumbling waves just as I was about to lower the mainsail. However, after rolling down to close reef, then dropping the boom on the gallows, it was stowed without much difficulty or having to alter course.

At sunset and sunrise the visibility is supposed to improve, but I looked in vain for any signs of land, which should have been on the port beam about twenty miles off. Tenerife was reckoned to be still one hundred and forty miles ahead.

It blew lively enough all night, and excellent progress was made under headsails. Several times I looked out of the hatch and stared into the windy darkness for the loom of land and listened anxiously for any foreign rumble of surf. Land should be abaft the beam, but one never knows. At this game an error of mathematics or lack of caution or even just a stroke of bad luck can cause disaster.

At half-past four, in the first paling of the stars, I was again shivering in the hatch. I do not know quite what I expected to see. Fuerteventura, according to Slocum, is 2700 feet high, and presumably Lanzarote is pretty high also. What I did see, apart from a rather fine dawn, was masses of black clouds dotted haphazardly about, and a great deal of unnecessarily agitated water. My warm bunk was sought again, honour satisfied.

As soon as the sun was decently high it was being spied upon by my sextant, and the longitude was again confirmed, with the additional check given by a steamer which was obviously heading for Las Palmas. The noon sight, however, gave a very different latitude from the dead reckoning, and although it explained why no land had appeared, it gave a line no less than forty miles to the north, thus showing that too much had been allowed for the current.

Leaving the mainsail stowed, I took the helm and watched the boat cream along at four knots under jib, reaching staysail and mizzen. It was one of those glorious days in which it was so good to be alive, and while having a cup of tea in the cockpit I could not help laughing out loud for the sheer enjoyment of it all. Everything seemed so simple and clean in that beautiful blending of colour. I thought how much better it was to have a greater interest in the condition of one's bowels than in what was happening in the Kremlin.

My poetic reverie was interrupted by a sustained whirring behind me which made me turn round in temporary alarm. But it was all right. The rotator log had somehow got gummed up with salt after the bad spell of weather and had suddenly reached its limit of resistance against the ever-twisting line. It proceeded to register one tenth of a mile in a few seconds. And so cleaning and oiling the log became one of the endless jobs required to keep a boat operating efficiently.

By late afternoon, wind and sea had eased away leaving calm and placid conditions. What a change from that first horrible week. From below the horizon to windward came a host of knobbly little clouds that looked like a mass of little animals scurrying to a feast. This was my first introduction to the typical trade-wind clouds, countless thousands of which I was to see in the next couple of months.

All day long there was the company of two stormy petrels which zigzagged repeatedly round the boat in their endless quest for food. These comic little black birds never rise more than a few inches above the surface of the sea, and their agility in rough weather is nothing short of miraculous.

It was nearly two hours before sunset, when the decks in the shady parts were already being stained with dew, that I had the thrill of seeing my first shoal of flying fish. Hundreds of white and blue darts precipitated themselves downwind, veered round in an arc, and plunged suddenly out of sight. Not long after I saw a white object floating in the water ahead. On running close I was excited to see that it was a Portuguese man-of-war. It was smaller than expected, only about seven inches long, and its 'sail' was a sort of narrow bladder, iridescent as a soap bubble and a delicate pastel shade of blue. Surely we were now sailing in tropical waters. All it needed was a little more warmth, for it had been far from warm on deck in the breezes of the day, and the nights struck cold.

The breeze freshened at dusk, and when the big staysail had been bundled down the forehatch and working sail set in its stead, motion became quite lively again as the boat was left to her night watch. Before going below to satisfy hunger, my eyes swept through the horizon arc and across the sky. All's well. No steamer lights. Already, braver stars were beginning to shine unafraid, while the first sickle of the new moon hung like a delicate piece of craftsmanship in the green, dark sheen of the illimitable spaces.

If cooking dinner is tricky in violent motion, eating it follows a pretty close second. In the erratic rolling which is always occasioned by the absence of the steadying effect of the mainsail, the swing table, the only type of table one can use, dances about in a most disconcerting manner. One moment the plate will be near one's knees and a few seconds later level with one's chin. Even when one has been able to spear some fodder with a fork, one often has to wait for an excessive lurch to expend itself, in case one misses the mouth or makes an inconvenient insertion of the instrument. That evening was no exception, although I managed well enough as I had now accepted such conditions as the normal way of living.

While waiting for the time signal to come through on my miniature short-wave radio, I listened to some music, which seemed quite incongruous and not easy to appreciate out there. One could not help thinking of the players of the orchestra, possibly rather soft physically, with sallow complexions, scraping and blowing away, conscious of the big audience but little realising their critic of a one-man band in the Atlantic, a critic jammed in the corner of a tiny cabin of a boat whose log was kept turning twenty-four hours every day.

Although the waves were much smaller than of late, the boat rolled heavily all night and allowed me but little sleep.

The day of May 30th dawned fair, however, and for breakfast there was still fresh bread, butter, and marmalade, although the bread was now ten days old and had to have the green cut off the outside before use. The butter had also gained an extra flavour which had a certain richness not usually apparent in more normal circumstances.

The morning sight again put me in a smug mood, as the position line had an intercept of only half a mile. Conditions for taking sights were almost ideal, as the height of the waves had shrunk to such an extent since the dropping of that boisterous wind that by standing on deck it was possible to keep the horizon in sight the whole time. This was very useful for the noon sight with the sun so high overhead. I was very painstaking over the sight, but on working it out I had all the smugness of the morning knocked out of me, for it gave me a latitude even farther north than the day before. In fact, on that course there was danger of being wrecked on the unlit and uninhabited Salvage Islands that very night.

The fix given by the two position lines was twenty-four miles off Great Salvage Island, and course was altered to pass south of it. Only one hour and a half after taking the sight there seemed to be a bump on the horizon, motionless, and a lighter blue than the waves. Binoculars were levelled. Damn. Lost it. Ah! Land! It was unmistakable, and on the exact bearing as calculated. At last I knew just where I was among those deceptive islands. Mainsail was hoisted in time to have the fun and games of a rain squall, which had me busy at the roller reefing gear. The pall of rain swept away forward, and by the time it had cleared the island had raised itself considerably from the horizon.

Short work was made of the distance in the squally wind, and at dusk the island loomed large to the north about five miles away. It was just possible to see the row of grey bumps that marked the Piton reefs farther to the west. A seagull flapped quietly round to inspect me, and it looked very unusual with its slow wing motion after the quick-wing birds one meets at sea.

With head sheets hardened right in, the boat sailed at two and a quarter knots through the night dead before the fresh wind, and although she has the odd bout of heavy rolling as she pays off on one way or the other, she remains remarkably steady when running true with the waves.

The only hazard between me and the vastness of the ocean was the island of Palma, about one hundred miles on the port bow.

The nine days of mostly rough weather had taken effect on the untried gear. The main shrouds were hanging in bights, and a general overhaul was required, as well as various work on deck. Thus a quiet bit of the ocean was required in which to do my repairs. Thinking that in the region of the islands the trade wind would be upset and it would be calm, I decided to sight Palma and made my plans accordingly.

The wind increased. Every now and again the jib started to shiver violently at the leech. At four o'clock in the morning the flogging started to shake the whole boat and quickly had me out on the deck. There was an amazing difference up above. The wind had risen to half a gale, and the crests of big seas could be seen glowing in the blackness. The sails were retrimmed and the helm lashed to keep the wind on the starboard quarter.

In the morning, on taking the helm, I found that a squid eight inches long had landed in the cockpit overnight while evidently escaping from an enemy. Conditions were unpleasant again. Black storm clouds covered the heavens and an angry sea rolled up astern, and I was soon happily scudding along at a comfortable four and a half knots, content to leave the mainsail stowed. This was the sort of day on which a ketch would have proved a better rig. The smaller mainsail of a ketch would have been simple to hoist in place of the mizzen, giving good increase in speed and possibly making the boat better inclined to steer herself.

Late in the day the cloud break-up occurred. How many times I have seen this welcome sight. To begin with, one has the whole sky obscured with black, the black sinks to grey, the pall scatters into individual lumps, then the famous patch of blue, the repairs for a Dutchman's trousers, foretells the lightening on the horizon and the gradual defeat of the clouds as they retreat in disorder to leeward.

Not having seen a ship all day, I gave a surprised 'Sail O.' My glasses made her out as a big gaff trading ketch coming from the islands and probably bound for Madeira or the Straits. Lying on the starboard tack she passed a mile ahead of me, lifting in an impressive fashion to the big head sea. There was a trysail set instead of the main, and no jib was set on the long bowsprit. She looked a real picture in that colourful scene, and her tan sails lit up by the now brilliant sun contrasted to perfection with the deep blue of the sea, which was itself slashed by the white horses and parabolic flights of the shoals of flying fish.

Visibility was obviously good, and it was only the clouds which kept the tall Canary Islands invisible to the south. As it was, there were several times when the cloud layer towards Palma, which was fifty-five miles off at dusk, appeared to take on a definite outline of land.

The day passed into a thoroughly dirty night. There was no dew, which is a bad sign in those parts. However, the boat charged on by herself under headsails happily enough. This headsail sailing is a great trick, and I would have made a much better passage from England to Gibraltar had I learned the drill then. In the trade wind area the wind increases at night, and it is, therefore, a waste of time to heave to during one's rest. Captain Slocum was exceptionally lucky with the extraordinary Spray, as this truly remarkable vessel sailed off the wind with mainsail set yet with no hand at the helm, and it is on this fact that he was able to make single-handed passages which have never been beaten to this day. Incidentally, he had some very bad words to say about the weather around the Canaries.

Down below it was difficult to appreciate how much the boat was moving about, and letting go for an instant I was flung across the cabin. I smashed a teak shelf right off and gave myself a nasty bruise on the elbow, which was to worry me for weeks.

At the crack of dawn the island of Palma was clearly visible in the haze, but there was such a poisonous sea that my only chance for some quiet water would be under its lee. There the rigging could receive attention before the start of the long slide to the west.

Taking the helm directly after breakfast, I eased the head sheets and hoisted the mizzen. Luckily I postponed hoisting the mainsail, for within two hours the wind had increased to such an extent that our speed went up to four, five, then six knots, and at a point seven miles off the land the wind piped up to moderate gale force with seas so bad that it was often necessary to run off dead before them to prevent heavy water crashing on board.

The morning had been overclouded, but after noon, when details of the island could be picked out, the sun broke through. There was no lessening in the wind, however, and the gusts, which were beginning to pick up dust off the crests, merged into one big blow, whipping spindrift off the surface and often just picking up the whole bow wave and scattering it to leeward. The seas acted as if in a tide race, and *Temptress* was behaving like a rocket that had misfired and was ricocheting along the ground. She did one sensational lurch as a wave caught her under the bilge and tipped her over so far that the little mizzen boom dipped under the surface and I found myself standing up on the inside of the lee cockpit coaming, with the deck near vertical.

People talk glibly about small boats clawing off a lee shore in a gale of wind, but in that sea and wind, if there had been a land to leeward, my boat would have been inevitably lost.

I had already been eleven hours at the tiller when the land at last began to creep abaft the port beam and the promised shelter of land became a reality. Half an hour later *Temptress* was dancing about in the swells with not a breath of wind to steady her, while easily visible astern was the seething mass of white water.

13

OFF PALMA

The change from gale force to flat calm under the lee of the high land of Palma seemed nothing short of miraculous. The engine was started, in order to run a few miles farther down the friendly coast. Leaving the engine idling in neutral to charge the batteries, I got busy on repairs to the gear up aloft.

There was still a fair amount of swell and it was strenuous work up the mast, but I managed to clear the burgee halyard, which had broken and wrapped itself round, and occasionally jammed, various blocks.

The main rigging was then set up, and several jobs listed as urgent were completed. After dusk, having worked by the light of a flashlight, broken two drills into the bargain (there was something horribly final in the sharp snap as they broke), and generally become tired and dirty, I felt that I had earned the soapdown with Teepol and the plunge over the side into the warm water.

Looking up at the boat looming unnaturally large above me as I swam round, it was astonishing to see how much motion there was, for she was leaping and cavorting about to such an extent that the bowsprit and the bumpkin in turn were dipping under the surface; yet when I climbed on board via the bobstay and stood on the deck she seemed as steady as a rock, in comparison with the turmoil endured for the last eleven and a half days.

There was almost no danger of any boats passing up that coast, but the electric riding light was lit and *Temptress* left to herself about three miles offshore with all sails neatly stowed, while I turned in with a quiet mind. Not expecting to be disturbed I probably fell into a deeper sleep than usual, and all the ruder was my confused awakening to the high-pitched screaming of a tearing wind, and all the greater my shock when my head was met with stinging spray at the hatch, while great masses of boiling crests surged around me.

It did not take long to collect my scattered wits and realise that we were again off the end of the island and that there must have been a strong current setting northward. It was the work of an instant to cast off the lashing and hoist the staysail. A few minutes later there was again that miracluous change to no wind, while astern the roar of breaking waters could plainly be heard. It took two hours under the engine to reach a point opposite the lights of a small town located about half way down the island, where I was able to continue my interrupted slumber.

It was not long after sun-up that we were half way to 'windy corner,' and I had only just time to do some refastening work on the bulwarks, which were coming adrift, when it was again necessary to start the engine and head south towards the smoother water. This time I went much closer in than during the night and stopped a bare mile offshore where there was little swell, no wind, and the sun beat down fiercely on the decks, causing the temperature below to soar to record heights.

The brown and green terrain ascended thousands of feet above me in a series of giant steps, while the indistinct skyline ran like a water colour into first the blue of the pure sky, then the grey of a passing cloud. It all seemed to me to be very quiet and motionless, and my glasses raked the hills in vain for any sign of life. The only indication that the hills were inhabited was the occasional glimpse of a white house and the zigzag mark of a track winding up into the heights.

It was a steep-to coastline with the perpetual white flash of breakers and sullen roar of surf as the incessant ocean swells clawed futilely at the unyielding rock.

The pangs of hunger had just given me thoughts about doing something about lunch when a white motorboat, built on the usual 'hipbath' principle of the country, was seen to be heading towards me. There was a group of men on deck all staring curiously in my direction, and when they were about ten boat lengths away and the exhaust note had died down, they were galvanised into activity launching a small boat from the stern. Deserting the *Olivo*, as she was named in two-foot-deep letters on her sides, they all tumbled into their tender and started to row vigorously to the attack. Heavens! Were the natives friendly in these parts? However, the flash of white teeth in their swarthy faces put my fears at rest, and they jumped nimbly aboard to my invitation of '*venga abordo*.'

While they examined everything with intense interest I was busy writing a letter home to England, and I chuckled at the thought of the surprise my people would get at seeing an envelope addressed in my writing when I was supposed to be in that other world which is the sea.

Evidently the houses that could be seen belonged to Puerto Dacacorte, where the *Olivo* was stationed. The inhabitants had seen me all day, first being swept up the coast by the tide, then coming back under power a mile or two. Having imagined that there was trouble with the engine, this lot had therefore come out to satisfy their curiosity and offer me a tow into their harbour.

They tried to persuade me to come into their port, promising me fresh fruit and good vino. Perhaps one day I will return to that sunny side of Palma and stay there many weeks; but at that time I had no urge to go ashore and meet all the complications of the customs and the publicity which could so easily be avoided by staying at sea. In any case, I explained to them, *Temptress* was bound for New York.

One of my ocean guests was a Venezuelan who wanted to return to his country, and his friends jokingly suggested that he come with me. He held up his arm in mock horror, and evidently considered that there were many other more comfortable ways of committing suicide. When they realised that I was serious about setting out to sea that evening, after much *adios* and wishes of good luck they dropped into their boat and rowed back to the *Olivo*, and after circling round to allow me to get a photograph, they headed towards their home port.

At that time, with the shimmering mauve heat haze enveloping the quiet beauty of that wonderful island, one could not help thinking how lucky the inhabitants were to be born there. Surely here was a place where the perfect climate and the proximity of nature allowed life to flow without most of the troubles of the cold and damp northern countries. Drinking in the scene, I had not the slightest thought of the tragedies and devastation which were fated to follow in only a few weeks' time.

Months later my father sent me the following clipping from the *Daily Telegraph*:

LAVA ENGULFS VILLAGE
FLIGHT TO BEACHES

As I flew over the island of Palma, Canary Islands, yesterday, lava was still coming from the crater of the volcano, 5,000 feet above sea level, in two rivers. Flowing in opposite directions, they were five or six miles long and half a mile wide and were expected to reach the sea today. The volcano renewed its activity on Friday.

The village of Las Manchas has been overwhelmed and others are threatened. I saw a lava stream engulf four farm buildings in a few moments. Pine woods and rich vineyards disappeared. Cattle were being led over the mountain sides to safer areas.

The lava streams are opening into several estuaries, endangering the rich banana plantations. If these are affected shipments to Britain would be reduced by 20 per cent.

So far evacuation of the danger areas appears to be in hand. But hundreds of people would be encircled if the lava estuaries became joined. Latest reports said the volcano showed signs of erupting in other places.

About 1,500 vehicles of all kinds are being used in the evacuation, and men, women and children are fleeing to the beaches, hoping to be picked up by the vessels which are speeding to the island. Schools are being used as rest, feeding and first-aid centres.

14

TAKEN SERIOUSLY

As the brassy sun whittled its angles away towards the western horizon, and the glaring heat of the early afternoon tempered off to the cool of the evening, my practised eye roved round the rigging, but all was now well. Above decks, the old boat was again all shipshape and Bristol fashion and ready to tackle the next stage of the marathon, while down below, the batteries were fully charged, cooking stoves cleaned and filled, bilges pumped dry, and the ship was cleaner and smarter than when she had left Gibraltar twelve days before. She had now been sailed over a distance of 850 miles and had completed her first lap.

It suddenly struck me that I would now have to treat this cruise seriously. Up to then, there had always been the comforting thought that there was a port within several days' sail if some untowardness had demanded special attention; but this was at the parting of the ways, and there was nothing but thousands of miles of deserted ocean before me. The real test was just beginning.

It started in a mild enough manner. A light cat's-paw of a breeze from the open sea entered the bight in the coast into which we had drifted, and, under full sail, the little yawl glided towards the west close-hauled on the port tack, with the rumble of the surf gradually dying out astern.

As the sun set out of a nearly cloudless sky, a cross bearing from each end of the island gave me a fix seven miles off. The light wind was not to my liking, being westerly and not enough to quiet the rattling of gear as the boat rolled to the northerly swell. This swell gave the only indication that the trade wind was still blowing somewhere, but nothing else did, and not for a moment did I think that the wind was still blowing gale force off the north end of the island, for surely being so far offshore there would be some indication, and not a variable head wind.

That Thursday night of June 2nd is the one that I remember above all the others of the whole trip. I was caught napping. The boat had been left hove to under rolled mainsail and staysail, slowly working out to the west. When I woke up, I found her sailing fast direct for the island, which was looming black ahead. I had hardly noted this fact when a squall leaped out of the darkness and I just hung on as *Temptress* went over… over… over, with the swirling water climbing relentlessly up the lee deck and the boom and part of the mainsail digging deep into the sea.

More to close the hatch than anything, I found myself on deck, kneeling on the cabin-top coaming and clutching the bulwark while heavy spindrift raked my naked body. There seemed very little of boat to hang on to at all. The night was black as sin. Then my right hand came in contact with the gunwale of the upturned dinghy, and I wriggled along the deck forward, expecting any moment to be blown overboard.

It seemed like minutes but it could not have been more than a few seconds before I reached the mast and started to feel for the halyards. Before I could do anything, the boat gave a sort of jump as water poured out of the mainsail, and without warning she jerked upright with jarring spars.

It was incredible, but there was not a breath of wind. It had been a warning, however, and now was my chance. That mainsail came down in double-quick time, although something got snarled up somewhere and the gaff took a little taming. Hardly had I lashed the boom to the gallows and passed the gaskets round the sail, when the second squall came hissing out of beyond like a rocket. *Temptress* heeled sharply but stayed on her feet this time, and leaving her on her own, I went below to put on shirt, jersey, shorts, and oilskins. It was obviously time to leave the neighbourhood.

When the third squall came along it was the real thing and was the start of a wild ride. The jib and staysail were now both set and sheeted hard in. The mizzen was also up, with sheet well eased. That little mizzen was made of the same canvas as the mainsail, and when that blows out I will buy some chickens and leave the sea.

The wind settled down to blow at moderate gale force. The seas were all breaking heavily, the crests glowing with an unnerving light, and over and over again I twisted round in the cockpit and gazed anxiously astern as the wind tore at my hair and heavy drops of spray flattened themselves out with their characteristic rattle on my oilskins.

Temptress was going like hammers to hell, but I knew her tricks by now. With a line round the tiller she ran true with the wind fine on the starboard quarter, and she only needed a quick pull to bear away from any sea which was heard to roar too ominously.

The sky was already beginning to pale in the east and I was looking around, making out the familiar outlines of the rigging, when there was a sudden hiss above me and a wall of water smothered the stern, knocking me forward over the compass, filling the cockpit to the top of the coamings, and burying the whole after part of the boat completely under water.

The boat seemed to be sinking, and my undignified position and the fact that I was up to the waist in cold water did nothing to ease my mind. In a bit of a panic I climbed forward and shone my flashlight below, expecting to see water sloshing over the cabin deck, but it all looked very snug and orderly.

With the boat upright the water took an age to drain out of the inch diameter drain holes in the bottom of the cockpit, and most of the water no doubt headed to the bilge past the locker doors. In my unnerved condition I still thought that the freeboard was low. No time was lost in rigging the pump, but it was not long before the handle worked free, showing a clear bilge. So that was that. No damage had been done. A canoe-sterned boat is not supposed to be pooped like that, but I feel that no stern could have lifted to that sea, which must have been one of the overhanging crest variety.

It was lucky that the boat had been dead before the sea. Had that wave broken over the quarter, there would have been a very good chance of losing the binnacle, the dinghy, or me, any of which would have been a regrettable affair.

With the coming of the red dawn the wind rose to gale force (Force 8 Beaufort Scale), and *Temptress* was staggering off before mountainous seas, with decks continually running with water. There was two hours of this before the spindrift stopped rising, and at noon I managed to relieve the long cold hours by making a dash below for an egg, which I drank raw in a cup. I also enjoyed a tin of cold beans at the helm.

It continued to blow hard, shifting between east-north-east and north-east, while huge waves rolled up astern, and it was not until I had been at the tiller for sixteen hours that it was considered safe enough to lower the mizzen and let her sail herself under headsails.

When I went below, I marked the log: 'Wind Force 6. Position 72 miles W. x S. of the north end of Palma. Big sea.' What weather! Oh, where are these authors who write about 'white billowing canvas aloft, as the yacht is wafted gently down the trade winds'?

'Wafted gently!' I thought grimly, as I prepared to jam myself in my bunk. The boat was rolling wildly, the wind was still blowing hard enough for yachtsmen to call it a gale, and coming up the whole time astern were the great masses of foam, rumbling and as powerful as a landslide, which at odd intervals would cascade heavily on the unyielding teak planks of the deck.

Children of Mother Nature must have their games, but she looked after me. My body needed rest and sleep, and in spite of the noise and turmoil, I got good sleep, for my mind was at peace. My navigation troubles were over for a long time. It was only the heaviest blows of the sea that awoke me, and I had the best night's sleep in days.

15

TRADE WINDS

A fortnight at sea and fresh bread for breakfast! But this was the last time. There were no ship's biscuits either, for these had not been obtainable at Gibraltar. There were on board only three small tins of biscuits which had already been in my possession for over two years. Two were the type which are carried as emergency rations in lifeboats, and the third was found to be of a sweet variety which pleases me little and is not suitable for butter. As it turned out, none of the tins of butter was opened the whole trip.

At first I missed the bread and butter, and what breakfast, for an Englishman, is complete without toast and marmalade? Not that my bread at that point was very succulent, as it was green, with the taste disguised with rancid butter.

As if to console me for starting my deep-sea rations, the day was a rare one of sun, with wind just a fresh breeze, and the steep seas of the day before had lengthened out into respectable rollers. It was cool enough for a jersey when sitting at the helm, and to while away the time steering I did the finicking job of freeing and oiling all the spring hanks of the big reaching staysail, which had seized up with salt and corrosion. Those little jobs! They are endless.

Several cuttlefish ejected themselves from the water and smacked against the sides of the dinghy. After a little time I went forward to pick up the largest, which had already started to stick to the deck, and threw it ahead over the side. It sank slowly for a moment before giving a furious squirt of black ink and scuttling (or is it cuttling?—shoot that man) away.

The following morning was a colourful delight. The sea was

an even dark blue, and what is more, free from those stampeding white horses. Studded in the paler sky were fair-weather white clouds, while round the horizon was that deceptive haze which makes landfall so difficult in the warmer latitudes. Probably visibility was no more than five or six miles. Off the Canary group, although there had been much better visibility owing to the bad weather, I had not been able to get even a glimpse of Tenerife, which towers up 12,180 feet into the air. Tenerife has a peculiar phenomenon, for its peak is high enough to be in the anti-trades and is bombarded by a prevailing wind from the south-west, although at sea level the north-east trades blow almost continually. It is a fact that in the trade wind area the winds undergo complete reversal in the higher levels of the atmosphere, although at what actual height the reversal takes place is not clearly recorded, except that it is apt to vary considerably with the season and latitude.

With the coming of the long-awaited fine weather, no time was lost in hoisting the mainsail. It was pleasant at the helm, with the boat slicing along comfortably at three to four knots with nothing but a smooth swell to lift her in easy rhythm.

It was much warmer, too, with the dropping of that hearty wind, and although it became cloudy again in the afternoon, I stood naked at the helm, with the air flowing around my body like warm silk, giving a sense of freedom from the trammels of civilisation which has to be experienced to be appreciated.

My course still edged me to the southward. Out in the ocean there is little need of worry about accurate navigation, but one should keep a fairly accurate plot within a day or so, in case the sextant is damaged or the radio dies on one, especially, as in my case, when there is no chronometer aboard.

The sun showed itself for a short time in the west, and the mean of three sights gave a longitude which showed that we had completed the first thousand miles. The actual sights of the sun were, of course, half blocked by the mainsail. The sails have the most aggravating habit of getting in the way, and this is made worse for the single-hander as there is no one at the helm to hold the boat straight and keep the sun in view of the hapless navigator.

The next day provided the best sailing day to date. Miraculously, it was cloudless. The trade wind was not too strong, and it blew over the sparkling sea as *Temptress* tramped along at speeds between four and a half and six knots with the variation of the wind. This gives me another chance to debunk a popular misconception that the trades blow at an even speed from exactly the same direction day after day. As I found it, both the Portuguese trades and the true north-east trades varied in strength from hour to hour and would shift direction up to a point or more during the day, this exclusive of the squalls which, of course, completely upset the true wind. It was, therefore, not possible to lash the helm with the mainsail up for any length of time.

Captain Slocum, in his description of crossing the Pacific in the trade winds in his seventy-two days' run from Juan Fernandez to Samoa, says, 'My time was all taken up those days—not by standing at the helm; no man, I think, could stand or sit and steer a vessel round the world: I did better than that; for I sat and read my books, mended my clothes, or cooked my meals and ate them in peace… Nothing could be more restful than my voyage in the trade-winds.' Well, he was lucky, owning about the only vessel which was able to steer herself before the wind with mainsail set. As for me, this was impossible, and I had not been able to afford any patent running gear such as fitted by my friend Marin Marie in his crossing to the West Indies from Madeira. So I had to do just what Slocum deprecates and spend countless hours at the tiller.

A ten-hour trick was normal, and on that sunny day we reeled off close on fifty miles during the period.

When at sunset I lowered the mainsail and went below, my face was smarting from the glare of the sun, and I thought that it was probably just as well that the first two weeks had been overclouded, thus allowing my skin to get acclimatised to the light rays.

Tuesday, June 7th.—Following a night of heavy rolling, the morning showed that the wind had hardened considerably, and a biggish sea was running. *Temptress* was doing quite well under her headsails and was left so while I busied myself below with some of the innumerable jobs. A revolting paper bag was discovered full of a soggy mess of stinking beans and onions, which were not long in polluting the Atlantic.

In return the old ocean played a rather dirty trick on me. While I was perched on the rail aft and doing what is known as 'my business,' some seas came along which made the boat do some exceptional lurches. Twice, a part of my anatomy was plunged beneath the waters. Is nothing sacred?

The engine was fitted with one of those patent folding propellers, but for some reason I had never got round to testing it under service conditions. Now was the time. After screwing back the rod which runs inside the main shaft and locks the propeller during normal use, I hung far over the stern to see what had happened, but all was well and it was neatly folded aft. I also saw two fish a couple of feet long swimming under the keel. Fresh food! Into my eyes came the gleam of the hunter.

During that afternoon, as *Temptress* rolled along by herself with decks glistening wet and cold from the odd wave crest which spilled aboard, a milestone was passed. One quarter of the distance to New York had been sailed in seventeen days. However, with the calms of the Horse Latitudes and possible bad weather off Cape Hatteras, I did not expect to arrive until my original estimate of eighty days, or at least seventy-five, had elapsed.

After reading below in the warmth, I had a look out to see the sunset. It was wild-looking and red. After dark when I turned in, it was blowing a full Force 6 and rough, and a proper sleep was found to be impossible, as the boat staggered along with the hull resounding to the shock and crash of seas. 'Do I have to endure this for the next two months?' I asked myself, and felt a stab of apprehension. Was the incessant strain of keeping the boat going twenty-four hours a day unaided beginning to tell?

In the morning there was the welcome sight of two flying fish lying on the deck, and as it happened, they were the biggest flying fish the boat was ever going to collect, a shade over eight inches long each.

It was another gloomy day, and when I eased out the headsheets, hoisted the mizzen, and took the helm, a pall of rain was sweeping across the stern, and the boat rolled first one gunwale under, then the other.

As I nodded over the steering, clad in oilskins against the cold rain of the squalls, with my left arm negligently hooked round the tiller and my right hand gripping a cleat to steady me against the violent motion of the vessel, I suddenly received a series of blows all over my body and sat up with a start. A whole shoal of cuttlefish had bombarded me. Although I have had food thrown at me in some London restaurants, I certainly did not expect it to happen in mid-ocean.

In spite of a headache, and a huge swell from the east-north-east with a sharp sea running over it, I managed ten and a half hours at the helm and twisted up forty-three miles on the log. Black rain squalls had been in sight all the time, and it was these which kept the seas whipped up, as a small boy keeps a top spinning.

Putting the boat under her night rig, I soon had flying fish and the squids in the frying pan. Having heard so much about the wonderful taste of the flying fish, I can only say that I was very disappointed. The potatoes and anchovy sauce turned out to be the best part of the meal. The cuttlefish tasted as they had in Spain, rather like a piece of decayed rubber. To add insult to injury, a minor disaster in the galley terminated this unappetising repast. The stove had already been turned out, with three cuttlefish left in the pan for the morrow's breakfast, when there was a sudden report. One of the little beasts had exploded, blowing the other two out of the pan and scattering smelly fat all over the galley. The meal had not been a success. And just as I had been congratulating myself on being able to cook at all in that sea and with that appalling roll.

Before turning in for a night of 'rest,' I scrambled over the deck on all fours and shone a flashlight into the face of the log to check *Temptress'* speed. Under headsails she was knocking up a steady three knots, and she was left thus to run on her own through the darkness, without even showing any navigation lights. The white light was only lit on alternate nights first, to save the batteries, and second, to test whether more flying fish came aboard if a lantern was exhibited, a point of argument with seamen.

If a steamer were to cut me down, it would not matter, as it would all be in the interests of science.

16

GETTING ON

At the end of three weeks at sea, I thought it about time to do something about my 'fresh wind' rig. My original scheme for 'day' sailing had been to hoist the mainsail in reasonable weather, but, when it was rough, to use the more easily hoisted trysail, which would supplement the area of the little mizzen and, of course, the two headsails.

Fantastic though it may seem, except for the look I had given it before the boat had been purchased, the trysail had never been unfolded, nor even, for that matter, taken out of the sail locker, much less tried up the mast.

After lunch and a morning spent working below as the boat sailed herself under headsails, the conditions improved, and the time was obviously ripe for messing about with sails.

The job was made no easier by the heavy rolling which, as usual, was in full swing. To begin with, it was necessary to emulate a snake in order to dislodge the trysail, which had somehow made its way right up into the canoe stern—quarters, to put it mildly, that are somewhat cramped.

After lugging the sail up on deck and measuring it up, on hands and knees, I came to the conclusion that a long time had been spent by someone in designing the most inefficient trysail imaginable. It had a foot as long as the main boom, little hoist, and the tack was a right angle. Hopeless. After various experiments it was finally set as a sort of a squaresail (except that it was triangular), forward of the mast, upside down and hoisted on the staysail halyards. One corner was lashed to the shrouds to starboard, and the port corner was boomed out with the boat-hook. It looked pretty queer, but it gave me an extra knot, and the helm could be left far longer than if the mainsail was up. However, it did not make her roll any less.

The next day all the mess was cleared away and full sail was set to a perfect wind. At last! A day corresponding to a storybook picture of the trades. A rippling breeze on the quarter, low enough to give one no worries about reefing, yet strong enough to hold the boat and gear steady and to temper to perfection the heat of the almost vertical sun, shining out of a cloudless sky. The sea was an unbelievable blue, and flecked here and there with white horses. The silver glinting of the flying fish made the beauty live until it almost hurt. The billowing russet-brown sails in their graceful curves made the perfect foreground as *Temptress*, the focal point of the vast canvas, scudded with a swing and a sway before the smooth rollers of the mighty ocean. 'Another few days of this,' I wrote in the log, 'and I will modify my somewhat harsh opinion of the Trades.'

That afternoon our passage through the water flushed an incredible shoal of countless thousands of flying fish which temporarily blotted out the horizon.

In the tropics, clouds always formed before sunset, and that evening the evil moment of lowering the mainsail was put off so as to enjoy to the utmost the wonderful effects in cloud-land. The sun sank like the upturned bow of a stricken ship which hesitates before being swallowed by the sea.

There must have been a big disturbance upsetting the weather somewhere, while we were on the eastern side of the Atlantic, for at six o'clock the following morning I was greeted with heavy rain. As a matter of fact, this early-morning rain was quite a feature during the whole crossing, and it was the coming of the dawn and, presumably, the increasing warmth that burned up these rain squalls and finally the dark clouds.

There was considerably more wind sending a jabble of a sea over the general swell, a sort of jabble that can be raised just as easily in Long Island Sound or the Solent as in mid-ocean. These long ocean rollers, which do not affect a small boat, are as good a myth as the one about sailing vessels not rolling. Anyway, *Temptress* was rattled like dice in a shaker as she parted the water ahead at a speed of six knots, and the gear sawed, groaned, and jolted as the demon chafe was busy at his work.

It was not long before full sail was too much for the strength of wind, but we crashed on without any reduction, which made steering wild in the fiercer puffs, and exciting with the wind so far aft.

One day, too much sail, while the next day, with a bit less wind, the mainsail was not even hoisted. Everything or nothing! And variety is the spice of life. And people ask, 'Weren't you bored?'

As it happened that day was a memorable one, for the good day's run took me over the crease in the chart, so that it was folded with America in view, instead of Europe and Africa. This effected a great psychological change in my attitude. I felt thenceforth that I was sailing towards New York, and not just away from Gibraltar. And all this through a mental unreasoning, as the little cross was by no means a half-way mark.

There was a minor celebration in the food line. Despite the heavy roll that started as soon as the mainsail was lowered, I cooked with difficulty but ate with facility a colossal dinner which, as far as quantity was concerned, would have done credit to any hotel.

There was difficulty in tuning in my little radio for Greenwich Mean Time. It was those Russians again. Radio Moscow, on the same wavelength, was pouring out some very uninteresting propaganda, making it very awkward to pick up the British station when reception was bad. What was the sense of it? What stupid animals most of us are.

Monday, June 13th—Did my first dhobying, and not before time. It was not necessary to use fresh water for the actual washing as I used a Shell product, 'Teepol', which washes well in salt. However, for the final rinsing my precious fresh water had to be used. It looked quite a homely scene with my washing kicking in the breeze.

Regarding clothing worn throughout the trip, in spite of the searing sun, which was worse than expected, it was not found essential to rig up an awning, and although we were on the sun's equator or elliptic for a good few weeks, I never wore a hat, nor anything else, for that matter, except in the interests of warmth. Down below, with the temperature never much under 80 degrees, I never wore anything, and therefore was not affected by the heat, even when the thermometer read 94 degrees in the calms.

With care, it did not take me long to become tanned nut-brown all over, and I felt all the better for it. In any case, laundry facilities in the Atlantic are not exceptional, and there was no shortage of sea water to keep oneself clean. Later on when rain squalls were more frequent, I used to soap and let the driving rain give me a fresh-water shower bath, although I remember once when the creeping pall of rain turned aside at the last moment and left me standing angry and covered with soap.

My position at noon was 24° 19' Latitude and 31° 43' Longitude, and it was surprising to note on my globe of the world that although we were near the Tropic of Cancer with the sun almost vertical (89°) at midday, our position was nearer both to Newfoundland and to the mouth of the Amazon than to the West Indies.

The wind eased in the afternoon, too late to bother hoisting and lowering the heavy mainsail for so short a time, so the big reaching staysail went up, boomed out as a sort of a spinnaker. She still steered herself for ten minutes and more at a time. Since the wind was exactly in the magnetic east with a compass variation of 20°, it was well aft, as I was edging south the whole time (I wanted to drop down to 22 °N.), and it was a day, if ever there was one, for squaresail and raffees, had there been any.

There was a great surprise for me when I looked up and saw a white bird framed in the hatch. My *Birds of the Ocean* told me that it was a White-tailed Tropic Bird which bred in Bermuda or the West Indies. My first contact with The Other Side. I was getting on.

This beautiful, snow-white 'bosun' bird fitted well into the colourful scene, and was extremely pleasing to the eye, except, perhaps, for the excessively long tail, which looks as if it had been stuck on as an afterthought. In the islands, evidently, the natives pluck out this tail while the unfortunate birds are nesting, without, however, any detrimental effects. There was ample time in the next month or so to study these birds. The first visitor, who flew round and round the mast uttering a cheep remarkably like the noise of a part of the gear (I never learned to distinguish the difference), was joined the next morning, presumably by its mate, and they used *Temptress* nearly every morning as a trysting place. This was, however, complicated by the addition of a third, thus making the Eternal Triangle. It was some time before my mind was put at rest when a fourth brought harmony in the bird world. They kept near me for over two thousand miles.

The only other bird which was sighted was a giant petrel, one of the birds which flies like an albatross, gliding effortlessly low over the waves and swooping along the troughs in remarkable fashion.

An amber beer bottle came bobbing along. It is very rare that anything foreign to the sea is sighted, and it had me thinking of its history. It looked so fresh and clean. Had it been in the sea for days, or years? There was the impression that there was another vessel only a few days ahead of me.

Perhaps my last boat, *Content*, had dropped this very bottle. She was West Indies bound. Stranger things have happened.

That day (the 23rd), the last of the onions were finished. Potatoes supplied by the ship chandler were already going bad, while the hard new ones bought personally in the market were still in perfect condition. There is a moral somewhere.

With the warm trade wind easing and the seas smoothing out, the next day was another of those wonderful days, with *Temptress* swaying easily along under full sail with scarcely a sound—just the rippling of the water past her curved sides and the slight, protesting creak of gear aloft. I basked in the glorious sun, drinking in the fair picture of my beloved sea, a canvas of ever-changing colour and movement. A feeling of contentment and peace of mind flooded over me, in a manner rarely experienced. It is in such moments that the freedom, the cutting adrift from bureaucracy and the escape from the unnatural life which one is forced to live in this modern world, are sufficient in themselves to justify the endurance of such a voyage as mine.

17

BECALMED

On the fifteenth of June it seemed that the trade wind was dying on me. It was queer to see no white horses, and with full sail and all light canvas it was only possible to proceed at three knots.

The sun was grilling. One advantage of a yawl became especially apparent, for as the sun rose directly astern to pass right overhead and drop down over the bow, the mizzen gave me welcome shade in the first part of the morning.

As *Temptress* waltzed slowly westward there was little enough to do at the helm, and I shortened the hours by reading Compton Mackenzie's *Monarch of the Glen*. Many and long were my chuckles over this gem of volatile literature.

There were a great number of Portuguese men-of-war, all of which were on the starboard tack, while farther east they had mostly been on the port tack. I saw no protest flags flying after *Temptress* had passed, nor is it true that on a quiet night one can hear tiny voices piping 'Lee O' in the darkness. Gerbault's studies of these delicately coloured jellyfish led him to believe that they were merely hove to, drifting slowly to leeward. I do not agree, but believe that they spend their whole life making up to windward against the trades and the current, not solely by their sail, which has not enough propulsive area, but chiefly by auxiliary power below. The so-called sail is probably an aid to direction. In choppy weather it is amusing to see the number of capsizes that take place, but they do not take long in righting themselves.

Sailing at this lower speed, it was possible to leave the helm long enough for refreshing baths under the bobstay. At two or three knots, with the water dragging at one, the power of her going was impressive. My favourite game was to hang onto the forward part of the bobstay near to where it meets the bowsprit. It is a wonderful sport. One moment one is plunged right under, and the next moment, as the bow lifts, one is wrenched upward completely clear of the water. Then there is the scramble on board via the bowsprit shrouds to gain the tiller before the boat is too much off course.

After sunset, with the mainsail down, the log did not even make any pretence of rotating, and for the first time on the cruise it was calm enough for dinner to be eaten with the swing table pegged.

Daylight on June 16th showed a white oily swell distorting the sullen reflections of the clouds. *Temptress* tossed and pitched disinterestedly—points off her course—completely becalmed. The kicking tiller was useless. I seemed to have passed into another world.

Taking this opportunity to wipe down the white topsides, which to my surprise were in remarkably good condition, I happened to drop the chamois leather into the water. The boat was creeping slowly ahead at the time, before a breath. Running aft to retrieve the chamois, I caught my second toe under a cleat and must have been within an ace of breaking it. As it was, it was a damned nuisance for days, and it received further agonising knocks. By the next morning the toe was completely black.

The surface of the water was covered with what looked like dust, as if someone had just shaken a carpet over it— evidently the initial form of sargasso weed.

As I lay on my stomach peering into the depths, it was easy to dwell upon the relative values of distance. *Temptress* was suspended over the great depths. In the brilliant sun and the surrounding powerful colours, it seemed uncanny that three miles and more beneath there was a grotesque world of utter darkness inhabited by beasts large and small, of species still unknown to man. It is difficult to visualise such long pillars of water, yet had the land been that distance off along the surface, it would have been very near indeed.

Without a breath of air to create even a suspicion of a draught, the fierce sun burned down at its maximum strength directly overhead, the glue bubbled in the deck seams, and for the first and only time blisters were raised in the enamel of the vertical topsides. The under side of the inch-and-a-half teak deck became hot to the touch as the thermometer in the 'cool' cabin hovered near the nineties.

There was plenty of work to do, heat or no heat, and the rolling was not too bad, although occasionally a series of beam swells would correspond with the boat's period of oscillation and several impressive rolls would result.

My occupations that day included modifying the generator seating and adjusting the belt, stripping down the W.C. pump and making and fitting a new valve, carrying out engine maintenance, overhauling my fishing gear and nearly catching a dolphin, renewing gland packing on a water pipe, filling the stoves with paraffin, renewing parts of the rigging, cooking various meals, and last but not least, taking many baths after first examining the water for sharks, about which I was still very vague.

The next day again found the boat rocking to a smooth swell, without even a cat's breath to ruffle the surface. Swimming round and round the boat was a shoal of seven fish about two feet long each. My eyes glinted speculatively as I tied a retrieving line to my grane-head, which an Irishman would describe as a five-pronged trident and about the size of one's hand. This was screwed to a nine-foot stave. A stout piece of marline was tied to both the head and the inner end of the stave, so that it would be possible to retrieve both should the fish break off the head.

I waited for half an hour with arm poised, but the fish were wary and would not come into easy range, and it would have been unwise to frighten them by a long shot. I then threw a sheet of paper onto the water and awaited results. They were curious, and after milling around while my shoulders were being grilled by the sun's rays, the leader decided to investigate. Putting my whole strength behind it, I drove the spear into their midst. I grabbed the stave, which vibrated excitingly, and a few seconds later there was my first fish flapping about in the cockpit—a bonito eighteen inches long. And did it taste good? It was worth a hundred of the tasteless little flying fish. This was the start of successful efforts in the ocean fishing line. It is quite untrue that fish cannot be caught far from land. In the end, I could catch them on line or spear with equal facility. I am no fisherman and knew nothing about it when I started on the trip.

My equipment was of the most meagre and would have horrified any real fisherman. As I say, I knew nothing about it, but just caught 'em.

Bolstered by my success, I cannot but pass on my experience to anybody who may wish to catch bonitos at a minimum of expense. The advice below includes the various events which allowed me to become a skilled catcher, thus:

1. Steal a boathook stave from a naval destroyer.
2. Accept the gift of a grane-head from a hotel proprietor.
3. Attach firmly 1 to 2.
4. Become becalmed in mid-Atlantic.
5. Throw a sheet of the *Times* in the water (the Times, for some reason, interests the fish).
6. Insert 2 into fish.

They, of course, soon get bored with the *Times* and it is essential to change the bait. One way is to dip one's feet in the water, but with this method it is wise to strike before the fish each and every time.

While I was swimming round the boat I noticed a number of queer flowers or shells growing on stalks and adhering to the bottom, especially aft, evidently by suction. Later on there were hundreds of these 'goose barnacles' stuck all over the underbody and they seriously impeded progress, although I did my best to pluck off as many as possible round the bow. After a time, the ones round the stern had to be left to multiply, as I became afraid of the sharks.

I took advantage of the calm to charge the batteries, a usually difficult job if any sea was running, owing to the side outlet exhaust system. Between England and Gibraltar it had caused plenty of trouble by stopping in a seaway, and flooding if the exhaust pipe sea cock was not turned off.

In Gibraltar I had written the manufacturers asking for their advice and also ordering spare parts for the engine, but they seemed more keen in absolving themselves of any responsibility for the original installation than in helping me, and as for the spares, they ignored this part of the letter. Therefore, I sailed without spares of any sort, but took the advice of their local representative to fit an eighteen-inch standpipe, which cured absolutely the tendency to flood but did not improve the running of the engine when the boat was rolling. On the port roll she dipped the exhaust outlet under water, then on the other roll the water ran up the pipe and the back pressure was sufficient to stall the engine. In New York I determined to have the run of the pipe brought out right aft instead of on the beam. Another disadvantage of the outlet on the beam is that a foul mixture of burned paraffin and dirty water can be blown aboard over the helmsman.

On that day of calm there was another trouble. The second cylinder plug repeatedly oiled up, so the simple expedient of running on one cylinder, with one spark plug removed, was used, and the engine ran happily for five hours in a very satisfactory fashion but with a somewhat unusual note.

Radio reception was very good that evening, and I listened with pleasure to that girl's harmonious voice from the B.B.C., London, saying, 'The time is now 21 hours, Greenwich Mean Time.'

After a grilling day of clear sky, there was a typical sunset with the sun being distorted and squashed between layers of black clouds—clouds which almost invariably formed at the same time, and which presumably were the forerunners of the nightly rain squalls.

By eleven o'clock that night the sea was still smooth, but a light and steady breeze from the north-east foretold the end of the two-day calm.

Watching the boat settle down to her course, I stood a while on deck before turning in, and let the warm wind flow luxuriously round me.

It was a fitting end to a delightful interlude.

18

HALFWAY WEEK

The first four weeks had exhibited many of the pictures of the ever-changing events which can be expected by a sailor, and the sea itself had played through its acts, from a battleground of elemental strife to a soft bed of peaceful reflections. Gone now, at least for weeks, was the chance of cold, the chance of gale-force winds, or any possible danger from the land. There just remained the vastness of the sea, and the endless drive to harvest the comparatively minute day's runs which, by painful addition, would finally span one of the great oceans of the world.

As it happened, the fifth week's run was only to be rivalled once again, and after seven days of pulsing trade wind, varying from fresh to light, a distance was marked off on the chart corresponding to 522 miles. In fact, on the last day, it could be said, without any fear of contradiction, that I had a nice offing, for *Temptress* was rolling and tumbling about at a spot which formed the centre of a huge circle of two-thousand-miles diameter in which there was not a speck of land.

The hull chose this somewhat inconvenient position to spring a not too serious leak, which sent me grovelling about the bilges in an ineffectual attempt to locate it. Henceforth it was to be necessary to pump the ship daily, or at least on alternate days, to keep the water and my worrying down to reasonable limits.

Following the old windjammers' practice in saving the best sails for the more stormy latitudes, I substituted my old jib for the new, but not for long. After two days the hiss of ripping canvas was its swan song as the fresh trade wind ended the useful life of this venerable sail. So up went the new again.

The new and expensive jib which had been sent out to Gibraltar had not been a complete success. To begin with, it had stretched so much that it overlapped the forestay, with all the resultant chafe and trouble while changing tacks. Why is it that sailmakers never allow enough for stretch, yet riggers nearly always cut rigging too short? Then again, the sail rolled up very badly with the patent gear, since the wire luff-rope was too thin. For a roller jib which does not often have to be stowed below, a ⅜-inch diameter non-flexible rigging wire luff-rope, preferably stainless steel, is the best, allowing one to roll up the sail without any trouble, even in strong winds.

On one day the most extraordinary things began to happen while I was taking the noon altitude. The sextant chased the sun all round the horizon until, finally, a reading was obtained while facing north. I had passed under the sun, which was to be in the north for some weeks. The sun was within a few days of its greatest northern declination of the year—23° 26.9′.

The following day my latitude was south of 23°, and my invaluable atlas informed me that we were now in the Torrid Zone, whatever that meant. The change of latitude was necessarily small, as we merely edged south, but the degrees of longitude were piling up in a very impressive fashion. The longitude of Gibraltar is not much more than 5°W., while in this fifth week the sharp line of 40°W. was passed over without the slightest trace of a bump.

It was getting warmer, too, and the temperature in the cabin did not drop below 80°F. Clothes were quite unnecessary, although around the hours of noon I usually draped a thin shirt over my head as I gasped under the searing sun. This would have been a good time for Lord Dufferin's cockpit umbrella. Who said that an umbrella and a naval officer had no place in a sailing boat?

During most of the week there was a huge swell coming from a direction north of the wind, denoting a severe disturbance which might have been the cause of the upsetting of the trades and the formation of that queer calm already experienced in the middle of the wind area.

One morning there was a perfect example of the antitrades. A

V-formation of mackerel clouds appeared in the west and marched steadily up to windward overhead across the sun towards the east, while below, the white puff clouds hurried across the sky in the opposite direction.

Generally the morning was overclouded after a squally night, but the sun managed to burn up the black clouds before noon. Rain squalls became more frequent as westing was made, but they usually passed to one side or the other of us.

Small bunches of sargasso weed became more numerous, although there were no signs yet of actual islands of the yellow weed.

I was at the point of greatest variation of the compass, which had altered more than 10° since leaving Gibraltar and was as much as two points or 22½° to the west. This had been one of the things which had baffled the seamen under Columbus no less than four hundred and fifty-seven years before. It was pleasant to think that all the beauty of the sea had been unspoiled by the scar of civilisation, and that I was lucky enough to enjoy exactly the same sights as the famous navigator himself, and all that without the grave worry and responsibility which was his.

I saw one sight, however, which would have surprised the ancient voyagers more than it did me. On the afternoon of June 20th, a big merchant ship suddenly seemed to pop up out of the depths and loom large on the horizon on the starboard bow, passing ahead only three miles away. I made haste to hoist my flags, but the so-and-so made not the slightest effort to close with me, an act which would have cost him nothing.

He appeared to be on the New York to Cape Verde Islands route, and for the next two nights a light was carried on *Temptress*, just in case.

All the time the boat rolled heavily, and I felt somewhat lethargic with an aching back. I began to dream every night. In one of these dreams I was at home in England trying in vain to reach the bathroom for a hot tub; in others I had not started the voyage, and when I awoke it took some seconds to work out just what was happening. But it was all right—I was merely in a small boat built of thin planks, rushing through the night with, more often than not, no lights exhibited and, of course, no lookout. Maybe a steamer was six feet off, or maybe a baulk of timber or some wreckage was ahead.

Occasionally, at night, there would be a terrific urge to look out, but there was never anything to see—just a distant blackness of a rain squall or, more likely, the mast silhouetted against the stars and rolling viciously. So back to the warm bunk and to the great thought ever present in one's mind… 'What is the present position of the boat?' 'Where will the boat be in a week's time?'

Good progress was being made and it was considered a bad day if I could not reel off fifty miles while sitting at the helm, during the hours of daylight.

There was a very wild sunset on the 22nd and wind to spare the following day, causing many capsizes among the nautilus fraternity. Also, that day I fell heavily into the cockpit. More bruises. Sores were also developing on my lips, and after a tiring day at the tiller it took increasing will power to force myself to cook a generous meal to keep me going.

For several days a grey haze formed round the horizon similar to that experienced near the Canaries, and this was logged, rightly or wrongly, as being caused by the meeting of the cold Canary Current and the warm Equatorial Current.

During the afternoon of Friday, June 24th, the wind fell lighter and was barely able to temper the grilling heat of the sun. The boat floundered along in an exasperating fashion, first dipping the end of the boom under water, then flinging it twelve feet in the air. The poor day's progress looked as if it was going to spoil the week's run, so the opportunity was taken to see what the night sailing conditions were like. They were not especially inviting and included freezing rain squalls, which kept me clambering forward to man the reefing gear, and sudden shifts of wind. After a spell of seventeen hours at the helm, I gave it up in disgust and hove to for six hours for rest and food until daylight. Finally, in the next afternoon, the mainsail was stowed, after I had spent twenty-six of the last thirty-two hours at the helm. I promptly had a refreshing dip from the bobstay, and noted that my pilot fish had been joined by four of his pals, none of which had the slightest fear of me. It was quite easy to prod them with one's finger.

However, 522 miles for the week was not bad for a little one, and this had put a different complexion on the vast distances. We were over the halfway mark to New York, and, what was more, the nearest land was the West Indies. It was now quite inconceivable that it would be necessary to put into a port on the eastern side of the Atlantic. It gave me a pleasant feeling that it was easier to reach the 'other side.' There now could be no anti-climax to my avowed aim.

19

TWO SUNDAYS

Originally, when mentally planning the trip, I had intended to heave to or let the boat sail herself on Sundays, thus giving me something to look forward to every week—extra sleep, as well as a chance to get some cleaning done. However, what with leaving later than estimated, and the imminent starting of the hurricane season, five Sundays had already passed without any easement from the exacting operation of driving a small boat single-handed across an all too agitated ocean.

After having hoisted the mainsail for seven consecutive days and knocking up a record week's run, it was felt that a day's rest was well deserved, so at dawn on Sunday, June 26th, instead of tottering out of my bunk, with gummed-up eyes and a mouth feeling like the bottom of a parrot cage, I just went on having a good sleep; not that my night's rest had been undisturbed, for at two in the morning the jib had started to flog and it had been necessary to harden in the sheet amidst cold, driving rain.

The boat was rolling heavily (one penalty of not setting the mainsail) but keeping course beautifully, running westward on the twenty-third parallel of latitude with the wind fine on the starboard quarter. Big trade-wind rollers were piling up astern after gathering force for many hundreds of miles, and they were generously capped with white horses spurred by the energetic wind.

It was obviously the day for cutting hedges, so after my oatmeal breakfast I could have been seen holding on grimly with one hand, and trimming my beard into a fancy Vandyke with the other. I also cleared away some of the hair falling over my ears, but dodged any attempt to cut my hair. As it happened, although it had not been cut for thirty-eight days (and it grows fast), it had kept well under control, as the sea air had turned it into a mop of unruly curls which, as well as being picturesque, prevented the hair from falling over the eyes.

After a good soapdown and rinse I felt a new man, and being seized with a washing complex, I tackled dirty towels, pillow case, and drying-up cloths—they certainly needed it.

What looks better than softly gleaming brassware? When my clock and barometer are shining it makes the cabin a thousand times more homely.

By the afternoon all the maintenance jobs below were completed, stoves cleaned and filled with paraffin, bilges cleared, decks scrubbed, guns cleaned and oiled, and so on.

The shooting of the noon sun, which was only half a degree off the vertical, and another sight in the afternoon, preceded a leisurely spell of mathematics and a touch of cartomania before I settled down to reading *Famous Trials*. It was satisfying to have the unaccustomed relaxation away from the tyranny of the tiller, and the relief from the tropical sun.

The fresh wind eased after dark, leaving a warm, silky night covered by a canopy of brilliant stars. This was but a mockery of the coming hours, for, without a doubt, the moisture sucked up by the daylight sun would form into black clouds and descend as vicious squalls.

Thus ended a day of rest as I washed and dried my hands on a comparatively clean towel and rested my head on a comparatively clean pillow case.

I decided this Sunday rest business was an excellent institution and I was already looking forward to the next one.

People have often asked me, 'Didn't you find it very boring sailing in the trade-wind area? Wasn't one week just like another?' One week like another, heck! Why, every day was somehow different. I do not think that there was one day during the whole trip which did not have something special logged, apart from the usual navigational data. Naturally, there were individual series of deadening hours which ran into weeks of broken time, calling for a mental and physical endurance without which it would not be possible to effect such a voyage and keep sane.

There is enough for me that goes on in the normal course of events, and although it could be said that I was in the heart of the 'boring' area, the six days between my first and second rest days produced their crop of excitement.

Here is a short descriptive log of those six days in the 'Monotonous Trades':

Monday—Entirely new departure in the weather, and an unpleasant one. The night's squalls carry on into the day and produce a morning of torrential rain but only occasional bursts of wind. Have refreshing but chilly fresh-water bath. Two huge blue dolphin fish alongside. In afternoon new wind from E.S.E. Have trysail hoisted as sort of squaresail. Stomach upset. Suspect corned beef giving me worms. In evening storm clouds gather and huge swell rolls up from S.E.

Tuesday—Terrific excitement. Look out of porthole soon after dawn and see a skyscraping bow of a liner coming at me at twenty knots. Dive for signalling flags already made up, rush out of hatch, rush back again to put on some shorts, give myself a nasty knock on the shoulder before reaching the mizzen flag halyards as the ship hisses close past the stern. I hoist my signal letters MDPV, then MIK— Please report me at Lloyds, London. He acknowledges smartly and I hardly have the time to read the name *Jagiello* before he has turned to port and is diminishing towards the west.

They were smart signallers, and within twenty-five minutes Lloyds in London held a telegram.

LLOYDS LONDON

AT 0920 GMT LAT 2225 N LONG 4642 W

PASSED BRITISH SCHOONER MDPV—MASTER

Lloyds thrilled my parents with this information. This was the first news of *Temptress* after thirty-eight days at sea.

The liner was Polish and very well turned out, although he seemed a little out in his navigation, and I do not think he allowed for the northing off his course to intercept me. Looking back at my records and comparing his telegrammed position, his latitude is ten miles to the south of mine, although his longitude seems correct. However, I did not ask him whether he wanted to know his position.

Wednesday—Estimate waves at twelve feet high. Rolling first one gunwale under, then the other. Trysail hoisted as a 'squaresail' and boomed out by the boat-hook, which is good for the setting of the sail but sometimes bad for boat-hooks. Squalls getting fiercer. Wind E.S.E. 5. Decks often running with water, as waves are so steep—more like the Channel than the ocean. Am in nervy and irritable state. What a rough and tumble all this is. Wild sunset.

Thursday—Squally. Big sea. Same rig during day. By afternoon am running before half a gale of wind and mountainous seas. Water pouring aboard both port and starboard. At 1830 two waves coincide and *Temptress* is suddenly hoisted up on a pinnacle of water over twenty feet high; it collapses, letting the boat crash down sideways into the next trough. Have headache all day but take helm for eleven hours.

Friday—Filthy sea. Will be glad when this road ends and I can turn right for America. Suspect bad weather in West Indies, if not hurricane, as the season has started. Giant petrel swoops over the waves like an albatross. Better sunset.

Saturday—During night am awakened by a heavy crash like the firing of a gun. Jump up expecting to see a naval ship, but there is nothing. Improvement in the weather. Trade wind back to E.N.E., with characteristic little white clouds. Hoist mainsail in spite of big sea and fresh wind while keeping her on course. Foaming along in great style under wonderful conditions. At noon find we have passed under sun again.

It was on this day, when taking a very tricky meridian altitude necessitating quick movement between the helm and a position on the deck near the boom gallows to take a sight, that I found difficulty in climbing out of the cockpit, and after the sight had been obtained it was found that my legs could hardly support my body. I immediately started daily exercises of 'knees bend,' but it was a full week before my legs were back near normal. This is the sort of weakness which one can get in such sedentary occupations as, say, bank clerking or crossing the Atlantic single-handed.

And then Sunday, July 3rd, was upon me, after a week's run of 472 miles—hardly a record, but one which made a big difference in the ship's position. On the previous Sunday the boat had been in the middle of a vast expanse of the ocean, but now all was changed. The nearest land was even British, namely the north-east West Indian island of Barbuda, only 550 miles off, although I did not expect to sail within 350 miles of it, and, of course, to the north.

To keep the fair current and to work the trade winds to their maximum, I had decided to aim halfway between the West Indies and Bermuda before striking north-east for New York.

At this moment, although 360 miles to the south, I was on the same longitude as Alain Gerbault when he complained so bitterly about the lack of Trades. He had only himself to blame, because all data and records show that the winds do not hold so far north. Had he had a sister who had given him a Philips Record School Atlas as a birthday present, as I had, he would have had none of that trouble and delay. My atlas has been laughed at, but it was found invaluable, showing to perfection winds, currents, temperature, and useful details of the land.

All the potatoes which had been supplied by the ship chandler were now finished, and good riddance, too, because for every three edible there had been one bad, and even the edible ones were wrinkled and soft as sponges, and some of them flew away in the form of revolting little flies. The other potatoes, hard new ones, which had been bought in the market, were still in excellent condition. I am sure that Mr. Ratsey will excuse the use of one of his new sailbags for stowing them.

The sea was still bad, with waves fifteen feet high, yet not much more than two boat lengths apart. It was fascinating to watch *Temptress* rise to the breaking seas, and often she seemed to turn her stern to a bad sea, although no one was at the helm and she was running under headsails, with wind on the quarter.

The leak was getting a bit worse and I spent an hour with floorboards up trying to trace it, but in vain. The bilges were certainly sweet enough!

Since it was Sunday, and the inevitable 'jobs' were completed, I had time for a leisurely afternoon tea in the saloon, and I broached the first of my three tins of Dundee fruit cake, purchased at great expense at Gibraltar.

I had expected to see a steamer, as we were directly on the Mediterranean to Panama route, and sure enough, one came into view heading west and passed about five miles away. From this time on, it was decided to carry lights at night.

Probably because of the after effects of a bout of cartomania, which I allowed myself on Sundays, and the studying of Gerbault's arrival in New York on the large-scale charts I had been presented with, I had a very real dream that night about *Temptress* anchoring off City Island, New York, and the detail was such that I laid out a second anchor astern. A note was put in the log to see how it would compare with the actuality. However, although City Island was the first place I stepped ashore in America, nothing else had the slightest sympathy with the dream.

20

SARGASSO SEA

The next week, under far better conditions, in fact for some of the time in real story-book trade-wind weather, I knocked out 475 miles without experiencing any great excitements. It was hotter, with less wind. Several steamers were sighted, but not close. One merely showed its presence by regular outbursts of smoke as the automatic bell clanged and some sweating stoker flung so many shovels of coal into the hungry mouth of the furnace. There is the entry in the logbook, followed by this somewhat painful rhyme:

> Ha Ha Ha, Hee Hee Hee,
> I can see you 'nd
> You can't see me.

During this time I began to see a difference in the cloud formations to the north. There were great vertical pillars of bulbous clouds, presumably thunderheads, which took up the most grotesque shapes and made me wonder just how lucky we were going to be with the trade winds. My latitude was already over 24° N. and increasing every day. It was possible to have the Trades for a week yet, before I would be caught in the blistering variables of Cancer, or Horse Latitudes as they are more commonly called.

On Friday, July 8th, my eyes were startled by a great gash of bright yellow floating in the deep blue sea. It was an island of sargasso weed and it gave a vivid contrast to the surrounding colours. For a week or more my course would lead across the western portion of the mysterious Sargasso Sea. The centre of this desolate region, about which so many tales have been told, was only a few days' sail to the north. It is an area completely deserted, devoid of wind or current, in which derelicts can drift eerily, caught in the greatest whirlpool in the world. Some stories cannot be believed. Dod Osborn, with one companion, and engine broken down, said that they were driven below by the terrible animals that climbed over the side to invade the deck. However, without a doubt, many strange creatures, great and small, live amongst the yellow weed, and they would provide an interesting study. One day when I am not in such a hurry to race hurricanes to New York, it is in my mind to spend several weeks in that fascinating area, and either come back with some heavy debunking material or, perhaps, with some stories to put all others in the shade.

On Sunday, July 10th, the voyage had lasted fifty days and all was well. My indisposition of the previous week was over. My water supply was not half finished. The sails were in good condition, and the hull and gear were standing up pretty well, although there was plenty of attention needed. However, I aimed to give her a thorough overhaul in the calm area, only a few days away.

When I finally did get up on this day of rest, I was surprised to see coming up astern a long storm cloud stretching across my wake from horizon to horizon. It must have been a type of line squall, with the cylinder of cloud about fifty miles long, and every five or ten miles a grey haze of rain meeting the sea appeared like ethereal pillars supporting the awesome black mass above. At the same time, to the south, there could be seen great clouds formed at all heights in the manner of a gigantic V, as were the cirrus of the day before. Without doubt, there was rain and storm over the West Indies, and I was about to endure a bit of local hate.

This whole great illimitable magnitude of the heavens gave me a sense of complete isolation from society, and a true realisation of the humility of the individual. It is in such powerful moments as these that one wonders just how far man has progressed in the last thousand years in the art of how to live, and one grows angry at the thought of the futility of wars, the fear people have of the future, and the lack of personal freedom.

An hour later *Temptress* was like a dot at the foot of a great arch, with a squall passing on either side of her. There had been little enough wind, and as the long cloud began to break up and evaporate, nothing happened except that the wind increased to Force 4 and the boat went faster, if one can use the word 'fast' when under headsails in these winds.

My position on the chart was still an obsession with me. It was impossible to curb one's impatience by living in the present. One lived one or two or three weeks ahead, probably basing one's prognostications on the maximum speed of the vessel, and ignoring little details such as head winds or calms. However, as I approached the edge of the trade-wind belt, my whole interest resolved into reaching the doldrum area. After passing through that region, I would merely be in a hurry, not to reach the land, but to pass as quickly as possible the notorious Gulf Stream and Cape Hatteras before a hurricane struck.

According to my records of the West Indian hurricanes, June and July were fairly safe, as there had been 11 and 13 hurricanes respectively, in the last thirty-six years, but in August there had been an average of one every year. I could not hope to get in before that month. It is an odd thing, but if there is any bad weather about, I always seem to be in the midst of it, and certainly did not want to tempt fate by dawdling.

If the previous week's run had made a big difference in the ship's position, this last week's run altered the complexion of the voyage entirely. The string of islands were now to the south, and I was actually farther west than Barbados. Far, far to the north was Newfoundland, and my longitude was even west of that. There was no longer any doubt, we were at last on 'the other side,' and my course from now on would be roughly north-west in the direction of New York, 1250 miles away. Nearly three quarters of the task had been completed.

There was very un-trade-like weather in the afternoon. It became overclouded above, black as sin towards the south, and it was only on the northern horizon that a strip of blue sky was visible. The moderate wind from the south-east started to blow in gusts, there was a shower of rain, a flat calm, then the floodgates opened and it deluged for over two hours without ceasing. The rain was so hard that at times the scuppers could not cope with the water which built up on deck. The glue in the deck seams had bubbled and planking shrunk away from the cabin-top coamings to such an extent that water dripped below, soaking my bedding. It was a good thing that the cabin top itself had been covered with canvas before leaving England; at least it was dry under that.

It had been an ominous sort of a day, and all evening, in the sombre distance, could be heard the throb of thunder, like the rumble of heavy gunfire.

I thought I would take advantage of the calm to swim round the boat, but at the last moment I was dissuaded by a mustard-coloured shark, which proceed to rub its back on the chain stay of the bumpkin. It must have seen me peering at it at close range and then going away, for when I came back with a loaded revolver it had sheered off. The cunning of these beasts is sometimes inexplicable.

A steamer four miles to the south heading towards England gave me an added navigation check, for the Panama to Bishop Rock route cut through my position.

A little later a smart breeze settling in from the east brought things back to normal as the disturbance cleared away.

The sunset that evening lacked nothing in colour contrasts, and it blew fresh all night. Several times I was awakened by a splash of water on my face as a wave broke over the quarter and part of it fell down the half-open hatch.

The heavy roll, as usual, made it difficult to sleep for long, and the thermometer stayed all night at over eighty degrees.

For some time I moved into the cot in the foc'sle. To begin with, it was much cooler there, but the draught coming down the forehatch and playing on one's naked body was a bit dangerous; however, the effects of rolling were very much less, since being near the centreline, one was nearer the axis of roll than was the bunk in the wings of the boat. The drawback was the swift vertical motion. After a few nights I went back to the after bunk, as it was more convenient in looking out, and handier to the sheets and the helm.

A French tunnyman in the Bay of Biscay

Gigantic swell, Bay of Biscay

Alongside the quay at La Coruña

The invisible helmsman

Approaching the Rock of Gibraltar

On a party to Spain

A Spanish trading schooner

Temptress on the slip

The new and stouter mast

Unstepping the old mast

Off Palma a fishing boat comes alongside

A fine sailing breeze

Shooting the sun

From the bowsprit

During the gale off Cape Hatteras

Temptress at City Island, New York

21

TOIL AND TROUBLE

On July 13th, there occurred an incident which proved to be the most dangerous throughout the cruise, and it was only by chance that there was not one of those mysterious disappearances which, as my friend Alf Loomis later put it, delight the heart of the chroniclers but not those of the disappearees.

At the time, *Temptress* was foaming along under full sail. Noticing that the luff of the mainsail was getting a bit slack, I lashed the tiller and went forward to give a good swing down on the throat halyard jig or purchase. The main part of the sisal halyard, rotted by the sun and damp of the tropics, broke short off at the upper sheave, and the jig block, released from tension, was catapulted to strike me on the edge of my left eye, blacking me out and stretching me full length on the narrow sidedeck to port as the boat rolled to starboard. I had avoided by a hairsbreadth being shot over the side. One can imagine only too well the thoughts of a lone mariner on seeing his boat sail away as he struggles in the water and the sharks turn in to investigate.

Meanwhile, the mainsail was hanging from the peak halyard with the boom dragging in the sea. It was with difficulty and in a shaken condition, with water pouring from my bloodshot eye, that I lowered the mainsail fully and secured the boom firmly on the invaluable gallows.

Oddly enough, just before the incident (it was almost an accident) I had been thinking that danger was not always apparent, and that one had only to have a shackle break in order to plunge, without warning, to one's death.

It was a day of surprises. Who would have thought that there would be fresh fruit for dessert that evening? But it was so. An orange was found at the back of a locker, and it was without a trace of mould, although rather dry.

A new halyard was rove that day. It was not easy up the swaying stick, and I obtained some more bruises and grazes to add to the arm which had been strained in the fall.

The next day, in order to prevent any further untoward incidents, there was a more difficult job of re-reeving a new peak halyard. One end had to be shackled aloft, while I stood on the crosstrees. A line round my body and the mast prevented me from being flicked off, since the masthead was switching about like a fishing rod as the boat frisked among the waves. While at this job I discovered to my alarm that the clamp fittings were slipping down the shrinking mast, and one would shortly be grinding into the eye-splices of the main shrouds.

The time for a refit was overdue. My position was already approaching Latitude 27°, and the trade wind was gradually easing away as the doldrum area, with its opportunity for repairs, drew near.

The lighter weather conditions allowed me to turn once more to fishing. After sticking my ridiculous toasting fork of a grane twice into large dolphins that shook it out, and losing two of my dwindling supply of hooks, I at last caught one on a hook attached to the line by Admiralty seizing wire. Dragging him alongside after furious play, I drove the spear in behind his gills and unceremoniously yanked him aboard into the cockpit. He was a magnificent blue fish over three feet long.

Sights fixed my position at less than a thousand miles from Sandy Hook. For fifty-four days I had calculated in thousands of miles; now it would be in hundreds. 'Dammit,' I said, 'I'll be anchored week after next.' Not that anchoring would give me much pleasure. I decided on a good dinner, an offering to Saint Thousand Miles, but not a celebration. What was there to celebrate? Getting near to the artificialities and impurities of civilisation, where money was god? Giving up the glorious freedom of the sea? No. The last two weeks had given me a second wind. I felt purified by the sun, cleansed by those baths, and animated by the laden sea air. Land was useful for the facilities of refit and stores, but perhaps my life would develop into living entirely on the sea and amongst islands, while my books would allow others to share my hardships and freedom—those others who cannot seek adventure but have the ache in their hearts. How many have said to me, 'You are doing just what I have always dreamed of doing.'

'As I pen these few words in my cabin, and the boat rolls her irregular way across the ocean, a magnificent sunset, almost frightening in its beauty, forms and fades. Yet how many there are who do not see, who are not even conscious of this, one of nature's more frequent marvels.' Thus reads one of my first hand entries in the ship's log.

My menu that evening:

Saint Thousand Mile Dinner
Yacht *Temptress* Lat. 27° N. Long. 64° W.
July 14th, 1949
54 days at sea
* * * * *

La Ina Sherry
Soup à la Tentadora
* * * * *

Steamed Giant Steaks of Dorado
Potatoes cooked in sea water
Beans cooked in tomato sauce
* * * * *

Pineapple Rings and Cream
* * * * *

Coffee Chocolates
* * * * *

Liqueur Brandy

Even if the cream was evaporated milk, and the brandy Spanish, the Ritz would have been hard put to supply such a repast. And there was no skimping in the quantities.

A few days of blissful sailing with the wind slowly dying made me so sure that the Horse Latitudes were reached that I started on the jobs scheduled for the area.

The engine had been due for top overhaul at Gibraltar, but there had not been time, so, with the boat jerking along in the swells and sailing slowly before the light easterly wind, I removed the cylinder head, decarbonized the engine, and ground in the valves. Not an easy operation, as every nut and spanner had to be carefully put in a safe place, and there was always the thought that one might break a thin stud or strip a thread, without exceptional chance of rapid replacement. A violent squall came up while I was at these games, and luckily the reaching staysail was not set, for that ancient sail would have departed this life with scarcely a word.

To clean off, I dived overboard and had a race with *Temptress*. She won, and after grabbing the bobstay to swing myself aboard I potted at the sharks to let them know that they could not trifle with me.

For some evenings the sunsets had not boded fine weather to me. They were just vivid gashes of crimson amidst a swarm of small black clouds, with mammoth lumps of cumulus piled up above the horizon, looking as if they were cut out of cardboard.

The light wind was often whipped up by vicious squalls and, after one exceptionally bad one, the mast-band holding the throat halyard twisted round forty-five degrees and seemed to be biting into the main shrouds. With the halyard half jamming aloft, the mainsail was taken off in double-quick time. The staysail followed suit. The jib fitting had slipped down some inches but I took the risk of leaving this one sail up, since the wind had freshened and the sea was getting up. All thoughts that I had reached the calm area were quickly dispelled. By nightfall it was rough, with storm clouds gathering.

Two days went by under the ridiculous rig of jib only during the nights, with mizzen added during the day. There was no possibility of hoisting the main or foresail, as both the halyards were fastened to the same fitting, which, had the downward thrust been continued, would soon have cut through the shrouds by means of its spur. The first day was fine but squally, but the second produced a strong trade wind out of a sky laden with ominous black clouds.

These days were enlivened by several incidents. Early one morning there was a motor vessel heading directly for me, but when he was a mile off he decided that I was evidently all right and altered course back to the south-west. He must have been from Bermuda bound for the Windward Passage and possibly Jamaica.

The next day a very battered and rusty steamer came groaning over the horizon and passed within a mile of me. I had my flags ready to hoist, but he gave not the slightest notice of me, nor could anyone be seen on his bridge. Although I was very eager to send a message home, I did not make any special attempt to attract his attention, for perhaps he could not afford the extra coal to alter course.

It was an unsatisfactory period, with the boat crippled. Had a real storm come up (Bermuda waters have their own specialities), there would have been nothing to do except drift out of control, as the mizzen alone would have been useless. And what if there was a weather freak and the calm area did not exist? The job of refastening the mast fittings would be quite a little business in harbour, and a physical impossibility in any but a smooth sea.

My mental harmony was not improved by having to open yet another tin of corned beef. I had failed to land two dorados, owing to my poor gear. The fish were just too big for my little spear. The next stab at fishing was successful. There had been a charming little yellow fish with long black eyebrows, giving it a permanently surprised air, which had been following the boat for several hundred miles. I hardened my heart, waited until he came back from inspecting a lump of sargasso weed, and scored a bull's-eye. He had turned as I struck and was impaled by all five barbs. It took a moment to cut him into four pieces, three of which went over the side, the last one being snatched by the excited dorados. The fourth piece, of course, concealed a Spanish swordfish hook. The big fish raced for it. Result—a huge dorado completely filling the cockpit, providing enough meat for over a dozen people. This was the most successful way of catching them, and I got so cocksure that I would only get my fishing gear ready just before a meal. Why was it that the female of the species invariably got to the hook first?

Unconscious joke on the Lime Juice Cordial—'Please shake the bottle.' That was one chore of which I was relieved.

I had a try at night fishing, by suspending a bright light over the water. It attracted the fish all right, but they would dash by at a furious pace, making it quite impossible to catch them.

Regarding the night harvest of flying fish, it was a rare thing to find more than three on deck in the morning. It would be a very good idea to have a net about five feet deep of any reasonable mesh strung vertically between the masts. It was found that the fish would stay aboard if they hit the small target of the dinghy or the stowed mainsail. A net would, of course, stop all that fly over the deck. By this means one could expect at least six on most nights, although there are not large quantities unless one is farther south than 21°N. latitude. M. Marin Marie in Winnibelle once found as many as thirty-seven on deck at once, and wryly makes the comment that they were more than even his appetite could cope with.

My latitude increased from 27° to 28°, to 29°, then to 30°N., where the wind eased right away, the sky cleared, the barometer gave a leisurely climb, and the swell went down. Could this at last be the beginning of the Horse Latitudes? I could not afford to wait and see, so not being able to persuade myself that there was too much motion to tackle the difficult labour up the mast, I started the preparations, which are half the battle. I collected spare nuts, all the spanners that might be wanted, and a host of miscellaneous gear, all of which were placed in the canvas deck bucket lashed to the bosun's chair.

I will never forget the toil on that morning of Thursday, July 21st, after sixty-one days at sea. With the boat floundering about unsteadied by sail, it took so long to hoist myself thirty feet up the mast that I was quite exhausted and running with sweat before the actual job was even started. A line round both my waist and the mast prevented me from being flung far, but the inside of my thighs received enough nips between the chair and the mast to bring blood, while my legs were being badly grazed by the shrouds in my attempt to hold myself steady.

When I had reached the lower mast-band and secured the bosun's chair, the boat started a series of rolls and pitches, so that for the first ten minutes I could do nothing but hold on. The seemingly leisurely motion on the deck was transformed into violent jerks up the mast, and I had nothing but bad language to relieve my feelings.

A quieter spell allowed me to position the spanners, one of which was required on each end of the bolts. It was necessary to slacken both bolts which clamped the heavy cast-iron fitting to the mast, then remove one, take out a washer, put the bolt back, lift the fitting, complete with all blocks and halyards attached, back to its proper position five inches higher, and tighten up the bolts. Then do the same thing to the next fitting.

Often, all that could be done was to hold on. I lost all sense of time. It must have been about an hour and a quarter before the jobs were completed to my satisfaction. Blood ran down the shrouds from my toes, which gripped them, and I was so weak that I felt like dropping to the deck. Never have I been so hot and exhausted. On regaining the deck I reached the hatch on hands and knees, and spent the next few hours in my bunk, completely exhausted.

After a bathe and lunch of fresh fish, I got busy scraping and varnishing the cabin-top coamings. They needed it. They had not been done for eleven years. The natural teak came up like a dream. I hoped to do all the deck brightwork and arrive in port smarter than when we left.

It seemed fantastic for a navigation check, but a peculiar flat-topped cloud formation slowly lifted itself above the horizon before dispersing. Allowing for the light wind, this cloud was in the direction of Bermuda, and I reckoned that it had formed over the island, 240 miles away. Visibility was startlingly clear, and apart from this one there were no clouds in the sky.

At sunset the great red disk of the sun seemed to balance for a moment on the sea before plunging out of sight.

Two hours later the light wind petered out, and when I had the last look round before retiring to my bunk to attempt sleep in the oven below, *Temptress* was rolling in a glassy swell reflecting the stars above. There was a final air about the quietness of the night. There was no doubt about it any longer. The trade-wind lap had been completed, and we were trapped in the Horse Latitudes.

22

HORSE LATITUDES

For three days *Temptress* lay utterly becalmed on white oily swells. Occasionally a cat's-paw would ruffle the surface and momentarily fill the flapping sails, but usually there was not a bee's breath of wind to temper the scorching heat. Patches of sargasso weed stayed motionless alongside as the bowsprit lethargically tried to box the compass.

The re-rigging of the boat was completed, servings renewed where necessary (what rotten marline one gets now), and the gear overhauled to such an extent that the vessel was in a more seaworthy condition than when she left Gibraltar. The engine reacted well to its decoking and ran sweetly in neutral for seven hours, until the batteries, which had got very low, were bulging with ampères and energy. She was made smarter above and below decks, too. It takes a long sea voyage to make a boat all shipshape and Bristol fashion. As a matter of fact, the boat was in better condition than she ever had been, and ready to tackle any weather the Gulf Stream or the waters off the notorious Cape Hatteras had to offer. I breathed more easily.

All sorts of queer creatures began to gather round the helpless yawl—creatures great and small. One was positively evil-looking—a thin fish about four feet long with a body shaped like a torpedo and a cruel protruding jaw. Apart from luring it near by dangling an old sock from the end of the boathook and making an unsuccessful jab at it with the spear, I did not bother with it when it took up quarters under the turn of the bilge. I used to bathe with it, as well as with the dorados, which examined me with interest, although one or two, I thought, gave me a rather suspicious look, as if to say, 'Have you any idea where all my friends are disappearing to?'

So it was a bit of a shock to me when I later found out that my friend under the bilge was nothing less than a great barracuda, and that in Florida they are more feared than sharks. I also read that they are not only highly inquisitive and quite fearless but are also ferocious to a degree, and will not hesitate to attack bathers. In fact, had I had a Frenchman aboard, we could have tested out the theory of Le Sieur de Rochefort, who once stated that barracuda are more likely to attack Englishmen than Frenchmen, owing to the former's meatier flavour!

One of the smaller beasts was circular, floated on the surface, and was jet-propelled, just to show that there is nothing new under the sun. There was also one of the ridiculous sun fish, which could proceed flat out at one knot. This was a small one; they grow up to a ton in weight but never seem to show much initiative, and if harpooned they die quietly in a manner which has been described as disgust.

There was an absolute army of small fishes. They were, in fact, a confounded nuisance when I bathed, since they had not the slightest fear of me. Later on they were to nibble the ends of my toes, which prevented me from lazing in the water. One time when I was floating, a large something suddenly scratched the length of my back and made me nearly jump out of my skin, but it was only a large piece of weed and not a shark. Sharks never came too near me when I was bathing; however, several times in the calm a shark came to scratch its back on the topsides, whereupon I would hold my revolver to its head and fire.

Aircraft radiate round Bermuda and serve as a useful aid to navigation. For two evenings an aeroplane crossed astern for the island. On the third evening, so complete had been the calm, that it crossed the bow. We had actually drifted backwards.

So many queer things had been seen that it did not surprise me when shrimps came out of the sea-water pump in the galley. And to go to the other end of the marine scale, I saw my first whale of the trip, blowing heartily and making tracks towards Bermuda, where, presumably, it had a date.

There were now hundreds of those stalk-like goose barnacles

adhering to the bottom, and I spent a lot of time while swimming picking off dozens of them. It took a strong pull to counteract their suction before they broke clear and spiralled into the vast depths of three miles and more.

After enduring the creaking and protests of the gear as the boat rolled to the low expiring swell of the distant Trades, I lowered all canvas to save chafe. We would have looked an unusual sight to a passerby, with all sails neatly stowed as if we were anchored in some creek.

There had been flickering lightning to the north during the nights, and on the fourth day there were all the signs of a coming storm. A light north-west wind darkened the water; it increased to fresh, making the boat smoke to windward in the smooth water, driven under full sail. After the refit I could snap my fingers at the wind. Water began to come aboard from windward and leeward, but *Temptress* carried gamely on close-hauled through the whole night and into the next day. The following evening it blew up to half a gale, making me roll down the mainsail and reef the foresail.

Heavy rain followed by a terrific display of lightning enlivened the proceedings. The sea was whipped up into violent tumult as the boat plunged as if she were trying to stand on her head. This unnecessary exhibition of a Bermuda storm blew itself out after twenty-four hours and after soaking my bedding once more through the leaky deck.

Of all things, a butterfly flew aboard, evidently having been blown out to sea from North Carolina by the storm. This was my first live contact with America. It stayed on board for several days, living under the dinghy. Its beautiful colours added a pleasant touch to the scenery. I suppose it lived by drinking the dew, which was so heavy at this time that it would run down the deck to the scuppers.

Generally, the heat was very clammy, and probably unhealthy, as I contracted a sore throat. During the day it was foggy around the horizon, and it is easy to imagine the difficulty of trying to find Bermuda under such conditions. The islands at this time were two hundred miles to the east.

Two days passed with light northerly winds, then there was a flat calm for twelve hours before it happened—the south-westerly arrived. It had taken me seventy days from the Mediterranean to reach the coastal winds of America, and over four thousand miles of tortuous wake had spun out astern. Only a hurricane or major disaster could stop me from making a landfall during the next week. It was Saturday, July 30th.

23

HEAVY WEATHER

That first day of the south-west wind provided one of the best day's sails of the voyage. A moderate wind on the port beam, calm seas, and all the working and light muslin I possessed were doing their best for me. There was even the luxury of steering in the shade of the mizzen.

It seemed queer at first to have the vessel lying over to starboard. I laughed. No ditch crawling, this! Over two months with the wind on the starboard quarter, then 'Gybe O' to make port, a paltry five hundred miles off.

A dorado gave me a wonderful exhibition of speed and agility. It was a usual sight to see a large fish launch itself into the air by its momentum after swallowing a small fry near the surface, but this one actually kept in the middle of a shoal of flying fish, doing a series of tremendous bounds and swallowing a fish at each jump. The fish could not fly any faster than he could swim. Incidentally, it was an odd fact, but I never found a flying fish or the wings of one in the stomachs of the dorados caught, but there was often a deep little fellow there of a type that I never saw swimming round the boat.

I never ceased to admire the beautiful colours of the dorado. And what could be better than its natural surroundings? Really, the fish is an incarnation of the Tropical Ocean. Its long single dorsal fin and back are of a brilliant blue, shading to silvery white below, with purple and golden reflections, and with a series of bright blue spots on head and back, while the fins and tail are a dazzling yellow, like sargasso weed. Contrary to what I had repeatedly read, these colours still show well after death. I used to cook the steaks by packing them into a pressure cooker. Not having any means of refrigeration, it was essential to eat what one could within twenty-four hours.

Sights of the sun checked my week's run through the Horse Latitudes. It was surprising that it was as much as 225 miles, considering the often glassy conditions.

Ominous squalls passed me on either side, enabling me to carry light canvas all day. At dusk the boat was snugged down, and she plunged along on her own. Away to the south, uneasy flickering lightning and black clouds gave rather an ominous air to the night, and it looked as if another storm was brewing. I went to tap the barometer, which promptly shot down in an unpleasant manner. What was coming?

After checking through the portents of hurricanes again, I was a bit relieved, but determined to keep going day and night till I reached shelter. We were now right in the path of any hurricane which might sweep up the Florida coast and follow the course of the Gulf Stream, as is their wont.

Fair progress was made during the night, but the wind veered to forward of the beam, and the head sea prevented good speed. In spite of this and a very foul bottom, I did my best noon-to-noon run of ninety-four miles. There very nearly was no noon for me, for at precisely 0925, when *Temptress* was bucketing along under full sail, the water immediately ahead suddenly parted with tremendous commotion, and a great black body of a whale threatened imminent collision. I jammed the helm hard down and spent some agonising seconds in the whirlpool of his descent, expecting the tail to flick me up to Kingdom Come. It was all over in a flash. I did not see him again nor did I want to.

I had just recovered when a steamer was sighted to the south, heading towards me. Now was my chance to send a message home, and no time was lost in assembling the Aldis signalling lamp. My course was more toward the land than his direct course to New York, and by the time he was level we were about two miles apart, and at once he was attacked by the lamp. No reply. More flashes. Then the hull foreshortened and the masts swung together. He was altering course towards me.

My pretty flags were then hoisted. Still no reply. Still he came on. Suddenly it was too late to get my camera. Ten lengths. Five. Then close alongside. There was great excitement on board, with all the crew crowding the rail. He was a real Yankee. To hell with lamps and flags and things. The captain just leaned over the edge of his bridge, looking down at the funny little boat foaming along his windward side, and he bawled through a megaphone, 'What do you want?'

'Please report me Lloyds London.'

'Lloyds where?'

'London. London. London. London.'

He raised his hand in assent and turned away to give some command. The great wall of steel rearing above me started to slide ahead. His stern drew level and was past. Across it in large letters was KATHRYN NEW YORK.

The next day the following letter was received by my father:

Dear Sir: Temptress
I confirm the report telephoned to you this morning to the effect that a cablegram dated August 1st, and timed 0937, has been received at Lloyds from Lloyds' Agents at Bermuda, reading thus:
KATHRYN REPORTS WIRELESS BRITISH SLOOP MDPV
3400 NORTH 7130 WEST

I felt quite emotional at the stir that the news would have at home. It had been thirty-three days since the last message via the Polish steamer *Jagiello*.

Although the wind was freshening it was like steering in a Turkish bath. *Temptress* was smelling her oats that day. Down came the mizzen. Up came a grotesque black cloud on the port quarter, with grey sheets of rain underneath. I had just decided that it would be possible to hang onto full mainsail, as the squall seemed to be passing clear, when there was a colossal clap of thunder, and with one bound I was at the mast with my little reefing handle, winding furiously. Nothing happened!

The weather in the Gulf Stream is, to put it mildly, somewhat peculiar. According to some reports it is the sort of place in which one is becalmed one moment, then, without warning, the masts are whipped out by a squall. But if one believes half the yarns about the dangers of the deep, he would never go to sea at all.

In a choppy sea and wind to spare I stowed the mainsail at dusk and let her chase on under headsails.

There was a damp heat of nearly 90°F. below, but on deck it was wet and draughty—an unhealthy combination.

Three times during the night the hatch had to be closed against the roaring wind and rain of a Gulf Stream Special, and in the last one I had to go above to adjust the helm. It was bewildering on deck. Visibility was nil. Just black wind and the bite of water. Only the flashlight played on the compass face brought sanity to my kingdom.

At dawn there was a wild, steep, breaking sea whipped up by furious squalls. By noon I could not kid myself any longer. The storm which had been slowly catching me up for the last two days was upon me. The wind had risen to moderate gale force, while a grey pall of rain swamped the view, as if a great wet brush had been sloshed over the heavens. Monstrous hissing waves surged up from the south-south-west, sluicing over the decks and adding their voices to that of the wind.

Temptress did not care a jot for the heavy weather, but just continued scooting to the north at three or four knots on her own, helm lashed firmly and headsails sheeted hard in. I was superfluous. There was nothing to do except wait for darkness again, with incessant rain and anxiety about steamers. Then another day. The sea had by then lengthened out into long majestic rollers with rumbling crests, in which occasionally one could see the outline of one of my tame sharks still gently waving its tail. If they stop, they sink.

White bosun birds looked out of place in that stormy scene, trying in vain to beat up to windward. This was the last sight I had of them. Instead, there was an unwelcome number of ships. One motor-ship came plunging toward me from the north and stopped, blowing his siren on my beam, but well clear. The captain must have been surprised to see my hatch open and to see a figure come half out to take a photograph, and give a casual wave before retiring below again, for it was blowing some.

An alarming thing happened before noon. Without hesitation the wind went—vanished, not a breath. The great seas at once fell out of their ordered ranks and charged about in all directions. Giant waves collided and reared up into the air before collapsing with an eerie swoosh. There was no sound but the fearful noise of crushing waters and the sharp slap on the surface as *Temptress* did her best to stay the right way up, dipping her bow, stern, and sides in turn under water. Ten minutes later the wind came back like a rocket, and off we went. For New York? Or bust?

The waves were higher than my aerial, so my attempts to get the time signal from London failed that evening.

On the third day it was still overclouded but merely blowing fresh, and the boat continued to scud on course in a remarkably steady manner, considering the sea running.

The sun even deigned to glimmer vaguely through the cloud wrack, thus allowing me a series of unreliable sights under appalling conditions. However, the wind piped up again for another dirty night, in spite of the steadily rising glass.

The next morning found me gaily hoisting the mainsail to a lovely breeze from the west. The gale was over. It had been remarkable. Had it been dry below it would have been the most comfortable gale imaginable. *Temptress* had steered herself for three hundred miles without any attention, and she calmly deposited me at a point about one hundred miles equidistant from Sandy Hook (leading direct to New York harbour), and Montauk Point (at the east end of Long Island).

More and more yellow weed, somehow harvested from the weird meadows of the Sargasso Sea, appeared all round, till ahead a continuous line could be seen stretching directly across my path. Above, there was a thin black string of cloud. It was a startling sight. 'The edge of the Gulf Stream!' I shouted.

We crossed it at precisely 0831, and for some seconds the bow of the boat was in the cold water and the stern was in the warm.

In an instant the water was green. The deep blue water was slipping astern.

It was the beginning of the end.

AMERICA

At noon on Thursday, August 4th, I threw up my sextant and obtained an observed altitude of 67° 23'. Only fourteen days before, the noon reading had been in the eighties. Those days were gone now—the days of tropical colours, of trade winds blowing over a deep blue sea, of shoals of flying fish, of beautiful dorados, of delicate Portuguese men-of-war. Gone and temporarily forgotten. My thoughts were directed towards the question of making a landfall. Within twenty-four or thirty-six hours, land should be in sight.

My noon sight crossed with a morning sight put me in a position with Montauk Point eighty-seven miles away.

There were two courses open to me. Either head slightly east of north for Montauk Point and travel the whole length of Long Island Sound before reaching New York, or steer 70° farther westward for Sandy Hook and use the big ship entrance to New York harbour.

The wind made the decision for me by veering west, then west-north-west, bringing up a series of alarming thunder squalls, hosts of black clouds, and then steady rain with much reduced visibility. Not only was it no longer possible to lay the course for Sandy Hook, but it would be madness to join the crowd of ships converging for New York. Montauk Point was the answer, and it would only be necessary to cross the shipping routes to and from the west.

I prepared myself for a long night's sail in the wet.

By ten o'clock that night, the wind had slowly died away, leaving an irritating drizzle.

Luckily there were better things to do than twiddle one's thumbs in the wet, waiting for a steamer to come out of the fog and run one down without the chance of getting out of the way. Instead, I gave a violent kick to the crank handle of the little engine, and it was not long before we were ploughing through the water, with a regular swell from the south giving her repeated pushes on her course.

By midnight there were but forty miles to go and I was keeping my eyes peeled for ships on the main track. Rain had ceased for the moment.

Sure enough the lights of a big liner showed for some minutes across my bow. Two hours later, more lights of a small ship crossed pretty close. Both were heading due west. After another six miles to the north, I felt that I was at last out of the range of the ships and stopped the engine, which had run like a sewing machine for five hours.

I dug out the sounding line. No bottom at thirty fathoms. Nor did I expect any. So far, so good, but just what the tides were doing to me could only be ascertained when land was sighted.

After a two-hour sleep I had a look round. The coming of daylight had turned the oppressive black into a grey fog, while a gentle rain was just enough for the lower scuppers to send a shower of drops on to the glassy surface from the dark and shining deck, as the boat rolled to the smooth southerly swell.

The evening before, a dragonfly had flown aboard; now a tiny moth came out of the mist, borne upon the light north-east wind.

There were no outlying shoals from the coast I assumed I was approaching, and visibility was such that there would be time to alter course to avoid hitting the beach.

I pumped half a pint of oil out of the sump of the engine into a bottle, which was then corked and thrown into the sea; then I topped up with oil, cleaned spark plugs, checked her over, and away we went.

One hour, two hours—three, four, five—noon again. I stopped the engine and the boat gradually lost way in the glassy calm. Plop went the lead in the water. Thirty fathoms said the chart, and, by heaven, thirty fathoms it was. Then a faint boooom could be heard. A fog siren! And from the direction of the shore. America!

Lunch, a bath, more oil for the engine, and once again into the breach. Still thick fog, and only an estimated ten miles to go, but I kept my eyes straining ahead.

Another six miles. Another sounding—twenty fathoms. I steeled my brain to curb the almost overpowering urge to stop every five minutes to take a sounding, and ran for a whole hour till my estimated distance to the shore was up. Fourteen fathoms underneath, but nothing, nothing in sight. It was maddening. It would have been nerve-wracking in the dark.

Then some anchored markers appeared black out of the fog. What the hell? They were oscillating violently in a strong tide setting to the north-north-east. Had I passed the end of the Sound and Block Island? Or was I miles away from my estimated position and about to tear the bottom of the boat open upon some outlying rocks? The swell had started to make up in an unaccountable fashion. Tension mounted.

A seagull, ice cream cartons, and bottles bobbing up and down like a fisherman's float encouraged my sense of the nearness of land.

It was when the sun was sinking low to the west that a high form silhouetted itself slightly darker than the fog. It was abaft the port beam.

I waited for a few seconds, then shouted, 'Land!' and altered course towards it, pushing the throttle open as far as it would go. Soon houses could be seen and it could be identified as Block Island. It had been a successful landfall after seventy-six days at sea.

I hesitated off the harbour, in and out of which fishing boats were racing with open exhausts. Several sailing and motor-yachts could be seen inside, but not feeling like coping with the publicity I was bound to get, I steered away to the centre of a big bay and dropped anchor off the island, and was soon rolling to the Atlantic swell which was breaking with a mighty roar on the beach.

It gave me a wonderful sensation to be in a safe spot out of the dense fog.

From the shore occasional bursts of music and the honking of horns drowned the booming of the surf. I stared wonderingly at the unaccustomed lights before turning in to a luxurious night's rest.

There was still over one hundred miles of Long Island Sound to negotiate without any tidal charts, and in the persistent fog and light head wind it was to prove an irksome business.

The first day I did only twenty miles before the fog became so dense that one could nearly step on it. I groped in under Watch Hill Lighthouse to anchor. The fog dripped on to my blankets during the night.

I had no money to buy any more fuel, which was nearly exhausted, and all that could be done under sail the next day, in a little better visibility, was to reach Niantic Bay, where anchor was dropped to avoid being swept back on a foul tide. Then on again at four o'clock in the morning. More head winds. More fog.

After doing a reasonable piece of seamanship by stopping alongside the Cornfield Light Vessel to hand them a message to report me at Lloyds, I had to anchor for some hours on the top of a reef to again avoid being set back by the tide.

After making very poor progress with those hundreds of long barnacles being towed through the water, and because of the lightness of the head wind during the day, I had an unwelcome change during the night when the wind suddenly increased, making me reef, and kicking up such a steep sea that progress still was not possible. And it was too absurd being out of sight of land. When dawn came I had only the vaguest idea of where we were, and the perverse fog continued until I had managed to check position by a Stratford Shoal lighthouse with bellowing fog siren, which was stuck on a rock conveniently placed by nature in the middle of the Sound.

During the afternoon the sun came out and a perfect wind off the southern shore allowed me excellent progress until sunset, when I was becalmed within sight of Execution Rocks Light, which guards the entrance of East River.

I sounded my fuel tank. There was enough. I gave a short laugh. New York was in the bag.

And so, after ploughing through the mirror-like calm water reflecting the magic of a full moon, and dodging innumerable vessels, I passed through the narrow passage inside the Rocks and picked my way slowly into a little bay opposite City Island, New York.

I had been on the go for forty-three hours when the anchor

chain rattled loudly over the stem roller in the quiet night. Then all was silence.

I had kept my word, for it was exactly eighty days since anchor had been weighed at Gibraltar. *Temptress* had sailed through close on four thousand eight hundred miles of water.

It was midnight on August 9th, 1949.

I had arrived.

APPENDIX

ADVICE TO DREAMERS

Soon after my stepping ashore at City Island, New York, the plague of reporters had carried the story of the crossing to the newspapers, and the United Boat Service Corporation, where *Temptress* was docked, was inundated first with telephone calls, then with an increasing delivery of letters for me.

These letters were from all over the world, but mostly from young Americans who had been fired by the news, and wanted advice as to how they, too, could sail the oceans and see the world from the decks of their own craft.

Other letters contained proposals for me to appear on radio and television, or to write articles for magazines (all of which I did). Further letters contained invitations for dinner or the week-end or longer. It was these last letters that eventually made it possible for me to remain in the States for the winter and to write this book.

I cannot be more grateful to those who extended their hospitality and helped to make my stay so enjoyable. One kind soul, after one horrified glance at my battered old typewriter, turned up the next day with a brand-new one!

Although the City Island yachting facilities are usually the most expensive in the country, the United Boat Service Corporation let me down very lightly in the matter of bills, and, incidentally, did some first-class repair work on the boat. It was a lucky chance that Bob Jenkins, the manager, was at the end of their pier when I gave a hail, asking for a berth. The other yards had already refused, after one look at the weather-beaten *Temptress*. But Bob said, 'Sure. Come right in.'

All the intense interest roused by *Temptress's* crossing the Atlantic shows without a doubt that there are many people who in their hearts cherish an urge to cast off the insidious chains of civilisation and live.

It is towards these people that this Appendix is directed.

When planning any operation, one must examine the reasons why others have failed. Most of the failures of prospective world girdlers have been due to the incompatibility of the crew. This is possibly the most important item of all. Conor O'Brien, who circled the world in *Saoirse* experiencing appalling crew troubles, once said to me, 'If you want a crew, marry one.' Somewhat drastic, maybe, but it is one solution.

Of course, going single-handed removes the worry at once, but one has to be born with the right temperament, and I do not advise it *if* one can get a congenial companion.

It is because I have seen so many large craft rotting in port too under-manned to carry on, owing to the desertion of half the crew, that I advise selecting a craft small enough to be handled by two, so that if there is dissention among the crew, it is still possible to continue with the cruise.

THE BOAT

So few boats have been designed in the last few decades for the purpose we have in mind, that it is sometimes as difficult to find a suitable boat as it is to find the money to purchase it.

All types of boats have cruised the world, but it is generally agreed that for deep-sea cruising it is better to have a hull with long length of keel to allow for ease of steering, heaving to, and self-steering. Short overhangs, good beam, and a moderate draft will provide some of the characteristics required, and the construction should be STRONG. Bad luck alone can put one ashore, and it is the heavily built craft that usually gets away with it.

I also tend to favour the type of stern which allows the rudder to be slung outboard where it can easily be got at.

Experience with nearly all rigs has brought me to the conclusion that the ketch rig is the best for off soundings work, either with marconi on both masts, or at least on the mizzen, and two headsails, with the staysail running on the main forestay attached to the hull and not the bowsprit. With such a rig it is possible for one man, without leaving the cockpit, to reduce sail by rolling up the jib and lowering the mizzen.

Regarding the actual length of the boat, it is merely a matter of what accommodation is required. Seaworthiness has nothing to do with size.

DEEP-SEA SENSE

Have your working sails of heavy canvas.

Have your sails made with vertical cut, cloths running parallel with the leech, in order that the stretch of the sail will be along the cloths, rather than on the seams.

If marconi rig, fit mast hoops up to the spreaders and jackstay above. All tracks tend to jam when the boat is off the wind.

If you can afford roller reefing—fit it: but use the heavy pattern.

Treat all your sails with anti-mildew solution. I always use some stuff that also prevents chafe, called Kanvo, made by D. Weston Company, 61 Dunlop Street, Glasgow.

Lash sails to spars with separate stops, not continuous lacing.

Have at least 60 fathoms of stout anchor chain, and mark it.

Don't use 'yachty' fittings. They are only good for the Solent.

Don't have a wood rudder stock. If it is, slide a steel tube over it, and weld steel flats to the cutaway bottom of the tube, extending them right across the rudder blade each side and riveting through.

Have extra stout rigging screws on the shrouds.

The mast and rudder should never fail.

Make the auxiliary engine very reliable, and fit to run in any sea. It is the best insurance.

Use big blocks.

Use stainless steel wire-rope. It is cheaper in the end.

Splice in a length of chain at the end of rope halyards and out-hauls, at the 'nip.'

Use metal to metal connections. Lashings part.

Don't have a big cockpit. Deck it in.

Assume one day that the boat will be temporarily submerged by a sea.

Have sound hatches and deck layout to prevent a submergence being permanent.

Have two non-choking bilge pumps. One to be worked from the helm, and one from below.

Twin deep sinks are the best for the galley, but fit non-choke waste pumps. Gravity outlets are no use for the heeled sailing boat.

Fit a sea-water pump in the galley—and use it.

One half-gallon of fresh water a day per man is enough at sea.

Have at least one stove slung in gimbals.

Position the galley aft where there is least motion.

Arrange it so the cook can chock himself in, and can administer with both hands in any seaway.

Have a swing table in the saloon.

Have no equipment that cannot be used both at sea and in port.

Wherever the ballast is, see that it stays there. Assume that one day the boat will be upside down, and bolt things down accordingly.

Don't have electric plugs and sockets on deck.

All deck fittings should be bolted down, not screwed.

Rattle the ship down.

Fit adequate lifelines.

Make and fit baggywrinkle.

Keep the deck tight. Canvas for thin decks is best.

Use chain or stainless steel wire-rope bobstay attached to a fitting secured by fore and aft bolts right through stem.

Don't catch gadgetitis. Simplicity is best.

Don't buy a boat without a professional survey.

Do all the work on the boat yourself, if possible; if not, get a written estimate.

Check compass for deviation, and take a spare.

Never make a line fast to a cleat or belaying pin with a half hitch.

Fit wide permanent boom gallows, not the flimsy crutch usually fitted.

It is better to lose twelve inches off the foot of the mainsail than to have the dinghy on the sidedeck.

Fit a wind vane that lasts—either the sock variety or the patent metal type.

Gas for stoves or light is a danger.

So is petrol—so, beware.

A ship is not complete without a vice clamped to a workbench, a sharp axe handy to the deck, and a coal stove below.

Finally, trust all men. Yea, even princes. Then cut the cards yourself. *Caveat emptor.*

Temptress Returns

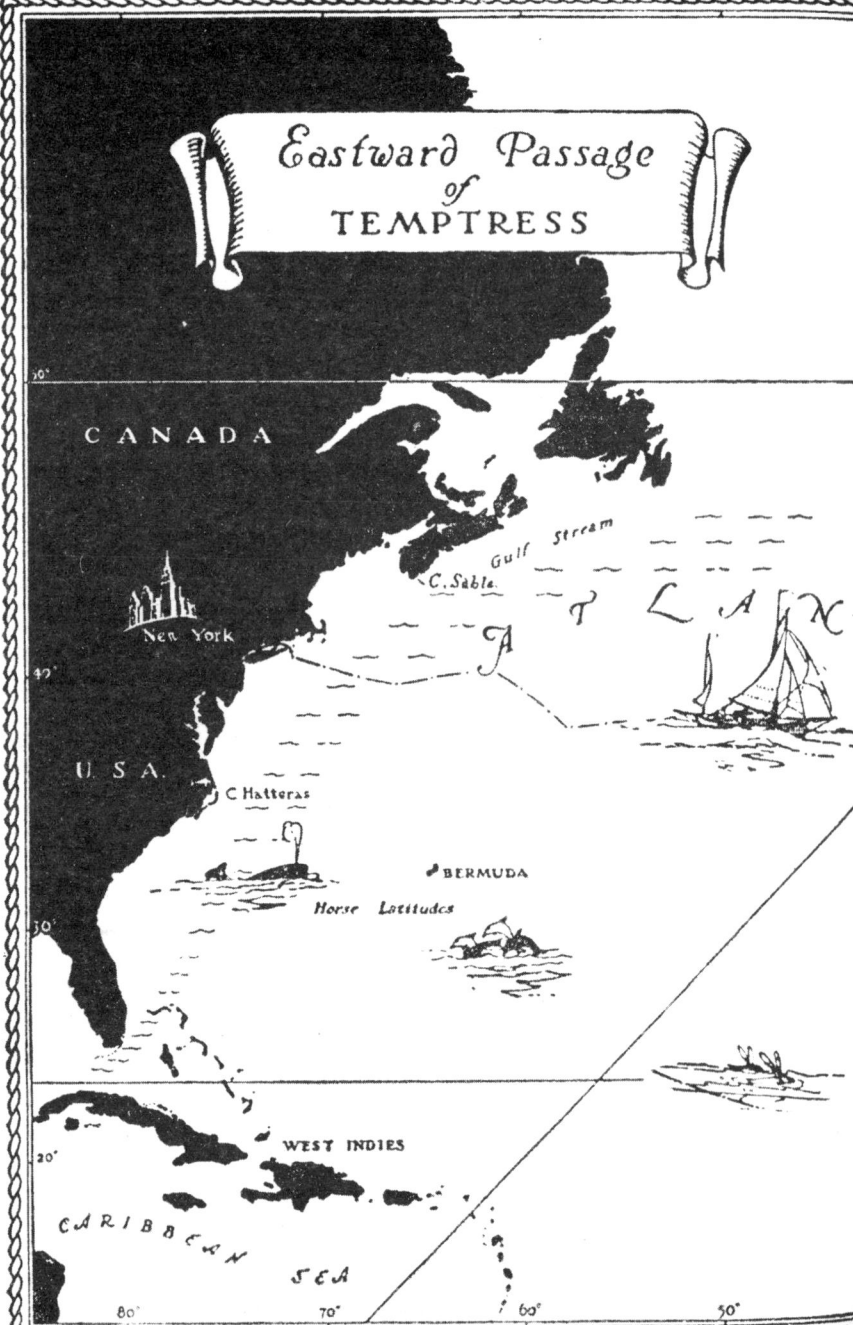

Eastward Passage of TEMPTRESS

CANADA

C. Sable

Gulf Stream

New York

ATLAN

U.S.A.

C Hatteras

BERMUDA

Horse Latitudes

WEST INDIES

CARIBBEAN SEA

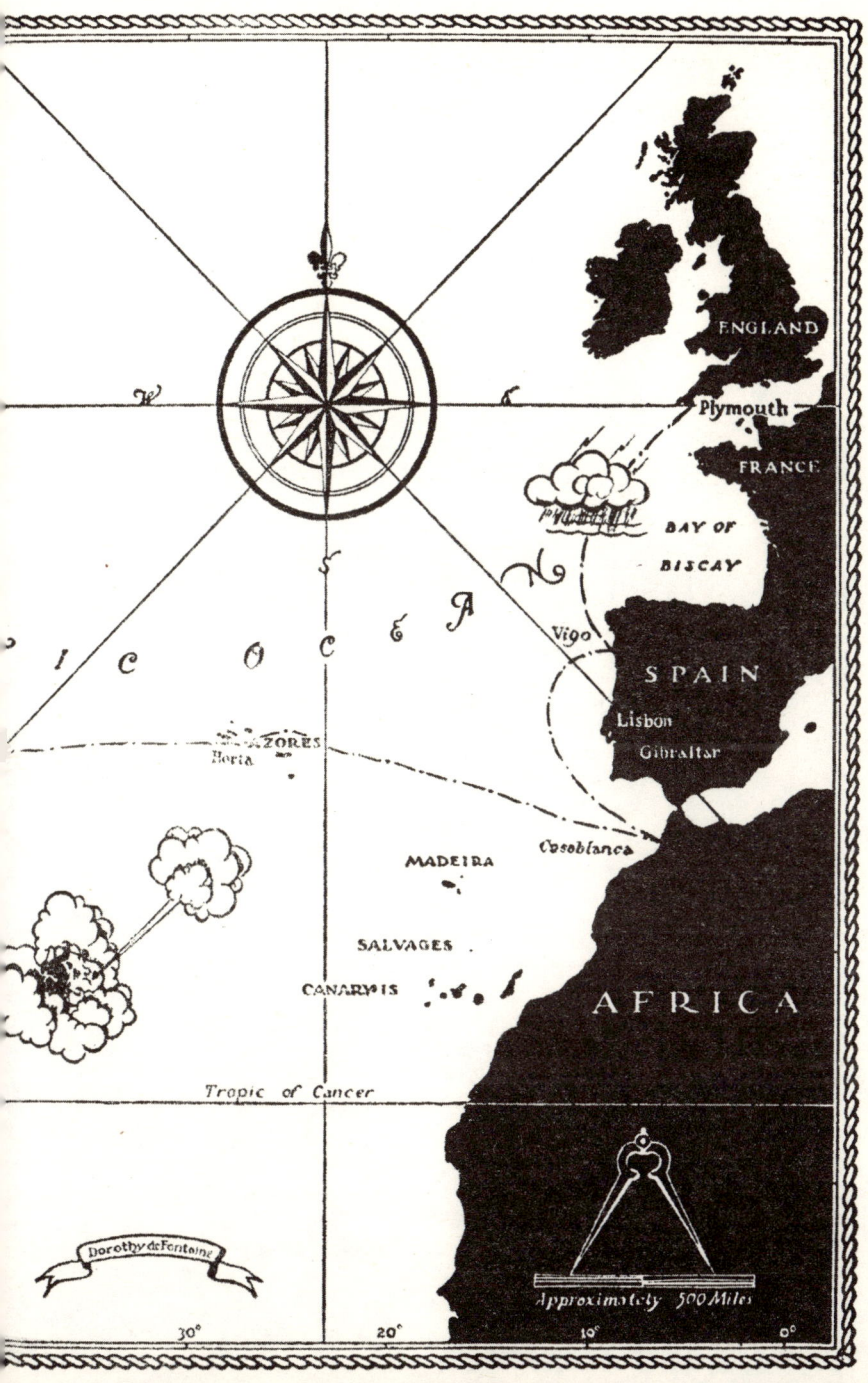

I

LEAVING NEW YORK

What on earth had induced me to announce a definite time of departure? Eleven-thirty on Tuesday, 15th August. The whole morning had been a hectic rush. Nothing was properly stowed. And it had been just too ridiculous that last minute drive in the Plymouth, dashing down to the shops, buying a heap of stores, then piling them aboard as though it were the beginning of a week-end trip, instead of a single-handed passage across the Atlantic Ocean.

'Fifty minutes late,' I declared. 'I'm going.' Suiting action to the words, I cast off moorings from the pontoon and prepared to push *Temptress* clear.

'It's heading up this way,' someone shouted. I turned round to see a man waving from the pierhead. 'The hurricane. It's coming up this way. You'd better look out!'

With these cheerful valedictory words ringing in my ears, I shoved clear with my foot, swung aboard and engaged the clutch. Without the engine, it would have been impossible to start, for there was not a breath of wind, and the sun burnt down from a cloudless sky.

Already the knot of people who had come to see me go were dispersing.

There was, no doubt, much shaking of heads that day on City Island, New York, at my departure in the hurricane season, but certain circumstances had almost forced the delay. Not being able to stay in America for another winter, for financial and other reasons, I had decided to risk the crossing, and expected to be in Plymouth, England, before fifty days were up. It was obviously going to be a hard passage. Had I then foreseen just how hard it was in fact going to be, I would have immediately put back, finance, promises, 'other reasons', notwithstanding.

Meanwhile *Temptress* clove through the still water on her course up the East River, heading to pass right through the centre of New York. I stood in the cockpit, steering with one hand and vaguely wielding a flyswatter in the other, my mind busy on the people and things I was leaving behind me. Some of these people would be watching me till the boat was out of sight. One would be Mrs. Gilman, who had lent me her green Plymouth—it had been an absolute God-send while fitting out, and had enabled me to speed up the roads of New York State, the previous week-end, to say goodbye to the de Langleys and other friends.

Frau Schoett would be another. I was to be agreeably reminded of her in the weeks to come, for below there were two large tins of the most wonderful home-made chocolates, and a vast fruit cake.

Perhaps my presence would be missed by some, but there were others who would be glad to see me go, the Immigration Department, for instance. They had been positively delighted on being told of my imminent departure—for I was that dreadful thing, a foreigner in their midst without an American visa. I was an irregularity. My arrival a year previously had strangely upset them. They had no special form headed 'Single-handed Mariners without Visas'.

Yet, before arriving in the States, I had visited four countries without a visa being considered necessary; but when I had sailed into New York, although my passport was perfectly in order and my official papers showed that I was full owner of a British Registered Vessel, a fat-transomed immigration official had woodenly informed me: 'You are D.O.B. Detained on Board, notify us when you are leaving.'

'Detained on board? What? After eighty-one days at sea?' I had felt like laughing in his face and shouting: 'Ha, ha, detained on board, RUBBISH.' Rubbish must stand for the shorter and more expressive word I had in mind, but I refrained. I countered by spending a week-end with Alf Loomis down on Long Island.

On visiting Immigration headquarters later, at the end of Manhattan, a high-up official (he must have been high-up for he had a carpet on his floor) blustered that they would fine me $1,000. I had evidently been very naughty, and imagined myself being led off to the electric chair. The idea of $1,000 was even more ridiculous than detaining me on board. Why! I had only managed to raise the subway fare because Bob Jenkins, of United Boat Service Corporation had lent me five dollars to go and get a haircut (I did have the haircut but the barber would not let me pay for it, anyway). Neither was it encouraging to be asked whether I had ever spent a period in jail, nor to be told that they had contacted Scotland Yard to inquire if British records listed me as a criminal! I kept quiet about the fact that my driving licence had once been endorsed.

Seeing that he was not impressing me very much he suddenly smiled and shook hands, saying, 'There will be a special meeting of the State Department at Washington on Friday,' adding, ominously, 'We will let you know their decision.' Of course, when the decision did come through it was happily to declare, 'Visa Waived!' I might remain in the United States on a business permit. The permit was valid for thirty days; I was there twelve months. Had they refused me entry after such an arduous voyage to reach the country, the newspapers would have descended on the story like flies on a dung heap. However, right to the end of my stay this lack of visa constituted a loose end of red tape which seemed always to trouble the bureaucratic mind.

The Bronx Whitestone Bridge passed overhead, though New York's famous skyline was still hidden in the murk caused by a thunderstorm which seemed to be making up, not an infrequent occurrence around New York and Long Island Sound. These storms command a very healthy respect. Indeed, *Temptress* had once been caught in one; the wind had changed from a light southerly air to gale force from the north, in a few seconds, with visibility nil. I had nearly put her on the rocks. After sailing 6000 miles of ocean.

The helm was left for a few moments to consult the barometer. Good! High and steady. Nothing yet to show that the first hurricane of the season was approaching. It would need watching—easy enough these days with radio. There were two sets aboard, a midget as used by secret agents and which operated well, and a larger one which at that moment lacked batteries. Although this latter set had only been manufactured in 1948, in England, the designers, by a humorous whim, had produced a set operated by a special type of battery which is absolutely unobtainable in the States—just the thing for export.

Weather reports are of little use to slow craft once outside range of shelter, but as I possessed no chronometer and was not versed in the art of the lunarian, it was necessary for me to obtain the time signal to calculate longitude. Obtaining latitude is a comparatively simple matter—a sextant sight at ship's noon is all that is needed. I therefore had no little interest in the working of my radios.

The engine, running like clockwork, performed its double duty of propelling *Temptress* and pouring ampères into the battery which, as usual, had become rather low. It is a losing battle trying to keep batteries charged, especially on an ocean passage when the engine is little used. I had an added difficulty because the engine would only run in smooth water; there was no separate charging set.

However, the strong fair tide was doing good work also, and as we shot past two small islands, there was a gust of wind, a sharp shower, and the weather cleared ahead, revealing the skyscraper forest.

The buoys marking the channel were nodding violently in the tide, surging from side to side and tugging at their moorings as if infuriated at being chained to the bottom of the river.

Hell Gate was the next excitement, necessitating quick action at the helm as the boat was thrown about in the tide-rips. Then came East River Drive with its giant wafer-like building of the United Nations. Diving to the cabin for my camera, I took various shots of these titanic examples of man's progress in modern civilisation. This meant steering with my thighs as the bow plunged in the wash of the many craft plying the river.

The newspaper business is run at such high speed that already one could buy a newspaper showing *Temptress* leaving City Island, and there was no doubt that many had done so, according to the people waving from the bank. But it was when nearing the end of Manhattan that things began to liven up. A big pleasure steamer surged by, whistle shrieking, while the passengers shouted and waved as a vociferous gentleman in the bows encouraged them by loudspeaker. Noisy people these Americans! Noisy, enthusiastic and likeable.

A heterogeneous collection of boats created further hustle and bustle as each threw its wash into the everchanging mounds and potholes of oily water. Each vessel seemed to have its own version of electric, air or steam hooter, and each vied to raise its voice higher than the other. Squawks, shrieks, and whistles mixed into a cacophonic medley of sound.

Gradually more and more people spotted my Red Ensign fluttering in the freshening breeze, and realised this was *Temptress*. Ships blared their sirens, swelling the sound to one deafening crescendo. This great city's salute to a tiny foreign vessel, made me feel both very small and very big at the same time.

2

LAST JOBS

All the excitement was left behind as we approached Governor's Island and began plunging to the first waves setting in from the Narrows.

KATHRYN, NEW YORK was inscribed across the stern of one ship docked on the Brooklyn side. 'Kathryn,' I cried delightedly. She had been the Bull Line ship which had sighted and reported me on the last lap of my westward voyage. Was this a good omen?

By half-past three that afternoon the Statue of Liberty was receding into the haze on the starboard quarter. A sudden shift of wind off the opposite shore gave me a powerful whiff from a garbage quay. Whew!

Having survived this, we reached the Narrows, where the masts and funnel of a sunken ship could be seen sticking out of the water—where her Master left her— a pleasant nocturnal hazard.

We passed Fort Hamilton just before the tide was due to turn, and I ran on for another half-hour in thickening visibility before casting anchor in Gravesend Bay—perfect shelter from both the south-east wind and the swell coming up the Ambrose Channel from the open Atlantic. Here was an ideal spot to finish the many jobs required before the boat would be all shipshape and Bristol fashion. What was more important, it was a safe place to ride out the hurricane which was expected to affect the area.

My first job was to clear my bunk, piled high with last-minute purchases. The next was the wretched task of filling the two gimballed stoves, the riding light, the two navigation lamps and the cabin lamps with paraffin. This messy performance is irksome enough in port, but at sea becomes loathsome and detestable. And I am supposed to rely on electricity!

While examining the food locker, which, like everything else, was in a chaotic state, I came across a tin of ham which had been opened only two days previously, yet was already a mass of writhing maggots. Just where do these animals come from? Surely any eggs would be exterminated in the process of canning? There is that mystery of how biscuits become weevily after being kept in an airtight tin. I once had a tin which was so old that even the weevils had died; it was a waste of energy even to tap the biscuits on the table—the age old custom of the sea. That problem scarcely arises nowadays as it is very difficult to buy proper ship's biscuits. The ship chandlers say that there is little demand for them since present-day seamen would refuse to go to sea unless there was fresh bread baked every other day.

For the last few days not only had I been working hard during the day but the nights had been spent in clearing correspondence; it was therefore a great relief to be free from the shore and its many worries and interruptions.

With the delightful anticipation of a quiet night's rest, after a somewhat hurried supper, I relaxed in my bunk, now made more comfortable by a newly acquired air mattress. I might have saved myself the trouble. At three o'clock in the cold morning I was rudely awakened by the heavy shaking and pounding of the boat on the hard sand. Aground! and on a falling tide. A hurried look out gave me my bearings. The wind had veered round to the west, blowing straight into the bay. Blessing the engine, which started immediately, I motored clear, rushed forward to get in the anchor chain, and directly the anchor was aweigh, dashed aft to straighten up into the wind. Anchor was dropped in four and a half fathoms. After twenty fathoms of chain had been veered, a sounding showed the keel to be floating safely eleven feet above the bottom. That was that.

This proved the usefulness of an engine. Further, if the breeze had blown up strong, all that would have been necessary to be safely moored, would have been to motor out at an angle to the wind until level with the anchor, then drop the kedge.

The sun streaming through the ports was the next, and more

pleasant, awakening. The boat was lying quiet again, the wind having backed once more to the south-east—a head wind; but that was of no import as I had plenty of rigging work to do before we could proceed to sea.

As a few things were needed in the galley, I launched the dinghy and rowed energetically to the shore—a stiff pull to windward. Breaking I do not know how many regulations, and caring not a jot, I landed at one of the Coney Island piers. What a contrast! One moment the quiet life on board, and the next, civilisation in its least aesthetic aspect, with a mass of ill-mannered and sweating humanity passionately exchanging discourtesies. Most of the feminine vacationists were doing their shopping in swimsuits. Lord! how fat those women were. This type of woman in America must own more pounds in weight per head than in any other country in the world—although, I must confess that the fact that they were well sunburnt did something to improve matters. White flesh exposed in large areas is depressing at the best of times.

I hurried through my shopping, which was an unpleasant task. The most important item to be purchased was a battery which could be adapted to my larger radio. The salesman, an unwashed individual whose two-day stubble went apparently unnoticed, made several rude remarks on my own perfectly respectable beard. He seemed not to care whether I bought anything at his shop or not. I thanked another man who sold me some lemons. He looked at me suspiciously but did not return the compliment. I fled back to the dinghy and the sanctuary of *Temptress*, to busy myself doing sailor's work which I love so well, and to soothe my ruffled ego with memories of kindness and hospitality at the hands of other Americans in places different to Coney Island.

The weather, next day, repeated the same pattern—an early morning south-west wind soon backing to south-east and freshening. From the anchorage, the leaping waves could clearly be seen on the far side of the point; even had the boat been ready for sea, it would have been foolish to make a start which would merely involve fruitless tacking across one of the busiest steamer routes of the world. In any case the radio reported that the hurricane had passed north of the West Indies, and was expected to brush Florida before pursuing its course northwards. To start now would be to court the risk of meeting this whirling monster after some days at sea—a thing best avoided. My chance would come after the hurricane had swept by; before the next one came, I should be clear of the danger area—or so I hoped.

A small boat sailor has to be a jack of all trades, and master of some. Rigger one day, mechanic the next. That was my lot. The worn sprocket on the magneto needing renewing. A simple job, one might think; but the sprocket was held on by four slotted set-screws. Only possible to use a screwdriver; it took forty-five minutes. Had the screws been designed with hexagon heads, a spanner would have removed them in as many seconds. It is, also, quite incredible how many inaccessible nuts one finds. When engine designers die, do their spirits float about the oceans of the world, in the engine-rooms of ships, splitting their sides with laughter, while watching hapless engineers fiddling with a nut around which it is impossible to place a spanner? I would like to believe in a just God, and the doctrine of reincarnation.

The next job was on the water-circulating pump which leaked abominably. In this case the gland nut was round and so positioned that it was impossible to get even a small wrench on it. Taps with a cold chisel shifted it, thereby stopping the leak but making the plunger bind. Ah well! To settle by compromise is supposed to be an integral part of the British character —so, a slight leak in the pump and a slight sticking of the plunger, and we will keep everyone happy.

It was a peaceful place to work—anchored out there in Gravesend Bay—no telephones, no camera-men, and no unwelcome visitors. Purposely the Red Ensign was never worn nor was the name of the boat painted on the hull. Occasionally I would stop work and gaze about me. Although only a few miles of the main shipping channel were visible, at least one ship was always in sight. Those inward bound for New York had their smoke all blown well ahead of them—a sure indication of the stiffness of the breeze. The Queen Elizabeth steamed majestically up the channel, remote and indifferent to her dash across the Atlantic, a mere matter of routine for her, but a hazardous undertaking for *Temptress*.

By midnight the wind had dropped completely, and the brilliant coloured lights of Coney Island reflected in the mirrored surface held a certain fascination for me, as did, strangely enough, the sound of the swing music wafting over the still waters.

The distant groaning of fog sirens aroused me. Looking out on deck I found a heavy blanket of fog weeping gently with fine drops of moisture.

The morning report placed the centre of the hurricane 360 miles off Miami, heading towards Carolina at 15 miles per hour, with its encircling winds blowing at 140 miles per hour.

I continued with the jobs. The galley salt-water pump was completely modified—it had never operated properly as originally designed. Another thing had just the same trouble; before leaving New York I had ordered a new bronze gaff saddle to replace the inefficient wooden one. It arrived bright and shining, presumably parts of it made with gold—judging by the price. After fitting to the gaff it looked well enough, the only snag being that it was impossible to hoist the mainsail without gouging the mast! However, my friends the hacksaw, drills and files had come to the rescue, and with a morning's work we confounded the designer's ingenuity.

The rubber inserts were renewed in the four opening ports; though the rubber had been bought in England two years previously, it was only now being fitted. These ports had leaked maddeningly on the passage to America, but now they should be almost watertight for the return passage.

By late afternoon the sun had burnt up the fog, but a strong and freezing-cold wind was blowing, presumably already affected by the hurricane screaming away in the south.

Having completed most of the work by tea-time, I tuned in my short-wave set, deriving considerable amusement by eavesdropping on a radio telephone conversation between a yacht and the shore. Evidently a husband on board his motor-boat at Eatons Neck was calling up his wife, and the following inspired conversation ensued:

'Hallo.'

'Hallo, is that you?'

'Yes, this is me.'

'How are you?'

'Fine thanks, how are you?'

'Fine thanks.'

'Guess who is on board?'

'I don't know, tell me.'

'Oh! it is Marion, would you like to speak to her?'

'Oh! all right; Hallo, Marion, how are you?'

'Fine thanks, and you?'

'Oh, yes, fine thanks; I don't know what to say.'

'No, nor do I, er... shall I call hubby again?'

'Oh, yes, thank you.'

'Hallo, dear.'

'Oh, hallo, is it you again?'

'Yes, it's me.'

'Oh, good; I think we had better stop now.'

'Yes, I think so.'

'Good night.'

'Good night.'

'Good night.'

3

WARNING

I heard an enthralling talk, on the radio, between a tug towing a dredger, and—presumably—headquartered in New York. The tug skipper said he was going as hard as he could for Delaware River, although bound farther south. He was getting very anxious at the reported velocity of the hurricane, and was already meeting a tremendous swell which was delaying his progress.

His headquarters were passing on to him each report of the hurricane as it was received. At that time it was only one hundred miles south of Cape Hatteras. Severe storm and high tide warnings were out over the entire area. It was already blowing full gale force off Hatteras, not far to the south of him. The tug-master and crew had plenty of cause for anxiety. For me, it was a true-life radio drama. One could hear and sense the anxiety in the skipper's voice and the comfort he was gaining from his contact with those safe on shore.

Sunday, 20th August. Tuning in at 7.45 a.m. to the Weather Bureau forecast for the Battery area I received 'All small craft advised to stay in port; hurricane near Cape Hatteras travelling north-north-east at twenty miles an hour, blowing one hundred and forty miles an hour, and expected to reach Nantucket after nightfall. North-east gale warning off Long Island.'

My conditions were easterly wind, heavy rain with thunderstorms. Humidity very high.

By midday the wind had taken right off but incessant rain fell, with bad visibility; barometer was falling fast. Heavy surf was beating on the New Jersey shore. It was not until the afternoon that the wind picked up fresh from north by east and sent me hurrying to lay out my second anchor. It felt more secure riding to twenty-five fathoms of anchor chain to port, and sixteen fathoms of stout mooring line to starboard.

The day dragged by, tinged with a certain amount of anxiety, the radio being switched on and off to pick up the latest reports.

Soon after darkness it was blowing gale force from the north. *Temptress* was beginning to pitch and snatch at her moorings—even in that sheltered position. A few hours later the centre of the hurricane was to the eastward and would get no nearer. The radio stated that it would pass about one hundred miles east of Nantucket next morning. Its forward motion had speeded up to twenty-five miles an hour and it was expected to hit Nova Scotia.

Following this report there was a Symphony Concert from the B.B.C., relayed from New York. This helped to drown the roar of wind.

By dawn the conditions were much quieter, the wind only blowing Force 4. The hurricane had passed, after brushing Cape Cod with full gale-force winds and exceptionally high tides. The previous day's rainfall had been no less than three inches.

It was over. I went on deck to cast off the halyards...

Temptress, in the train of a lifting sweep of gulls, glided through the still water under the hot sun. Gradually the bay, which had provided such a timely shelter, was hidden; it was a relief to be on the move again, after waiting over five days. I had become very weary of the Parachute Tower on Coney Island, as well as the unpleasant flotsam and jetsam floating on the dirty water. Now the petrol-perfumed air of the City would be changed for the ozone-laden atmosphere of the ocean.

In the afternoon the hardening breeze veered, allowing *Temptress* to scud down the main Ambrose Channel, cheekily joining the procession of ocean-going ships. One by one the great cargo carriers thudded by —flags of all nations—name after name—*Uruguay, Robert E. Hopkins, Exchange, Ivorville, Crotton Trails, Fort Mercer...* an unending list, each a challenge to the sea, and each a separate adventure.

With the faltering breeze barely filling the curving canvas, *Temptress* stole out of the tide, into Sandy Hook Bay. The anchor splashed down, with the chain rattling over the fairlead and echoing off the nearby breakwater. The day's sail had only gained ten miles, but we were now poised in perfect position, ready to plunge into the open Atlantic.

It was a lovely cloudless evening, but the soft breath of wind, warm and laden with the scent of land, filled me with an uneasy nostalgia for what I was leaving. To the north the famous skyline of New York was faintly outlined in the grey haze. I gazed at this with attachment, for, mellowed by distance, it was indeed an an enthralling sight.

*   *   *

In the early morning mists, with sails trimmed to a light south-westerly wind, *Temptress* nosed slowly out of the bay. But as she rounded Sandy Hook this feeble breeze died away, leaving her drifting eastwards on the tide, kicking about in the hurly-burly of water stirred up by passing steamers.

A slight clearing of the haze showed the tall buildings of Coney Island again, and even to these, distance lent enchantment on that fair and peaceful morning.

Not wishing to be becalmed all night amongst the thick traffic, before the tide turned against us I started the engine and the bowsprit swung round to point for East Rockaway Inlet. For hours the yawl had been lying like a log in the water, now she was transformed by the thrust of the propeller, and bubbles creamed along the waterline, to be lost in the turbulence of the wake.

The twisting channel had to be negotiated without a chart, but as it is so well buoyed this presented little difficulty and we anchored in Long Island creek just before dusk.

Being able to reach shelter proved again the advantage of having an auxiliary engine, however small, for otherwise I would have been left in a bad position and lost a night's sleep into the bargain. Later a steady rain further reduced visibility. It would have been a cold, wet and anxious night outside.

It was raining hard, with a gusty wind from the south-east, next morning. I remained at anchor. It cleared by midday and I rowed ashore in the dinghy to top up my water and fuel tanks. It was a hard pull back in the fierce current. To get some exercise I dived over the side and was swept downstream where I landed on a bathing beach, and sunbathed for a couple of hours; the tide then changed and carried me back to *Temptress*.

The next excitement was provided by some clam fishermen in a motor-boat bearing down on my bowsprit, missing it by inches. For some peculiar reason, still unsolved, they were towing a sixty-foot fire hose, which promptly wrapped itself round my anchor chain. With this extra weight, from holding their boat as well as *Temptress* in the strong tide, the anchor began to drag. A large individual called Johnnie came blundering out in another motor-boat in an effort to help, but he merely added to the general confusion, while *Temptress's*, topsides began to suffer in the battle. Despite their noisy and landlubberly endeavours, the hose suddenly cleared itself, and the motor-boats were whisked away by the tide. Single-handed the job could have been done in a few minutes. The present generation of fishermen are often longshoremen, whereas in the old days of sail they were all seamen.

Not in the sweetest of tempers, I was manoeuvring the dinghy aboard when one of these fast motor-boats dashed by, sending a terrific wash, making the dinghy inflict further damage on the long suffering topsides— another instance of thoughtless bad manners from the legion of marine motorists. Luckily there were few of them on that side of Long Island compared with the numbers that infest the Sound.

I had had enough of these false starts. Would the morrow provide conditions favourable for heading out into the ocean? I asked myself, while giving a last look round before turning in that night.

4

'TEMPTRESS'

I bought *Temptress* in early summer of 1948 at Dartmouth, Devon. I had stumbled on her quite by chance when visiting this town after an unsuccessful attempt to sail to Gibraltar in my cutter *Content* during the previous winter. I saw at once that although she was considerably smaller than *Content*, she would be easier to handle and cheaper to maintain. A four-figure overdraft at my bank paid for the boat, and after a few weeks *Content* was sold to Len Greenwood who eventually sailed her to the West Indies and America.

While in New York Tom Tothill helped me to measure up *Temptress* and draw her lines and accommodation plans. The dimensions in Lloyds Register were found to be wrong; here are the correct ones:

Length overall (on deck)	34ft
Length on waterline	31ft 6in
Beam (extreme)	10ft 4in
Draft (fully laden)	6ft 8in
Displacement	14 tons
Sail area (working)	600 sq ft

Temptress is rigged as a yawl, with a gaff mainsail and marconi mizzen. The mainsail is a stout sail roped all round and fitted with roller-reefing gear which proved to be almost indispensable; it rotates the boom by a worm drive and rolls up the sail like a blind. This sail can stand anything that a trysail would, thus saving the cost of a special storm sail. I once had to shift from mainsail to trysail in a gale in the Irish Sea, an experience which I have no wish to repeat.

She is a fine seaboat, always light on the helm, able to stand up to her canvas in a squall, and to look after herself in gale conditions. She could have been improved by less draft and a more modern bow, but this would have increased her price by a thousand dollars or more.

Since my return I have received many letters concerning the boat; this one was from the brother of her designer:

North Wales,
4th October, 1951

Dear Mr. Allcard,

In the September number of the *Yachting World* I have read about your wonderful single-handed cruise in the *Temptress*, designed by my brother H. G. S. Robinson in 1910, and I feel that I would like to congratulate you on your safe return. You may not know that my brother was killed on the Gold Coast in 1913, which was most unfortunate because he, like myself, had always been very keen on designing, building and sailing all types of craft... *Temptress* must have been well built and cared for to stand the strain of your long cruise so many years afterwards.

Wishing you every success in the future,

I am, yours sincerely,

E. P. M. ROBINSON.

There is no doubt that the yawl was very well built. The timber used, even for those days, was exceptional.

There are no butts in her planking; that is to say that every plank (in the hull and deck) goes end to end in one piece. All her frames are selected oak crooks cut to shape by saw and adze. Fastenings are of copper and bronze. Hull planking is 1-inch thick pitch pine, and her decks 1½-inch teak.

I received also a letter from the family of her first owner:

Hertford,
17th August, 1951

Dear Sir,

I am writing to you, somewhat belatedly, to congratulate you on your recent voyage in the *Temptress*. I followed your voyage in the papers with particular interest as my father had the *Temptress* built. I thought that you would like to know that he is still alive, but an invalid.

She was built about 1909 by Brabyn at Calenick in Cornwall. Some of the wood, including the teak deck, came from an old Ship-of-the-Line which had been broken up at Falmouth. My father was in the Sudan Goverment service and could only use her during his summer leaves. She was first commissioned in 1910 for my parents' honeymoon. Each year, they cruised in the Channel, between Falmouth and Dover, and never went farther afield.

In 1914, she was laid up at Fowey and subsequently her lead keel was requisitioned. After the war, she was sold to Clyde owners.

My father has been very thrilled to hear about the old yawl again and has read your last book. We would very much like to know what is happening to her now.

Yours sincerely,

J. E. C. BEVAN.

I think that new boats have something missing, something intangible, the difference, for instance, between modern furniture and antique. Not only had I bought *Temptress* but I had bought her history as well. It makes life more interesting for me and the many others who have sailed in her. She has led me to new contacts, new friends, as well as to new horizons. What a yarn I had when, in Scotland, I met one of her crew who participated in several outstanding cruises in the late 'twenties—when she won the Coats Challenge Cup of the Clyde Cruising Club three years in succession.

In 1929 she was chartered for a voyage to Spain. On board was Humphrey Barton who has since sailed across the Atlantic in a twenty-five-foot boat, *Vertue XXXV*. She has done her share in training many in one of the healthiest sports in the world.

After her Spanish cruise she was bought by a man who used her for pottering about in the West Country. She was hauled ashore and laid up in 1938, and remained in a shed until I rescued her ten years later. After a hurried fit-out I sailed to Gibraltar, refitted, then sailed to New York in eighty days. And now, here she was, ready for the second crossing of the Atlantic in the hurricane season. Her history and her strength gave me confidence.

5

TO SEA

At last the voyage started—genuinely. On Thursday morning, 24th August, I got under way for (presumably) Plymouth, England. The wind was not too encouraging, being just faint airs blowing over a low glassy swell from the south-east. The sun struggled to break through the early morning mist.

With the strong fair tide, and under power, we soon dropped the inlet astern; but after a run of some hours the engine was switched off, and we waited for Boreas to throw his dice for the day's chance of wind. It was not long before a breeze came away steadily, allowing *Temptress* to sail close-hauled to the eastward, parallel to the shores of Long Island.

Gradually the mist dispersed leaving a perfect day, but I was not yet sufficiently composed mentally to enjoy it fully, being saddened by the thought of leaving the country where I had been so richly befriended. Despite this feeling of loneliness, I still would not have cared to have anybody else with me and merely looked forward to the time when this depressing mental attitude would be shaken off.

To banish these unpleasant workings of the mind, I picked up one of Agatha Christie's Hercule Poirot books and read a page or two at a time, sitting in the cockpit, looking round between whiles at the fair scene and thinking of the subject which claims sixty per cent of one's thoughts at sea—namely: What is the position of the boat? Where will we be in two or three days' time? and, What is the wind going to do?

The day passed very quietly until the red sun, looking like an enormous poached egg, was absorbed into the fog, and the moon apologetically lifted out of the haze towards the south-east; it was nearly full, and would cheer me for some nights to come.

The wind gradually fell away, leaving *Temptress* gently rolling to the beam swell, with the gear protesting and snatching.

We lay becalmed all night, about five miles off shore. I took cat-naps below, occasionally looking out for coastal shipping. Increasing fog gradually blotted out the shore lights and by daylight no land was in sight. Wanting to check my position before finally heading out to the ocean, I lay close-hauled to the north towards the shore until it was identified, about two miles off, then tacked ship and headed eastward once more. With little wind all day, *Temptress* merely nibbled at the miles.

The only yacht met on this trip, a beautiful schooner, with a magnificent array of light canvas hoisted, was heading in the opposite direction close inshore, evidently bound for Sandy Hook. Very few yachts appear to venture outside Long Island Sound.

As on the previous day, the wind slowly veered to the south and gradually faded away towards sunset. It seemed that America just would not let me go, or perhaps the hurricane had stolen all the available wind.

The evening colouring was beautiful, with huge light patches of pale green on the water, reflecting the mauve of the sunset haze— but still there was little wind, and as night fell the log line took a steeper and steeper angle, as the yawl barely held steerage way. Again the snatch of gear and rattle of blocks raised noisy protest at the lack of a sailing breeze. This calm, which would be quite welcome in mid-ocean, was now nothing but an anxiety and nuisance, so near the land and shipping tracks. Besides, the lateness of the year and the coming winter made it a very bad time for delay.

Only fifteen miles had been gleaned during daylight. We were getting nowhere very slowly.

The day faded into a magical night; so absolute was the calm that the reflection of the full moon wobbled grotesquely on the uneasy water. Except for the screak of gear I might have been anchored in some quiet bay.

To the north faintly flickering lights on the shore stabbed over the dark waters. These lights were to be my last positive indication of land for many weeks. The silence was broken only by the mournful moan of a whistle buoy far astern, and the faint rumble of the surf on the beach.

Before starting my nocturnal cat-naps I switched on my mast-head light—an important safety measure. Instead of the usual red and green side lights, which are very difficult for steamers to pick up, there was this powerful all round white electric light fixed on the main truck. It not only advertised our presence to all and sundry but also illuminated the red nylon wind-sock—a great convenience for night sailing, especially when running before a light wind, with the danger of gybing. At this time, of course, the sock was just hanging down dejectedly and swivelling erratically round the mast at the short rolling of the vessel.

By daylight, although fifteen hours had elapsed since passing the confounded whistle buoy it could still be plainly heard. Looking back at my descriptive log, I note with amusement that although I had described it in the evening as a 'mournful moan' by the morning it had changed to a 'plaintive bleat'!

In spite of the oily calm there were at least signs of wind, in the form of huge bell-shaped 'mares' tails' across the sky, all pointing towards the north-west. From the radio came talk of cool winds from the Great Lakes. Nevertheless, when the wind did come, it was from the south. No time was lost in hoisting the reaching staysail. Temptress was soon cutting along nicely on her course, lifting slowly and easily over the restless swells, with a tintinnabulation of the bow-wave.

A long straight-stemmed fishing boat loomed out of the mist, crossing astern. I scrambled below for the binoculars to study her more closely. At the same time a little land bird with yellow breast flew aboard. Insignificant incidents perhaps to the reader, but all happenings at sea, however small, assume the greatest importance.

After these two epoch-making events, I got busy with the oil-can, lubricating the patent roller-reefing gear and the rudder stock bearing, the squawking of which had been disturbing my sleep for some time.

Then once more to the helm.

A heavy drone from a number of aircraft flying directly overhead, allied with Fitzroy Maclean's war adventures fresh in mind from the previous evening's reading, brought back to me memories of bombing during the War. I remembered how sometimes I used to lie back in bed keeping my thoughts off the fireworks by dreaming of sailing across the Atlantic. Well, here I was sailing across the Atlantic, dreaming of bombing raids. Something to do with what Dunne would call 'Serial Time' perhaps*, each experience being a separate pea in the same pod.

In those peaceful surroundings it seemed a far cry from the time when my own blood ran freely in the gutters of London, and the subsequent period when I lay in hospital, wracked with anxiety as to whether I would finally lose my arm—and my chance of sailing the oceans alone.

My thoughts roamed on... through the post-war period when, in an endeavour to fulfil those dreams I decided to escape the masses of regimented people who appeared to be content to exist in little concentric circles, clinging to life but afraid to live it. People would say to me, 'I wish my ties and responsibilities did not prevent me doing what you have done. If only I had the time.'

Of course I am not suggesting that it would be a good thing for everyone to jump aboard boats and rush out into the Atlantic! But it is the principle of the thing that counts. The principle of a healthy and happier life.

Given the incentive anyone can make the time. As for ties and responsibilities, these can usually be boiled down to grubbing for an unnecessary amount of money (to keep up with the Jones's), or living far more softly than nature ever intended man to do.

The basic laws and instincts of nature are inherent as much in man as in the lesser animals. There is no counterpart in nature of a few controlling vast masses, and this is one reason alone why the world cannot be on the threshold of spiritual advancement, not while these 'isms' exist, forced by seekers of egocentric power on

---

* See J. W. Dunne, *An Experiment with Time*—Ed.

those whose only alternative is death. It is to be wondered at, that the salt sea itself is not swollen by the tears of tragedy brought upon the defenceless by the wicked machinations of man's rulers.

A State should exist by a procedural pattern of collective individualism which would encourage those prepared to work on the fundamental processes which help the Country and Community. The whole system of contemporary life would seem to drag down those with initiative to an unnecessarily low common denominator...

At this point, my chain of theories was completely broken by the sudden flap, flap, flap of the reaching staysail, showing that we had wandered off course. Leaning forward, and peering into the compass, I straightened out the curve in the wake. A floating black object was sighted dead ahead. Course was altered again. A submerged plank bobbed just below the surface, and standing on it was a bird looking so depressed that I burst out laughing.

A couple of hours later the wind hardened appreciably and we began to foot it at good speed, with the bow busily carving a slice out of every wave.

The change of conditions and increase of sea made it seem as if I had passed into another mental and physical world, for it is 'wind in a man's face that makes him wise'.

The evening wind eased but became colder. A few steamers were occasionally sighted on the course to New York. Ships give a pleasant sense of companionship to the lone mariner.

To facilitate navigation my clocks had been changed to Ships' Mean Time, so it was seven o'clock when the sun, a red ball of fire, sank down towards the sea, while above, a thin scattering of cirrus cloud marked the sky. Half an hour later the full moon, huge and pink, appeared low over the horizon; the first scintillating reflection was of pure gold, until, as she rose clear of the haze, the colour imperceptibly changed to silver.

It became too dark to see the compass, but by keeping the planet Jupiter sighted through the rigging it was a simple matter to steer the speeding *Temptress*.

After a continuous fifty-mile run, the staysail sheet was hauled to windward (to keep her on course) and the boat was left to forge through the clear night unattended. The estimated position, twenty-six miles south of Block Island, was plotted on the chart.

Had my luck now changed? Could this good day's progress continue?

*   *   *

The wind gradually fell away until, at a crystal-clear dawn, *Temptress* was rolling lazily to the southerly swell, becalmed. So much for my hopes for more speed. At seven o'clock I tried to pick up the Fishermen's Forecast, but we were out of range; from now on I would have to rely on my own weather predictions.

Only two vessels were sighted the whole morning—one steamer, hull down to the south, and one sail. Any vessel in sight at sea is of the greatest interest, much more so if a sailing vessel. This one proved to be a big ketch, Bermudian rigged with three headsails. She gradually overhauled me to port, and at lunch-time she was two miles away on the beam, most likely a yacht bound for Nantucket Light Vessel. Where did they think I was bound?

6

FIRST LAP

Climbing on deck with my sextant I took a sight of the sun and went below to work out the problem.

But horrors! I had forgotten how to navigate! I had not taken a sight for over a year, and, as every seaman knows, one becomes rusty without practice. Assuming my calculations to be incorrect (for they placed me in the middle of South America), I then slavishly followed an 'example' which was in the navigation book, but obtained the same result. After spending about half an hour, and being unable to find the mistake, I impatiently threw all the navigation instruments back into the drawer and rolled up the chart.

The proper navigation books were on board; it was merely a matter of getting used to them again. Later that day, in the afternoon, I took another sight, this time managing to obtain an accurate position. We were ten miles west of the dead-reckoning position, evidently due to a foul current.

After a nine-hour calm a darkening on the south-western horizon heralded the day's breeze; the sails softly filled and the log slowly began to turn.

A shoal of tunny surrounded the boat. I lost no time in getting out my new Abercrombie and Fitch fishing grains*. The retrieving line was attached both to the head and the top of the stave, so that if the powerful fish broke the head off, it would not be lost. Adjusting the helm, for an instant I waited poised with the grains; as the fish turned, I lunged forward. Ouch! Being too

---

* A barbed and spiked weapon for spearing fish—Ed.

near the boom, instead of catching a fish I caught my little finger a resounding thwack on the spar, frightening the fish away—result—no tunny and a very numb finger.

During the day the wind backed to the south and freshened, but by late evening the increasing sea reduced the good progress. Black clouds began to form to windward. Humidity became so high that dew was dropping on the decks long before sunset.

To my astonishment, a steamer which I was watching suddenly disappeared; the black cloud was nothing but fog.

As dusk gathered in, the wind gradually fell away. All round me these great fog banks crept over the darkening waters, and in the distance I could hear the hoot of ships' sirens. I felt somewhat apprehensive at the ominous change in the weather; it was going to be an anxious night. This was the actual entry in my log:

20.00: *Log reading 38.3. Heave to. Little wind. Barometer 30.08 steady. Black fog banks, lovely! and right in steamer track.*

The whole night was spent with me dodging up and down the hatch, portable fog-horn at the ready. Once, the sound of a ship's siren became increasingly loud. I pumped my gadget, making the best noise of which it was capable, until, just as I was becoming seriously alarmed, the boo…m of the ship's siren inexplicably receded in the same direction.

Another time, while I was peering into the damp atmosphere, the fog lifted for a moment revealing a big liner, an absolute blaze of lights, heading towards Sandy Hook. I had not heard his siren; presumably he was navigating on radar, and might or might not have picked me up on the screen. Though I have never seen one fitted, it would be a safety factor for all yachts navigating in foggy waters to carry a radar reflector installed, possibly, on the crosstrees.

The heeling of the boat and the whistle of wind awakened me from one of my quick snatches of sleep. Up again! The wind had come away fresh from the south-south-west. A huge fog bank was approaching and quickly smothered the vessel. Having furled the jib and rolled down two reefs in the mainsail, I stood shivering in the hatch, straining my ears for more sirens. Light rain began to fall as daylight slowly took over from night, leaving a grey sky and cold grey waters.

On the radio I picked up a report of two hurricanes, one 2,000 miles off Miami heading north-west, and the other in the Gulf of Mexico. The first one gave me cause to worry as it would probably pass over my present area in a week or so. It was essential for me to get clear of its path in the meantime, and I decided on the grand plan; instead of following my pre-determined course to England by way of the Gulf Stream, I would now sail east and south to get away from the main storm tracks, marked only too clearly on my American Pilot Chart.

The first few pieces of Sargasso weed showed the proximity of the Gulf Stream. This weed becomes very tiresome, for, unlike normal seaweed, it catches on the log rotator and stops it turning. After some hours of repeatedly clearing the rotator I lost patience and took it on board, deciding for the future to rely on celestial navigation and only keep a very rough dead reckoning.

The wind eased a bit during the morning but the rain continued. With all light canvas hoisted, we made satisfactory progress towards the south-east. To my delight we gradually passed through the fog banks; suddenly it was quite clear ahead, but the breeze came up fresh again in the evening with more fog, and I prepared myself for cold, damp hours at the helm. After a miserable stretch of this I remembered the hot water in the thermos flask and, leaving the helm for an instant, made a very welcome, steaming cup of coffee.

That hot drink made an amazing difference. Before, I had felt cold, hungry and apprehensive of the coming night, but now I felt a completely new man and even started to sing—at least that is what I called it. There was no one there to contradict.

People often ask whether I talk to myself at sea. I did at first, when, on rare occasions, I felt the need to combat the lack of companionship. However, the ensuing silence seemed so complete and desolate that the sense of aloneness became even more poignant.

Loneliness, either on land or at sea, has before now led even to suicide. A friend of mine was once on a ketch and the cook shot himself, rather inconveniently, before breakfast was prepared. But lone-liness in a town can be much more acute than on the ocean. London or New York can be the loneliest place on earth. At least, on the ocean, one knows there is no one—no one for friend, no one for rival. Man's actions are said to be chiefly governed by his competitive instinct; therefore the single-hander, however small his boat, is in a position of supreme dominance.

There are times when one does not dare break the silence of the sea, but normally I sing when particularly happy or to while away a long trick at the helm. Singing, curiously enough, does not leave one with such a sense of forlorn solitude as does talking. And it helps to keep one warm. There is another reason for singing; without exercise, the vocal chords become soft. One can easily get a sore throat from a song or two following days of silence. But how strange it would be for someone to hear, unexpectedly, the haunting refrain of 'The Mountains of Mourne' wafting through a foggy night in the Atlantic!

*   *   *

After being at the tiller for thirteen hours (and fifty miles), I hauled the staysail to weather and went below, leaving the boat pitching to an unpleasant jabble of a sea whipped up by a squally wind. A tin of beefsteak and beans, tipped into a saucepan, was soon hotting up over the hissing primus stove. It was warm and comfortable out of the cold and wet on deck, where everything was so saturated by fog that drops falling from the rigging sounded like heavy rain. My blankets seemed exceptionally inviting.

*   *   *

During the night the fog rolled away towards the north. The sparkling clear dawn and sunny day was in marked contrast to the gloom and wet that preceded it. Radio reception became good again, and the news reported that a hurricane was heading direct from Louisiana in the Caribbean area; that was one at least that would never hit me! At that moment I could not care a rap for the affected areas. In these affairs one becomes quite callous of the other unfortunates: it was their turn; mine might come later.

As the forecast also told of thunderstorms and the possibility of winds from the east, I was at the helm early, driving the boat under full sail, in order to seize as much advantage as possible from the fair wind. I shot the sun as soon as it was high enough in the heavens, working out the position line while steering—an exasperating procedure with the wind blowing all the pages about.

The wind freshened further, making the boat charge along at five or more knots through a confused sea. There was definite evidence of the Gulf Stream: the yellow weed was more extensive, the first flying fish sighted shot out of the sea and, to the south, immense thunderheads reared into the blue sky.

A navigational 'fix' was obtained by bringing forward the morning position line to the latitude obtained at noon. The ship's position was already east of the longitude of Nantucket.

The first lap of the voyage was complete.

7

PHOTOGRAPHY

Sailing conditions on the afternoon of 29th August were absolutely perfect. A spanking fair wind just abaft the beam drove *Temptress* along at a six-knot clip. The sea which had lengthened out was that magnificent tropical blue, flecked here and there with white horses.

Between whiles of basking in the hot sun at the helm, I endeavoured to capture the beautiful colours of those shining hours with my camera, loaded (or so I thought) with colour film. Months later the film was developed; eagerly I tore open the packet, only to find that they were all ordinary black and whites.

On the westward passage I had begun to lose the use of my legs; remembering this, I spent some time doing my daily exercise of 'knees bend', hanging on to the boom gallows to steady myself against the lurches.

This remunerative day was brought to a close by a sunset which, although very tame in itself, was reflected in the east by a chain of grotesque and gigantic thunderheads. The growing dusk trembled with great flashes of lightning in the enormous series of slow-moving clouds, which imperceptibly changed from mauve to black. At one instant the full moon appeared, framed, in awesome beauty, in a window amongst the great masses. Above shone the bright light of Jupiter.

These thunder squalls move so slowly that even a small boat can sometimes avoid them. After several hours when one of these vast clouds had not altered its bearing but was converging on us, I could see that, inevitably, at its present rate of progress, we should meet. I checked the boat's way by backing the staysail and rolling down two turns in the main; this allowed the storm to pass ponderously across the bow. It was another two hours before it passed clear, leaving a fresh breeze and a hearty head sea.

The increased motion did nothing to help re-load the Leica with 35-mm. film strip, a tricky enough operation at the best of times.

In order to keep films in good condition I first put them in a metal container sealed with adhesive tape; then this is placed in an airtight jar, holding half a pound of tea, which acts as a hygroscopic substance. In this manner my films remain in perfect condition even after several months at sea.

I never feel safe at sea unless I am at least one hundred miles from land, and now at last Nantucket was this distance away. But my satisfaction for the fine day's run was spoiled by a radio report stating that a hurricane was centred 430 miles south-east of Bermuda, heading north-eastwards. This was somewhat disturbing.

Wednesday, 30th August.

03.15: *Pig of a sea: fresh S.W. wind.*

06.45: *Getup. Find weed hanging on end of bowsprit.*

07.45: *Take helm: course E.S.E. filthy beam swell and westerly sea building up: sunny with cloud to south-east.*

09.15: *Rig foreguy: boat rolling heavily.*

11.15: *Wind drops to Force 2 from the west. Fiendish, exasperating, erratic roll, with boom first dipping in the water before being flung into the air. Am in a vile temper and doing my best to check vituperation. Hot sun. Chain of thunderheads stretching over the horizon from south-west to east. Poor progress: unable to set light canvas as it would tear to ribbons in this motion.*

The wind veered slightly and it was necessary to alter course south-east, heading directly into the big swell which was increasing every hour. This was probably due to the hurricane off Bermuda.

In vain I tried to pick up the radio station to get the latest news.

Gradually the thunderheads retreated in disorderly fashion towards the south-east. The sky and sea remained a very deep blue, which belied its character, for the sea prevented even reasonable progress.

Swooping round the boat was one of those giant petrels, looking very like an albatross as it swept through the air without any perceptible movement of its wings.

The first Portuguese man-of-war to be sighted on the trip bobbed by on the port tack.

In the late afternoon, with the vessel making hardly any forward progress, I decided to have a bathe off the bowsprit, and was just about to plunge in when a shark, with three pilot fish in attendance, ranged alongside; when I put my foot in the water they sheered off rapidly. Nevertheless, I took my bathe, but was careful to keep a foot on the bobstay, and let the plunging of the boat do the work.

As I was towelling myself, a large school of porpoises came cavorting by. I dashed below for the camera, but, of course, by the time it was ready, they were too far off for a shot. These complicated cameras (I had invested in a Leica Mark IIIa, F2 Summar, in the States) take an unconscionable time to adjust. Previously, with my simple folding type, all I had to do, to take a photograph, was to grab it from the cockpit locker, open it, and press the button. My present apparatus is kept protected below decks; one has to perform the following ritual:

1. On sighting a suitable object, lash the helm.
2. Dive below.
3. Seize the camera, the filters, the lens hood and the exposure meter from their special locker.
4. Open the lens.
5. Choose the correct light filter.
6. Screw it into the lens hood.
7. Attach the lens hood.
8. Dash carefully back on deck.
9. Set the exposure meter.
10. Adjust the shutter.
11. Adjust the focus.
12. One is now ready to fire, but as by this time the object is out of sight, one then reverses the whole performance.

Missing this shot of the porpoises decided me to have the camera always ready, and, after that day, every morning I would set the adjustments to the prevailing conditions, and leave the camera on my bunk handy for instant use.

Taking pictures when sailing single-handed is seldom satisfactory because there is usually one vital split second for every shot, and if one is constantly tending the helm, that crucial moment is easily missed.

*   *   *

The first week at sea, a disappointing week of poor progress, terminated with *Temptress* rolling heavily in an alabaster swell. To ease the perpetual punishment given to the gear by snatching, the mainsail was lowered, leaving just the staysail set.

There was no change in the weather the following morning. I sweated up the mainsail again and pinned in the sheet, which helped to check the worst of the motion. It was hot work—the temperature in the cabin was up to 80°F. The boat continued to dance ill-humouredly to the tune of the crowding cross-swells until a light south-east wind came in, bringing with it, however, a new and nasty sea. Progress was still almost nil. Trying to sail in those conditions, with not enough wind and a vile sea, was like knocking one's head against a brick wall. The delay, too, was dangerous: September was starting on the morrow—the worst month for hurricanes—and there I was wallowing about in the middle of the worst zone. The main swell had increased mightily, the crests passing at ten-second intervals.

It is not true that ocean seas do not affect the small boat, for—

Great seas have little seas upon their backs to bite 'em,
And little seas have lesser seas and so ad infinitum.
And the great seas themselves, in turn, have greater seas to go on:
While these again have greater still, and greater still, and so on.

(With apologies to A. de Morgan.)

Changes come quickly. At sunset a freshening southerly wind

smoothed out the smaller waves and, lo! *Temptress* was thrashing along in great style, racing and swooping amongst the massive volumes of heaving water.

Dusk hardened into true night, and I steered, lost in admiration of the brilliant stars, until the moon rose, her face adorned with a moustache provided by a thin black cloud.

After thirteen hours at the tiller, I had had enough. Thirteen hours is about my limit, not of endurance, but of patience.

Three turns of the boom struck the right sail balance, and I could safely leave the boat with her helm free, while I went below to cook up some food before turning in.

After sleeping soundly for one and a half hours, I looked out to find a comparatively quiet night, with *Temptress* slipping along at a steady three knots through slight fog.

I returned to my bunk, and had a very vivid dream; I was at home in Surrey, arguing first with my sister, then with my mother, as to whether I had sailed back across the Atlantic. They said 'Yes,' and that it was not a dream; but I said 'No,' and that I did not suffer from amnesia, that the log recorded eight days and therefore I had travelled only eight days.

Having been so sure of myself in the dream, I did not feel disappointed on awakening.

At breakfast, the last loaf of bread was finished. Regarding bread, it must be confessed that I never became fond of the American variety. It has been described as an over-advertised, undernourishing mass of dried bubbles joined together by holes, rather like foam rubber. If one squashes it between one's hands it can be reduced to almost nothing, but on releasing this peculiar substance it returns to its original shape and size—not my idea of the staff of life. However, it is always prettily wrapped up in cellophane.

After the position was plotted, estimated to be 200 miles south of Cape Sable, we were off again at fine speed under full sail. The hurricane swell was subsiding.

We were now getting the full benefit of the Gulf Stream: a push of fifteen to twenty miles every day.

One of those white long-tailed tropic birds was flying round us.

We were periodically passing islands of Sargasso weed about twelve feet in diameter, the brown type, not the brilliant yellow which one meets south of the Sargasso sea.

It was encouraging to be making steady progress after all the delays. *Temptress* slid sublimely along at four knots, with a happy chuckle at the bows, increasing to a gay whoosh one side and whoosh the other at the occasional roll. It was peaceful and immensely satisfying among those smooth hills and valleys of the sea... the delicate colouring, the few birds and fishes, and the soft wind blowing the evening sunlight on the russet brown sails.

8

FIRST GALE

S witching on the lights, I found them to be dim.

The batteries down again! Owing to the reduced motion it was possible to run the engine, but the generator registered a bare ten ampères; it should produce twenty ampères, dropping to fifteen when the batteries are half charged.

Before leaving England I had bought an expensively large generator with the new electrical system, so that charging could be done in a short time at a high rate. Part of the equipment was a black box labelled VOLT-AGE CONTROL, which cut down the charge so much that the engine had to run for ten or twelve hours before fully charging the batteries, which of course, is absurd for a sailing vessel, quite apart from a prodigious waste of fuel. Unfortunately, there had not been time to test the system before leaving England. From Gibraltar I had written to the suppliers, but they seemed more interested in trying to avoid responsibility than in helping me.

I decided that when conditions became quieter I would break the seal on this wretched Voltage Control regulator and try to readjust it, ignoring the warning THIS MUST NOT BE TOUCHED.

Temptress kept going through the night under mizzen and reefed mainsail with sheets eased, but the headsails sheeted in flat. With the helm left slightly to weather she maintained direction, spinning out astern a fiery phosphorescent wake. The engine was left running in neutral, but I managed to sleep well in spite of the racket three feet from my bunk.

In the early hours of the morning the engine first hesitated and then stopped, owing to the increased motion of the vessel. Looking out I found that the wind had dropped almost completely, but a gigantic southerly swell was surging past, caused by the hurricane which I expected (and hoped) would pass well ahead of me. All this time, however, there was that other demon let loose off Florida. It was a delicate situation because, to avoid the second one, I had to make as much easting as possible, yet this meant heading into the first and nearest. Anyway, *Temptress* was merely marking time and, all day, floundered along, the gear sawing and complaining, with the wind shifting at each wave to such an extent that its true direction swivelled round 180° and back again, causing a terrific crash and slap of sails. This was provoking enough, and in addition the sun grilled down like a hot iron on my shoulders.

I did not take a noon sight; this was one of the rare occasions when, in spite of the small wind, the sea was too big to make it worth while.

Part of the day was spent trying to take a decent photograph of the tropic bird which had now been joined by its mate; but those perverse creatures would never come together when near the boat, or come at the right angle to the sun. Losing my patience with both photography and the weather I stowed the camera away, and sat down on the galley seat to prepare lunch.

The unpleasantness continued as the day wore on; it was worrying—that weather, and having the hurricane to the south.

A number of trade wind puff clouds were scattered about the sky, but later on bigger and bigger rain squalls formed to windward; the wind freshened with every hour, over a gigantic sea. My descriptive log says:

18.00:   *This colossal sea itself is bad enough. It would be hell even with a fresh breeze blowing over it. A gale blowing over it would be the worst party I have ever been in, and if a hurricane!!*

In the meantime I rigged the bilge pump and cleared out the water which had leaked from the water-pump during the night. Why is it that man can invent radar and atom bombs and yet cannot make a simple thing like an efficient water-pump?

I had not seen such monstrous waves in all my east-to-west crossing; in fact, the only time I had seen anything approaching them was in the Bay of Biscay gale on my passage to Gibraltar. It is difficult to gauge the size of waves from a small boat; these were possibly 25 feet high and 400 feet between the crests.

About two hours after dark I hove to, after yet another thirteen-hour trick at the helm. The barometer was tending to fall. The gear and sails were banging cruelly; the motion was very violent. Luckily, radio reception was good and a clear report about the hurricane nearest the American coast stated that it was now 115 miles north-west of Puerto Rico, with the wind blowing 160 miles an hour, and still heading north-west. Another small one was also reported as being stationary on the north-west of the Caribbean sea, increasing in intensity. Long may it remain stationary, I wished.

During the night and into the following morning conditions were terrible in the extreme. A steep, confused, breaking sea yet no wind, and the motion; it defied description. Absolutely no forward progress was possible. Those few days ago when *Temptress* was making great strides across the chart, seemed already like a dream.

Wind came away fitfully from the east and a large black rain squall bore down on us. The weather looked so forbidding that I crawled forward to reef the staysail. Bounced up and down on the foredeck, I saw a rather beautiful sight: a gigantic wave fled across the bow and the back draught, caused by its speed, scattered its crest into dust in the form of a perfect rainbow—not that I gave it its full appreciation, then!

It was like an oven below with a temperature at ninety degrees. The barometer had fallen to 29.66in. Not being able to do anything else to help the boat on her course, I sat in the cabin and pulled out my charts to study them for the millionth time. Perhaps I could make Nova Scotia, only 240 miles to the north? However, I decided it was safer out at sea even if the hurricane did come up that way.

The afternoon breeze veered, but directly I started the sheets to allow the sails to take up the correct angle to the wind, the crashing and jerking of the gear became so bad that I had to pin in all the sheets again.

The sun disappeared; the heavens covered with black cloud and soon rain began to fall. The barometer still fell. The great swells were pumped by so fast that each wave was throwing up spindrift against the wind, so swift was its forward motion. I sat in the cockpit wondering what was going to happen and endeavoured to amuse myself by cracking nuts with a pair of pliers.

(Note: Next voyage bring more nuts; they are filling.) At dusk the weather looked so ominous that I rolled up the jib and just left the boat with reefed staysail and close-reefed mainsail, and no mizzen. It was still very hot; there was little wind between the squalls, and the whole time *Temptress* was being murderously thrown about with canvas and gear slatting and banging cruelly in the massive hurricane swells. Barometer down and still down. Radio reception nil.

After we had suffered another five hours of appalling motion, the wind at last came on to blow, at three-thirty in the morning, making me very glad of the reduced sail. The barometer was down to 29.5in. Black clouds were racing across the face of the moon. By four o'clock it was blowing gale force from the north. I went out to roll down the mainsail to close-reefed position. Half an hour later, a heavy sea thundered aboard absolutely solid, and water poured through the closed hatches and skylights as if they had been part open; never before had one wave deluged such quantities below, not even in the Bay of Biscay gale. Water washed over me lying in my bunk; I wished for the chance to design my own hatches. Actually it was really my own fault that water had streamed all over my books and radio, as I should have sealed up the skylight before leaving New York.

At dawn the bilges were pumped out as much as the angle of heel allowed. It was blowing full Force 8: spindrift and wave tops were continually sweeping the deck. I kept my clothes dry by the simple expedient of stripping, when it was necessary to go on deck; naked, it did not matter how great the shower-bath; on going below I could rub down with a dry towel and put on my dry clothes. After blowing hard for eight hours the wind moderated slightly, and the rising of the barometer came to slake the dust of my anxiety.

By midday I wrote in the log:

12.00: *The storm, I think, is over: now merely blowing fresh from north by west: sea surging in from N.E.: still very rough.*

I went on deck and played about with the camera, taking several shots of the sea.

With the dusk the wind had taken right off leaving a fiendish sea, and *Temptress* rolled and crashed about once more—any progress eastwards was impossible.

With great difficulty I just managed to hear the weather forecast, and it stated that one hurricane was expected to hit Florida that night, while the other one, 400 miles north of Puerto Rico, was almost stationary and blowing up to 150 miles an hour.

This second hurricane was bound to curve up the Gulf Stream eventually, and I prayed that it would stay just where it was until we were well clear of the danger area.

9

BAD WEATHER

The weather still looked very unsettled. Leaving *Temptress* to dance about through the night on her own, under very reduced canvas, I went to my bunk to get some sleep. However, after a few hours the whistle of wind and crash of seas prompted me to roll out of my bunk, tap the barometer, which immediately started to fall again, and look out.

The wind had shifted right round to the south and was blowing hard, with driving rain.

At seven o'clock in the morning it was blowing moderate gale force and very rough. Deciding that to sail with this exceptional sea on the beam would be too much punishment to the boat and gear, I left her hove to, but drifting on her course, with the twenty-mile-a-day Gulf Stream current bearing her onwards. For a time I sat in the cockpit, watching the boat's behaviour in the breaking sea; it was remarkable to watch her rise to a steep sea and lurch over the top, taking only light spray on deck. This type of boat may not win races, but certainly makes the most comfortable sea boat. During this blow it was even possible to have the slot of the main hatch opened for ventilation.

The poor advancement along the course became increasingly dangerous, for the pilot chart showed the majority of hurricane tracks passing directly across my present position. 'If only the winds would allow me a decent week's run on my right course, I would be in a comparatively safe position,' I thought. While at the back of my mind was that hurricane to the south, which, at its present rate, could strike at me within four days.

After this blow the wind again died right away. The whole atmosphere took on a steamy, yellow look; it felt like a Turkish bath. Once more without the wind to control the gear, the boom and spars snatched inordinately.

Heading round the stern of the boat was a mustard coloured shark, quite small, only six or seven feet long. There was also a school of small dolphin in range, but the rough conditions were not suitable for spearing.

Surprisingly, there was considerable bird life. My friends, the two tropic birds, were squawking round the boat, while a minute striped bird was hovering near the surface, evidently picking plankton out of the water. The third species in sight was a type of gannet, which swooped round, hovered in the air and then plunged with a great splash among the waves, to reappear jerking its head in an attempt to swallow its prey.

During the afternoon the procession of menacing rain-storms which had been marching steadfastly across the waters gradually merged into one evil black mass; a cold curtain of rain drew across the entire area. No minutes were lost in reefing the sails right down. A sharp gust of wind suddenly filled the canvas, making *Temptress* accelerate so quickly that the large shoal of small fishes gathered round the boat were left far behind. Turning round at a great commotion in the water, I saw the school of dolphin attacking the small fry until there were apparently none left.

The pall of rain passed ahead, leaving me shivering at the helm. The wind once more dropped, and with the increased swell the boom smashed from side to side so violently that the sheets had to be pinned in, killing all possible forward motion.

It was a threatening evening and the sea and sky appeared, to my apprehensive mind, to be fraught with malice.

I was below working out a navigational problem when a sudden 'switchoo' sounded alarmingly close. I rushed on deck with my torch expecting to see a whale alongside; but the beam stabbed the emptiness of the night.

The heavy rain had knocked down the sea. There was just this inky blackness and the odd, uneasy flicker of lightning. During the night the wind was squally and variable in direction; but when I took the helm at eight o'clock the wind steadied from the east, with rain.

On the port tack I steered off towards the south-east at a good speed of six knots in the smoother water, with jib, full staysail, and main with three rolls in the boom. The atmosphere was still heavy and sultry.

The dolphins were showing incredible activity, leaping in all directions after the flying fish, which were taking off in clouds in an endeavour to escape their enemies.

Wind veered to S.E., forcing me off my course, and two hours later fell very light, leaving a nasty cobbled sea. I unrolled to full mainsail, but little progress was possible. Maddening!

The wind and sea were giving me a rough deal. I felt an accumulated mental strain causing increasing irascibility, especially as each day without progress meant more chance of the hurricane striking me. I wondered, 'Can the gear stand up much longer to the everlasting wrenching, jerking and battering caused either by a gale of wind, or no wind and rough sea? There must be a limit to endurance, both of boat and man.' Deck fittings were already beginning to work loose.

At 12.45, while I was writing my journal below, the boat heeled very sharply in a strong gust of wind. I bounded to the deck and rolled down two more turns of the mainsail, upped helm and chased off downwind, travelling fast. I expected the squall to blow itself out in half an hour; but half an hour passed; I was getting bitterly cold; one hour passed, and no let-up in the wind which increased to gale force with driving rain. The jib was furled from the cockpit by the patent roller gear.

After two hours the sea began to break dangerously, forcing me to bear away more and more to the south, and preventing my making any further easting. It was necessary to heave to. After many hair-raising dashes forward to the reefing gear, I rolled many turns in the mainsail, then backed the staysail. *Temptress* rounded up sharply to meet the gale.

The barometer was falling fast, worse was to come. Washed continually by the blood-warm seas, I reefed the staysail. Even under this reduced canvas the lee deck was often under, and every now and again a breaking sea would descend and smother the vessel.

It was a relief to get below into dry clothes, and I did not forget a nip of the cup that cheers. It was cooler down below, the temperature being down to seventy-eight degrees.

More waiting! I lay on the lee settee and, making a grimace, picked up a 'shilling-shocker' Western. In such circumstances it is impossible to concentrate on worthier literature, or to indulge in philosophical theorising.

Five hours passed; conditions were worse than ever. It was the hardest wind velocity yet met on the voyage; it had come without warning, except from the torrential rain. Just when it looked as though this was going to continue indefinitely, one became aware of the lulls indicating the gale was beaten. I crawled round the decks examining the gear, keeping a very careful eye on the serried ranks of advancing waves. The mainsheet horse was working very badly in the deck after the severe strain of the last two weeks.

By nightfall it was merely blowing fresh, but more and more rain fell. The huge swell left over from the gale meted out more punishment to the long-suffering *Temptress*. Several times during the night it was necessary to go on deck to bowse down the rolling tackle. It was enough to drive one crazy; if one eased the mainsheet to try to sail there was too much danger of breaking gear, and yet if one pinned the sheets in one could not make progress. So much for surface thinking; in the mind's hinterland lurked the spectre of the hurricane.

With the dawn freshening of the east wind, I made haste to set the jib and unroll some mainsail, to let her sail herself on the port tack. The beam swell, estimated at fifteen feet to twenty feet high, still struck relentlessly, but the increase of wind at last almost steadied the gear (almost, I say!).

An advantage of a ketch over a yawl or cutter was impressed on me; with the shorter main boom it is far simpler to rig a rolling tackle well outboard, which would enable one to make progress even in a light wind and rough sea.

For over an hour I had seen a bad rain-squall heading for me; less than half a minute before it hit I rolled up the jib. It blew very violently for half an hour and then, after a flat calm and fiendish sea, the wind came away fresh again from the east.

In the afternoon I was driven into an almost frantic state of mental frustration. A morning sight was impossible; conditions were as bad as ever; the barometer was trying to fall again. I was completely fed up with the incessant violent motion and lack of progress. It always seemed to be either a gale, stiff head wind, bad sea or no wind, yet the pilot chart had shown an encouraging number of wind arrows from the south-west.

Another disadvantage of the gale was that we and a big school of dolphin had somehow parted company; and I was in need of fresh food.

FINE WEATHER

The weather gods, playing their sadistic game with impotent man, evidently considered they had, for the time being, carried things far enough, and relented sufficiently to provide a miraculous change—a clear, starlit night, with a light east wind, and motion so much easier that I was able to start the engine to charge the batteries.

Being intolerant of the mere seven-ampère charge produced, I decided to take matters into my own hands, and broke the seal of the special Voltage Control Box, exposing the whole mass of coils and maze of wires. By tickling a trembler with a match and finding out where the fault lay I made several readjustments, until the ammeter was showing a healthy fourteen-ampère charge. This put me into a cheerful humour, and then when I got good radio reception of the B.B.C. and managed to check my wrist-watch (the first time for several days) I felt almost happy.

A sunny morning after a period of depressing black clouds was like the lifting of a heavy weight from my shoulders. My luck was changing.

Excellent sights fixed my position, which had become rather doubtful. The dolphins came back; with one throw I drove my grains into a perfect specimen and he was unceremoniously yanked aboard into the cockpit. Withdrawing the spear and jabbing it into his head, I killed him instantly. Propped up on the boom gallows, he was immortalised with the camera. His luck was in inverse ratio to mine.

It was a great treat on that sparkling day, under a tropical blue sky, to have the chance to dry my sodden blankets, and to ventilate the boat with hatches wide. All I wanted now for perfect contentment was for the wind to change one hundred and eighty degrees!

After a good noon altitude, the morning sight was brought forward on the chart, giving latitude 37° 28′, longtitude 59° 30′—360 miles N.E. of Bermuda—but after sixteen days at sea we were a mere 740 miles from Sandy Hook. None the less, out of the eight average storm tracks shown on the pilot chart, seven of them were already between me and America; every mile took me farther away from the most dangerous area. I was by then working on the ocean chart of the Atlantic; the grand day's run of ninety miles was represented by a mere half-inch. Patience! There were still another eighteen inches of chart to travel before the English coast could be raised.

A big swell set in from the south-west, which might have been formed by the hurricane previously reported between Bermuda and the mainland; this too would provide winds away from the prevailing quarter. It was fine enough though, and *Temptress* also was enjoying the respite, rising and falling regularly to the head sea, on her way up to windward and ever eastward.

Mentally exhausted after my morning orgy of mathematics and cartomania, I put away all the paraphernalia and turned to preparing the dolphin for a magnificent lunch. After gutting him, to the delight of his previous companions, five big steaks were battened down in the pressure cooker, with potatoes. My small type of pressure cooker would automatically swing with the primus stove on gimbals. This method of cooking makes it comparatively simple to prepare quite elaborate meals even under bad conditions. It also means a great saving in fuel.

It is essential in a small boat that the galley should be positioned aft, where there is least motion, and the cook should be able to sit close to the stove and chock himself in, so as to be able to attend to the cooking with both hands. This was the lay-out in *Temptress*.

Oddly enough, it was often in the worst weather that the best meals could be produced. It is mostly a question of time, as every good cook knows, and hove to in head winds is one of the occasions when one is freed from the tyranny of the tiller.

Nothing is more calculated to lower morale than to do without regular hot meals, and even under the very worst conditions I make a point of providing some sort of hot nourishment. When I did not feel inclined to do this, and desired only to drop exhausted into my bunk without bothering with food, I would take a short nip of brandy which would stimulate me sufficiently to make the effort.

It was a treat to have dolphin for lunch, when normally I had to be satisfied with rice and corned beef, although, as a special reserve, there were tins of meat, vegetables and fruit.

The wind eased off again and the gear started its rattling tune, but it was such a perfect day that I contented myself with dozing over a book on the lee settee and digesting an unusually large meal.

The nearest land, Nova Scotia, was 500 miles away; the bad weather was over (for the moment, anyway) and the temperature perfect. Now the cares of civilisation could be shed and the much sought after peace of mind pursued. It was, in truth, a colourful scene of dazzling beauty outside: the intense blue sea and paler sky framed the tanned canvas. Disporting themselves around the boat were the blue-green dolphins, while two snowy white bosun birds provided a happy contrast of form and colour.

My reading was disturbed by the blowing of whales. I charged up on deck to see three humpbacks—quite small, not much bigger than *Temptress* herself, and close by—but by the time my camera was at the ready, they were too far off for a shot. These three were travelling north at the moment, not that it had any special significance. I went below and pulled out from the bookshelf my *Giant Fishes, Whales and Dolphins*, a book no sea-voyager should go without, and looked up the humpback's migratory habits. Evidently winter is the time of calving and pairing, and for these purposes the animals migrate into warmer waters. They are also noted for their amorous antics—indeed for all sorts of antics, as they think nothing of breaching, rolling, finning, lob-tailing and scooping. I would like to see one breaching (but not too close), during which it performs the remarkable feat of leaping clear of the water and falling back again with a tremendous splash.

*   *   *

For dessert that evening I, alas, came to the end of Frau Schoett's wonderful cake; for many a mile, for many a day had this rich and satisfying cake sustained me through adversity! Having consumed the very last crumb I casually looked out and received quite a shock to see a steamer quite close and coming up dead astern. My masthead light was hastily switched on (no doubt much to the surprise of the officer on watch). He altered course slightly to pass along my port beam, heading geographically east, direct for the Straits of Gibraltar.

Our position was close to a route marked on the Pilot Chart for 'low powered steamers'. Well, I guess he was a low powered steamer. The thought passed through my mind to have a talk with him on the Aldis Lamp, but my morse had got a bit rusty; he might stop, or worse, come alongside. I do not trust steamermen (both Alain Gerbault and Harry Pidgeon on their world voyages were nearly sunk by a steamer's clumsy manoeuvre).

During the night, *Temptress*, under full sail, lifted steadily and easily over the waves, close-hauled on the port tack, steering herself while I, from my bunk, at intervals checked the course by watching the brilliant stars sway past the open hatch. Once in every one or two hours I would look out to see if any rain-squalls were forming, but, to my wonder the night remained clear, quiet and uneventful.

TROPICAL SEAS

One of the most horrid and recurring ordeals on a long sea voyage such as mine is not bad weather nor physical hardship, but, oddly enough, that same bugbear of shore life—'getting up'. For me this is always the worst part of each day. After stealing that 'five minutes more', so welcome at sea or ashore, I would roll painfully out of my bunk, hanging on grimly to combat the incessant motion, my eyes half gummed up through insufficient sleep, a nasty taste in my mouth, and a hollow feeling in the pit of my stomach. I usually feel a bit grey until I have eaten some breakfast. This meal invariably consists of porridge with plenty of sugar, and coffee.

Overnight the big south-westerly swell had vanished, so at least one storm had missed me. It was the start of another typical tropic sunny day, with the dolphins leaping after the flying fish. The course which brought us clear of the storm tracks had already had the effect of getting us out of the beneficial current of the Gulf Stream, but perhaps it was better to lose the advantage of that current and have smoother water.

While in Providence, Rhode Island, I had been lucky enough to meet Fred Thurber, who was one of Thomas Fleming Day's crew of three during his great passage across the Atlantic in 1911. He had advised me to keep south of the Gulf Stream and avoid the almost consistent rough sea. Evidently the *Sea Bird*, although making good days' runs, had undergone a very rough and wet time. Maybe this had been the cause of this twenty-six-footer being loaded on to the deck of a steamer at Gibraltar, to complete the voyage to Rome.

While dining with Fred Thurber and others, I had been presented with a piece of the old S.S. *Savannah* by Mr. William Munsey. This American ship, 130 feet long and 350 tons, had been the very first to cross the Atlantic under steam alone, in 1819. However, after her return she was converted into a sailing ship; on a voyage from Liverpool to New York she was driven ashore, at a place now known as Cedar Beach, on the southern shore of Long Island. Mr. Munsey's great-grandfather, who had discovered the wreck, was given the spars and timbers by the Wrecking Master, Elbert Carl. Some of the timbers, filled with home-made copper spikes, were used as fencing posts around an old pond at Great East Neck, Long Island. When the fence had been torn down, Mr. Munsey had salvaged one of these posts of hard cedar and, as far as is known, it is the only piece left of the old ship. I am very grateful to him for presenting me with a part of this interesting relic of marine history.

Meanwhile the head wind hardened, forming a steeper sea which did nothing to help the labouring yawl as she plunged onward unattended, whilst I, taking a busman's holiday below, read right through my own book, *Single-handed Passage* (which, incidentally and perhaps egoistically, I thoroughly enjoyed!).

Sunday, 10th September, was another tropical day, almost cloudless, and, with the easing of the head wind, wonderful sailing conditions prevailed. *Temptress*, heeling under her graceful symmetry of canvas, lifted naturally to the oncoming rollers in a fashion which can only be achieved by a sailing vessel. Great clouds of flying fish repeatedly flashed through the radiant air. I wished that these fish flew just for the joy of living, but it is only to escape their ravenous and implacable enemies, the dolphins. Even when they do take to the air it is still a losing battle, for on dropping back into the water, the swift dolphin is there to meet them.

There is much controversy amongst seamen whether flying fish can direct their flight. The Natural History Museum notwithstanding, my observations have shown me that they can, and do, but I believe that as soon as their wings become dry the fish immediately lose altitude.

As an example, one shot out of the water directly for *Temptress*, but it banked round, with its transparent, beautiful wings silhouetted for a delicate instant against the blue sky, before veering to starboard, only to fall, I fear, into the mouth of the waiting dolphin.

Never has a flying fish landed on deck during the day, but overnight it is a common occurrence. Surely this shows that without any doubt these beautiful creatures can direct their flight, and it is only when they cannot see that they hit the sails or rigging and fall on deck.

All sea life seems to eat or be eaten. The dolphins eat the flying fish and I eat the dolphins, so where are we? Even when the dolphins are leaping, it is not in play, for they snap at a flying fish just under the surface and their momentum carries them several feet into the air before they stall and fall with a thwack back into the water again.

Among all the creatures of the sea it is only the porpoises or mammal dolphins that seem to be continually at play. It is a delight to watch these graceful creatures twisting and corkscrewing, apparently from sheer exuberance.

The person who invented the same name both for the fish and the mammal dolphin should be strung up, as it causes the greatest confusion. I would like to make it clear here and now that the dolphins which eat the flying fish, and which I eat in turn, are the colourful fish of tropical waters; their name is *Coryphæna hippurus* and they are in no way whatsoever connected with the mammal dolphin, named *Delphinus delphus*, which is similar to the well-known porpoise.

At this particular time, we were accompanied by an unusual dolphin, ostracised by the others, which usually took up position just by the rudder; its back was more green than blue with half a dozen thick but indefinite black stripes across it; as I hesitated to catch any fish that might be poisonous I spared him (spared not speared).

My companions, the two white bosun birds, were circling above; something unfortunate had happened to one of them. Its long white tail was conspicuous by its absence, completely spoiling its appearance, but not apparently its flight.

Six o'clock found me in the hatch gazing westward at the setting sun, a fiery ball sinking inexorably towards the horizon—a blood-red full stop to the story of the day.

With phosphorescent water streaming out astern, *Temptress* carved her way through the night under the star-studded sky, across which, in unusual brilliance, meandered the cloudy path of the Milky Way.

Even during a spell of fine weather one has to keep careful watch for random rain-squalls, especially at night. A formation of clouds to windward had me jumping up and down all night, anxiously watching to see if there was a pall of rain, which would herald a vicious gust of wind, risky to the yawl with full sail set. However, my fears proved groundless and I merely lost a lot of sleep.

So restricted is one's actual area of life in a small boat, that one's eyes remain focused only on short distances. I am quite certain that often a steamer must have passed unperceived. For instance, that afternoon, I happened to look up and was startled to see a steamer only two miles off, already across my stern, heading towards New York. Had I seen him earlier it would have been possible to heave to, when he would have passed me very close, giving me a chance to signal my position home after nearly three weeks at sea.

Having watched the steamer out of sight, I resumed my meditation at the helm, my thoughts swinging back to my stay in America and to various talks I had given to yacht clubs and schools. I recalled with amusement one talk I gave to the High School at Tenafly in New Jersey. Although the lads were only about fourteen years old, the questions were as good as those asked by members of the yacht clubs, and perhaps more intelligent. One boy asked me a question which was hardly to the point: 'What do you think of nationalised medicine?' In my answer I had avoided the pitfall of being dragged into the platitude and longitude of politics.

This recollection started a train of thought on the health of the poorer masses living in their unhealthy and crowded conditions: Of what use were doctors to them and what is the use of providing them with free medicine, when all they need is sunshine, fresh air and decent houses in which to live? Here again I pondered on my pet theory which is the value of the individual. It seems to be a negation of life for man to barter his individual rights and powers for a spoon-fed, herded and directed existence. The French have a word for it, *avachi*... Such a condition places man little above that of his own domestic animals, and he is even less free than they, for he must always be goaded by an evil conscience, of mortgaging his birthright for a mess of pottage...

My thoughts drifted on to the conditions at home, Britain's difficulties which can really be judged arithmetically. She is self-supporting for only three-quarters of the population. When will a foreseeing government encourage emigration of a cross section of the community? The spirit of adventure and initiative of the individual is there—that is proved by the vast numbers of letters I have received. Some braves have acted. Have you heard of the Fisk family, for instance? Their whole future and the future of their two children (aged three and five) was at stake. But it did not stop them buying an old fishing boat, and sailing it out to New Zealand in order to give these same children new and broader horizons, rather than shelter them in the stultifying atmosphere of home.

Yet many are so often afraid of striking out for themselves (in business equally as in any other enterprise) for fear of losing what they call security. This attitude seems to me a denial of our national heritage and an obstacle to the development of individual character. In any case, what is security? Unless it is earned, it does not bring happiness, and happiness should be the one foundation stone of life. Security does not exist in nature as a gift. It has to be toiled for to become rewarding. How can we lose anything that is false in the first place?

12

MORE BAD WEATHER

After five days of head wind, it suddenly veered and freshened considerably. It was dusk. Taking advantage of the last of the daylight I rolled down six turns in the mainsail, and let the yawl plunge on in lively fashion. The deck was black and shining from the increasing quantity of spray. On going below I was not surprised to find the barometer dropping, and feared that a storm was overtaking me from the south-west. I ate my simple dinner pensively—more bad weather coming.

Taking a glance out of the hatch I was amazed to see a chain of lights stretching from my starboard beam all the way to the horizon, and looking, to my startled eyes, remarkably like Southend Pier. After a time, it proved to be four vessels, probably Destroyers, in line ahead. My masthead light brought immediate response from the leading vessel, who attacked me with his signalling lamp, but in the big swells it would not have been possible for him to read my lamp so low down. Seeing that they were passing clear, I switched off my light. Let them work that one out!

Ten hours later, after a bumpy night, I was at the helm, with *Temptress* pressing through the cross seas at her maximum speed, with a hard wind on the starboard quarter. There was considerable weight in the seas and every now and again a wave would spill aboard over the bulwark and *Temptress* would give a sensational lurch to leeward.

It was a great day's run. Sixty miles in ten hours. After the violent ride, the boat was hove to at dusk in order to reduce the motion. A stronger man than I would have her turning off downwind under headsails alone, but I felt like escaping from some of the turmoil.

By dawn a breaking sea was driving down upon us, and by the size of the waves I reckoned a big storm was passing up the Gulf Stream, not very far away. By noon the wind had risen to gale force and we stayed hove to, making leeway towards the south-east.

The few days of fine weather were already forgotten as I lay in my bunk, listening to the crash of seas and the shrill whistle of the wind in the rigging. Running underneath the toppling seas, whipped up by the gale, there was a gigantic and awe-inspiring swell from the west, so large that I was convinced that it was formed by a hurricane. For a good many days now I had been unable to pick up the American station, but had estimated that the hurricane previously reported would be between me and the American coast, and would, presumably, head up the Gulf Stream.

All that day and right on into the night the great wind roared overhead; wave after wave smote at *Temptress* in relentless onslaught; every hour or so a giant sea would cascade over the entire vessel, heeling her right over to a fantastic angle. At these moments I would half sit up in my bunk with wildly beating heart, and every nerve tensed, only to relax back when the boat resumed a more normal angle, and the characteristic gurgling of water running off the deck could be heard.

Even in these fierce conditions it was not a great difficulty to prepare dinner in my well-designed galley.

Damn the weather! A long anxious night ahead. The thumping of the rudder shaking the whole ship made me wonder whether the bearings were working loose under the tremendous strain.

After fourteen hours of punishment the gale blew itself out early next morning, only to be followed by some torrential rain-squalls.

The foul atmosphere and stink below in a small boat is appalling in bad weather. I was doing my best to ventilate the boat, holding the main hatch open, my hand ready to slam it quickly when I guessed a wave was going to break on board. The wind-veer built up yet another sea; the motion caused by triple cross seas became extreme. Each gale lasted longer and blew harder than the preceding one. And which was it? the third or fourth gale? I had lost count. And what had the future in store, with that giant hurricane swell flooding in from the west?

As usual the batteries were very low, and of course the engine would not run in that weather. The carburettor has a long float-chamber running athwartships. The jets, which by a laughable mischance had been positioned at one end of this float-chamber, were either flooded or starved as the vessel rolled, thereby stalling the engine—a delightful habit for an auxiliary which is usually only needed in adversity! Before the reader jumps to any conclusions about an otherwise excellent engine, I must add that this carburettor is not now fitted as standard.

Subsequently I wrote to the engine manufacturers regarding this trouble and (hoping to get something for nothing), asked them what remedy they could suggest for such a well-known vessel as mine. They wrote back saying they would be delighted to help me, and would immediately supply a modern design of carburettor— but for £18. The old carburettor remained.

It seems that most petrol or paraffin engines are affected by a list over twenty-five degrees; I would say that thirty-five degrees should be the minimum safety factor. Also, seeing that carburation and ignition are the causes of nearly all trouble with auxiliaries, it points to the fact that diesels or semi-diesels are a more reliable sea-going proposition, and minimise the danger of fire at the same time.

The aftermath of the gale was typical and just as unbearable: angry black clouds to the north, big seas, light wind, sails and spars flung mercilessly from side to side. The windvane rod on the mainmast was doing its best to cut wide circles out of the clouds.

In the greenish evening sky, and in direct contrast to the violence below, the slender sickle of the new moon posed remote and unconcerned.

Although a steamer was rarely sighted in day-time, one at least passed every night. Sure enough, at ten o'clock, I noticed some lights to the westward and paid careful attention until the ship was level, about a mile to the north. My lights were not necessary after all, but he would have been surprised to know that a small yacht lurked in the darkness.

During the morning of 15th September black rain squalls and heavy seas persisted. The bad weather was far from over. Fed up with continually changing sail to suit the varying outbursts of wind, and myself feeling tired and exhausted, I finally furled the jib and mizzen; hove to once more.

The only plan possible was to lie to in heavy weather, then take full advantage of any slant. I began to worry about whether my stores would last out. There was, however, enough rice and porridge to prevent me from actually starving.

Revived somewhat by the 'rest' below, I took the helm at noon after setting the jib, but leaving the mainsail well reefed. We battered off downwind. The motion was indescribable.

In spite of the gale just passed it looked as if another storm was coming. High overhead, between the black clouds, great V's of cirrus swept up in arabesques, denoting plenty of strong wind to spare.

By late afternoon, bulbous clouds had wholly covered the heavens, attended by eerie, motionless pillars of rain standing up like tree trunks in a dark forest.

It was wild sailing, but the end of every hour showed six miles nearer home. Finally, a squall hit us fair and square, sizzling over the steaming waters, with torrential rain for twenty minutes. It passed ahead, but the true wind had been killed. *Temptress* lost way and was thrown about so wildly that, without great effort, it was impossible to stand or sit. I threw myself exhausted on my bunk, picturing, in my mind's eye, *Temptress* at that moment, a victim rolling and crashing around in vast swells, as a great storm advanced.

To take my mind off my unenviable position I switched on the radio and was electrified to hear: 'It is Saturday the 16th; would you like to hear some music?'

I made it Friday, 15th! Was it possible I could have lost a day? For days afterwards I had a gnawing doubt that my navigation was completely upset and totally inaccurate. It was not until the following week that I managed to re-check on the dates and found all was well. This controversial date still remains a mystery to me. The actual time of the broadcast I made to be nine o'clock in the morning, G.M.T. (Perhaps it was Australia. Work it out, if you like.)

The punishment to the mainsail and gear became so bad that I went to lower the sail; as soon as the halyards were slackened away the seventeen-foot gaff slammed from side to side, making the job a very awkward and dangerous operation.

My next boat will have Bermudian rig, i.e. no gaff. Generally, as far as I can see, the rig of a small oceangoing sailing vessel should be designed to cope with two things:

1. Winds of gale force.
2. No wind, but rough sea.

All the other conditions can look after themselves.

As the boat bludgeoned slowly forward under headsails in that fiendish sea, a ghastly mauve sunset cast an air of unreality and evil over the entire area; threatening what? My log read: 'It might mean a hurricane.'

It was exactly one month since I optimistically cast off moorings in New York.

13

HURRICANE

Saturday, 16th September. Soon after midnight I was awakened by increased motion and whistle of wind, and got up to find *Temptress* holding course well towards the east under the two head-sails and mizzen. The wind was strong from the south. Although it was a clear night a peculiar veil seemed drawn across the heavens, and only the brighter stars were visible.

Two hours later it was blowing up to a moderate gale. Again I went out on deck. The boat was heeled to the gunwale even under this reduced canvas, and breaking beam seas smashed against her windward side. I cast off the mizzen halyards and grabbed down the flogging canvas. Expecting things to get worse I bore off and ran downwind long enough to furl the jib by the roller gear.

The barometer was falling; still this unnatural veil covered the sky; so back I went to my bunk for more sleep, while *Temptress* crashed on under staysail alone. Sailing was hectic, with seas beginning to come aboard increasingly.

Dawn showed a frightening seascape. The clouds opposite the rising sun were a bilious orange, whilst, in frightful contrast, the sky to windward was a livid green. It was blowing harder and I was very glad that the sails had been stowed in time.

An hour later the barometer had fallen farther, and a great wind was shouting defiance overhead. Obviously, neither the staysail nor sheet could stand up to any more wind; I decided to reef it. The decision was easier than the accomplishment; it was to be a dangerous and wet job, with the deck continually swept by heavy seas. But it had to be done. As usual, to reduce my wind-resistance and to keep my clothes dry, I stripped, then hesitated for several shivering moments under the closed hatch. It was comparatively safe below, but working on deck appeared to be fraught with every peril.

Summoning up courage, I wrenched open the hatch. The volume of sound was a shock to the senses. I climbed out of the hatch and slammed it quickly. The wind roared solid out of the south and whole areas of ocean were scattered into driving spindrift; lower, not reef, was the answer!

I crawled forward until I was able to hang on to the mast. Casting off the halyard and pulling on the downhaul, the whipping and slatting canvas was lowered to the stemhead. It was still essential to lash the sail to the deck; the wind tore at the untidy folds, threatening to rip the canvas into bits. I watched my chance between two seas and, quickly abandoning the mast, found myself lying full length on deck alongside the windward side of the bowsprit; hanging precariously to the forestay with one hand, with the other I clawed wildly at the sail which seemed to have converted itself into some kind of an obstinate demon. All the time the bow was plunging into a trough, then being hurled into the air, threatening to catapult me off the deck for ever.

I had just got one lashing round the sail, when a great roaring of a sea made me look round to face the screaming wind; there was just time to grab hold with both hands and feet, before the bow dived into the ocean, which poured in a solid cataract of water over the fore deck. As the wave descended it flashed through my mind how wise I had been to discard my clothes; the sea was unable to get any grip on my naked body. Grasping with all my might, I maintained my position and emerged safe but breathless.

With the hard and sodden mass of canvas lashed firmly to the mooring bitts I crawled my way aft and thankfully regained the protection offered below. Everything possible had been done. It was now just a matter of hoping for things to improve.

Temptress, all way off her, lay in the water, beam on to the seas in a way which has been described as a 'fisherman's float'. As each crest passed under her, she would be flung far to leeward, then would suddenly right herself as she slid down the back of the wave into the trough. She would be wrenched upwards by the next, once more to be attacked by a curling crest.

With a really bad wave the boat would not rise fully to the top, and the broken water would fling her down on her beam ends. During these knock-down blows, water would pour in on top of me, as I stood underneath the hatch. With my back against the wash-basin compactum and both hands pressing on the coaming opposite, I could stare out through a porthole and watch the advancing white avalanches.

The temperature below was 80°F. The wind was undoubtedly increasing every moment. Horizontal driving rain, mixed with the smoking spindrift, made the whole sea appear as a single mass of white.

My descriptive log written throughout the hurricane gives a more graphic and true reproduction of the circumstances, than any narrative written after the ordeal. The following description is based on actual entries.

> *08.00: Must be blowing hurricane force. Tremendous seas breaking aboard. Wind solid. Barometer falling $\frac{1}{10}$th of an inch every half-hour. Difficult differentiate between wind and water. If only skylight had been boarded over. Water pouring below, forcing its way through hatches and skylight. With the wind pressure on the mast alone, the boat is heeled to the gunwale. Impossible to know whether raining or not. The whole boat writhing and trembling in the screaming wind. Nothing more to do but wait and hope.*
> *No visibility. The barometer down to 29.13 and still falling, (It seems impossible that things can get worse.) Very serious position. A sudden lull: then the roar of an advancing wave and a tremendous crash as tons of water thunder over the vessel.*

As each heavy wave smashed aboard, the boat would get spun round in another direction, and I would see water racing past the lee portholes. Sometimes she was driven astern, other times ahead.

Half an hour later the worst sea of the lot came green over *Temptress*; everything went black below; she was rolling over so far that, although standing on my feet, I was in fact horizontal. In the darkness I could hear objects and cutlery being flung out of their stowage. The boat burst to the surface and the light filtered once more through the portholes. It was a little shaking to see my pillow creep up the ship's side and nestle among the deck beams.

To take my mind off the ghastly force of wind, blowing then from I know not which direction, I tore up two floor boards and started to bale out the rising oily water into the sink, with an enamel jug. Still there was no sign of improvement. The barometer dropped below 29.00.

The bilges dry, there was nothing to do but stare dully and anxiously out on the raging elements. The whole view was like a mad snowy landscape, and I wished desperately it was. At regular intervals I took sips at the brandy bottle to provide a little Dutch courage; since one must eat, I sustained myself with half a tin of cold beans, taken with a teaspoon.

At ten o'clock it suddenly grew lighter; a glimpse of sun revealed to my apprehensive gaze the overhanging watery mountains bearing down upon us. There must have been some blue sky above, but seventy or eighty feet of driving spindrift acted like fog. The power of the hurricane was such that the whole upper parts of those waves were so scattered and rent that, beneath the white, they showed green instead of the ocean blue. It was also unnerving to watch the barometer pumping up and down a tenth at a time as each wave raced past.

Dominating the shriek of even that paralysing wind, there came an unearthly bass moaning, a noise which sent more shivers down my spine than anything else. The hurricane must have reached its peak at ten-thirty, for, *mirabile dictu*, the barometer at last started to rise. The wind was still raging, accompanied by that horrible moan. The boat was pinned down by the pressure of the wind to an angle of forty-five degrees, and was repeatedly hurled over much farther. The cabin-top portholes remained permanently under. There was danger everywhere; it only needed one sea, a certain shape, to strike us, at a certain angle, to send us to the bottom. I consider that the boat was only saved by the very force of the wind itself, which tore to destruction any solid mass of water bearing down to annihilate us. 'Hold on, *Temptress*,' I shouted, 'hold on,' as the whole boat shuddered in that maelstrom of devilment. My overlying fear was that the dinghy, skylight and hatches would be sucked off by the vacuum which was formed over the deck by the steep angle.

Forearmed with the knowledge provided by the rising barometer that things should get better, in spite of the continued roaring and bursting of great seas, I had a sudden reaction, and thought of boiling some water for a cup of tea—an old British custom. More than once had I cast envious eyes upon a saucepan which had remained, somehow, on the gimballed stove —the only measure of sanity in a topsy-turvy world. A cup of tea in a hurricane? Ridiculous! No! It would be tempting the Fates too much! The hurricane might think I was not paying it due respect.

The barometer started to shoot up as quickly as it had fallen. Another glimpse of the sun through the spindrift showed that the wind had veered. It was still blowing like fits but not quite so violently. Through the porthole it was impossible to see any regular formation of waves, and seas continually swept the reeling *Temptress* from end to end. Everything was in chaos below. Potatoes seemed to be everywhere; an extraordinary collection of objects was piled high in my bunk.

I ate some more beans, then back to bailing.

There were occasional lulls—dared I whisper it at the time?… Another ninety unbearably slow minutes passed, before I could state in the log:

> The hurricane part is over: it is merely blowing gale force.

The great curtain of spindrift disappeared. Patches of blue sky and sun were visible overhead; the seas lost their threat of imminent danger. Although still more seas would come aboard, and the actual motion of the boat might increase, without a doubt, this particular battle was nearly over.

14

FIRST BLOOD

I opened my eyes; a grey light of dawn was filtering through the porthole opposite my bunk. It was the morning after the hurricane. The sodden clammy blankets gave me some warmth if I did not move. I lay, hunched up, weary; my stomach ached for food; a foul taste was in my mouth; there was a smell of wet, an all pervading wetness; bilge water gushed and sucked under me. Added to the general rattles, clunks and knocks, a series of heavy thumps would shake the hull, the rudder working in its bearings; it had become worse after the trouncing of the previous twenty-four hours.

Dragging myself out on deck at six o'clock, I first pumped out the bilge water, then set the jib. With the tiller lashed amidships, *Temptress* paid sluggishly off from the keen west wind and pointed towards the south-east; progress! A tangle of halyards and sheets were trailing over the side, and the fall of one topping lift had been blown upwards and lodged in the mast. Caked salt was everywhere, and woodwork had been scoured as white as snow. There was not a vestige of varnish left; it was all blown off.

The air below had a mephitic odour, but there was still too much sea to open the hatches for ventilation.

The simple acts of brushing my teeth, and eating a large bowl of stiff porridge, made me feel, physically at any rate, a new man. But I was still mentally exhausted by the hurricane. During the blow it had seemed impossible for things ever to return to normal, yet now I accepted the improvements with a sense almost of indifference.

Breakfast gave me sufficient energy to hoist the sopping staysail; the yawl moved ahead at three knots, under two headsails sheeted hard in.

It was still rough; I did not feel in any way disposed to hoist the heavy mainsail, with its clumsy gaff, and have all the trouble of lowering it again in the evening. Had the mainsail been Bermudian, I would have hoisted it and been doing six knots. Anyway, there was enough to satisfy me—three knots in the right direction was almost sensational compared with what I had just endured.

The weather had not yet cleared properly. A weak sun shone through a peculiar muggy haze. At midday it was still blowing half a gale of wind, with a big breaking sea. Great storm clouds could be seen towards the north-west; *Temptress* rolled heavily. Every now and again she would be caught out of step and would give an excessive lurch to leeward, tipping up the deck to an angle over forty-five degrees.

For lunch I finished the last of my fresh eggs. Although twenty-five days at sea, these eggs, which had not been treated in any way, were still perfectly good; eggs will keep an amazing length of time on board a small vessel. The Finns are reputed to keep their eggs fresh almost indefinitely by turning them over every twenty-four hours. *Temptress* did this for me.

Gradually the ugly clouds rolled back, the sun gained in strength, and the sea slowly lost its spite, allowing me, thankfully, to open wide the hatches. The better conditions permitted an orgy of navigation; by evening I had obtained an accurate position. At last the first 1000 miles had been completed from Sandy Hook. We were exactly halfway between New York and the Azores. The nearest land was St. Johns, Newfoundland—a little nearer than Bermuda, which was 650 miles off to the south-west.

At dusk, a steady rain began to fall, but little wind, which is very rare; the general atmosphere was so damp it just had to rain.

The engine, with everything else, had received a good shower-bath during the hurricane, and in the smoothing water I decided to give it a trial. To my surprise it started immediately. After running it for three-quarters of an hour, I festooned it with wet articles of clothing.

Leaving *Temptress* to look after herself, heading eastward through the rain, I turned in for a couple of hours until midnight, when I was awakened by a change of motion; it was a change for the worse; I was disgusted to see that the wind had swung round to the inevitable south-east—another head wind.

To windward the night was black with lightning-riven clouds. Standing shivering in the hatch for half an hour, I waited to see what was going to happen. It got no better, no worse. Pah! A man must sleep. In a fury of impatience I rushed up on deck, lowered all sail, then turned in again.

It is astonishing how little one feels the motion when lying in a bunk. Awakening at daylight I thought the vessel to be hardly moving, but as soon as I had got up, I had to hang on grimly to counteract the uneven rolling and pitching. I was delighted to find that the south-westerly wind had come back. Set jib! Hoist staysail! Get going *Temptress*! It's all yours!

But five o'clock in the morning is a devil of a time to get up—so, back to moist but comparatively warm blankets.

After a period of rain, it turned into a kind of day that I had prayed for: bright and sunny with a gentle breeze. By midday the boat looked like a stall in Petticoat Lane on a Sunday morning; spars, rigging and deck were concealed under wet blankets, mattresses, clothes and in fact almost all movable objects from below. I sacrificed some of my precious fresh water to sponge out lockers and drawers which had been soused with sea water, and were now studded with crystals of salt.

Adding to this great clean-up I went for a swim myself. It was very exhilarating hanging on to the end of the bowsprit as *Temptress* capered in the swells. One moment the bowsprit would plunge beneath the surface, completely ducking me; the next moment it would soar upwards, plucking me out of the water and dangling me in mid-air before splashing me under once more. But this pastime became pretty exhausting and, letting go, I swam ahead of the boat. Swimming breast-stroke I gazed in front of me where there was nothing to see except the vast Atlantic Ocean. It was a singular sensation. A 2000-mile swim would not have brought one in sight of land—a big enough swimming-pool for anyone. There was adequate depth below, too—2750 fathoms (over three miles, to save you working it out).

Getting aboard is sufficiently exciting in these circumstances, because of the ever-present danger of being knocked out by the descending bowsprit, or cut by the chain bobstay. I used to grab the bowsprit shroud as the boat immersed its bow into a wave; I would then be wrenched into the air and, by twisting my body round, could get my feet on the bobstay from where it was relatively simple to regain the deck. I am, fortunately, acrobatic enough to repeat this performance without difficulty, but it is extraordinary how many normally agile people I have had on board, who cannot climb back to the deck after bathing, even if the boat is absolutely still.

At dusk, with all the blankets and belongings dry once more and back in place, the voyage again reached normality, and the horror of the hurricane was forgotten.

To help dry out down below, and to charge the batteries, the engine was started. This was the cause of a catastrophe. The forward bearing on the dynamo had one of those screw-down grease cups for lubrication, but this cup had been, not too cleverly, placed only one-eighth of an inch from the cooling fan. When the bearing began to protest at lack of grease I decided to give it a turn. While my thumb and forefinger were on the cup the boat gave a violent lurch; the edges of the hard fan blades ripped through the top of my thumb, right down to the bone, with a horrible rasping whirr. I jumped back, blood streaming from the wound.

All other feelings were submerged in the rage which welled up within me at the crass stupidity of the installation, but still more at my own carelessness. As if I had not endured enough already from things beyond control! Even more aggravating was the fact that the engine was not even running properly, as the rolling of the boat upset that ridiculous carburettor. Oh! my friends the engineers; if only you had to operate your own products, the world would be a better place for those you supply.

While the thumb was still numb I cut off, with scissors, the broken bits of nail, and hinged back the loose skin. Holding it up vertically, I glared at it angrily, doing my best to persuade myself that it was not as bad as it really was. Then I looked out my so-called medicine chest—one bottle of iodine, Elastoplast, and a tiny first-aid kit. Meanwhile, the generator was still whining. I decided to screw up the grease cup with a pair of pliers.

It was a beautiful dry starlit night, but this meant nothing to me. It would be a week or more before my thumb, and my right thumb at that, would be properly useable, and I could not risk delaying its recovery by handling the heavy mainsail. Days would be lost.

This was the start of an even more exasperating period, for although the next day the wind was from the east, it was light enough and the sea was smooth enough for me to have been soaking up to windward, had I been able to hoist the mainsail. I found during this day just how much one uses a thumb, even in such a simple operation as taking a match out of a box.

In the evening, after several hours of over-clouded conditions, a very vicious squall, with little or no warning, struck us, making me very glad the mainsail was not set.

By dawn the following day the wind had veered round to south-south-west, blowing fresh, a fair wind at last, but I was in no condition to take full advantage. I rebandaged the thumb which seemed to be doing as well as expected; luckily there was no swelling or signs of poison.

Temptress, continually buffetted by the beam sea, painfully plodded on. I had now made all the southing wanted and should have been well clear of the storms queueing up to pass up the Gulf Stream. The Pilot Chart showed encouraging long arrows from the south-west, and it seemed to me then that henceforward I would be able to enjoy very pleasant weather towards the Azores, where I could refit if necessary.

The shades of dusk were falling when a big tanker suddenly appeared as if by magic, close astern. No time was lost in rigging the signalling lamp, it being too dark to use the International Code Flags. I knew that after a month at sea without any news, my parents and friends would most likely be worrying; here was the ideal opportunity to signal Lloyd's my position. However, although continually flashing my signal letters MDPV, I received no answering 'T' to show that they were understood. Instead, the ship's light, which was badly trained, just flickered erratically in my direction, making it impossible for me to distinguish the difference between the dots and dashes. At fifteen knots she had soon passed and receded into the distance. It was a bitter disappointment; an hour earlier and it would have been light enough to read my flags.

My small radio was working spasmodically, and I switched on to hear a voice say '… every Thursday evening…' before it died away to nothing. The devil take it! Surely it was Wednesday? Another flurry of doubt about the correct day; it seemed impossible that a whole day could have been lost, yet I would not be happy until it had been proved one way or the other.

The distance between the crests of the beam sea was only thirty feet, and *Temptress* rolled systematically and inexorably all night. I slept on my left side, with my knees against the bunk-board and my back against blankets jammed in between me and the ship's side.

I dreamt again, thus: I was sitting in a theatre in England with my mother, and said to her: 'I am dreaming now; you might also be dreaming at this moment, so, when you wake up, remember that I told you that my position was half-way between New York and the Azores.' I then went on to tell her about trying to signal to the oil-tanker and failing to make proper contact.

Evidently this anxiety to get some news to my parents was preying on my mind, whether I was awake or asleep. Was she attuned to telepathy, either in the conscious or subconscious? (Twelve months later I asked her whether she had received my message. She said, ' No.' But, of course, she may have received something through the subconscious—this we will never know. Her dream might have been as vivid as mine, but she could not remember it on waking up.)

An ugly dawn, with a profusion of cirro-stratus draped across the sky, and palls of rain dogging our wake, was more than enough to tell me that another storm was imminent. The wind, already blowing lively, steadily increased to moderate gale force. Although only under headsails, *Temptress* scudded faster and faster but, as the wind veered, tended to point more and more off course.

The wind rose to full gale force, and breaking seas began to surge

over the weather rail, and flood across the decks in a cataract of water. I took the tiller and bore away on to the correct course; it was a
cold and wet performance; the bandage round my thumb was soaked
with a mixture of sea-water and blood. Reaching the limit of my
patience I lashed the helm, then, watching my chance, slid quickly
along the deck to lower the staysail. Under jib alone, *Temptress* twisted and turned in the cauldron of angry seas, as she ran unattended
before her fifth gale of the voyage.

The worst of the blow lasted twelve hours, and the weather
cleared slightly at sunset: a green sky, and orange clouds deepen-
ing to bronze. Life was far from comfortable, but easting was being
gained. The cry 'Make easting! Make easting!' was ever before me. It
had become, indeed, an absolute obsession.

Later the moon showed intermittently, with cloud wrack flying
swiftly across its face. The great swell increased hourly and, as the
clouds rolled away, the strong moonlight flooding on these gigantic
seas created an eerie sensation that was a mixture of awe and longing, of loneliness and yet of being one with the elements, newly created and age old. Timeless.

These giant seas were out of all proportion to the force of the gale
that had blown the previous day; it was therefore obvious that there
was some big disturbance, or even another hurricane away up to the
N.W. In this case my southerly course was paying dividends.

15

FAIR WIND

Four flying fish were lying on deck in the morning, providing a good breakfast. It was a fresh sunny day with wonderful sailing breeze, but the fifteen-foot seas crowding in from the west made the vessel roll in an extremely aggravating manner.

Had it not been for my damaged hand the full mainsail would have been up and *Temptress* would have been cracking along on her course. Bad language was a relief to my feelings! In compensation for those benighted head winds I now had a marvellous wind and yet could not use it. Ah! the uses of adversity! To make things even more maddening the batteries were almost flat again, and it was impossible to run the engine in that sea. Had the designer of that carburettor been on board I would have gleefully set him to charge the batteries by hand.

Opening a food locker below, I was met by a foul smell ascending. It was an alarming discovery. Almost all my reserve stores were ruined. A large tin of plums had corroded through and, with the help of this acid, the bilge water had attacked all the other tins—most of which were old, anyway, as they had crossed the Atlantic with me already. Splash after splash sounded as the spoiled tins were flung overboard. This made the food position critical. Potatoes also were going bad.

Luckily a flying fish leapt aboard in the evening.

I grabbed him quickly and had a very welcome all-fresh dinner. This helped to mollify my jaundiced outlook, already made better by a peaceful sunset and a heavy dew which presaged fine weather.

Usually one of the pleasures in a boat is being able to jettison things over the side, and after the heartrending ditching of my stores, it was a relief to fling out a pillow which had got sodden in the hurricane, but which, when dried out, stank like a badger. The potato peeler followed it; it had only been on board for five weeks, but the blade was badly rusted right through. Before leaving America every effort had been made to buy a stainless steel one, but without success.

I appreciate so many things in the States but do not agree with the insistence on quantity and size as against quality. This was a typical instance. Apparently they would not make a potato peeler of stainless steel because it would last. No, 'Give the man a poor article and make him buy another.' Well, I beat them that time; there was not an ironmonger in sight. (For the outward crossing I had used a wonderful stainless steel peeler, but on a week-end cruise, Bobbie, one of those long-legged American girls, in the unpractical way women have, left it in the bucket of peelings, and then added insult to injury by handing me the bucket to throw the lot over the side.)

There was another loss that evening: I ate the last of Frau Schoett's chocolates, the most wonderful homemade chocolates I have ever tasted. *Danke schön* Hilda Schoett!

With a moderating sea under a steady westerly wind, *Temptress* cut through the moonlit night, with no lights showing, while I had my usual interrupted sleep, looking out at irregular intervals.

Saturday, 23rd September, was one of the best days of the voyage. With a view to hoisting the mainsail later, I stowed the reaching staysail, but knocked my thumb enough to dissuade me from further action. After making an ineffectual attempt to keep the engine running, I hoisted the mizzen and took the helm; steering all day in the hot sun which shone over a dark blue sea, I dreamed of my ideal boat...

The sinking sun looked so much like a burnished copper gong that I almost expected a soft clang as it touched the horizon.

The twelve-foot high swell, rolling down from the north, was the only thing to show that the weather was still venting its spleen on some other unfortunate quarter.

The beauty of the night tempted me to remain in the hatchway, fascinated by the heaving waters reflecting the silver light of a full moon; but the dew-wet air struck cold, and *Temptress* was once more left on her own, while I sought the warmth below.

Thirty-one days at sea and all well, and the lights were not burning bright. It was quite absurd not being able to charge the batteries. However, the sea had gone down sufficiently by the morning to allow me to start the engine; many times it would hesitate, almost stop, then stagger on. It reminded me of a friend's parrot in Scotland, which had learned all but the last note of Laurel and Hardy's signature tune. This wretched bird would whistle the first part, then hesitate; everybody in the house would stop talking and listen for the final note—it never came. Agonising.

I was determined to catch a dolphin for lunch. After nearly three-quarters of an hour wait, one at last came into range. Hurling the grains with all the force I could muster from my weary arm, I speared a fine specimen about three feet long, and pitchforked it into the cockpit; captured. It had been so long, however, since I had had such a lot of fresh food, that I ate far too much for lunch. Seduced by surfeit of fish and a temperature of 85°F. I took to my bunk, sucking a chocolate-covered toffee.

Outside, conditions were exactly those I had experienced for weeks on end in the north-east Trades: a few puff clouds, pale blue sky, and a fresh breeze on the quarter, amply flecking the dark seas with flashes of white. *Temptress* rolled on her course at a mere two and a half knots. Two and a half knots! Did I hear the rustling of bushy eyebrows from the Ocean Racing gang? and a snort 'What! No mainsail?'

'No. No mainsail,' I replied, 'that would chain me to the helm. I am just living as one might live in port: busy the day long with navigating, fishing, the leisurely cooking and eating of a good lunch, followed by a siesta and quiet browse into my books, interspersed with contemplation of the enchanting scene without. Shortly I will bathe in the blue water surging under the bowsprit. You see, I have paid for this glorious day by enduring those gales, head winds and a hurricane. Later, I will doubtless pay more, but this is my day.'

*   *   *

While lying in my bunk reading about Slocum calling in at Horta, I made the definite decision to visit the Azores. As things were, it would be impossible to reach England until November, and the boat needed a refit before coping with winter gales; already there was a list of ten items which required urgent attention.

Meditating more on Slocum's book I realised that, had I met *Spray* then, she would have been running before the wind, with full mainsail set and yet nobody at the wheel, a performance which was one of the most extraordinary features of his voyage. Normally, a boat rigged thus would automatically round up into the wind, hopelessly off course, and if the helm were lashed to weather to prevent this, there would be the chance of a dangerous gybe. There was a replica of Spray built but, strangely enough, this boat did not have the same remarkable characteristic—maybe because she did not have the same remarkable captain.

I hope to solve the difficulty whilst running in my next boat by rigging her as a Bermudian ketch. By dropping the mizzen, thereby bringing the centre of effort well forward, I could leave the helm for a good many minutes at a time, and, for a longer period for rest or food, the mainsail could be dropped in a twinkling and the boat could run under headsails. It would be an easy matter, without a clumsy gaff, to hoist the mainsail again when required. For long runs, however, such as in the Trades, the twin-staysail rig with sheets led to the tiller seems to be the best answer.

After an unsatisfying breakfast of two small flying fish, I started the day's work with the usual morning sight. Under a steady wind from the south-west, the big swell was no more than the eternal pulse of the ocean; I was not dissuaded from hoisting the mainsail. Finally this job was completed without too much difficulty and, to my surprise and relief, without hurt to my damaged thumb.

Under full sail for the first time for a whole week, *Temptress* leapt forward joyously in an abandonment of motion. An increase of wind made sailing even more exciting, but the tumultuous waves prevented me quitting the helm to prepare my food.

By pulling the staysail to weather and tightening in the jib sheets, I rounded up into the wind to heave to. With a fresh wind thrumming in the rigging, the yawl was thrown up and down by head seas that now met her bow. The motion was worse; she was no longer keeping her course, but she might be left, allowing me to take the noon sight, then cook myself some lunch. Rolling the boom four turns to reduce the mainsail I let draw the staysail, upped helm and away we went downwind, the broken, twisting wake reeling out astern.

Polka dots of rain stained the deck, without warning, out of a pure blue sky; immediately a vivid rainbow formed right ahead— the lowest I have ever seen. From where I was sitting in the cockpit, the arc, with its exceptionally bright colours, could be seen curved over the boom gooseneck, so close that the horizon could be seen through each end. I had the ridiculous feeling of wondering 'Will the mast clear the top?' I twisted round in the cockpit to see if there was anything further to this rare phenomenon, but no. When I looked back the bow had vanished.

The pair of tropic birds flew in to inspect us, and were soon joined by a third. There ensued much squawking and flapping as they circled round and round.

There was no need to wet the decks down that evening; the fresh beam wind looked after that. Spray continually sniped at me, while every now and again a dollop would fall down my neck.

Sunset was about six o'clock, but for an hour previous to that I had been continually looking westward in an endeavour to catch the first signs of glory. However, it was the east that held the stage; gargantuan thunderheads reared themselves extravagantly into the limitless heavens, as a billowing mass of flaming orange which was slowly and relentlessly extinguished by the shadow cast by the horizon, as the earth spun on its axis.

The wind eased, as if hushed by this awesome sight, but freshened again in the gathering darkness. I remained steering under the moonlight for another hour while *Temptress* bucketed along with a cough-cough of bow waves.

The wind had backed sufficiently to the south to allow the main-sail to be carried overnight; after rolling down two more turns in the boom, I lashed the helm. Having prepared and eaten my evening meal, I turned in for another disturbed night's rest, watching out for squalls and steamers.

In the early hours of the morning I was surprised to find the sky lit only by stars. Where was the moon? The full moon? I then managed to distinguish it as a feeble orange glow, very small and scarcely visible. I wondered, 'Can there be an eclipse?' and went back to my bunk, meaning to lie there for five minutes, but I fell asleep; when I awoke, strong moonbeams were dancing through the ports.

Rain drumming on the deck next awakened me, and almost immediately the sudden wrenching of the main boom being flung from side to side galvanised me into action. I rushed out on deck to rig the rolling tackle, receiving a fresh-water shower-bath, only appreciated after an exhilarating towelling down below.

The barometer was very high, and the seas the smallest I had seen for many a day. After a shower or two the wind came back with some strength from the (magnetic) south, but as the compass variation for this area is no less than 22°W., it was really a head wind.

The short irregular seas prevented the boat's way so that we just floundered along with violent motion; every yard was gained painfully. Every now and again we would come across a smooth patch; *Temptress* at once would leap forward, only to be knocked back by the next cobbled area.

The wind headed us even more, so, completely disgusted with the conditions, I hove to and went below for lunch. That was that, as regards a decent day's run. However, the last 'noon to noon' had been seventy-four miles, the best for a long time.

It was not until two hours later that the seas lengthened out; with the increase of wind *Temptress* began to walk out to windward, driving through the irregular seas and maintaining speed. The sunset was completely disappointing, being hidden by grey clouds, but the moon, huge and red, rose out of the sea on the starboard bow. By keeping the rigging silhouetted against her face, there was no need for me to strain my eyes at the swaying compass card.

The end of the day's sail is recorded as follows:

> 19.35:   *That is all for today, girls.*
> *Backed staysail, rolled four turns in the main boom:*
> *lashed helm slightly aweather and let* Temptress *start her*
> *night watch; after a good day's work.*

After eating dinner I fell asleep over the table, waking with the most frightful crick in my neck. Holding on to my cramped muscles, and blinking the sleep out of my eyes, I beheld a night of surpassing beauty. The wind had eased away, and the yawl was gliding serenely under the silvery light of the full moon which was dancing on the waters with mystic radiance.

16

BECALMED

Temptress, close-hauled to a gentle breeze, slid over a smooth sea. The barometer was high and steady. Above, the even blue of the sky was scarred by only a few upswept mares' tails, to the south.

I took my time over breakfast, then went on deck to take the morning sight. 'Now!' I said, looking at my watch and noting down the time. The sextant reading was 31° 6'; the angle between three very dissimilar objects, (a) the blue horizon, (b) my (much less) blue eye, and (c) (of all the strange things) the sun's lower limb. I always think that there is something rather naughty about the last one.

The time and the angle is all I need to work out my navigation problems. Mind you, one sight cannot give you a definite position, but merely gives a line, at right angles to the bearing of the sun, on which the boat must be. However, one can wait several hours till the sun has moved round to a new bearing, then get a second position line which can be crossed with the first; this is known as a 'fix'—an accurate position, well within the arms of the little cross you pencil on the ocean chart.

Ship's noon is when the sun has reached its zenith before descending and is directly south (geographically) of the observer. A sight taken at this time is important because it gives the latitude; an accurate time is not required. One merely watches for the maximum reading of the sextant. The calculation is quite simple.

For a sight taken at any time other than noon, an accurate Greenwich Mean Time is essential, and it requires a comparatively awkward calculation to obtain the position line.

As I had no chronometer on board, I relied on my wrist-watch,

checking it daily, if possible, with the radio; this method of obtaining G.M.T. is all that is needed for navigating the Atlantic, which is
remarkably free of reefs. An experienced seaman could navigate in
the Atlantic without even knowing G.M.T., by fixing his latitudes
at noon, then finally running down the parallel of his landfall. So for
me, all would not have been lost if the radio or wrist-watch had failed
me. However, for the Pacific, with its reefs and uncertain currents, a
chronometer is considered essential, at least by the best navigators.

One can learn how to do the calculations from a book; but taking
the actual sight with a sextant from a boat which is jumping about
requires considerable skill, only to be obtained by practice. A sort of
mystery seems to surround the art of navigation; but actually working the problem out is no more difficult than looking up a complicated railway time-table. One does not have to know why one is getting
various figures from various tables; in fact, I have a shrewd suspicion that half the old sailing-ship masters, with their rudimentary
education, had not the faintest idea what they were really doing, yet
generally they made successful voyages throughout their whole lives.

For the information of students of navigation I would say that I
use the old-fashioned Marc St. Hilaire method, using the small Burton's Tables. I did have, however, two volumes of the American H.O.
214, which had been presented to me by members of one of the U.S.
Power Squadrons after I had given them a talk on my voyages. I used
these tables for some time, but finally went back to the old method,
as my whole area of the Atlantic to England was not covered by the
two H.O. 214s, and also I found these big books unhandy in a small
space.

H.O. 214 is now superseded by H.O. 218 which, although double
the number of volumes, fits easily in a normal bookshelf. It is expensive, but, as it is much quicker to use and gives less chance of error
than the old methods (needing but one book of tables), it justifies
the extra cost and space taken up. The safety of the boat might be
at stake. In the future I intend using H.O. 218 or the British A.N.T.
tables. The latest Nautical Almanacs have been altered to suit the
new tables.

My usual practice was to take a sight after breakfast, then another at noon to obtain my 'fix'. If the weather was rough, I generally did not attempt a sight for fear of damaging the sextant. In practice, navigation takes up very little of one's time except when approaching land. I must confess that being able to find one's position by sights of the sun still amazes me; I am always secretly surprised at each accurate landfall.

On this morning of 27th September my sextant sight did not check too well with the dead reckoning, so I climbed up on deck with the intention of taking another one; but, lo, there was a ship, close by, coming up from the east. Discarding the idea of the second sight, I dashed for my flags and hoisted first the Red Ensign, then my signal letters and finally the International Code letters meaning, 'Please report me at Lloyds London.' Would this son of a gun alter course by one degree? Not he. I then flashed my lamp at him; no reply.

After he had passed, a mile to the south, he gave a few erratic flashes, then he was gone. The dirty little low-powered steamer. Is there no courtesy of the sea left? It would have cost him nothing to pass me close, and in the dull life of a seaman nowadays, one might think that the sight of a little boat out in the middle of the Atlantic would prove interesting. In the good old days the ship would have backed topsails to have a 'gam'.

It was pleasing to note that, in spite of the calm conditions, the sights showed that the 'noon to noon' had been eighty-three miles; at long last the tip of Newfoundland was no longer the nearest land, this being the island of Flores (685 miles away), one of the most north-westerly islands of the Azores.

From that moment the sense of sailing away from a place was lost; now I was heading towards a destination.

All this time the engine was idling away in neutral, charging the batteries; the opportunity was taken to check up on fuel consumption. I was disagreeably surprised to find that no less than ten gallons of fuel had already been burned, merely for charging the batteries; there appeared to be practically no difference in the amount of fuel consumed with the engine under load or running idle. There were only eleven gallons of fuel left; quite likely three gallons or so had evaporated; the temperature had never been much less than 80°F., and under the deck locker by the tank the temperature was possibly in the 90s.

As *Temptress* drifted idly along, the boom occasionally snatching as she rolled to swells of liquid pewter, I whiled away some of the time by taking coloured pictures of the yellow islands of Sargasso weed. A refreshing dip followed; I contemplated fetching the Leica to take a photograph of the boat; feasible, treading water. But in the end I rejected such a ridiculous idea; the camera was too expensive a toy to risk spoiling. One really could do with a rubber dinghy or a small canoe; it would not have been easy to launch my wooden dinghy without it being damaged in the roll. Instead, I climbed aboard and, making myself comfortable, picked up Jack London's *Mutiny of the Elsinore*.

So ended the fifth week at sea.

*   *   *

Daylight found us completely becalmed; not a breath; the gear protested, creaked and groaned as *Temptress* moved uneasily in the undulations. Faint airs ruffled the waters here and there, but left great patches of glassy surface to mirror the wobbling reflections of the horizon clouds; from the clear sky above, the sun burned down with increasing brilliance; below, the mercury in the thermometer mounted steadily.

Lying naked in the hot sun, peering into the blue depths, I became so interested in the marine life abounding that I missed the time for the noon altitude. Many species of fish surrounded the yawl; all sorts of sizes, all sorts of shapes; large, small, long, short, fat, thin, round, square, oblong; some fast, some slow; all sorts of colours; all sorts of different expressions on their faces, disdainful, dismayed, surprised, scared, sad, querulous, contented; some were beautiful, some were ugly; but all shared one thing in common—they all approved of the protection provided by *Temptress*—protection from the rays of the sun, and protection from their enemies.

Each one was watching the chance to gobble up a smaller one, as indeed was I. For instance, one from a shoal of steely blue-black fish, about a foot long, with white spots on their heads, would have made me an excellent dish, and easy to spear; but, being wary of fish poisoning, I only caught those depicted in my book on ocean fishes—or, to be more accurate, tried to catch; for, to my chagrin, because of catching the end of the spear on the mainsail, I missed a throw at a dolphin.

Even the faint airs of the morning then died away, leaving an utter calm, a very rare condition. The opportunity was taken to air my clothes, all of which had a musty smell, and some of which were covered with mildew. It was surprising that my two nylon shirts had been attacked in this manner, although the cotton ones had escaped.

It was an excellent opportunity to indulge in the profound satisfaction of throwing things over the side. In the end, a good many garments were floating round the vessel (some I fear might well have been retained), but one good riddance was my old Naval battle-dress top—a bad garment even when new, because it does not extend far enough down to protect the small of the back. (The American style is better.)

It was ten days since I had damaged my thumb and, after the skin had been softened during my evening bathe, it was possible to trim it with a pair of scissors. Nature had certainly done a wonderful job; the lump of flesh which had been pushed back into place had grafted on beautifully, and all that had to be done was to cut off the dead skin as the fresh pink skin grew beneath. The bandage had been discarded five days previously; the sun and sea air had done the rest.

Watching the sun lowering towards the horizon I revelled in the calm conditions, but the swell, north-west in the morning, had changed direction to north-north-east, rolling down as an echo of some disturbance happily passed by to the north, and now no doubt proceeding hot-foot for the British Isles, as one of the equinoctial gales.

Just for the fun of it I put on a snow-white shirt. It looked incongruous against my deep sun-tan and ruddy features, surrounded by long unruly hair and untrimmed beard. I decided that should a steamer come along, I would rig my black bow tie and bend on my black trousers, just as a joke. How amazed and impressed the crew would be to see the immaculate Englishman on deck, dressed for dinner in midAtlantic...

The sunset that followed was quietly beautiful and a real fine weather one—pink and pale green to the west, while to the east, great masses of bulbous dark mauve monster clouds blotted out the horizon. This type of cloud in more northern waters, would mean a tremendous storm, but in that area it was a normal sunset phenomena which split the east from the west, leaving them joined on that evening by the heaving white rollers of absolute calm.

My happiness was completed by the crystal-clear radio reception, and after listening to the time-signal from London I was delighted to hear the strains of my favourite tune—'The Donkey Serenade'.

Before turning in, I looked out at the night. *Temptress* rocked idly. The moon flooded with light the eerie swells; wayward airs tried ineffectually to quieten the shaking sails.

The calm had come slowly upon me, but it ended abruptly with a vicious squall of wind and rain at three o'clock in the morning. By the time I had rushed out on deck and reefed the sails, the wind had almost gone again, only to be replaced by torrential rain which fell incessantly for eight hours. Then the wind returned, slowly freshening, and once again from the east—a dead head wind. *Temptress* was soon plunging into the head sea, thrown out of step by a ten-foot-high cross swell. Conditions were normal once again. My holiday was over.

Having no proper waterproof garment, I let the yawl sail as best she could, with the helm lashed, while I lay reading Darwin in the saloon below. I was pained to note that he, a scientist, repeatedly makes the mistake of referring to 'knots per hour'. Of course 'knot' means 'one nautical mile an hour', which is a speed not a distance. One would have thought that this mistake would have been rectified during Darwin's voyage in the *Beagle*, commanded by Admiral Fitzroy.

Closing my eyes and pondering on Darwin's theories put me in mind of the question of apes being trained to serve the human race. An American physiologist at one of their universities has stated that if anthropoid apes were barred from their trees and made to stand upright, they would gradually develop a larger brain and a more effective nervous system, until they could perhaps be brought into the home and used as a somewhat unusual but adequately efficient butler. It is rather disturbing to think, on the basis of this theory, that the ape, standing like a guardsman, would eventually reach intellectual genius; while the wretched human, whose habits become more and more sedentary, bent forward as he is over desk, machine, television and other fetters of civilisation, becomes less and less intelligent until the ghastly question arises: 'Who buttles for whom?'

Would it be better to leave the ape happy in his tree, and the man unhappy at his desk, or reverse the procedure and give the man a chance to regain his freedom?

17

SIXTH GALE

29th September.

> *15.30:*   *Rain stopped: sun glimmers through haze clouds:*
> *weather conditions look ominous. If the barometer*
> *were falling I would say we were in for a gale. Cloud*
> *with east wind and swell: maybe storm to the south.*
> *Progress absolutely nil again. Food lockers beginning to*
> *look very depleted. Temperature 70°F. in cabin—cool-*
> *est yet. Only one more day of September—the worst*
> *hurricane month which has probably upset all the*
> *Atlantic weather. Need a week or two only of south or*
> *south-west winds to put me near the Azores.*

I stared at the Atlantic chart trying to work out just what was governing the weather, still thinking there was a storm somewhere to the south, but that we were also in the south-east corner of an anti-cyclone. This would explain the chill of the wind which, hundreds of miles away to the north-east, would be blowing from the north, bringing a stream of cold air from the Labrador current. It would also account for the excessive cloud. Far to the east this would be part of the norther which sweeps down the Portuguese coast.

No sunset was visible. The barometer showed a tendency to rise, but, nevertheless, wind and sea were increasing; the moon could be seen shining mistily through a sky haze—a presage of bad weather.

These contradictory portents and unnatural conditions instilled in me a strange sense of uneasiness. For the first time on the trip it was cold enough for a blanket all night; the first breath of winter.

At breakfast, while I was filling the kettle with fresh water, the pump sucked dry. My first tank was empty, twenty-five gallons had been used in fifty days. There was another tank of the same capacity. Each of these two twenty-five-gallon tanks was situated under the settees in the saloon, but apart from these fifty gallons, there were loose containers in the fo'c'sle holding twelve gallons. I found that half a gallon a day was ample.

Each morning I washed my face and also washed my teeth in fresh water. Where possible salt water was used for cooking; in porridge, for instance, one-third of the water used could be salt. On the very rare occasions that clothes or galley cloths were washed these were done with Teepol and salt water, although, of course, rinsing had to be in fresh water.

By the time breakfast was over, fed up with my long sojourn below, I hoisted more canvas, took the helm, and, after gybing, headed northwards of the true course, to look for better winds.

On the beam there was a small mustard coloured shark, which could not have been more than three feet long.

I was sailing again, but pretty unsatisfactorily. The course was straight into the north-easterly swell and *Temptress* was not long enough to cope with the short seas.

After the previous days of sun it seemed very cold and gloomy under the overcast sky. After giving me two hours of pitching up to windward, the sharp wind became squally and abnormal for the ocean; without warning it would suddenly increase until *Temptress* was carrying too much canvas, but by the time another turn had been rolled in the boom, it had dropped again.

I finally got so disgusted with the conditions that I backed the staysail, rolled down two more turns and left the boat on her own to worry herself to the north; the dirty cross-sea had done its best to soak me at the helm.

The barometer had at last decided to fall and showed that the storm, which had been presumed to be in the south, was coming nearer. I resumed my occupation of staring dully at the chart, to see whether I could work out any means of using to advantage the weather systems prevailing. But there was nothing more to be done. I had the satisfaction, however, of discovering a mistake in the Pilot

Chart: a distance near the Azores was given as 549 miles and should have read 249 miles.

There was either a fault in the taking of a sight, or my calculations were wrong, because the position put me in the South Atlantic! After checking and rechecking the maze of figures I merely became more and more provoked until I was in no state for further 'navigating'.

In the evening, the clouds melted away leaving an uncanny fog into which the pale sun slowly disappeared, while overhead the steely blue sky could be seen with one bright pin-point of light—the planet Jupiter. I took a sextant sight, as the horizon appeared to be well-defined, but with some difficulty owing to the jerky motion.

All next day, the signs of a coming storm became increasingly obvious. The sea was rising every instant as the head wind gathered force. During the last few minutes of daylight I furled the jib and well-reefed the mainsail.

For the first time on the cruise, apart from a general feeling of depression, I did not feel at all well, obviously due to the cumulative effect of the lack of proper vitamin and protein food. All that was now left was rice, corned beef and beans, apart from one or two tins of fruit and meat.

The sails were standing up quite well, although two small holes that had appeared in the working foresail needed repair. The deck fittings were not in good shape; all the time in rough weather the rudder was thumping and jarring in its bearings; every day the tiller jaws seemed to work looser.

In an endeavour to revive my flagging spirits I made a cup of strong tea, and for the first time in my life used one of those extraordinary 'tea-bags' so favoured by the American public. It is not a satisfactory way of making tea, to a tea-drinker. The idea is to put one of these paper bags in a cup, pour in boiling water—which is immediately chilled by the cup, preventing the leaves from infusing properly. It is alleged that the type of tea in these bags dismisses the possibility of making the equivalent of English tea. Some wits maintain that, after tea has been made in England, the leaves remaining in the pot are exported to America for use in these little bags.

*20.00: No more chocolate left. Radio reception almost nil.
Rough seas throwing* Temptress *all over the place.
Very dark night and blowing hard. Sidelights of a
steamer to the west and obviously coming towards me,
so switch on masthead light. She passes close but too
much sea for signalling. In my next boat there will be
a masthead light connected to a morse key, which will
allow signalling under almost all conditions.*

*22.30: Gale force: am below again after great tussle on deck.
Rolled down main boom to close reef, but left staysail.
Seas spilling aboard and heavy lurches put lee deck
under.*

*22.50: Sixth gale. Wind tearing over the boat with driving
rain. Very rough.*

The gale rose to greater heights, until it was obvious that *Temptress* was overpressed even under the very reduced canvas. During that savage black night I had to lower the mainsail in the rampaging wind; the roller-reefing gear proved exceptionally useful, as the boom was rolled until the gaff jaws were on the boom; then, with the boom on the gallows, the gaff was gradually forced down and lashed. The only sail now carried was the reefed staysail.

On arriving below after these exertions my whole body was shivering excessively; a good rub down with a dry towel and a hot drink of soup put life into me again.

Right on through the following day we were inflicted with the monotonous assault of the elements. The wind slowly veered clockwise round to the north-north-west (completing a 180° change), building up a conflict of heavy cross seas. More and more water came sprawling on deck.

In the afternoon, while I was writing up the log, a tremendous sea broke over the entire vessel—a sea as bad as in the worst of the hurricane. Everything was flooded below; the cockpit was completely full, with water pouring past the locker doors; the sea was driven in a waterfall all along the slides of the main hatch and even poured in a cataract through the skylight, in spite of the canvas cover nailed over it.

I struggled out on deck to pump the bilges dry and to put more lashings on the sails. The gale was as bad as ever, in fact the worst to date, barring the hurricane. I thought grimly: 'Who said the west to east crossing of the Atlantic is the easier?' It was I myself.

As far as one could see, battering down on the yawl, were those white-streaked masses of water, quite unheeding of the destruction they could cause to her.

The second night of hate dragged wearily by; not until the strong gale had blown for thirty-eight hours did it begin to waver, leaving me mentally and physically exhausted.

Extreme fatigue can so easily add lethargy of mind to lassitude of body. In matters of physical endurance, a man can fail in his task if he cannot separate the mind from the body. The mind must first prescribe, then force the body to act in accordance with its commands. It is only thus that one can lift oneself out of a *laissez-faire* attitude, and continue one's duty.

Shortly after dawn the jib was set and the angle of the lashed tiller was modified to midships. The bow paid off to leeward. *Temptress* first hesitated then dashed off, like a mad hare, before the huge seas; she rolled, lurched and corkscrewed in such a frantic whirligig of gyrostatics that the only way of preventing myself from being thrown round like a dice in a shaker was to lie on the cabin floor, jamming myself between table and settee.

Two hours of this was two hours too much. The only thing to do was to lie to again under bare poles. Moving slowly and carefully to combat the dizzy evolutions, I slid out of the hatch and gained the cockpit. Repeated jerks on the roller furling line of the jib gave no result; the line had dropped off the reel, and was caught underneath; a hazardous journey to the end of the bowsprit was the only way of putting matters right.

My jacket was thrown down below, followed by my shirt and shorts—I was stripped for action (I did not wear trousers, or anything on my feet, the entire voyage). There is plenty to hold on to—up to the mast and shrouds; the foredeck looked impossibly bare, and the bowsprit was shovelling out ditches in the water. Watching my chance, I made a quick movement to the bitts, then another one, over the bow and on to the bowsprit shroud. The spar smacked down then sucked clear; I swung my feet on to the bobstay, and gripped the chain with my toes. Sitting on the shroud, and resting my stomach on the spar, left my hands free to do the work of clearing the line, but several times I had to hold on with all I had got as the descending spar immersed me, right up to my waist.

I could not help remembering the oft-quoted instance regarding a yacht which was found untenanted in the English Channel; the last entry of the log was: 'Going out on end of bowsprit. Will I return?' It was not without reason that I had renewed the bowsprit shroud rigging screws, before leaving America. One cannot take liberties with a spar ten feet outboard.

The job was at last done. It was not till the afternoon that the jib was reset, and the boat allowed to shoot off downwind before seas that were (to quote a well-worn expression) as big as houses; as it happens they were bigger than most houses one sees nowadays.

Feeling that I had deserved it, I opened the last tin, the very last tin, of beef stew. There was just the corned beef left, a substance that now stuck in my throat when I tried to eat it.

> *This bad weather convinces me that an ocean going*
> *vessel must have all deck openings and all superstruc-*
> *tures capable of withstanding a heavy sea aboard from*
> *any direction. All hatches, etc., must be designed by*
> *seamen rather than naval architects.*

The above was written in my log during the gale, and is followed by the note:

> *Plates, even soup plates, are useless: one must eat out*
> *of bowls.*

The continuing wind gave the sea no chance to go down; it was not breaking heavily nor was it in any way dangerous to the boat, but a sudden shift or increase of wind would, like a touch from a wand, instantly have made it serious.

While working in the galley, I looked up just in time to see the five-foot high compactum tear away from the bulkhead, and fall towards me. I fended it off and, with it still tottering, managed to push it back into place and secure it with some handy line. It was another piece of evidence to show what a beating the boat had taken in the gales—even interior fittings were beginning to carry away.

After a restless night, in sodden blankets, I opened the hatch to find that the sun had actually come out. The swells had reduced to about fifteen feet high. *Temptress* was maintaining course eastwards at two knots.

A solitary flying fish was lying on deck. Later, it made a pitifully inadequate lunch.

Bird life was considerable. There were no less than four bosun birds, a bird I took for a shearwater, and several stormy petrels. But unexpectedly, the wind fell away during the day to a mere breath from the north; the spars and sails started their fiendish fandango, upsetting my spearing aim so much that, instead of having fat dolphin for dinner, I had to be satisfied with sardines out of a tin.

Those long white swells, the last relics of the gale, allied with the very openness of the sky, gave an air of vastness and desolation, which was accentuated by the unaccustomed quiet, following the clamour of the last two days.

Darkness brought the stars. *Temptress* lay halted, rolling consistently, squashing out phosphorescence at each side as she swayed.

Thus ended the sixth week.

18

PROGRESS

The moods of a woman are said to be as changeable as the weather, but it would have been a woman of innumerable moods who could rival the changes I had experienced on this trip.

October 5th dawned bright, with a beautiful south-west wind, for which I had scarcely hoped, and two hours later *Temptress* was skipping eastward under a hazy blue sky, while I happily tended the helm, all depression swept away.

Swift progress kept us ahead of a long cloud astern. This cloud gradually swept across the heavens and must have formed the father and mother of a squall. Within two hours it reached to the north-east horizon and stretched out of sight to the south-west. It must have been a funnel of cloud fifty to one hundred miles long and about twelve miles deep. The whole cylinder appeared to be supported on great pillars of rain, connecting sea and cloud. Several more hours passed before this system passed away to the north. It was a typical example of local conditions. There was I sluicing along in brilliant sunshine, yet another boat only twenty miles away might have had a day of violent wind and rain.

The northerly swell from the previous gale was still operating; the whole disturbance must have been big enough to affect the entire Atlantic Ocean.

At sundown the wind lost its strength of the day and we sailed on until the compass could be read no more. With mainsail lowered, *Temptress* slipped quietly through the night under headsails, after a perfect day's sail.

Chancing to look out some hours later, I was surprised to see a blaze of lights from a liner five miles away to the north, evidently heading for New York. A steamer seemed to pass almost every night; if only one would have passed during the day for me to signal.

Now, as a change from the usual excessive nodosity, the sea went down with such good effect that, at breakfast, I was able to peg down the swing table. With legs wide apart, one could even stand up without holding on. It was quieter than it had been for many a long day. However, there were no signs of the beautiful sailing breeze of yesterday; *Temptress* moved impatiently in the glassy swells.

With the calm sea and clear horizon, conditions were ideal for celestial navigation; having checked my watch with the radio, I took a series of sights, and plotted an accurate position of Latitude 37° 41′ Longitude 41° 40′. The nearest land was the island of Flores, now 500 miles away. The distance to England was still 1850 miles, yet there we lay, becalmed, half-way between New York and Lisbon. Each day lost would bring us nearer to the frosts of winter, at the end of the route.

The last onion which I had been hoarding and which, incidentally, had not improved in the many weeks aboard, went raw into the rice and corned beef for lunch. I would not risk cooking it, lest some of its beneficial effects be destroyed.

A light breeze filled the sails and whispered through the rigging. *Temptress* heeled very slightly and bubbles in the water began to slide slowly astern. Ahead appeared a white streak across my path looking like a calm patch, but, no, it was caused by a wide broken lane of Sargasso weed, extending as far as one could see to either horizon, its direction undoubtedly caused by a south-easterly setting current. Unaccountably, there was more wind on the far side of this yellow carpet. Another of those strange and inexplicable phenomena…

I had forgotten that such objects as aircraft existed, and a distant drone had me at first scanning the ocean for a ship, before I sighted a big four-engined plane, all glistening and silver in the sun, heading towards the west. From Lisbon? From Santa Maria?

After sunset the sky grew grey, the horizon less distant, and, to the east, Jupiter suddenly appeared, shining strong. The sky in the west gradually faded; star upon star waxed brighter in the heavens until the transformation was complete.

I steered for some hours under the magic of the stars, bright and sharp, like pegs in the sky, on which one can hang one's thoughts. Each gentle swish of the bow wave sent a mass of sparkling phosphorescence gliding past the sides, whilst astern a veritable cloud of scintillating silver eddied and swirled.

The following day, after eleven hours at the helm, I had managed fifty miles to the good, sailing through quiet seas to a beam wind.

The boat was still leaking about a gallon an hour. I do not like a leaking boat. To my idea, a boat should be pumped once a week, say every Sunday, and not morning and night—and what about Slocum's Spray? When he arrived back in the States he said he had not rigged his pump since leaving Australia! Perhaps thickness of plank has much to do with this. *Temptress* has one-inch while Spray had one-and-a-half-inch thick planking.

I began to feel my first pangs of hunger. Even for breakfast now I had to cut down on my porridge, being on the last tin. I began to have visions of three fried eggs with bacon, followed by toast, butter and marmalade...

The second quiet night was brought abruptly to an end by a squall from the south-west. The first green light of dawn was showing to the eastward. The mainsail was already stowed, so, an adjustment to the helm, and I could return to my warm bunk.

This was the start of a grand day's sail. It was quite a job to hoist the heavy mainsail in the lively motion, before *Temptress* was prancing swiftly downwind.

Clouds and squalls came and went. We rushed on; it was not until late that night that I rounded up into the spirited breeze, and dropped the mainsail, after fourteen hours at the helm. There had been no necessity to use the compass. First I had used the square of Pegasus until it swung out of range, then came Pleiades, and finally the great constellation of Orion rose majestically out of the sea. To the north, the handle of the Plough dipped below the horizon.

At seven o'clock next morning the wind had fallen right away; *Temptress* was wallowing heavily in the swell, with thrashing of booms and slatting of sails. It just shows that one should never let up with a fair breeze. Had I hove to at dusk the evening before, I would have lost many miles of easting.

In spite of the lack of wind in the morning the sights showed that the noon to noon run was no less than 103 miles. It is an extraordinary thing; never have I been able to try seriously for a record day's run. By a series of peculiar circumstances, twenty-four consecutive hours of fresh fair breeze have never been granted to me; this run of 103 miles was to be the best run of the whole voyage, yet we had been becalmed for over five hours during the period.

The distance run from New York now was looking very impressive on the ocean chart and so it should—after forty-seven days!

Had this been the beginning of the century, I would now have been sighting windjammers bound for the English Channel, from Cape Horn, Cape of Good Hope and South America. The square riggers had to come far west on account of the north-east Trades. All one can hope to see nowadays is the odd rusty steamer plodding its unromantic way.

After eight trying hours of calm, at last a pleasant breeze set in from the south-west and the yawl, steadied by full canvas, ploughed ahead at four knots.

While the glorious sun scorched down from the bright limitless sky, a rain-squall in the form of a low arch overtook us. *Temptress*, in an apparent desire to perform her own square dance, ducked gaily through the arch as the pillars of rain passed close on either side.

After this squall had passed, leaving a slight increase of wind, as I steered nonchalantly with one arm hooked over the tiller, my thoughts dwelt on the problem of arriving at the approaches to the English Channel, and I worked in a dream of various weather conditions, imagining being off Ushant, the Lizard, and approaching Plymouth. Gales, head winds, fair winds, fog, and even snowy conditions, passed through my mind.

It is astonishing how one's morale is affected by the weather. Just because it was a fair wind and warm, I was planning to miss the Azores and risk making for England with poor stores and the boat needing many repairs, and yet I knew perfectly well that there only had to be the threat of a gale or strong head winds, and immediately

I would reject all ideas of heading straight for England and would be pricking off the distance on the chart to the nearest port.

As usual, no ships came in view during the day, but two hours after sunset a ship appeared quite close abeam, and called me up, saying: 'What Ship? What Ship?' but, alas, he could not get my message; my signalling light seemed quite cock-eyed. Anyway, I pumped out my signal letters MDPV MDPV over and over again at him, in the hope that they might be read.

After he had gone, I spent some time with the lamp, trying to find out just why it was not working properly. It really needed an object to spot on, half a mile away, to test the angle of beam. However, aimed at my windvane on top of the mast, the light seemed to miss it by about thirty degrees. While fiddling around with the lamp, I came across a loose screw on the reflector adjustment. It was quite loose and about three-eighths of an inch out, with the lock-nut inoperative. After screwing it back, I again tested the lamp on the vane, and became fairly satisfied that now it would be possible to signal with sufficient accuracy.

The second night's wind was used to the utmost; we romped towards home, bounding and lurching over the swells.

Midnight came and still we kept going—leaving five miles astern of us at the end of every hour. After steering eight hours through the night I adjusted the sails and lashed the tiller. The barometer was falling, and the wind had backed to the south.

Meteors were falling, flashing past the galaxy of stars.

The number of shooting stars must be very great; I doubt if one can watch the sky for a quarter of an hour without seeing at least one. We should be very thankful for our protective band of atmosphere, which throws off the millions of meteors which are attempting to bombard the earth.

I had hardly dozed for three-quarters of an hour, when I was jolted wide awake by the scream of wind and excessive angle of heel. *Temptress* was travelling like an express train; by the time the deck was reached a squall had hit her fair and square—driving rain, with the seas whipped into a frenzy. I clambered forward to the mainmast, rolled down two more turns of the boom, and crawled on all fours in the pitch black, groping my way aft to the cockpit, to take the helm. We fled before the shrieking devils, while I rolled up the jib from the cockpit with that wonderful furling gear.

By the time the boat was rounded up to heave to, under staysail and six-rolled main, the worst of the squall was over; before the next snorter came, the mainsail was stowed, both headsails were again set, and the helm lashed to suit self-steering to leeward.

The wind had veered to the south-south-west with the first squall, and kept blowing, but I returned to my bunk to continue my short and interrupted rest, happy in the knowledge that *Temptress*, now dressed for the occasion, could well look after herself.

19

SIGNALS

By dawn, a steep breaking sea was snapping at our heels, with the odd wave-top spilling aboard over the starboard quarter. Sweeping across the sky a mighty rabble of wild cirrus formed a scattered V to the western horizon. Another milestone of the ocean was passed; every fifteen degrees of longitude one passes into another time zone, and on that day, 10th October, I had to put the ship's clock onward one hour, making it only two hours different from G.M.T.

All day *Temptress* reeled and staggered drunkenly eastward, under headsails, pushed on by the irresistible surge of the sea. As each crest passed forward, her speed would suddenly drop, then the sharp rolling would temporarily increase as she sank down into the trough. The next wave would come boiling up, the stern would be flung into the air, and as the crest struck at her quarter, she would give a violent lurch to port, righting herself as the wave passed underneath. Wave after wave—hour after hour.

The sharp wind turned bitter with the setting sun. The yellow colour of the sunset, a mackerel sky and falling barometer gave no hope of better conditions. *Temptress* scudded on while lightning flickered incessantly to the north-west. It was the start of another bumpy night. I turned in, ready to keep a look-out. The batteries were low, so no lights were showing, nor had they been for the past week or more.

There was an increase of wind at midnight. The motion was bad, and sea-tops washed continually. At two o'clock in the morning I logged 'Moderate Gale'; it had been only a week since the previous one. Dawn showed a rough, big and broken sea of gale dimensions.

Temptress skipped along and occasionally tipped over at a frightful angle, as she slowed down the advancing front of a wave. Good progress but somewhat alarming.

Breakfast was being prepared when a heavy sea poured aboard through the chinks in the hatches, sousing the saloon and my bunk. Two hours later another sea broke heavily over the rail. It was detestable weather. By the afternoon, conditions were worsening; seas were coming aboard in greater quantities and more often; I felt that it was about time the crazy racket was checked.

I lowered the staysail and lashed it firmly to the bitts, leaving the boat under jib alone. She still maintained course, slightly more downwind and, travelling a little slower, rode more comfortably.

Temptress had travelled for thirty-five hours under two headsails and, in the noon to noon period, knocked up eighty miles on her own; I deserved a bit of a rest. It certainly takes nerve to tear through these seas day and night. Of course, one can always stop the boat by heaving to in comparative safety, but every advantage had to be taken of a fair wind to wrest more miles from the sea in our perpetual struggle eastwards.

The wind jerked round to the west, building up a new set of vicious cross seas. Lowering grey cloud covered the sky. An hour later the wind shifted ninety degrees.

17.00:   *Wind suddenly to the north blowing hard as ever.*
        Never a dull moment. Thick with rain. Seas like a
        tide rip. It will be over soon. Sopping below.

A cold wet night, black as sin, brought a failing wind from ahead. Any sort of progress became impracticable. I felt tired, wet and dispirited, and had a lump in my stomach, caused either by the motion or by lack of reasonable food. Little did I realise that I would never have another fair wind on that passage.

Later that night it was necessary to lash the helm harder down. The fresh wind struck bitterly cold. The boat was rolling horribly. Somehow I found it impossible to sleep in the wet, smelly bedclothes. I felt grey and out of sorts.

Another nut securing the tiller arms had slipped off the thread during the gale. The barometer was high enough but the dark glowering clouds and heavy seas gave no sign of improvement. I was too jaded to hoist the mainsail and left the boat under jib, barely moving with the wind just abaft the beam. In any case, even under full sail, progress would have been negligible in the jagged sea.

Jammed on the lee settee of the saloon I spent the day going through old yachting magazines, cutting out anything of interest, and flinging the rest overboard—and about time, too.

After preparing a very uninteresting rice dish as first course for dinner, I was reduced to eating one blackcurrant lozenge for dessert.

At half-past ten, on that cold and rough night, I made out a light bobbing occasionally into view, to the east. Eventually, two lights, one above the other, showed this to be a steamer heading directly towards me. Without delay, my masthead light was switched on and, from the cockpit, the sails floodlit with the hand lamp. I watched anxiously as the ship approached.

The red and green lights became visible. Then the two white lights spread out from each other, gradually, masking the green; the Captain had altered course to pass under my stern. In spite of the big sea running, it was an opportunity too good to miss; I pressed the trigger of my signalling lamp, sending out the call-up letters AAA AAA AAA... But only when *Temptress* was on the crest of a wave was it possible for him to see my flashes.

He swung round to port and stopped, close abeam, a huge black shadow in the obscurity, pinpointed by many lights. Even near as the ship was, intervening waves would momentarily blot out all except her masthead light from my vision. Conditions for signalling were deplorable, but I repeatedly spelt out MDPV MDPV MDPV REPORT OK. His reply winked in the darkness; first acknowledgment, then a message; only half of the letters were visible, but I managed to understand: 'What do you want?'

Again waiting for a crest, I pumped back: 'Report MDPV OK.' An acknowledgment followed. Then I realised that the great mass was moving. Another flicker came: ' R—U—O—K.' *Temptress* surged to a top of a breaking sea. 'YES.' 'YES.' Down she dived into the next trough. The ship's masthead lights swung together as she turned away. 'What is the matter,' blinked erratically out of the inky light. But we were too far apart. I switched out all my lights.

I could not know, but his radio transmitter was operating. It was the first news received of *Temptress* sixty-two days out of New York. It made a great stir at home. The following appeared in one English newspaper:

News Chronicle, Wednesday, October 18, 1950.

WAS IT THE CALL OF THE TEMPTRESS?
AS SHIPS PASS IN THE NIGHT
News Chronicle Reporter

Light signals seen in mid-Atlantic were thought yesterday to be the first clue to the whereabouts of Edward Allcard and his 34-ft. yawl *Temptress*—unheard of for sixty-two days.

The British whale-oil tanker *Thule* reported an encounter 300 miles south of the Azores in the early hours of Friday, the thirteenth.

At 2 a.m., her twin screws pounding in a heavy sea, the 7,500-ton Thule slowed down to exchange signals in the darkness with a craft asking to be reported at Lloyd's of London.

Nothing could be seen from the bridge of the *Thule* except the blinking of the signal lamp.

'ALL WELL ON BOARD'

If it was *Temptress* this is the first news of Allcard since he left New York. He had planned to take only fifty days for the 3,000 mile voyage.

Frithjof Holst, Norwegian master of the *Thule*, signalled Lloyd's: 'Encountered MLDV 02.00 hrs. position 3423N. 3410W. All well on board.'

Lloyd's were puzzled because MLDV are the code letters for the British coaster *Sussex Birch*, which they knew was lying in the Thames.

However, they guessed it might be *Temptress*—whose

code letters MDPV are very similar.

They radioed for more information and the master answered: 'Morse lamp difficult to read due to heavy swell and bad sending.'

Hope spelled out in Four Letters

Here, first, is the code signalled to the *Thule*—contrasted below with the code call of the *Temptress*. It would be easy to confuse the two groups if conditions for sending or reading were difficult:

M	L	D	V
— —	. — . .	— . .	. . . —

M	D	P	V
— —	— . .	. — — .	. . . —

I must say that, on reading the above, many months later, I was rather annoyed at the Captain's remarks about my sending!

20

THREAT

Those former six golden days were certainly being paid for: first a gale, and now, with the barometer ironically pointing to 'Set Fair', a searching easterly wind tearing over grey water under lowering skies. The height of the barometer was, in fact, phenomenal—30.45 inches. The weather was past comprehension; maybe the previous gale was then attacking the Portuguese coast? Whatever was happening, it meant more waiting, more days lost, more desultory reading below for me.

When forced to suffer poor sailing conditions, it is always a balm to read about people in an even worse state. What about Fred Rebel? He sailed from Sydney to San Francisco in an eighteen-foot boat, with his only shelter a rough canvas cover such as roadmenders use. However, he certainly had good ideas for stores which he kept in painted paraffin tins with screw tops. Here he kept his flour, rice, wheat, pearl barley, peas, beans, sugar, semolina, rolled oats and powdered milk. He already knew the secret of food stores—a secret I myself was only just beginning to comprehend. The more one goes to sea the more one realises the inadequacy of tinned foods, in all of which there is a horrible sameness of taste and little goodness. Dried food is the secret. The only tinned stuff necessary, in my opinion, is orange or tomato juice and milk.

Just at ship's noon the sun glimmered for several instants in a cloud gap, and I managed a sight, lashing my hips to the boom to prevent myself being catapulted overboard, complete with sextant. Later in the afternoon a chain of sights was obtained and, taking a mean of these sights and the time, I obtained an accurate position which came within only three miles of the dead reckoning.

A reeling cabin is not the best place for an intense bout of mathematics, but it was not long before a course was pencilled on the chart. Horta was only 280 miles away and the course—well, you can guess it—exactly against the malevolent wind.

Shortly afterwards, the sky cleared to windward and the clouds retreated in a scattered mob. This improvement in the weather was but a mockery; before sunset a blanket of grey clouds had been drawn across the sky. The wind swept the spray before it, as gusts sweep the autumn leaves across a field. The rudder thumped; the bowsprit slammed repeatedly into the excited seas.

The couple of hundred miles to port could just as well be a couple of thousand in those adverse conditions. A strong head wind and steep sea creates a barrier as effective as a brick wall. A twinge of something like fear ran through me, as I thought of my dwindling stores. Only a few days more, and I would have nothing except some rice, tins of corned beef (which I could scarcely force down my gullet) and some tinned beans.

Uneasy, I could not settle down to any definite occupation. I would look out, try to read a bit, and make a cup of tea with no enthusiasm, then fiddle with the miniature radio, when suddenly, loud and clear, I picked up Santa Maria Ground Staff trying to contact a Clipper which evidently was attempting to overtake other air traffic at 1900 feet. It was so loud that it almost made me jump, but it had the effect of making me realise how near were the Azores—in distance though, not time.

There was nothing to do but turn in. I drew the log towards me and wrote:

> 22.00:   Damned if the barometer has not gone up to 30.48
> in.—an all time high: yet a stiff east wind and
> cloud—not my idea of an anti-cyclone. Paraffin light
> in the rigging. Filthy motion in this jerky irritating
> sea. Well, Friday 13th is nearly over, so let us hope for
> improvement.

More wind with pouring rain was the best the dawn could produce, and the rest of the day inflicted black squalls upon us, between which there was little wind, and an abominable sea. It was not until the evening that I had my first sight of the sun; even that was followed by a gloomy sunset, blocked by a black square wall of cloud.

While listening to the radio I was startled to see two lights through a porthole; leaping to the deck it amused me to find that it was only Jupiter—made into a double image by the glass.

Oddly enough there were also lights of a steamer away to the south-east.

As the Azores were then comparatively close, it was essential to have accurate G.M.T.; luckily I obtained a radio check from London—crystal clear reception, usually a sign of better weather. It seemed odd to me that Australia could be heard as clear as London, and far clearer than the United States.

On the morning of the fourth day of this fiendish easterly wind, I had the unusual sight of a steamer slowly crossing my bows, about three miles off, black smoke pouring far ahead. The Captain actually had the decency to alter course to pass near me to see if any assistance was needed. All my flags were ready to hoist, but I left them on deck; the ship looked so rusty and decrepit, she probably had no radio transmitter. My position was right on the low-powered steamer route. ' Low power! ' this poor old thing was almost dead in her tracks. I took a photograph, only a few cables off, then waved energetically. A whole forest of arms were raised in reply by the crew lining the bulwarks—all very heartening.

The yawl tumbled and sparred as best she could, beset by that thrice-damned wind. I did not help her. It was too much for one man to drive to windward in that weather; he would soon get cold and soaked. In any case, all my clothes were already clammy with salt. Then there was the problem of bedclothes which only got dry by the morning—dried by the heat of my body overnight. My only pleasure (pleasure?) was eating— but what food! Boiled rice and corned beef for one meal, and fried rice and corned beef for the next; it was tantalising to know that the Azores, rich with fruit and vegetables, were only a few proper sailing days away. As it was, if similar weather continued, I would probably starve.

The afternoon sight was not very encouraging; it gave the same longitude of 44° 14'. It was galling to know that in the last forty-eight hours I had made absolutely nothing towards Horta, and was back where I had been before.

October 16th did its best to give me some improvement; the wind was still from ahead, but had abated to Force 3, while the sea became more regular. Sailing on a bowline, *Temptress* hurdled over the waves, as if eager to shake off the stagnation of the previous days—as indeed was I.

It was cold at the helm, especially to bare legs and feet. Shorts are preferable, for bare legs dry easily; nothing is more horrible than pulling on a cold and wet pair of trousers... and trousers are always cold and wet. A full length oilskin, though, would have been useful and acceptable.

After a profitable day the fine wind petered away and, after sunset, vanished completely; it became necessary to lower the mainsail to stop the chafe. Of course, this was hardly done when a steady south-easterly breeze sprang up; but it was too much trouble for a jaded body to rehoist the heavy gaff mainsail; too late in the day, also.

Before retiring for the night, I tapped the barometer, which fell slightly from its high position. Black clouds still covered the sky. All during the day visibility had been exceptionally sharp, and now the deck was white and unstained by dew. These portents indicated that bad weather was not far away.

*   *   *

The eighth consecutive week at sea ended; the morning of Thursday, 19th October, found *Temptress* with all canvas hoisted, sailing, it is true, but in a disconcerting manner. The swell had grown in immensity and as each crest swiftly surged under the hull, the sails and spars snapped aggressively; the wind varied from Force 1 to Force 5 in a matter of seconds.

There were certainly many signs of wind, and woven through a mackerel sky were great sweeps of untidy mares' tails. The cirrus cloud was drawn like a veil over the sun, forming an immense halo.

It was going to be a race with the bad weather to reach the Azores.

Rain-squalls were never absent and sent, across the great swells, a splintered sea through which the yawl had to struggle for every inch of her way.

Exceptional visibility, allied with immense swells, produced some very curious effects. The horizon seemed to be the same distance off the whole time, but actually varied in distance and height at every moment. Above the apparent horizon one would first see the bulbous top of a cloud, which would then mount rapidly into the air like an atomic bomb explosion; then its progress would suddenly be arrested by the false horizon of a huge swell, and the cloud would drop out of sight again.

In spite of the various weather indications which pointed to a huge storm far away to the north-west— 1000 miles or more— and another one closer to the west, my fears were alleviated by a fine-looking sunset, although there was much cloud, of every conceivable size and type, travelling in diverse directions.

Being, as I thought, near the end of the road, I ate the very last potato for dinner, one which I had been saving up for over a week. Meals at this time were only giving me momentary satisfaction, and generally I felt an aching void in my stomach. The worst meal I have ever eaten on shore would have seemed a feast; the dizziest height of mental gastronomy I could achieve was to think of a large plate of simple, boiled cabbage.

*   *   *

A cloud, looking remarkably like land, and looming large above the horizon, on the bearing of Flores, filled my brain with conjectures and some doubt as to my true position. I knew Flores could not really be as big as that.

Occasionally in my log I would subject myself to self-criticism. This 'landfall' was faithfully recorded, with the added:

*Come now don't lose your sense of proportion, just because you
have not seen any land for two months. You know perfectly well*

that Flores is far below the horizon, and even if it was not, it
would be merely a little blue bump.

It was not until noon that I could fix my position; the sun obligingly showing itself when it was needed.

Latitude was 38° 30'; bringing forward my morning's position line, I made a little cross on the chart some hundred miles from Horta to the east; Flores was sixty miles away to the north and slightly abaft the beam. Already amongst the Azores, in fact. An eighty-eight-mile noon to noon run and the fine wind continuing, made it look a certainty that land would be sighted on the morrow, with a good chance of making port before nightfall. (The Gods laughed.)

The bulk of black cloud in the west slowly advanced, inexorable as fate; the wind, which had been so helpful from the south, veered ahead, blowing straight from my destination. This change, in one fell swoop, annihilated every vestige of hope of either making an early landfall or missing the coming gale.

It was half-past five, and already growing dark, when a frightful livid mauve gash appeared between horizon and cloud. A chill went through me; I had only once seen such a terrible coloured sunset—before the hurricane!

As if itself aghast at this appalling sight, the wind faltered, then dropped away to a complete calm.

Spars and gear broke into that clamorous dervish dance.

A halo of vast diameter formed round a blurred moon. This fitful light, with indistinct black squalls lurking in the darkness, gave the night a haunted and ominous air. The wind came in uneasy gusts, clouds thickened. The feeble light of the moon was almost imperceptibly extinguished.

There was nothing left. Nothing. Just an awful cloaking blackness. Complete and absolute.

The reaching staysail set to a fair wind

Temptress sailing into T-Wharf at Boston, Massachusetts

Temptress, ready for the ocean again, takes a quiet sail in Long Island Sound

Temptress has a gaff-rigged mainsail; note the nylon windsock fitted on truck

Temptress with Edward Allcard's new *Wanderer* tied up astern on the river Hudson, New York

A large dolphin, still transfixed to the grains that speared him, poses for a photograph

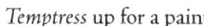
Temptress up for a paint

Running under headsails before a big sea

Becalmed in mid-Atlantic

Looking down on Horta harbour, Fayal, Azores

Looking across to Pico. The harbour wall of Horta can be clearly seen

Hoisting the damaged *Temptress* on to the quay, Horta;
the mizzen mast is conspicuous by its absence

Repairs to rudder, Horta. Manuel da Silva
with hand on rudder

The Portuguese stowaway,
Otilia Maria de Mesquita Frayao

Otilia at Casablanca

A company of Atlantic navigators on board *Temptress*, Casablanca:
left to right, Edward Allcard and Otilia Frayao of *Temptress*,
Eleanor and Ben Carlin of *Amphibious Jeep*, Marcel Bardiaux of *Les 4 Vents*

Temptress at Casablanca

Temptress at Casablanca

The Société Nautique, Casablanca, as seen from *Temptress*

Edward Allcard in the interior of Morocco

The roller-reefing gear

Bowsprit plunging into head sea

A French tunnyman *EL 5170* tries to overtake *Temptress* in the Bay of Biscay

At Plymouth, Devon; *Temptress* tied up alongside the ill-fated *Nellie Bywater*—later sunk during a winter gale in the English Channel

21

GALE DAMAGE

S aturday, 21st October:

    01.15:   Wind increases to moderate gale. Rough night.

I was still intent on making port. *Temptress*, steering herself, charged on under jib, full staysail, reefed mainsail and mizzen. The squally wind would suddenly shift a couple of points, then revert. As best as could be seen in the inky blackness, a uniform pall of cloud stretched overhead; darker lumps in the night heralded further squalls.

Between bouts on deck to record the course and distance run, by flashing the torch into the compass and rotator log, I sat on the weather side of the saloon, my feet braced on the opposite settee. Occasionally I would drop into a doze, bearded chin resting on my chest, only to be jolted awake by an abnormal lurch. It would have been too risky to turn in; approaching land one cannot let the boat wander where she will.

Late in the night a fine rain saturated the atmosphere. Not even the mast was visible from the hatch. At one instant a pocket in this fog revealed the misty lights of a steamer, quite close. In a moment it was gone. We were near the shipping track passing between Flores and Fayal.

The seas growled louder in the darkness. I prayed that daylight would come before a further reduction of sail would be necessary, but only an hour later the whistle of the wind had reached a higher note, promising worse things to come. I decided then to reduce canvas before the difficulties became too great, and struggled out on deck, to be met by a blast of driving rain.

I crawled aft, cast off the mizzen halyards and grabbed down the flapping sail, lashing it firmly to the boom. Running the boat off before the wind, I rolled up the jib with the roller line led to the cockpit. As I was giving a final heave to make sure it was fully rolled up, the line slackened in my hand—broken. However, there was no thunder of flogging canvas, so it was at least already furled, but at any moment it might unroll and tear itself to ribbons. Clawing my way along the deck I slid forward out to the end of the bowsprit, to lash down the end of line. Over and over again I was plunged into the sea; it seemed hot compared to the biting wind.

With way off her, *Temptress* lay quite comfortably under backed staysail and close rolled mainsail. So far so good.

It was difficult to say when dawn came; the blackness of night slowly dissolved into a cinder-coloured rain. The change in the sea overnight was staggering. The last hours of the previous day had shown great smooth rolling swells; now they had been converted into overtowering, down-toppling monsters intent on licking the truck.

The barometer was falling slowly, but very steadily, showing that the storm system was almost static. It pointed to a long drawn out combat; also, as the east-south-east wind gave not the slightest sign of backing or veering, it indicated that the centre of the storm was heading remorselessly my way.

After three hours of so-called daylight, things became far worse. The wind was blowing a gale that ever in recurring squalls increased upon itself. Once again courage had to be summoned to send me out on deck. With my bare back whipped by stinging rain and spindrift, I toiled at the roller-reefing gear, until the main gaff-jaws were down to the boom.

> 10.00:   *Barometer 29.75in. Still falling: damn it. Blowing and raining like hell. No sign of break in pall. Estimated position midway between Flores and Fayal—about sixty miles from each, and right on steamer track.*
> 10.30:   *Worse: must be Force 10.*
> *More must be done.*

On my way forward to lower the staysail, a gigantic sea reared up and bore down on the boat; I had hardly embraced the mast with my arms and hooked one leg over the gaff, when it thundered over the beam, smashing on top of me, forcing the boat almost down to her beam ends. She surfaced with water pouring off both sides. In the comparative calm which followed I managed to drag down and smother the staysail without damage. The wind force was now terrific.

With the gaff-jaws on the boom, the vessel was now under the mainsail triangle only. It would be a very hard fight even to hinge the gaff down to the boom, and I decided to leave this tiny sail area; it tended to steady the boat, allowing her to present a less vulnerable target to the breakers, as more hull was exposed and less deck. Leaving sail up turned out to be a grave mistake; but a very severe gale was already blowing, and I hardly expected it to blow stronger; not only was it now past the hurricane season, but we were outside the hurricane area.

It was midday. The barometer, down to 29.65in., began to fall much faster; alarming gusts, in increasing numbers, laid *Temptress*, shuddering, over on her side. The seas grew into veritable avalanches.

It had always been my boast that I can cook in any weather; to bear this out, I jammed myself in the galley seat, and brewed up a cup of beef cube.

I wished perhaps that all canvas was down, but the gallant yawl did not seem to mind the scrap of mainsail still up. I felt somehow that a crisis was at hand.

Spindrift and rain were beginning seriously to reduce visibility. The log was entered up every hour; every hour things became worse.

> 13.00: *Barometer 29.61in. Worse. As I write a heavy sea comes aboard with minor waterfalls below. Damn the weather. After all the rough breaks it has given me, it might have let me make Horta. This is severe. Heard note of the wind rise past the shriek of gale— that harrowing moan which I had heard during the hurricane. Rain still driving. No sign of break in clouds.*

*If only the barometer was rising. All the sea streaked
with white.*

An hour later the barometer was down another half a tenth, and still
falling. The wind howled and screamed its explosive tune of destruction. Mountains of water with jagged peaks flung *Temptress* forward
and skyward in a welter of broken foam. Scarcely had she recovered
from one blow, when she would be sucked down to the bottom of
the world, only to be attacked by the next, and the next, and the next.

Down below I bailed out the bilges with a tin can, tipping the
water into the stainless steel galley sink and pumping it out through
my blessed non-choke pump. It was something to do. I was angry
and fed up at having to endure the mental anxiety of severe weather
again on a half-empty stomach.

The barometer still fell.

Several times the boat had been flung over on her beam ends at
the onslaught of that odd exceptional wave, but she had each time
righted herself without damage.

Wedged in with my knees against the sink, and back against the
compactum, I had just written in the log:

14.20: Must be hurricane force,

when my whole body tensed at the mighty rumbling and booming of a bursting sea. A report, like a cannon shot, was followed
by *Temptress* reeling away—rolling over, over, over; in an instant
pitch darkness engulfed everything. Water poured below from
every direction in hissing torrents. The paralysing shriek of the
wind was cut off by the volume of water above. Far worse were
the ensuing heavy thuds and crashes pummelling somewhere,
somehow, this stricken yawl.

'It is the end. She is sinking,' I muttered.

My senses were bemused, beaten into a kind of oblivion. All
sense of gravity was gone. Water continued to flood the boat. To
open the hatch, even if I could have found it, would have only speeded up the process of choking death.

In moments of peril the mind, apparently, forms a carapace for itself and is protected from panic.

Completely unexpectedly, I found myself on my hands and knees trying to collect my scattered wits. A grey light filtered through the ports. The boat was upright! Unbelievingly, I started to raise myself up. The movement had the effect of unlocking my numbed senses and releasing me for action. The hard battering of some sort of wreckage grew more fearful every second. Clinging to the ladder, I frenziedly tried to open the hatch; it opened three inches before stopping against some immovable object—evidently lying across the cabin-top. At that moment a second sea spouted green on board, and a solid cataract of water gushed below. Blinded and smothered I managed to shove the hatch to.

The wave passed. I had another try at opening the hatch, but in vain. Driving my fist into the hinged part of the fashion board, I made a gap sufficient for my head and shoulders to pass through.

It was impossible even to breathe in the wind, and the seas were gigantic toppling walls of water reaching skyward. At that moment yet another wave swamped tons of water over the rail; I was jammed in the hatch; panic welled up within me in my struggles to get out or get below. It was impossible to move; the wave swept over my head; I could feel it clutching and racing past my sides into the cabin below. The moment was desperate.

The tremendous reserve buoyancy of the hull finally forced the cabin-top out of the water with a terrific wrenching heave.

I wrested myself out of the hatch and slammed it to, just in time to see the dinghy seized and carried off out to windward. I grabbed for better shelter as it was brought furiously aboard again, borne on the crest of the following wave. It rammed itself up between the mast and the shrouds, and, watching my chance, I seized one of the lines that were trailing over the deck, and strapped it across the boat as a preventer.

Then I looked aft. There was nothing there. It was as if a giant with a massive sword had razed every fitting down to deck level. The boom gallows had gone; the compass had gone; the mizzen-mast had gone; the bumpkin had gone. The centre of the main boom sagged on deck like a broken wing.

Pieces of broken wood and lengths of wire and line were scattered all over the boat and around her in the water. As I looked, half the mizzen mast poised itself like a battering ram and crashed into the topsides, sending a shiver through the boat from end to end.

Not only was the canvas cover ripped off the skylight, but the metal rods were bent and twisted up in all directions. One more such wave would smash through the hatches and sink the boat out of hand.

There was one last chance—to run off before. Fighting my way to the cockpit, I cast off the lashings and pushed the tiller hard up to windward. I eyed the distorted triangle of the mainsail with mixed feelings, but *Temptress* paid off and gathered way downwind, towing a mass of wreckage still attached to the boat by the mizzen shrouds. This wreckage, acting as a sort of sea anchor, made a 'smooth', flattening out the more dangerous crests.

The situation was still critical but the immediate danger of foundering was shelved—anyway, for the moment. The worst of the seas, however, had to be taken exactly astern; the effect of bringing the wind directly aft, and the violent lurching of the boat, caused the rag of mainsail to smash over in a gybe, scraping half the broken boom across the cabin-top.

Waiting for a crest to pass underneath us, I made a perilous dash forward to cast off the halyard, but to no avail. I kept leaving the helm, to drag frantically on the leech of the sail, but the mighty wind pinned the rope in the blocks and held fast the gaff end against the topping lift. This vicious gybing played such havoc with the steering that I prayed the sail would be torn and blasted into ribbons. But the tough flax endured.

I steered mostly facing astern, half-deafened by the wind. One overtaking wave towered above me; silhouetted in its green transparency, I viewed with surprise and disgust no less than three sombre shapes— sharks waiting for the kill. Those beasts swimming with such nonchalance and ease in their element beneath the crests, as safe in that weather as in a flat calm, made me think: 'I don't belong here. Man was never meant to go to sea. It is only his ingenuity which allows him to achieve the seemingly impossible and survive.' Or was it really some atavistic urge? Having largely divorced himself from nature it becomes a battle between him and her.

One hour passed, then two, and still *Temptress* fled before the storm, pursued by tempestuous waves, angered at being cheated of their prey. After three hours at the helm there was a sudden lull, then the wind came back as hard as ever, but not for long. Lull followed lull; now was my chance. Jerking savagely at the leech to lower the mainsail, I felt the halyards give way and had to duck as the gaff crashed on to the deck. Even then it was no easy job to lash the splintered spar and sail firmly, so violent was the motion.

In an instant, there was not a breath—as if the gale had been cut off with a knife. This total lack of wind was almost catastrophic, as the seas were left without its controlling power, yet seemed to have absorbed its latent malice.

This was the dreaded centre of the storm in which small boats are said not to be able to exist.

22

STORM CENTRE

The centre of that atmospheric whirlpool imparted a hell of motion that entered into my very soul. 'Was there anything, anywhere, that was still, quiet, peaceful? Could I ever have experienced such a thing?' I wildly wondered. 'Had it been in a former life when I had seen, say, a green lawn bathed in warm sunlight?' It seemed a fantasy of another world.

Top-heavy pyramids of waves, provoked to a frenzy by some hidden force, hurled themselves skyward, jostled, collided and whirled in a maelstrom of insanity.

There was a noise, yet no noise. With the demented howl of the wind lost, there remained a stunning pseudosilence in the air. One wanted to shout, but who would dare to shout in that awesome void? The world seemed concentrated in the sound of crushing mighty waters.

Temptress was in imminent peril. The wreckage which had been streaming so conveniently astern, now closed in on the vessel, in an attempt to stove in the hull.

Scarcely knowing where I was—on the deck or overboard—in the flurry of water continually flooding the deck, I feverishly unscrewed a seemingly endless number of shackles until, to my great relief, the broken spars and wreckage drifted away.

As I was lashing down the dinghy more securely, from behind me came a series of cracks like pistol shots; it was the jib. The roller line had chafed away where it was hitched and, in the wild abandon of movement, had flicked itself free. Balancing myself as well as possible on the dizzy platform, I lowered it altogether, unbent it, and stuffed it down through the forehatch. I wanted to have the minimum of resistance exposed to the coming wind.

What was now going to happen? One thing was certain: at any moment—maybe five minutes, maybe five hours—the wind would return and blow even harder than before, and from the opposite direction. The very thought of hurricane winds blowing over that demented sea made me sick with apprehension.

The barometer was sluggish and still inclined to fall. Rain at last ceased, after falling incessantly for sixteen hours. Individual clouds appeared. Away to the south-west a whirling funnel of dark brown vapour writhed and parted. For about five wicked minutes, orange rays of the sun pillared down to the sea. The entire gloomy area took on an unearthly livid hue of mauve and black.

That sunset was an awful thing.

The whole atmosphere was charged with the silent, uneasy flickering of lightning. Surely such devilish sights were not of this world but of very hell itself?

As far as possible all had been done to prepare the vessel for the second bout. My eye ranged round the deck; the dinghy was firmly lashed, there was no chance of the wind catching under the tightly furled canvas, and all my warps had their ends attached to each quarter, ready to throw over in a bight to act as a drogue, if and when it was necessary for us to run before the wind.

Looking up at the mast I debated whether to unreeve all the halyards, but decided against this; I might not be in a fit condition to re-reeve them, when it was all over. The staysail, perhaps, could have been unbent, but one never knows... maybe it would be urgently required to manoeuvre away from land or shoal. The engine, of course, could be discounted; it certainly would not run in those seas.

I made a mental plan that should the mainmast go as well, and should the head wind persist from the Azores, *Temptress* could be worked south under jury rig to reach the Trade Winds, and then run down to the West Indies. My food would be fresh fish from the ocean, and my water from the skies. It would take three or four months, but it was feasible. We were far from beaten yet.

My idea of position was vague; I estimated it to be only thirty miles from Flores, and about ninety miles from Fayal. South-west of this latter island was Princess Alice Shoal—about seventy miles off. Should conditions force me down to this shoal, *Temptress* would have no chance whatever.

Midnight! Yet no sign of the coming wind. The barometer was 29.4 in. and, if anything, still inclined to fall. The boat was leaping about like a cat on hot bricks, but less water was coming aboard; the seas had gained some control of themselves and no longer reared up vertically in mushrooms of insupportable weight.

In spite of the motion, the accommodating Primus heated up some very necessary Scotch broth.

At one o'clock in the morning, the barometer had reached 29.35in. and was steady. With the hot food in me, and the saner atmosphere down below, sudden fatigue possessed me. With the thought that the noise of the wind would awaken me when it came, I rolled into my saturated blankets to get some rest, but too much was impending for me to sleep much.

It was bitterly cold and very wet below. The barometer had been steady for five hours but, at my anxious tapping, seemed inclined to rise.

It was not until dawn, with its dirty grey clouds, that I first looked out, and there they were—fitful puffs of wind and rain—the first deceptive mutterings of the waking monster—180 degrees from the previous direction. There was no escape from a second battle. So be it.

07.00:   *Barometer 29.39in. started to rise. Here comes the wind, and fresher. Blowing against yesterday's swell, which has luckily gone down considerably during the remarkable twelve-hour calm. Weather very thick. Temptress rolling hectically from side to side: the wind rising to a whistle, as she heels back to windward.*

07.30:   *Gale Force.*

Half an hour later the seas were beginning to get serious again. It was blowing full gale force. Struggling out on deck I tipped my warps over the stern in the form of a huge 'U'. The boat was lying as well as could be expected, beam on.

At the end of each hour, increased wind and sea were logged; the barometer reluctantly crept upward, showing how slowly the storm was moving.

At midday the seas were becoming really bad and began to crash aboard with added violence, and more frequently. Then a short lull allowed me to take some photographs of the damage. Unfortunately there was a coloured film in the camera; the conditions were not exactly ideal for colour photography, so these priceless shots were not a success.

That sole lull was short-lived. The wind ripped over the sea and, expanding explosively, renewed the mad fury of the first half of the gale. The wind must have reached its maximum, but all the time the sea built up and up into terrifying proportions. The old swell had now been completely obliterated by this second onslaught.

Then for two hours the barometer remained absolutely stationary. Had the storm stopped its forward motion altogether, or was *Temptress* being sucked along with the storm? Were the seas going to continue to rise in magnitude and destructiveness? The chances of survival seemed to be diminishing.

I have often been happier in my thoughts.

All this time I was watching the seas through the porthole, planning to stay below as long as it was safe.

On that dreaded afternoon, *Temptress* already had been rolled over several times on her beam ends, and whirled away to the leeward in the seething mass of broken crests. I perceived through the port a great tottering, terrifying mass of water rearing up above its fellow waves; it collapsed into ruins with a thunderous roar before disappearing out of my view.

My heart beat wildly; that one wave could have smashed in the hatches, driving us downwards, down to the black marine forests whence there is no return.

I had left it almost too late.

There was barely time for a scribble in the log:

14.30: *Sea serious—must run before it. Hurry.*

23

MARATHON RUN

On reaching the deck, I was aghast at the immensity of the seas, and the pandemonium. The whole surface from horizon to horizon wore an unnatural white. Waves were bigger and more dangerous than when the yawl had received her catastrophic blow. During that very first moment I could see at least three mighty wave-top explosions, under which it would be scarcely possible for a small boat to survive.

The only hope was to give in to the storm; to the best of ability, to run before the wind and sea, cutting down their overwhelming velocity.

I lodged myself in the corner of the cockpit, on the port side, then using the spare headsail sheets, passed a double lashing round my waist and secured firmly to three deck cleats. I had no desire for swimming.

With tiller up, although there was no sail set, *Temptress* paid off downwind; the bow pushed round by the resistance of the mast and rigging, while the stern was held up by the drag of the warps towing in the wake.

Now the boat was before it, the wind was unable to pin her down as before, but the arcs of rolling increased to one hundred degrees and more of included angle.

I had not been at the helm for more than a quarter of an hour, when a giant wave, standing high above the others, approached from dead aft. It came nearer and nearer, roaring, towering right above me, tumbling like a landslide. A solid wall of white water, the crest, seven feet deep, came leap-frogging down the frontal surface like an avenging demon.

The water pooped the boat high above the stern, sweeping up above my shoulders and over my head, tearing over the cabin-top and dinghy, burying everything completely from sight. My beret was lifted right off, and as my head broke through the foam, I could see nothing but the mast, alone, black, rising out of a seeming field of snow. However, the enormous buoyancy of the hull was exerting itself; suddenly the dinghy and cabin-top broke through the surface; water poured off either side in a solid torrent. The hatches, thank God, were still intact.

Grabbing the bilge pump handle I worked it frantically up and down until, to my joy, the bilges were dry again.

Hardly had we recovered from this blow when a similar wave hurled its broken peak upon us, half-burying *Temptress* and leaving me waist deep in water, allowing me to see with amazement and fear that we were travelling at the same speed as all the waves in sight. Wave-riding at twenty-five knots in a hurricane! Had the bow wavered even a few degrees one side or the other, the boat would have been twisted round, tripped up on her keel, and the whole deck would have been shattered into its component parts.

It was not yet over. There was more to come.

There was a sudden jolt as the bowsprit pointed up almost vertically into the sky, and the stern dropped into the cavernous trough. The following wave was a twin, and rushed at *Temptress*, picked her up, and flung her forward as from a giant's catapult. The tiller was vibrating with the fantastic speed of water tearing past the rudder.

Suddenly I had the feeling that the boat was beginning to turn to starboard, but before she actually moved, once again there was that tremendous jolt; the sea tore off ahead of us and we slid down again into the trough. We had escaped our greatest peril.

Hour after hour went by, but there was no sign of easing. Great seas thundered down with endless repetition; *Temptress* performed her seemingly impossible feat of keeping afloat. Time and time again she was buried by pooping seas; each time the fear struck me that the hatches had gone, for I was only assured that they had resisted the impact, when they once again rose clear. At other times the mass of water stayed so long covering us that I thought surely the boat must be breached, and was already being dragged down to her doom.

All sense of time was lost. Daylight had given way to darkness, so it may have been five, six or seven hours after the start of this nightmare run, when another of those monstrous waves caught up the yawl and, like an arrow, hurtled her through the air, wave-riding perilously on the edge of this world and the next—but she steered straight and true.

During that reign of terror there were four waves in all which forced *Temptress* to fly along at a speed out of all proportion to her length; but times out of number she was smothered temporarily by those frightful seas.

It became bitterly cold and I was becoming weaker as the hours ground by, for I had started the run already exhausted. The only respite from the cold was when the warm seas swept up above my waist, but when the water receded the icy blast froze me to the bone.

Shivering fits became more and more frequent. My muscles ached and wracked me through and through. I was bruised and sore, with only the one position possible, lashed down as I was by two stout ropes. These ropes themselves were grazing and cutting into my skin.

Quick judgement and concentration were necessary at the helm to keep the boat dead before the seas, and an added complication came after about ten hours, when my eyes got so encrusted with salt that I became completely blind. This could only be cleared by sucking my fingers and rubbing in spittle. My eyes were soon raw and painful.

Still the wind battered, roared and slapped as I watched fearfully the approach of my unrelenting enemies.

Always to windward was a hateful white 'V' in the clouds, always in the same place, always mocking me in my grave distress. I shouted and swore with every obscenity known to me towards this 'V', but the hours passed and still there was not the slightest sign of improvement. *Temptress* and the gale appeared to be irrevocably locked in embrace by an occult super-imposition of two 'Vs'—the one in the clouds astern and the other cut in the air by the mast swaying to the rampant roll.

I had no idea of the time except that it was dark. Surely night could not last so long?

'I cannot go on,' I cried; but I went on—there was nothing else to do. To stop was death. And I wanted to live.

The pain from my whole body became worse and worse; the strength of my arms was weakening. Time and time again that heavy tiller had to be pushed as hard over as it would go, and with anxiety I would watch the slowness with which the boat would straighten in her course. And all the time to leeward somewhere, perhaps one mile away, perhaps twenty miles away, was that shoal line, right across my path. I could pass over one side of it, but could never come out on the other.

Then a time came when I was so exhausted that I shouted out aloud: 'I am going to stop now—no, not now, five minutes more, and I must stop.' Five minutes passed, and another five minutes, and still another. Where was the dawn that always brings renewed strength? I knew the light alone would give me added power could I but endure.

The skin was beginning to tear off my white and wrinkled hands which had long before lost all sense of feeling. My bare feet pressing hard on the cockpit grating were swollen and caused me agony at every lurch; my back, continually scraping the deck coaming, was bleeding and raw; and over all, that searching, bitter cold. I had reached and passed the limit of my physical endurance; but there remained the will not to fail.

Looking down from a height at those ranges of snow-capped mountains, *Temptress* would scarcely be seen, just her mast oscillating wildly in snowdrifts of heavy foam. The dark hull would occasionally leap upwards out of the water, showing the deck—a mass of broken and splintered wreckage. In your imagination the boat would be unreal, non-existent, like a phantom of the ocean; the helmsman would seem to be a ghoulish apparition—the great wind tearing at his long, wild, matted hair surmounting a gaunt salt-encrusted face and sunken eyes, and as far as you could see there would be only that fearful unutterable sight that filled those painful eyes.

At last it came. My dulled senses were sharpened by a change—the grey light of day, and as the last smudge of darkness was obliterated, that 'V' of cloud to windward melted away as if in defeat.

Looking around me I realised that the seas had grown so enormous that it was no longer possible for the existing wind to build up the water in overhanging crests.

It then became apparent that the wind itself had undoubtedly abated. The flying spindrift was no longer everywhere. Peering as far as I could to windward, there was not one crushing pinnacle of water. It was safe, but only just, to end the hell and lie to. And down to leeward, somewhere, was still that dreaded shoal.

With some trepidation I lashed the helm half down, and waited to see what would happen. *Temptress* slewed drunkenly round and took up a position beam on to the seas. She passed over one, then another, then another, in safety. I could go below.

Casting off the double lashing round my waist, I crept on hands and knees to the hatch and climbed below.

My glazed eyes blinked at the clock—five minutes past six. On top of all the previous day's exertions, I had been fifteen hours at the helm. The barometer had only risen a little over two-tenths in all this time, showing that the tropical cyclone was barely moving.

Peeling off my sodden clothes, and making an ineffectual attempt to dry myself down with a wet towel, I collapsed into my bunk. As I lay on my back and dragged the cold wet blankets up to my chin, I felt my lips crack into a self-satisfied smile. Ah, the luxury! All things are a matter of comparison, and to me this was heaven—to be in shelter out of that terrible wind.

After a few moments of this mental bliss, I tried to turn over on my side, but it was impossible to move; my muscles had given their all; even the uttermost reserve had been drained away.

AFTERMATH

From the time that I collapsed into my bunk, after surviving my ordeal on deck, it took seven hours before my morale recovered sufficiently for me to decide to get up for some very necessary food, but the painful process of climbing out must have taken me ten or fifteen minutes. Any deep breathing or movement of my chest muscles sent a searing pain through my left side. No bone could be seen out of place, but it was obvious that one or two ribs had been fractured against the cockpit locker when I was being thrown forward by the pooping seas. Also I could hardly put my right foot on the deck; two toes appeared to be broken.

The barometer told a depressing tale; it had only risen one-tenth in these seven hours. Would this never end? It was still blowing gale force and very rough; every now and again a heavy sea would crash brutally on to the exposed topsides, squirting cataracts of water below.

I prepared hot porridge and coffee.

During the afternoon, things got momentarily worse. The wind shifted more northerly, and the heavy cross seas were breaking aboard one after another.

Another night fell, but it was still blowing a gale; hazy white cloud covered the heavens. Despite the noise of wind and crash of seas I managed a fair night's sleep, but as well as the bone damage, all my muscles were very stiff and aching, not much improved by the hours lying in wet bedclothes.

Tuesday, 24th Oct:

06.30:   *10,000 curses on this flaming wind: still blowing 7 or 8
          with rough breaking cross seas from N. or maybe N.E.
          Weather clearing slightly but plenty of that indefinite
          white cloud which I have grown to hate so much. This
          is the fourth day. Went on deck to pump out bilges,
          and have only just got below when a sea smashes over
          the stern, fills the cockpit. Water can be heard pouring
          below through lockers, chinks and hatches. Is this
          never going to end? To think last Friday I expected to
          be in Horta on Saturday.*

09.30:   *Very, very bad and violent motion. Check wind
          direction with hand bearing compass. Is N.E. by N.
          Force 7. Now clear and sunny but thick haze all round
          horizon. Barometer 30.06in., almost no movement
          for 3 hours. Wet is so bad below that even dish towel
          hanging free is going black with mildew. My palm
          and little finger of my left hand are still numb. One
          of the bolts through the tiller arm has sheared off and
          disappeared overboard.*

11.40:   *Dragged myself on deck to obtain noon sight—40° 41'.
          Tried to take an accurate sight in the gale but it was
          just a guess, there being no horizon. Terrible motion
          and big seas. This is hateful—hateful—hateful. Four
          days is too long. Food is very short. Half-way through
          last tin of porridge. Then only rice and corned beef
          left. No biscuits. Nothing.*

While on deck in the afternoon, I was concerned to find the after
starboard main shroud broken at the upper splice. It probably went
at the same time as the mizzen. Thank goodness I had not noticed
it before; it would merely have resulted in increased anxiety. In some
pain, I rigged up a jury shroud out of the stout masthead gantline.
Almost at the same time it was observed that all tiller arm bolts had
sheared off. I strengthened it all by screwing on three steel carpenter's clamps.

The boat looked a complete wreck and every lurch sent her farther from port. And the engine? Well, it was designed only to run in smooth water.

In the evening I cooked first some rice, then the miniature radio, over the primus, and dried the latter out sufficiently to get a faint time signal from the B.B.C. on the Brazilian programme.

Through all the last few days, some alteration of wind had manifested itself at dawn or dusk. After a somewhat wild sunset, the wind fell away to a mere good sailing breeze. I retired once more to the pleasures of my bunk, leaving *Temptress* lying to with no lights. If only the engine could have been run the batteries could have been charged and my clothes dried. Before going to sleep I mentally composed an impolite letter to the engine manufacturers.

The hot sun, burning out of a cloudless sky, looked down on *Temptress* rolling lazily to a gentle swell.

Clambering out of the hatch I found it very pleasant to feel the warmth of the sun, and to watch the even turquoise of the sea unmarred by white horses.

A movement in the water showed a dolphin circling round the boat. My eyes gleamed with the anticipation of fresh food; keeping low down on the deck, I prepared my spear to strike. With my heart beating fast, I saw it glide quietly under the bobstay and run parallel with the boat towards me. I lunged forward; the pain in my side making me gasp. The spear splashed and disappeared beneath the surface—too weak.

The warps, still hanging over the stern, were coiled aboard. The creased and sodden staysail was hoisted. *Temptress* crept forward with the light south-easterly wind on the beam. I hobbled about the deck; my right foot was terribly swollen and tender. However, I managed to bend on the jib, clear up the tangle of rigging, and install the spare compass.

The mean of a whole chain of sights taken in the morning and crossed with the noon altitude gave me an accurate position. It was very disappointing. Fayal was no less than 110 miles away to the north-east. But what a joy it was to have the hatches flung wide open, and clothes and blankets baking in the hot sun.

The light breeze petered away to a complete calm; after a painful tussle I managed to start the engine and put it in ahead to cut down the miles to Horta—elusive haven of safety. I found myself quite numb between the shoulder blades, every now and again getting unpleasant tweaks in that region.

Night came. The lack of wind, and the full moon riding serenely over that quiet and beautiful night, made it almost impossible to believe that this was the same stage which had presented the nerve-wracking drama of the previous days.

As I gazed up into the pale sky in which only the brightest stars attempted to rival the light of the moon, a large green meteor floated slowly down near the horizon. It was a splendid and wondrous sight, enhanced by the setting of utter solitude.

25

LANDFALL

The sound of a big aircraft had me tumbling painfully out of my bunk. He circled across my bow—maybe to look at me—and then headed off in the direction of Santa Maria, or at least my calculated position favoured that conclusion.

It was essential to have the boat under control; there was only a gallon of fuel left, after the night's run of twenty-four miles. Sail would have to be set. 'Impossible in your condition,' some might say. They would be wrong. It was possible whatever the pain would be. My damaged ribs prevented me straightening up, and the broken toes caused me agony each time my foot touched the deck. I must hastily add that I am not one of those that think that all things are possible, for that is foolish—many things are impossible. (I remember at my prep school one Sunday in chapel when the theme of the sermon was that all things, absolutely all things were possible, if one had faith. How absurd, thought I, and bending sideways, whispered into the ear of the boy next to me: 'Could a blind man, in a pitch dark room, find a black cat which is not there?')

I was certain that the next gale would finish me, so set to work immediately to get *Temptress* into seaworthy trim, or rather mobile trim, for only a major refit would attain the former state. It took a good many hours, but it was done, not without suffering, and that very afternoon I was filled with pride at the spectacle of my boat sailing along at two or three knots with everything set—full mainsail bent to a patched-up boom, jib, and reaching staysail. At least everything was set, barring the mizzen, which was no doubt still floating as wreckage in the Atlantic.

I wondered if my two lifebuoys with *Temptress* written on them, which had been seized to the mizzen shrouds, would be picked up by some steamer captain who would report me lost.

My first surprise that day was to sight three birds, each with a long tail ending with an unusual knob— harbingers of land?

The second surprise almost petrified me. It was just after three o'clock. I could not believe it at first, but the growing realisation burst upon me like a flood—Land! Land ahead!

Amongst the clouds there was a motionless grey-blue cone, which could not but be the mighty summit of Pico rising above the horizon. I waited for minutes, fearful of some hallucination, but although the clouds were the same colour, the shape of this cone remained unchanging. There was no further doubt—LAND!

It was LAND! It was the greatest thrill of my life! The first land sighted since Long Island, sixty-four days before, with the boat a battered wreck, myself scarcely better, and food almost exhausted.

A single-hander does not have to control his feelings in periods of excitement and, on that incredible day at that incredible hour, I gave full and complete rein to my natural emotions.

Recovering myself, I took a bearing on Pico. It was eighty degrees. Crossing this with the noon sight I plotted my position—sixty-three miles from the cone.

So there were but fifty-six miles to Horta on the island of Fayal—only six miles from Pico, but still well below the horizon.

Such is the wonder of celestial navigation that even after many weeks at sea, and fogs and gales, it was not necessary to alter course one degree to point for harbour.

It was probably raining over the Azores at that time (it usually is), and nearing sunset there came a most curious cloud effect in the form of adjacent windows showing red, green and blue through the frame of a black cloud.

Before the sun had disappeared, there appeared ahead an amazing contrast of indistinct pink and heliotrope, while astern, clear-cut black clouds were set in a pale white sky. The sea, unruffled by the falling breeze, reflected the whole.

Just before darkness shut *Temptress* from their view, the Wind Gods must have peered down on her, and discussed what final form of amusement they could supply before she made port. Having provided plenty of fog, calm, seven gales and one hurricane, interspersed with head winds, they had now been decent in giving me a day of calm to allow me to sort the gear. I was hopeful for a south-westerly breeze, so they sent me a squally wind from the east instead, and a bickering head sea.

> 24.00: *Plunging into dirty sea. Expecting some major part*
> *of the gear to break at any moment. Course should be*
> *E. but am forced to steer N.E. Not even on the final*
> *approach to port will the damned wind be fair. The*
> *broken shroud is, of course, the windward one.*

Dawn broke at six o'clock, and a faint outline of land could be seen to the east—Fayal. There was no sign of the great Pico, which was completely enveloped in cloud.

The port was now dead to windward; the following twelve hours were spent at the helm tacking against the stiff head wind and choppy sea. A cautious mariner would have lowered the mainsail (and drifted away from port), but I cast all caution to the winds and drove her under full sail; it was a hard grind in that confused sea.

I approached the lighthouse on the west point of the island and feasted my eyes on the green and red colouring ashore. It was pretty certain that I had been sighted from the shore, and if dismasted could have counted on help. It was impracticable to reef, as directly the strain came inboard from the end of the boom, it would have broken immediately. Somehow the worn and patched-up gear stood the pounding.

The lack of sleep, and aches and pains besetting me, did nothing to improve my temper, and at each soaking I would swear and shout vile oaths into the unheeding wind. It was enough to make a Saint blaspheme—a head wind to the bitter end.

Working my way along the south side of the island, past a peculiar rock on a point called Castello Branco, at dusk, I was not many miles south of Monte da Guia, a small extinct volcano, breached by the sea.

The wind was beginning to abate, but gusts still swooped down after cannoning off Pico.

I made a long tack until I was certain to weather Monte da Guia, and, tacking ship, headed for the centre of the Fayal Channel, between the two islands. By midnight, *Temptress* was entering the channel, where the unnatural twinkling lights of the port could clearly be seen.

In the middle of the channel the wind, blanketed by the great mountain of Pico, completely evaporated; the resultant kaleidoscopic sea set the spars and gear thrashing wildly. Everything was threatening to come tumbling about my ears. I somehow succeeded in lowering the mainsail.

There was a little fuel left, but I doubted my strength to start the engine. I cleaned the plugs, cleared the carburettor and primed. Down came my foot on the starting handle; to my joy (short lived) the engine broke into life, only to die an instant later. Another prime, another kick, and away she went—erratic, but working. The bowsprit swung round and pointed at the lights.

It was exactly one o'clock on the morning of Saturday, 28th October, when my anchor was let go in the little artificial harbour of Horta. I was safe. Oh! the stillness, the peace, the magic of it all!

26

IN PORT

Surely it was another dream—to be safe in port again. The abrupt change, after nine weeks at sea, was almost too much for me, in my weak condition, to appreciate. My body acted automatically during the whole period of my arrival, driven by a mind of separate entity. I found myself taking a sounding, noting the sandy nature of the bottom, veering more cable to suit the depth. The deck was in a shambles— that could wait.

My legs gave way under me; the cabin-top was handy. I looked dully about me; it was a sight for sea-weary eyes, that little harbour in the dark. There was now not a breath of wind; on one side of me an untidy queue of yellow lights, reflected in the water, stretched a mile or so along the shore; on the other side the long arm of the breakwater was a mere intensification of the darkness; the lighthouse on the end glowed a silent welcome to me.

Giving a shiver of chill I rose slowly and felt my way below. I was so weary, so weary.

I slept soundly for several refreshing hours. Dawn broke with a crash—a crash alongside; it was the Port Captain's launch. Having exhausted all the usual questions as to my voyage, they said: 'We will have to move you. This is the fairway.' Two sailors jumped aboard and started to raise my anchor. The launch towed *Temptress* across the harbour, far too fast; white rocks could be seen flashing in the clear water. These pilots were used to big ships, or their light schooners which lose way rapidly; but my heavy displacement boat charged on with her momentum. My shouts and waves at last had some effect. They reversed the tow, snubbing the yawl round just as she was about to hit bottom. We chased back again into the deeper water. Finally everything was sorted out and *Temptress* was anchored, but rather precariously, I thought, amongst some round boulders. 'Senhors, if there comes much wind, my boat not safe,' I protested, with all the anxiety that a captain has for his boat. It was a pity that the only good holding ground was in the fairway which, anyway, was only used for small craft. 'O.K. O.K. If too much wind, we take you to big buoy.' They sheered off.

Being at anchor was better than being alongside the quay which they had first suggested. Tied to a quay in an exposed harbour, with an incessant swell, was not my idea of fun. In any case, even at the best of times, I detest being alongside; warps need continual attention; dirt blows aboard; people jump down without invitation; and last but not least there is the inevitable 'crowd' destroying any peace or sense of privacy.

Bilge water was up to the deck below*; sitting weakly in the cockpit, I pumped out with one hand, while the other was held against my ribs. This became a regular pastime; it gave plenty of time to admire the scenery.

The sun broke through, revealing the surroundings in all their beauty. Indeed, Horta is best appreciated from the water; the tortuous main street runs all along the shore; the town consists of a scattered jigsaw puzzle of small square houses, some yellow, some blue, but most of them white—white as bones found on the seashore, and with the same salt-roughened texture. The boats at moorings, these houses, a church, the ruins of a castle, all acted as foreground to rolling green hills rising to the interior, and generously brushed with splashes of good red earth.

As to the harbour itself, however much it appeals to the aesthetic senses in fine weather, it is not one of those sheltered nooks safe from all the winds of Heaven—as beloved by seamen. It consists of a massive harbour wall, several hundred yards in length, built north and south. One portion of it is a different colour to the rest—this part was breached by hurricane seas some years ago. Fortunately, Pico

---

*   The author presumably meant the cabin sole—Ed.

prevents any seas coming in from the eastward, but to the south-east there is nothing but the Atlantic Ocean. Yet it is the northerly gale which causes so much damage to small craft; the boat-repairing yards call it a 'carpenter's gale'.

My charts had already informed me that each island of the Azores consists of a mountainous interior (most of them are over 3000 feet) bounded by high basaltic cliffs without, regrettably, any inlets—hence no natural harbours. Actually there are only two harbours of note in the whole archipelago, all 400 miles of it; one is at Ponta Delgada in San Miguel, and the other where I was—Horta, Fayal. Both harbours are artificial, and both have their troubles in certain weather.

A passing motor-boat took me ashore. Limping slowly, on account of my weak legs and broken toes, I made my way along the cobbled main street in search of food. This picturesque quarter looked much as it must have fifty or even one hundred years ago—the gay houses cannot have changed much, and as for the wooden axles of the carts hauled by oxen, well, they creaked and groaned as they had creaked and groaned throughout the ages.

A man made a sign to me and crossed over to my side; he was Senhor Labescat, member of the Yacht Club; he invited me to the Fayal Hotel to eat. I accepted with indecent haste and had a noble repast. Before the fascinated eyes of the waiters, I ate the full four-course meal as well as two plates of bread rolls and a bottle of wine. I had been almost starving. (The next day, I weighed myself; two and a half stone under normal weight, despite this meal.)

Late afternoon found me pumping out the battered yawl again. The clouds had rolled back from Pico, that inspiring mountain with her great cone lifted up in splendour 7613 feet about the sea; one never tires of watching her changing face, whether it is the different shades of colour or the varying formations of the clouds. Pico dominates the lives of the ant-like mortals below, and is a never-ending source of discussion. Its effect on Fayal, which is an island about eleven miles long and seven miles wide, is immense, geographically, climatically and spiritually.

The next morning, the British vice-consul, John Collins, and his wife came down to see what all the rumours were about. He was a short, square-shouldered, rather dapper man in his late forties—the unruffled type of Englishman. He had a somewhat changeable attitude according to which had the upper hand, his sense of humour, or the diplomacy of his calling. He was the greatest help to me and, forthwith, did all a consul should do, and much more. They invited me to celebrate my birthday by having a party at their house, which I did, three days after my entry. His father-in-law was staying with them; in spite of the fact that I once nearly dropped him in the water, and another time nearly broke his arm, he never bore me ill-will.

27

THE AZORES

Before visiting this area of the ocean, I had held the idea that the Azores basked in almost perpetual sunshine, and were caressed by balmy winds. The great gale which had caused me such damage had disillusioned me, and in the first week of my stay it blew another gale, starting from the south-west and gradually working round to the dreaded north.

The panic party arrived as promised. *Temptress* rode out the gale to fifteen fathoms of anchor chain shackled to the big mooring buoy—even then, the kedge anchor, which was secured on the chain half-way between boat and buoy, was often jerked right out of the water. I was marooned aboard as it was too rough to get ashore. Seas and spindrift raked the quays; black sand was whisked off the beach, blown along the main street, and built up in doorways and corners like snowdrifts.

That little lot blew for three days. 'I think your harbour is a little dangerous, Senhors,' brought voluble explanations. The Hortenses are very touchy about the safety of their (to me) dubious harbour. 'But,' they said, 'our port, is it not the best in the Azores? And that gale...' raising shoulders high, '... it is true that we have had nothing like it in twenty-three years.' However, I was not interested in the last twenty-three years. (They had a hurricane a year later.)

Summer in the Azores is said to be perfect, but the other nine months provide weather that is anybody's guess. They have less sunshine than London, and the changing atmospheric conditions rival the British Isles. One can have days of gales and rain, then, without warning, a baking hot day like our mid-summer.

The erratic weather prevailing over the islands is a question of location: it is an intersection of three great weather zones:

(1) the Atlantic sub-tropical anticyclone,
(2) the unsettled westerlies,
(3) the north-east Trades.

The islands can be affected by any one of these or all of them at once. Incidentally, Pico is supposed to act as a weather barometer. Some wags say that if Pico is clear of cloud, it is a warning of bad weather, and if it is cloudy, then it is bad weather.

The depressions that produce the heavy rainfall and excessive wind start off as minor gales running up the Gulf Stream. Some of them break off south of the usual track and head for the Azores where they appear to fetch up against some great air-mass. Their forward motion is arrested but wind blows harder and harder. This is the famous 'stagnant depression' of which the meteorological experts are so fond. 'Stagnant' to me is a misnomer; call it what you like, the best procedure is to hang on to your hat if you are on shore, muttering a prayer for the poor so-and-so's at sea.

If anyone should imagine that I am exaggerating the effect of these storms he has only to watch the newspapers. It was not long afterwards that an old battleship broke its tow and disappeared in this area. Nobody seemed to be able to think where it had gone. I could have told them—to the bottom—capsized by the force of the wind, after a series of gigantic waves had built up one final catastrophic roll.

While my strength slowly came back and my bones mended themselves, I amused myself with short rambles over the countryside, working lightly on the boat, and catching up with my reading, the latter mostly to find out more about these islands which I had so unexpectedly taken unawares.

It is not difficult to visualise the discovery of the Azores in the fifteenth century. A Portuguese trading vessel, possibly trying to beat round Finisterre, got caught in a gale from the north-east, and had to run or founder. Day followed day and still the wind blew; but just when the crew were becoming resigned to a slow death by thirst or starvation, they were electrified by the age-old shout 'Land O!'

The central and eastern groups were settled on, but it is quite extraordinary that the group comprising Flores and Corvo were not discovered till many years later; they are only 120 miles off Fayal. It makes one wonder whether discoveries were often due to chance and not to daring and initiative. One would think that, in this case, these hardy mariners would have ranged out to the west for a day or so to see if anything lay beyond, a simple matter in summer time.

There is a remarkable book, with a copy of the original manuscript held in the British Museum, dated 1593, written by G. Fructuoso, containing a vast amount of information not only about the Azores, but also about Madeira, Cape Verde and Canary Islands—oh, happy Fructuoso! I am sure that he was a great enthusiast, and in a job after his own heart.

Back to the present. Nature was looking after my bodily ills, but stronger action was required to cure *Temptress*. I had first dallied with the idea of remaining in Fayal for the whole winter, refitting and repainting the boat, before continuing to England. But this was soon dispelled when I ascertained that the steamer came only once a fortnight, and that importing gear and supplies took impossibly long owing to red tape (everything had to go to Lisbon). It would have been summer before I would have received them.

I decided to do a temporary refit, enough to make the boat seaworthy, and sail for Gibraltar. The immediate problem was to place the yawl clear of the water in order that the frightful leak could be stopped; it was in the sternpost. The local schooners are hauled ashore every night—a practice much to be recommended in an area afflicted with superabundance of wind and paucity of harbours. For *Temptress* this was not practicable owing to her deep draught and the feeble range of tide.

There was a huge electric crane newly installed at the inner end of the harbour wall. It was all nicely painted in red and supposed to lift fifty tons (*Temptress* weighs fourteen tons); so the problem would seem to have been solved. However, either someone had forgotten to attach the motor or there was not enough electricity, for it did not work. Nevertheless, this put the helpful and enthusiastic islanders on their mettle; 'Here is a boat,' they said, 'that must be lifted on to the quay. Esta bem. Pronto! We will lift her on to the quay!'

The Portuguese may often be short of materials or equipment, but they are wonderful improvisers, and most likely a completed job will be stronger than normal. They are apt to overdo it sometimes. I remember a huge sheave chock, twelve inches by three inches, which the carpenter riveted to the top of the mizzen mast, and which had to support only a light line for the lift of the tiny boom; the chock looked big enough to upset the boat's stability—but I had not the heart to ask them to change it.

The great day for lifting the boat on to the quay dawned bright and calm. From the anchorage I could see swarms of men surrounding the crane. The hook was festooned with a Heath-Robinson arrangement of rusty chain purchases reputed to be stamped ten tons (I had been told fifteen).

For me it was an anxious and exasperating day. It started off by João and Antonio trying to break out my anchor, which had caught round a heavy mooring chain, by brute force. I came up from starting the engine to find the bows pulled down by the anchor chain which was stretched like an iron bar—ominous creaking came from the windlass. Fools! It took the united efforts of the three of us to get in the quarter of an inch necessary to allow us to throw back the pawl. By letting out quantities of chain we dragged the anchor clear; but it was bent two inches out of true.

The actual lift to the quay caused some harrowing moments. Added superficial damage made *Temptress* look more battered than ever. But the job was at last done, and repairs started.

I left the boat and slept ashore, for I had received a welcome invitation from one of the English members of the Eastern Telegraph Company, Brian Moorhouse, to stay in his bungalow, and to share his magnificent view of Pico.

It was on his lawn, while I was relaxing in a deck chair under a hot sun, with a glass of local wine at my side, that faint but insistent stirrings in my brain made me conscious of 'peace of mind'. 'Can it be possible,' I wondered, 'that one day my restless nature will be satisfied and permit me to live happily and contented in one place?'

Each morning after breakfast I would walk along the main street on my way to the boat. 'Too much goddam wind,' Faria would shout from the Pilot House.

'Finish work quick,' another would shout, 'a gale from the south-east and your boat, poof!' raising his arms in an extravagant and expressive gesture. He was disappointed, though occasionally lumps of water would be lobbed over the wall on to the deck.

Then Henrique, of the Café Sport, sitting lazily in his doorway, would give me a sly wink. At the last moment before departure he was to give me a packet of food, which turned out to be far more appreciated than he ever expected.

Then as I passed the workshops of Fayal Coal Co., old man Costa would come waddling slowly out, blinking through his glasses, smiling a query at me while holding possibly some broken part of *Temptress*, or a sketch on the back of an envelope, wanting to settle some doubt of what was required. His engineering shop was an everlasting source of entertainment—his merry men would tackle anything—casting, forging or welding. The skilled blacksmith would turn out a perfect job without ever looking at a plan, or even hearing about it—for he was both deaf and dumb.

Old Costa, himself, is a genius, his light hidden under the proverbial bushel—an engineering wizard. He would just as soon undertake to repair a damaged merchant ship (indeed he did 'impossible' jobs during the war) as cast you a new cylinder head for your old car. He would probably make you a new engine if you asked him—and design it as well. His opposite number on the wood-working side was soft speaking Manuel de Silva, and I could not have wanted a better man to see to my new spars, and repairs to the sternpost and rudder. The remains of the old mainboom served for a mizzen boom and bumpkin, while an old forgotten log, covered with dust and cobwebs, was fashioned into a gleaming new mainboom.

A new mizzen mast was offered me by José Christiano de Souza. In one of the fast diesel launches Moorhouse and I crossed the five-mile channel to Pico, and spent some hours with him to select a suitable spar and examine his whale factory. A fine spruce pole was found, just the right length and thickness, but doing duty as a clothes prop—we took a photograph of the washing.

The whale factory was interesting but a trifle overpowering as regards odour. There was one whale half cut up, and we could see another one being towed in. Whaling in the Azores is still the he-man stuff of old; not for them steel ships armed with guns—they row into the attack in the traditional whale-boats, narrow, open, with a crew of seven, and get fast to the big fish by hand harpoon—ready for a hectic ride. Fast motorboats tow them out. On shore a watcher is always at the look-out post.

28

SHORE ADVENTURES

Brian Moorhouse and I had taken the early morning launch to Pico, so, with the business of the new mizzen mast satisfactorily settled, there was still plenty of time to take advantage of the rare cloudless day. We decided to make a tour around the whole island, a seventy-mile circuit.

A car, complete with piratical looking chauffeur, was hired at off-season rates. Off we went—in a clockwise direction. Up steep hills, across valleys—sometimes one thousand feet up, sometimes at sea level, always amidst colourful scenery. Often we would cry halt, and start walking, telling our driver, Pedro, to follow after us in twenty minutes. At one place we stopped, the view was breath-taking. To the north, the horizon was hidden by the browny grey island of San Jorge, long, precipitous, clusters of white dots indicating villages. The wide channel was dark blue; from above the sea looked still. On our side there were two black shapes of fishing-boats, like toys. Five hundred feet below us was the jagged shoreline, white flashes growing and fading at the death of each swell. The foreground consisted of green and red shrubs growing on black lava which had solidified into fantastic shapes two hundred odd years ago. Behind us rose the quiescent volcano itself—the last eruption had been in 1720. The hot sun threw the most grotesque shadows of the misshapen whorls and spurs of lava—a scene that would be changed to evil without the benign influence of this sun.

The driver went up at a moderate speed at first, although he had the disconcerting habit of twisting right round in his seat to speak to us, usually at a corner.

We stopped at Prainha for rest and wine. Thereafter Pedro drove somewhat faster.

We stopped at Calhao Gordo for rest and wine. Pedro drove faster still.

We stopped at Villa das Lagens for rest and lunch.

'Pedro,' we said, 'no more wine.'

'No. No. Never, Senhors!' he expostulated. But there was a whole carafe of the raw local wine in front of him at the table.

Never once did we see him touch it, yet, miraculously, each time we looked the level of the red liquid had fallen. We watched in vain to catch him. Ah! he was an artist, that one.

Our crude wooden chairs scraped on the stone floor as we stood up to go. We looked. There was no wine left!

Pedro, swaying slightly, bowed us out, a huge grin spread right across his flushed countenance.

Brian and I looked at each other apprehensively. 'Come on,' he said, 'there's only twenty miles. It'll soon be over.'

'Yes. It'll soon be over,' I said, 'One way or the other.' We solemnly shook hands and got in.

The car jolted forward, flinging us back in our seats. The interesting return drive had commenced. Five minutes elapsed. Five miles less. We were still alive.

'It is better,' said Brian, 'to close the eyes just before each corner.'

He was right.

The speedometer was in kilometres per hour, which made it seem even worse. The needle swayed back and forth alarmingly near the hundred mark. The road was narrow and twisting.

Carts, houses, people would appear suddenly ahead for a fleeting instant, rush towards us and vanish. Astern great billowing clouds of dust swirled high enough to affect the weather reports. Then, across the channel, Horta came into view.

'I believe we'll make it,' I said. Four minutes later the car stopped with a screech of tyres. It was Magdalena, and the ferry. We got out, both wobbly at the knees, and breathing deep sighs of relief. Do not believe anyone who says sailing across the Atlantic is not dangerous—if you stop at Horta!

The authorities, members of the Yacht Club, were generous and helpful to a high degree—as indeed was everyone with whom I came into touch.

On the language side, my not too fluent Spanish got me by, although I had great difficulty in understanding them—I will have more to say about the Portuguese pronunciation.

There was a little trouble with the Customs. The smaller a country is, the more absurd are the regulations enforced. Perhaps it is because the smaller the frame the greater the importance things are apt to assume. My first brush with the Customs was when I tried to take ashore my broken tiller for repair. I was stopped. Such a thing was forbidden without a special permit! Fuming, and thinking of the hundred and one things that would have to go back and forth to the repair shops, I marched off to see the Consul. We visited the Customs Headquarters. Alves da Cunha could not have been more helpful, and special orders were issued forthwith. There was no more trouble.

In return, when repairs had been completed, I asked da Cunha if he would like to join in a trial sail. He accepted at once, also suggesting bringing a girl friend. It sounded a grand suggestion. Off we went for a short sail, out of the harbour and back—three men and a girl. She was called Otilia, and added lively fun to the sail, but it must have been quite a sensation for Horta, where a girl may hardly breathe without a chaperone in attendance.

A party of us drove right round the island one fine afternoon—a decidedly more peaceful jaunt than the previous road race round Pico. We climbed the lip of the crater (most of the way in an inevitable jeep), and peered down to the three lakes 2000 feet below. The island was beautiful but it was too late in the year to see in flower the banks of blue hydrangeas, which line both sides of the roads.

The general populace lives in a roughish way, but feeds well on meat and vegetables—not much mutton but plenty of beef. Most people have a side line to their main jobs, such as fishing, whaling or farming. On one of my climbs up the hill to the bungalows in the evening I was surprised to meet one of the Port Captain's crew leading a large cow.

'Your cow?'

'Si, si, Senhor, my,' he returned, with a flash of white teeth in his swarthy features.

It transpired that most of them have a cow, much as we might have a dog.

Petrol, or any imported fuel for that matter, was a terrible price, but there was plenty of one source of power—wind. On the crest of most hills there were windmills—on the high land to the north of the harbour there were half a dozen, one of which carried, instead of the usual square sails, a number of triangular ones. This must be about the only Bermudian-rigged windmill in the world.

There is no airstrip on Horta, which makes communications bad by modern standards. One airmail letter I wrote to London took over a month to get there. The lack of landing facilities does not stop emergency medical supplies being flown over, and one evening there was great excitement when a small aeroplane swooped low over the harbour and dumped a large package on the quayside.

Gossip and intrigue form the major part of conversation, but apart from this there is, of course, the weather and what Pico is doing, any unusual happening in the harbour (the fortnightly steamer is a great event); and then there may even be a small earthquake to discuss.

Several times during my stay, earth tremors made the ground rock and vibrate. The last real earthquake was about twenty-five years previously; they told me another was about due. During the tremors one has the false impression that the crust of the earth is only a few inches thick, and one may fall through.

It has been my idea for many years, and it always has amazed me that pretty well nothing has been done to tap the illimitable source of energy of molten lava, at our very doorstep, so to speak. The central heating at Reykjavik, Iceland, is a tapping of the natural hot springs, but that seems to be all. So if anyone wishes to become a millionaire, develop the harnessing of subterranean energy. You have my idea, free, gratis and for nothing.

Apropos of nothing, as early as 1940 I thought of the war expedient of pumping fuel across the sea by flexible pipes on the ocean bed;

I received official thanks. A couple of years later this very same idea from someone else was placed before Winston Churchill; it formed the basis of the fuel supply to the invasion forces. (I know that the above is hardly relevant to this account of my Atlantic adventures, but what's the point of writing a book if you cannot record what you want?)

*   *   *

Now where was I? Ah, Yes. On the quay, hoping the weather would hold. In short—it did not. On the night and morning of the day fixed to drop *Temptress* back into her true element, it blew a fierce gale from the south-east. This was not too bad as the harbour is sheltered from this quarter. Then the wind dropped to nothing.

All laughed at my fears of a northerly gale. 'The gale,' they said. 'Why, it is finished. Look. Here comes the sun.' But my barometer told me it was the centre of the depression.

The stern was manoeuvred over the edge of the quay, to ship the rebuilt rudder, but the job took longer than expected. It was just on dusk when a shower of rain was followed by a burst of wind—from the worst quarter—north. The very unexpectedness of it threw some of my helpers into a panic. The crane-master thought of nothing but his precious crane, and to hell with my boat—I thought of nothing but my precious boat, and to hell with his crane.

'Lower away,' he screamed to the men.

'Keep her on the quay,' I shouted, but any support I might have gained from the audience disappeared in the wind and rain. Down the boat came, nearer and nearer, until she was plunging violently— the waters whipped up into a frenzy by the gale.

Immediately the crane hook was clear, bedlam was let loose. Warps parted as soon as they were made fast. Some hero, however, kept his head, and, just when it appeared certain that *Temptress* was going to be battered and sunk by the stone quay, a heavy warp miraculously materialised, leading from the nearest lighter. We were dragged clear. In the raging darkness the yawl was moored, all fours, between the lighter and the quay—temporarily safe.

It blew for two and a half days. My boat received considerable damage. The steel mainsheet horse, newly repaired, was pulled in two; the bowsprit driven inboard by a drifting launch; the mizzen chainplates torn off; and all along both sides extensive scars told the sorrowful story. *Temptress* was merely one of a number.

The carpenters rubbed their hands and grinned. It had been a wonderful gale.

*   *   *

The yacht club boat was now laid up, luckily, so I was offered their moorings, of massive chain. It is a fact that a boat is only safe, in the harbour, if it rides to moorings out of all proportion to its size. Even the owners of big launches prefer to have men aboard, or even to cruise round and round during a gale from the north.

Temptress, alas, leaked worse than ever and there she was, afloat it is true, but showing more damage than before she was landed. Feeling very depressed, I pumped her dry, and dolefully sought the bungalow and Brian's commiseration. After a couple of gins the problem took on a more cheerful aspect.

The next day was fine and bright. To my joy the boat had taken up. Three days after launching she hardly leaked a drop, nor has she since to this very day.

Work then became constructive rather than destructive; the new mizzen mast was stepped, new spars came aboard, and new or repaired fittings were installed. Sails were bent by Christmas Day—by that time I was living aboard again—and the first sail took place on December 31st, exactly nine weeks after arrival.

The two jolly teen-age daughters of Mr. Payne, the Manager of the Cable Company, used to use *Temptress* as a bathing base and sport themselves overboard if the sun was shining. When there was no sun they used to polish the brass. What a difference below when the clock, barometer and stoves are shining bright.

Unfortunately, even on a calm day *Temptress* used to move in the swell, making one of them 'incommoded'. So the brass was allowed to dull after all.

Nothing can be kept secret at Horta. One day the most unlikely people came up to inform me that there was fifty pounds waiting for me to collect. Everyone knew but me! Perhaps that is why my bill came to fifty pounds. But if they took every penny in my pocket I was still very grateful, because a bill for double this amount would not have been unreasonable.

My sentiments were deeply genuine when, shortly before departure, I wrote to His Excellency the Governor, the Port Authorities and the Yacht Club to thank them for their co-operation and help. On my part, maybe my visit had caused them interest and pleasure. To what wide extent the *Temptress* episode was going to interest them I could not then foresee.

My unheralded arrival had been a sensation, but my now historic departure was going to shake the islands to their very foundations.

29

UNTOWARD DEPARTURE

A trial spin outside the harbour in a squally wind showed that *Temptress* was ready for sea. Senhora Faria, the pilot's pretty wife, cooked me some biscuits to add to my two weeks' stores. I gave out that my departure was 'any day now'; no definite date this time; it leads to trouble. A gale brews or a head wind blows—the date comes and goes; one is met with 'Not gone yet?' in reproachful tones which seem to indicate a personal slight.

I had secretly decided to drop moorings early the morrow morning, and sail for San Miguel, 150 miles to the east. From there I could wait my chance to continue to Madeira, and thence to Gibraltar.

The Port Captain was warned; he would come out to take a photograph. Good. One never seems to have a decent picture of one's own boat under sail.

I spent the last evening with Brian, then gave an evasive round of good-byes. After collecting an enormous bunch of bananas from the Paynes at Fredonia, I hurried down to the harbour and rowed out in the darkness; clambering aboard, I immediately started preparations for an easy getaway.

By the time that the dinghy was lashed down, sails were ready to hoist, and a stout slip line was rove through the ring of the mooring buoy, it was eleven o'clock. It was a period between gales, but, better still, there was a rare north-west wind which, instead of dropping as it usually does at nightfall, continued to gush down from the hills, making the yawl surge fretfully as if eager to be off.

A fair wind—a wind one must never waste. To go or not to go? The real question was, to sleep or not to sleep? But it was a problematic sleep; my mind was too full of anticipation.

One hundred and fifty miles, and five knots! Why, we would be in San Miguel in thirty hours; Ponta Delgada would be made in daylight after the loss of only two nights' sleep. It took me about a quarter of an hour to make up my mind for an immediate start; but really, as in all these cases, it was a foregone conclusion. In my heart of hearts there was no real intention of wasting a fair wind. It was just self-indulgence to dally.

Getting away from moorings single-handed, when there is no tide, is a delight, even on a pitch dark night. One can first hoist the mainsail, and, disregarding the shaking and slatting canvas, have plenty of time to coil and stow the halyards.

Lashing the tiller over to port, I waited until *Temptress* surged to starboard, then quickly let go the slip rope and pulled it aboard; it took only a couple of seconds to unroll the jib; she heeled sharply and gathered forward speed towards the harbour entrance. The helm steadied her course. Up staysail. Up mizzen. We were off.

If there was to be no sleep for me that night why should others get away scot free? Twice I sounded four loud blasts on the fog siren. A few would understand but for the majority, when they woke up in the morning, we would just have disappeared as unexpectedly as we had arrived. That is how I like it. Nobody saw me come; nobody saw me go.

The wind was squally in the Bay. *Temptress* skidded round the end of the breakwater, gybed viciously on to her correct course, and began to lift immediately to the ocean rollers.

Farewell, Horta.

The lights were being extinguished one by one as the promontory of land cut them off from view. A sudden shout, and close, clove the darkness: 'Boa Noite, Senhor'. A returning fishing-boat. My reply echoed through the night. We were soon past and the dark blob disappeared astern. My last contact with Fayal had been broken. I was alone once more.

Clear of the island, the wind settled down to a good sailing breeze from the north-west, while a big swell lifted *Temptress* high, sending her foaming through the water in a series of rushes. The course was south of the direct route in order to avoid the blanketing effect of Pico, and to bring the wind more on the quarter, giving more speed and making the boat easier to steer. Later I would gybe and head eastwards for port.

A grey dawn showed the islands well astern, surrounded by massive lumps of drab cloud. We rushed on. The needle of the log completed its first revolution. I was in need of a hot cup of coffee to warm me after the cold and cramped hours at the helm. I was just watching the seas chasing us, and judging whether they would allow me a dash below to light the stove, when a movement at the hatch caught my attention. I started. Then my heart rolled over in momentary fear at the sight a of clutching hand, followed by a frightened white face half-hidden by straggling black hair.

Unbelievingly I stared; open-mouthed; speechless.

It was the girl Otilia—the one who had come on the trial sail.

In an instant, alarm turned to wild anger, and I shouted and spluttered at the apparition until the triple realisation came over me that she could not understand, half my anger was due to the previous fright, and that I was making rather a fool of myself. I subsided into mutterings.

All this time she remained half out of the hatch, eyes wide, motionless, like some wild creature trapped without hope.

My mind switched suddenly to Horta; Santa Maria! The commotion exploding, the Port Authorities, the populace, the British Consul! My sense of humour triumphed over everything. I just gave myself up to shouts and shouts of laughter, motioning her to come to the cockpit. But she still did not move. A long time later, she told me that she thought I had gone mad, and feared for her life.

A wave splashed on deck. The boat was right off course; it broke the spell. I spoke quietly to her in Spanish; she climbed awkwardly out of the hatch and sat beside me in the cockpit. Frightened. Silent. She gave me a fleeting smile.

'What is your name?' I asked.

'Otilia Frayao.' By the time I had pronounced this correctly, we were laughing together.

An extraordinary discussion followed, complicated by the language set-up.

'Why did you come?'

'To go England.'

'I am not going to England.'

No reply.

'I take you San Miguel?'

A flood of Portuguese followed this statement, with a hint of tears in her eyes. I felt I had been an awful cad and hastily changed the subject.

Conversation followed for about half an hour without my making a definite decision. This conversation was carried out in Spanish, French, English and Portuguese, in that order of importance.

It is a peculiar thing that any Portuguese can understand Spanish but no Spaniard can understand Portuguese. This is due to the widely different pronunciation. Spaniards have the sense to pronounce the words as they are written, while Portuguese differs very much from the written word (as does English). For instance, how can a race expect a foreigner to learn their language if they pronounce 'oes' as 'oynch'!

There was one thing I was definitely not going to do and that was attempt to beat back against such a wind and sea to Horta. In fact, there would be no point. It would help neither my (not too welcome) stowaway nor me.

The main decision was whether to call in at San Miguel or Madeira; at either place she would presumably be taken ashore and sent back to Horta, where life would become so unbearable that she would probably commit suicide...

In a country where it is against social convention for a man to take a girl, unchaperoned, to a place as public as a cinema—even in broad daylight—what would be the reaction to a girl who had committed the terrible sin of 'being alone with a man' and 'at night'?

To gain time and quiet her obvious distress, I said that my verdict would be reserved until I could think more, and judge her behaviour. Her whole life lay in the palm of my hand. It was not a time for hasty decisions.

A gentleman should not take advantage of a girl, nor should a gentleman refuse any request from a lady. Therefore, strictly speaking, I could not refuse to take her to Europe…

Although feeling sick and apprehensive, the girl not only offered to take the tiller, but did so.

I altered course to the south, explaining that the large S on the compass card must be kept near the black line (the lubber line). I pointed out the position of the sun, impressing on her that, as the bows swung to and fro, it must never appear right ahead, or terrible things would happen. This unusual explanation seemed to have the desired effect, for she handled the boat reasonably well, although she had had no previous experience, and the boat was yawing downwind before a breaking sea.

Somewhat dubiously, I left her and went below, feeling that she had gained one good mark. I needed sleep, but stood undecided, fearing that she would gybe the ship.

My brain was racing uncontrollably with this unexpected development, so it was doubtful if sleep could come to me, in any case. I stole a look, through a gap in the hatch, at my stowaway. She was not tall; slim, I remembered, for she was now swaddled up in various clothes, including a coat of mine which was far too big.

With the sun's rays falling on her small head, it was an ideal chance to study her features. Her black hair was swept loosely back and was being blown about with the wind. She had large brown eyes accentuated by a small nose. Her full lips were pressed together in concentration. It was her lips that expressed her transient emotions. Her rounded chin hinted at determination, but of no aggressive quality. Generally her main characteristics of large dark eyes and olive skin, slightly flushed, were typical of the beauty which we associate with the Latin races.

My luck had evidently changed—but which way?

Finally I rolled into my bunk, conscious of the boat's course by watching a sunbeam spotted through the port. In agony my eyes would follow this light as it crept almost out of sight, and I was ready to jump up to prevent a disastrous gybe, when, no, the little circle of light would gradually work its way back to its proper position. She was steering well. Some of the blood of the old Portuguese navigators must run in her veins.

Sleep had seemed out of the question, but a minute later I was deep in slumber.

30

DECISION

After several hours below, I rejoined Otilia in the cockpit, with the intention of trying to dissuade her from continuing. It was the only fair thing to do. I did my best to point out to her that it was now the worst month in the year as regards bad weather and cold; it was going to be very rough, very wet; there was only proper food for little more than a week, then she would have to live on rice; the boat would have to be driven day and night, which would mean that she would have to take the helm while I slept, and then cook meals below to sustain me during my much longer hours at the helm. It was a grim picture.

Women have some queer reserves of bravery; she just shrugged her shoulders (a mannerism of hers) as if all these horrors were a matter of course. I suppose after her tremendous decision to leave home in such extraordinary circumstances, and to trust herself to a total stranger, all the rest seemed of very minor importance. It was all very trusting and naive; but then nature loves rough wooing.

On the basis of her attitude, there was no other alternative but to go on. Who was I to ruin someone else's life? Besides so many coincidences had occurred to allow her to get aboard in the first place, that I felt it would be challenging Fate herself not to help with her plan.

I turned to her and said, dramatically, 'I will take you direct to Gibraltar.' If I expected any great show of emotion, I was disappointed; a slight shrug again, an imperceptible movement of the lips which might have been 'Thank you', and that was all.

She had a friend living in Gibraltar, with whose help we could get her papers straightened out, and she could then carry on to England under her own steam. To my great relief she had a passport, having received it, if you please, the very day of our departure.

'How many years have you?'

'Twenty-four.'

I thought she was pulling my leg. Surely, I thought, she cannot be more than eighteen, but, sure enough, she showed the date of her birth on the passport. Must be right. I felt a bit better then, somehow. I cannot imagine why. It seemed a big improvement to have a girl of twenty-four on board rather than one of eighteen, although there is no reason why it should make the slightest difference.

Meanwhile, *Temptress* scurried south—surprised at the change of course, but seeming to accept the circumstances in a casual manner.

So adaptable is the mind that even after only a day it seemed quite normal to me to have a girl on board. It was just our own business and the rest of the world became exceedingly remote.

The jostling seas crowding up astern were not enough to splash the decks but Otilia gazed apprehensively to windward:

'This sea bad?'

'No, not very bad,' I replied. 'And it will get better later on.'

I smiled inwardly. She was going to learn something about whether the seas were bad before the trip was over.

It transpired that when the girl had first climbed aboard in the darkness from a small boat and whispered a last farewell to her accomplice she had gone into the fo'c'sle, pulled the spare sails aside (which were always kept in the cot hinged up at forty-five degrees), crept in between and lain cramped in that uncomfortable and restricted space. Evidently she had at first intended to stay there for two days, but the motion upset her so much that she decided to give herself up, hardly caring what happened. Sea-sickness has that effect, as every victim knows.

Actually it was a lucky thing for her that she did not stay in her hiding-place for, had she done so, she would probably have emerged just as we were entering San Miguel's harbour. The attack of nausea was another coincidence to add to all the others.

'Momenta,' I said to her, and went below and forward to see what could be done to make the fo'c'sle more habitable. Having hinged the cot down, I added a pillow and a couple of blankets, more comfortable than the rough sailbags.

There was a large parcel stuck in with the sails. Evidently her luggage. I went aft again to ask her what she had brought with her. For a poetess who had never left her little island, except for the short trip across to Pico, she had been amazingly practical. She had come aboard wearing slacks and a jersey, and the parcel included one suit of shore-going clothes, a bathing costume, toilet articles and a Portuguese-English dictionary, which latter seemed to be the height of forethought.

She went up further in my estimation.

31

THOUGHTS

Our first noon to noon run was 132 miles; this was sailing. During the afternoon the weather broke out into a rash of squalls. Two turns were rolled up in the boom—it was child's play with somebody else at the helm.

At dusk I myself took the helm, ready for a long night's trick. Otilia went below, leaving me alone with my thoughts, such a jumble of thoughts to the pattern of which the shapeless dark presented an inscrutable face, while *Temptress* sped on her way bearing now two entities instead of one.

At least one conclusion had been reached—Otilia Frayao would stay—anyway, till the next port of call on the mainland; that was certain now. My mind, freed from the fretful bonds of indecision, ventured on a disturbing variety of possibilities.

What strange trick of fate had sent this girl stowaway to me—to me of all people! In Britain some had dubbed me 'Woman-hater'. Heaven knows why. The title is a myth that grew around me, due, possibly, to the fact that I have generally been too busy and engrossed in preparations for my ocean passages to have time left for the normal sociabilities which form the life of an (almost) eligible bachelor.

Since a very early age, in fact so early that it is impossible for me to remember just when the idea was formed, my one dominant ambition has been to traverse the world single-handed in a small sailing-boat. For me, there has been no other true love but the sea, for it is only out there, alone, that a yearning inside me is satisfied, and the oneness of Nature and the oneness with the infinite becomes a conscious feeling, so that the pain and sometimes agony of hardship is seen merely as the negative field of which the joy of achievement is the positive. For myself, a nobody, I seek neither fame nor riches, but freedom, a spiritual need, for which I would give my life. Without freedom there is no life, just a physical existence of the body.

This then was my singleness of purpose which had induced me to decline the most tempting offers of companionship on various stages of my travels, and, earlier still, had prompted me to refuse no less than offers of marriage. I can never be happy till my ambition is freed from my system, and have long since decided to be ruthless with any hindrance to my destiny. Was this now to be upset because a beautiful girl had dauntlessly, and just as determinedly, crept aboard and hidden herself under my spare sails?

What difference was a stowaway, and a female one at that, going to make to me? Her help could certainly make life easier on board—but then, did I want life made easier? If this was so I would not have chosen the rough path of the single-hander. And yet, and yet, already, a change had come, for I would have resisted strongly any attempt to take her away from me. Could her warm presence now possibly spoil me for my future single-handed trip around the world?

Those thoughts would not be disciplined—they marched, counter-marched, jostled in confused, increasing circles, both sublime and ridiculous. They then turned to my friends in England and America, and how they would laugh at the inevitable romanticised journalese. But mostly my thoughts were of Otilia herself. What courage it must have taken to leave everything she knew, to face an unknown world and future which she hoped would hold greater things for her than could be encompassed in that small island of Fayal. And how did she feel when, cramped in her restricted hiding place, half smothered by evil smelling sails, she had heard the unmistakable sounds of my preparations for departure? Did she have a last minute impulse to leap overboard and swim ashore to safety and security? And having mastered such impulse, did she shake a little with apprehension as the yawl gathered speed? Or did her heart thrill with excitement that the great adventure had begun? I remembered all those people, strong men some of them, who had told me their 'I wish...' stories, and who had sullenly lamented the destiny that had tied them to one particular place or job. And now? It had been left to a slip of a girl to put them all to shame. She, too, had wished, but had not been content with aimless wishes. She had acted, in a most original and courageous manner, to further her ambition. My admiration for her was great, even though her scheme had interfered with my own plans. Nonetheless, I commended her to the special department of Guardian Angels who must surely look with benevolence on such a fearless soul.

I knew only too well how very small a small boat can be, and wondered how we would fare in the weeks we would have to be together. We knew nothing of each other. For two complete strangers to be flung together in that confined space is a prospect at which most would hesitate. Old and tried friends have been known to loathe each other within a week of close proximity in a small yacht. It has caused the break-up of more than one marriage. Perhaps then total strangers would have better luck… I pondered on how she would react to the inevitable lack of privacy, and cast about in my mind for ways and means of easing the situation.

Thus I mused throughout the long night—one moment warmed by the prospect of the voyage with such an attractive companion, and the next torn with doubts. Over all was a faint but steady feeling of anxiety, for in making the final decision to accept the stowaway, I had automatically shouldered a responsibility both in actuality and morally—for had I not, by my action, severed the last possibility of her returning to her old life? For a time at any rate, apart from myself, she would be completely alone in a new and strange world. Imagine being acquainted with only one person, and that person unknown! For weeks to come I was to be everything to her. By coming aboard she had renounced her all and put her faith in one man, with nothing more than her intuition and generosity of mind to guide her.

I have tried not to betray her trust.

At the first chill light of dawn I banged energetically on the deck, and after a time Otilia, looking far from cheerful, and wondering what on earth had induced her to embark on such a crazy escapade, took over the helm, with scarcely a word.

I went below to snatch a few hours' sleep. Cold and weary I

turned into my bunk to find it warm. Motion during the night had got so bad that Otilia evidently had forsaken the fo'c'sle and retired into my bunk. To come down from a cold watch to a warm bunk was an excellent idea, and at sea the best arrangement; the fo'c'sle is almost untenable in rough weather, and the settees in the saloon have no bunk-boards. I had not suggested anything to the unknown factor about the most practical sleeping plan, but she had come to the same instinctive conclusion.

The matter was not mentioned between us, but I wondered what they would have said at Horta.

*   *   *

It was Otilia Frayao's second day at sea, and she wrote:

> I have a feeling of non-existence in mid-ocean in a boat only a hand and a half long, which is taking me to a faraway land with an unknown man. I must say that in spite of his most unattractive beard I feel far more reassured when he is by my side... He must be sound asleep: otherwise my jerky steering would have disturbed him.

32

SEA ROUTINE

At last we ran into fine weather. The wind eased to such an extent at midday that the boat was almost stopped. The sun burnt down out of a cloudless sky.

I had slept during the morning and at noon I went up to see Otilia who was holding the almost useless tiller. When displeased she used an odd word, or rather ejaculation, which can best be written as 'oof!', but said very quickly. She used it now,

' Oof! Never have I been so dirty. At home I have two baths every day.'

'Have a bath now; in the cockpit. I will get you soap and bucket. I am going to wash and swim.' Naturally, although she was a better swimmer than I, she could not go overboard as she would never get back. I had visions of a descending bobstay cutting her ear off. She would have to do the best she could on board.

I foresaw a slight difficulty ahead, for the only way to get clean was to soap all over with the special saltwater soap, then dive over the side, or dowse with buckets. How was she going to take this? I was not going to let her presence upset my whole routine. One cannot have a bath in a costume. It would be too ridiculous.

We both went below, one forward, one aft. Clad in nothing but my towel I mounted to the deck and made my way to the foredeck where I threw the towel off and got busy with the soap. Noises of buckets being drawn came from aft. A quick look round for sharks and I dived in, swimming down level with the cockpit. I had to duck my head to hide a smile; she was making a very ineffectual attempt to bath in a full costume; but she then realised how silly it was to try and pretend that living on the ocean in a small boat has in any way its counterpart on land.

Otilia was not afraid of cold water. Later I poured bucket after bucket over her.

For those who might think otherwise, I would like to state that in those clean and pure conditions of both the sea and the mind, the idea of anyone having an open-air bath, wearing a costume, seemed degrading and positively indecent.

A slight breeze sprang up, enough to keep the sails asleep. Sitting in the cockpit we both looked unnaturally clean and tidy. I told a joke about an experience I had been involved in before leaving New York. She laughed heartily, with a flash of attractive teeth between her red lips, then started to scribble Portuguese.

> *I was at the helm 6.45-12.00. Our first sunny day. We had our first wash and the non-existence of my captain's swim-suit made me feel terribly embarrassed. Now we are sitting at the helm. While I do some sewing, Allcard is telling me a story which amuses me immensely although I do not understand.*

*   *   *

A quiet night followed. *Temptress* slipped through the pale darkness under the first positive light of a new moon.

With the tracery of rigging swinging gently past the stars we sat in the cockpit talking until late. Indeed the romantic setting was conducive to confidences.

By noon the next day we had only managed a run of forty-two miles. I was at the helm in the hot sun whilst *Temptress* pushed through the glassy water under power.

Otilia was lying on the foredeck in pyjamas reading philosophy in French, or writing up her diary. That diary! I had given her a school exercise book and all her spare time was spent feverishly writing in Portuguese. She never really told me just what it was all about. I imagined it recorded her thoughts; anyway, it helped to keep her mind clear of doubts as to whether she had done the right thing.

Having never left home before, she had bouts of homesickness and would look up at me with a pitiful expression, saying, 'Why I come?' By then we had gained a certain understanding of each other, and managed to respect each other's need for privacy.

My decision to continue the voyage with her made some of the responsibility obviously mine, and I endeavoured to quieten her doubts by pointing out that homesickness, or any doubts and thoughts she would have during the voyage, were ultimately unimportant, since the decision was now irrevocable; besides she was now leading an existence which was so unreal and strange to her that the thoughts that were troubling her were not a true representation.

As my philosophy was too complicated for translation into my poor Spanish or (to me but not to her) easier French, the longer dissertations would be in English, which, although she would not really understand, gave her a certain amount of comfort.

She got her own back by an insatiable desire to speak her Portuguese; I let her ramble on, talking about her childhood or her mother's childhood, or it may even have been the history of Portugal; I never knew, for I could hardly understand a word of it, though it was quite pleasant to listen to her attractive voice. She had written a fair amount of poetry, and this too would ripple forth in a stream in which the boulders were the recognisable characteristics of the language such as 'swish-wish', 'ow' and 'oinch', appearing at regular intervals.

As domestic help is plentiful and cheap at Horta (Otilia's maid bore the unusual name of 'Brilliantine'), my companion had little experience of housework or cooking. Nothing daunted she would attack the chores with terrific energy, especially laundry; any sunny day would see her pattering about the deck on her small feet, festooning the rigging from stem to stern, until poor *Temptress* looked like Dress Ship in the Chinese Navy.

Daily I scanned the water for fish to supplement our somewhat bare larder, but without success; in fact, being in a cold water current, we were not rewarded with one fish, not even a flying fish, far less a fat dolphin.

*   *   *

All during the night the swell had been rising from the south-east, the barometer dropped. Darkness faded. A streak of red sandwiched between clouds and sea indicated a sunrise stillborn. Bad weather was imminent. A strong southerly wind forced us to heave to. A day passed and a stormy night.

(Otilia wrote: *The wind is blowing furious tonight. I feel excited. Temptress is dancing nervously. Allcard has not said a word.*)

Another day passed, with us hove to in a moderate gale; *Temptress* drifted away to the north-east. Water breaking over the foredeck completely flooded out the fo'c'sle.

The girl moved her belongings into the saloon.

The barometer was fairly high but little inclined to move, showing that another of those slow-moving depressions was passing into the area.

I drew rough weather charts, trying to make out what was happening, and suspected, and hoped, that the centre of the depression was directly to the westward; if it should move north-east we would have a lovely fair wind.

Hour followed hour and *Temptress* was trounced up and down by growing seas. Otilia was sea-sick, but after a while recovered sufficiently to cope with the cooking. On the third day she said, with a little nod of conviction, 'If I had known it was going to be like this I would still have come.'

Thank God, she had a sense of humour too. We had a special joke; every hard knock of the sea caused us to look at each other and say: 'Aye, it's a hard life, it's a hard life.'

But the weather was hard on her. She had not yet attained my instinctive knowledge, which told me just when a bad sea was going to cause a heavy lurch; she hardly dared move from the lee settee for fear of contracting yet more bruises. Oh! Why had she left her quiet room in Fayal? And her bath? And her warm bed with clean sheets? And now this hard-hearted man seems to be living in a world of his own!

(Otilia: *Allcard keeps reading the barometer: but the weather re-*

mains obstinate, and any forecast is quite impossible. I have the joy of listening to music for the first time since leaving my island. Allcard allowed me to use up some of the precious batteries in the miniature radio: music for five minutes. I was starved of it. He uses the radio only as a navigational aid.

The weather is frightful. Swiftly flying clouds seem to race the wild waves below. Temptress is in a state of inebriation. The fo'c'sle is completely drenched. I have had to move into the saloon. Chains, tins, glasses and waves set up a fantastic concert of noises which nearly drives me mad.

17th January. I spent a dreadful night. Two or three occasions I awoke to find Allcard drinking Oxo or eating porridge. Two or three times I tried to go back to sleep, and forget I was hungry too.

…four whole days without sunshine: all ports tightly closed. We have completely forgotten the art of conversation. I feel so wretched that I can't even cry. Allcard spends the days gazing at the sea through the portholes. As a heavier sea hits us, I hear him murmur 'well done': then silence again.

A strange sunset: a deep golden yellow.)

I spent most of the time in my gale position, jammed between galley and the compactum and the girl lay down, unable to read, almost unable to think in the hectic motion. We hardly spoke a word. The awful waiting again for things to get better. Alas, for my hopes for a fair wind—it was one of the very rare depressions that pass well south of the Azores. *Paciencia!*

The centre passed even south of us, and far from getting a fair wind we had a vicious easterly wind blowing hard in our faces. There were three cross seas running, and waves were colliding obliquely. *Temptress* was completely bewildered, not knowing which way to point, and she rolled, corkscrewed and flung her self around like a bucking bronco.

The only dry place on board was the saloon. My efforts with the skylight, screwing down the flaps on to a generous amount of bedding compound, had been quite successful.

We had completed no less than ninety-six hours of being hove to, and still the wind blew viciously from the east. A large sea caught the boat unawares, knocking the bow round up to windward, causing a thunderous flogging of the mainsail and boom as they lashed furiously from side to side. The boat rolled in great sweeps to port and starboard. Otilia was chucked off the saloon settee on to the floor, and hung on with an expression on her face as if she thought the end of the world was at hand.

Leaving her to work it out, I dashed for the hatch and thrust my head out to find *Temptress* racing through the melée, stern first, as if intent on driving the stern right underneath. Had the helm not been lashed, some part of the steering would surely have been broken.

By the time I had reached the cockpit the yawl had slewed round on to the opposite tack, and arresting her progress for an instant, started to spring over the stormy head seas in a series of leaps and bounds. The boom was jammed hard against the runner backstay, but the gear was now strong. Casting off the lashing and pushing the helm hard up, made her gallop downwind. Without gathering in the main sheet, I gybed her all standing. The boom snapped over with a God-Almighty jolt and a few seconds later, with the helm down, the boat sheered up into the wind, taking one breaker green over the bows, sufficient to stop her dead in her tracks. She was once more hove to on the starboard tack.

Opening the hatch I was met by dense and evilsmelling fumes. During the operation the primus had run out of fuel. When the smoke cleared away I found a very frightened stowaway who had no idea of what was happening on deck, or even if I was still aboard, or what had caused the fumes below—tears were trembling on the edges of her eyes.

'What is?—I don't want,' she gasped.

33

BETTER WEATHER

At night the wind diminished into a fresh breeze, but was still from ahead. The sea was very confused and *Temptress* was left hove to overnight. There had not been a chance to charge the batteries which were getting low; we were showing no lights. It occurred to me that Otilia would be very alarmed at this, but in fact she was completely indifferent to the danger of being run down. Ignorance is bliss.

Nothing was more welcome than sun after an overcast period and the following day the colours were so brilliant that they almost hurt.

The wind still blew keen and bucket baths on deck, although wonderfully exhilarating after our long sojourn below, were not prolonged.

My newly acquired cook was more enthusiastic than skilful and that evening we had a somewhat singular meal. There had been some rice and potatoes left over from lunch; Otilia, having fried the potatoes, not too successfully, in butter, then fried a little of the rice, also in butter, and handed me a small sample, which I pronounced (as Admiral Smirnov did the meat), 'Excellent'.

However, when the whole dish arrived it appeared that this method of cooking had been carried too far. She handed me a gelatinous mess, absolutely solid with butter (which, in any case, was slightly rancid), and sat down beside me as I peered apprehensively at the congealing substance. Then, stealing a look at the girl, to my relief I saw her shoulders starting to shake with laughter. My own laughter bubbled up and neither of us could stop for about five minutes. It was certainly a great joke, but as a repast not a complete success. We ate the last of the bread.

Another sunny day followed; *Temptress* ratched up to windward on a starboard tack, after the longest spell hove to I have ever experienced—five days twenty-one hours.

I took a series of sights to plot the position and, believe it or not, found a mistake in Burton's Nautical Tables, where it states oo minutes instead of 30 minutes. We were 340 miles off Madeira, which bore 120° true. The sea remained choppy.

A good sunset at last gave promise of better weather to come. We had now been at sea for twelve days, and owing to the depression had made very poor progress after our flying start.

The stowaway was getting affected by the emptiness of the ocean—'Oof! Why don't we see any ships.'

It was about an hour after this that I looked round on deck and called down: 'If you want a ship you will have one, come up.' A ship with a blaze of lights was passing a few miles to the north.

We were gradually getting east, however, and we passed another milestone of time. As we sailed into the new zone the clocks were put forward one hour. We only managed a sixty-five mile run, held back by that wretched head sea.

I nursed *Temptress* over the waves, smiling to myself, still not yet really used to having Otilia aboard.

It seemed amusing somehow. Sometimes she would catch me smiling—she never let anything pass, so 'Why you smiling,' would come promptly. 'At you. Because you are my little joke.'

This always annoyed her; her dark eyes would flash with fire, and lips would purse petulantly. If further provoked, she would stamp her foot, or even, if reclining, drum her heels.

'Ah! I not joke,' she would protest vehemently.

It was a shame to tease her, but better that than allow her to brood—she would occasionally meditate for hours, hugging pessimistic thoughts. It was different for me, for if I ever had worrying thoughts, I could always switch them to the problems of navigation or the big subject of 'boats'. While Otilia had nothing to think of except her life—or me.

At this moment, however, I was smiling at the noise of activity below; it was nearly lunch-time. Suddenly there was a crash of something falling, followed immediately by 'Oof!' and a short burst of Portuguese. Nothing happened for several minutes, then a quick movement of a hand sent several white fragments over the side. They sank rapidly. It appeared that there had been a reduction in the galley equipment.

The log propeller disappeared. It is a thing one expects to last forever; it had been towed thousands of miles. The spare one was fixed, but the log itself was suffering and in spite of repeated oilings would jam at intervals. It took only a knock to free it and the wheel would whirr round and twist up on the dial one-tenth of a mile or more in a few seconds.

We saw our only whale of the trip—the hump-backed variety—which crossed the stern, blowing heartily.

The wind luckily having veered to the south, a better course could be picked up. Previously, when Otilia had been steering, our direction had been more southerly; that sector of the compass card was to her an old friend. It was now very different, and she became quite bewildered at the new part of the compass between east and south-east. I had started the engine which tended in any case to turn the boat off wind, and, while below, I heard a 'crack' and dashed up to find the vessel nearly 180 degrees off course. She had gybed the ship for the first, and, I must say, the last time.

Otilia's diary at this stage, translates as follows:

> The sun at last, and not so much water falling on deck. Special lunch to celebrate. A good wash with buckets of water, in the cockpit. After his wash, Eduardo put on his best flannels and we had a Portuguese lesson: I am sure he is not the least bit interested in my language: he just wants to make me laugh because I am feeling so very homesick.
>
> Later he showed me the plans of Wanderer, his other boat in which he plans to sail alone round the world. I am terribly igno-

rant regarding single-handed sailing, but it seems to me he must be extremely brave!

In a few moments, the sun will be setting—our chance to see some colour.

21st January. Temptress is making good progress to Gibraltar, A week from today we should be dropping anchor in Spanish waters, if all goes well. Eduardo told me he would take me as far as England if I wish. I am beginning to realise that his beard is not altogether lacking in interest.

22nd. January The whole day at the helm with Eduardo. In the morning a ship passed fairly close: but I am not sure whether they spotted us: Eduardo tried to use his signalling lamp, but was unable to, owing to the position of the sun.

Three birds followed us for some time, swooping and rising magnificently.

The sunset promised fine weather. Opposite, against a rose-coloured background, the moon ripened gradually from green to yellow, just like a fruit.

23rd January. Afternoon: I was at the helm. There was a strong wind and several times the sea leapt up and washed on to Temptress—an unpleasant sensation. Rocking and rolling all day long. Sometimes I feel more like a pendulum than a human being.

Eduardo at his usual meditation…

The sea looks more vast than ever. Temptress seems to rejoice in such abundance. I do not feel well. I was sick and feel deeply humiliated.

A brilliant moonlit night, light enough to read the compass by, a smooth sea and quiet breeze pouring over the water from the south, gave ideal conditions for my night watch, and as the girl Friday slept below, I remained hunched up over the tiller, beset by the unfamiliar nature of my thoughts and emotions.

The more days that we were together, the more my girl pleased me. Explain it in terms of proximity, lack of competition or what you will. I did not care or bother to search for any other explanation than that she was a woman—attractive—a good companion.

34

SHIP ALONGSIDE

Although Otilia could steer quite well during the day, she had found it too confusing to do so in the darkness, even with the stars to guide her, or a light in the binnacle. However, it was now a night so brilliant with moonlight, with only a gentle breeze blowing from before the beam, that I thought she could manage. At half-past one I shouted down the hatch, 'Wakey, wakey, show a leg, show a leg, watch on deck.'

Well muffled up, she took the helm. After impressing upon her the importance of keeping the moon in a certain position relative to the rigging, I thankfully turned in.

Three hours later, after a hot drink of Oxo, I returned to the deck to find Otilia half perished with the cold.

'Oof!' she shivered, 'but so beautiful, so beautiful. Very good to make poetry, but…' she clambered cautiously out of the cockpit, then turned as she descended the hatchway, and added '…too (Portuguese adjective) cold.'

It was six o'clock when the moon set behind clouds low down in the west. *Temptress* was cutting along with a 'chop, chop' of wavelets on the bow. Although at its last breath, the night, at the dimming of the moonlight, plunged, for the first time into real darkness; the voice of the sea rose and fell. The sky gradually lightened over the eastern horizon, with me yawning ungracefully at the fugitive stars. Another half-hour passed before the familiar outlines of the rigging could be picked out, and the compass card clearly read. Colour strengthened. Little by little it spread across the sky. Marble-shaped clouds merged from red to orange, then yellow. Lo! it was daylight. One more night was over; a beautiful day at sea had commenced.

It was another two hours before I had the heart to awaken Otilia sleeping peacefully below, but hunger overcame sentiment; a loud tattoo was banged on the deck.

A feeble noon to noon run of fifty-five miles put us equidistant between the most south-eastern of the Azores, and Madeira—distant 240 miles. We were in the region of the cold current from the north-west, which is in itself a mystery; presumably it must be the Labrador current which plunges underneath the Gulf Stream. I was surprised to see a whole fleet of tiny Portuguese men-of-war, each only about an inch long. Later on there passed another, six inches long. I pointed it out to the lightly clad Otilia, who was sunning herself, sitting on the sidedeck, with her back against the cabin-top coaming.

'I am feeling poetic,' I said. 'Just look at that beautiful animal, so pretty, so graceful, so translucent that one can see its digestive organs working.'

'That not poetic. That horrid.'

I relapsed into silence, content with the easy steering, half my mind on keeping a straight course and the other half on admiring, somewhat abstractedly, the excellent example of the female form posed in front of me. A good figure, I thought. Filled out in the right places, curved in where...

She looked up, with questioning eyes.

'What is?' (I knew that 'What is?' in Otilia-language meant 'What are you thinking about?')

'Oh. Thinking that your waist is pinched in just enough to make room for a man's arm.'

She did not understand, and inclined her head on one side interrogatively,

'What ees peenched?'

I waved her attention back to the sea, and said:

'Look! More Portuguese men-of-war?'

'Why are they called Portuguese men-of-war.'

'Oo-er, well,' I replied rather vaguely, then with an inspiration: 'It is a tribute to the great Portuguese navigators of yore.'

'What is 'yore'?'

I gave up the unequal struggle and, leaning forward, frowned into the bowl of the compass.

*   *   *

A slight fall in the barometer, and complete overclouding of the sky, was followed by uncertain breezes, first from the south-west, then north-west before falling away to nothing. Such a huge swell rolled in from the west that the sails were taken aback in each trough, causing so much chafe that, for the first time on this leg of the voyage, the mainsail was stowed. *Temptress* swayed eastward, steering herself under the two headsails, allowing us both to turn in.

*   *   *

A second person at the helm makes most operations a hundred times easier than when one is single-handed; in the fine breeze of the morning Otilia steered with skill downwind, as I hoisted the full mainsail. Six knots and a flowing sea. 'How much longer?' 'How many more miles?' the inevitable questions came.

'Only a few more days at this speed,' I said, which was both true and untrue; I knew the ocean too well to think that a fresh wind on the quarter would last. It was wonderful sailing over those smooth rollers, in the fresh bracing air, after the sultriness of the preceding day.

How much easier it is to take sights of the sun when there is someone else at the helm, and how pleasant to be at the helm oneself yet hear noises from below indicating that a proper hot meal is being prepared. I was the donkey engine at the helm. It was up to Otilia to provide the fuel.

Night came once again, flooded brilliantly with the light of the full moon, and still we kept going. It was a long and somewhat uncomfortable trick at the helm all night. Single-handed I would never have had the patience to stick at it all night through, because there would have been nobody to appreciate my efforts, and it would not have made the slightest difference to anybody but myself whether I slept or not; but I happily steered until eight o'clock the next morning—after no less than twenty-four hours at the helm.

Conditions were tricky for steering but I went below, leaving Otilia at the helm. I was a little anxious as to whether she could manage, and kept looking out of the hatch, but each time she saw me she flapped her hand at me and shouted: 'Go sleep, go sleep.'

When I appeared on deck again the wind was stronger and the boat travelling well. I read the log. We were getting a move on now—107 miles noon to noon despite choppy seas holding us back.

There were three common kittiwakes playing around the ship. People think that gulls follow ships at sea. This is only true in coastal waters, for no self-respecting gull would think of staying out all night and not returning home to its rocky base. Gulls are the best known of all sea-birds, therefore, people who are unacquainted with ornithology, think that any bird seen at sea is a seagull. Actually, gulls are pre-eminently birds of the coast, and the flocks of seagulls which wheel and scream round the sterns of liners, melt away one by one as the ships head for the ocean.

Usually the only birds sighted on the ocean are the various types of petrels; it is only near the tropical regions that one sees the white and long-tailed bosun bird. Not till way down in the South Atlantic does one come across the much-publicised albatross. Only in the North Atlantic, throughout the winter and spring months, can the common kittiwake be seen.

Seventy-one miles was the best we could do by the following noon. I called Otilia up on deck and pointed to the south. 'Madeira is down there—ninety-three miles away,' but she did not appear to believe me. After two weeks of nothing but sea she could scarcely believe that there was any land left in the world, and, after all, it was only by hearsay that she knew of vast continents.

'Is it possible to miss Africa?' she asked.

'I don't think my navigation is as bad as that.'

I tried to check our position by an afternoon sight, but there was too big a sea running.

During the previous twenty-four hours the wind had veered forward of the beam. We were hard on the wind, which tore boisterously out of the north, ripping over the big swells.

The wind dropped in the morning of 25th January, after a night that had struck bitterly cold. I could hardly believe the thermometer which read only fifty degrees.

As always at the onset of better weather, I seized the chance to obtain accurate sights of the sun, also, to complete the horrible job of filling stoves and lamps with paraffin. Otilia busied herself by cleaning up below, while the hatches, wide open again, allowed the stale air to escape.

Towards midday, I shouted down for Otilia. A ship was heading straight for us, coming from the east. At last a chance to report, and remove any doubts about our safety from those at home.

A cargo ship of about 5000 tons, high out of the water, weeping rust, plodded leisurely by, rolling (as Otilia later put it) slowly and voluptuously; the blades of the propeller, lifting out of the water at each turn, beat up fountains of spray to the tune of that characteristic thud, thud, thud, thud—as regular as a metronome.

Otilia was beside herself with excitement as the ship came close abeam.

'Quick. Take the helm,' I ordered, picking up the Aldis signalling lamp and aiming it amidships. But there was no reply. The flags were ready, and it took only an instant to hoist them on the mizzen halyards. But still no reply.

'Damn it. Are they blind?'

Both of us stood in the cockpit gazing avidly at this (to us) thrilling sight. The only movement to be seen was on the nearest wing of the bridge, where the white faces of three men could be observed. One had binoculars. I raised my arm in salutation, and these little figures, like puppets on a stage, each lifted a right arm.

The stern passed; MARDIN ISTAMBUL was painted on it in large letters. Already she was drawing clear. Otilia looked crestfallen. I was just about to say something sarcastic when the masts spread apart.

'Otilia! Look! She's turning.'

The ship swung round in a wide circle to port, obviously preparing to overtake us on the lee side. She was still going at dead-slow, and I had to back the staysail to let her approach. It was going to be a wonderful chance for an action photograph.

Leaving the slightly bewildered Otilia at the helm to cope as best as she could, I dashed below for my camera which was stowed away, went through the ritual until it was ready to fire, then climbed back on deck. Crouching amidships, on the weather side, I took a picture of Otilia holding the tiller, and looking back past the mizzen at the huge advancing bow of the ship.

It was only a few moments before the great steel wall of the steamer reared above us, only a few yards away. Click! Another shot of the officers crowding the bridge. They seemed amused at this.

'Are you in difficulty,' the Captain shouted, in a strong foreign accent.

'No. OK, OK. Please report Lloyd's, London.'

They turned to each other as if they did not understand. We were very close. I held the tiller over with my foot, then repeated slowly: ' Report OK. Report OK. Lloyd's London,' pointing to my four signal letters, fluttering energetically in the breeze.

The Captain nodded and raised his hand in understanding. 'Bon voyage,' then 'OK, OK.' (Surely the most international of words).

His telegraph jangled. I got a final close-up of the giant propeller as it thumped round, driving the ship forward and to starboard as the Captain manoeuvred to regain his course westward. The Captain was a good sort and he kept his word. The following letter was sent to my father from Lloyd's:

26th January, 1951
Dear Sir,

Yacht 'Temptress'

I confirm that a radiotelegram, timed 19-05 and dated 25th January, has been received from the Master of the steamer *Mardin* via Portishead Radio, reading as follows:

GMT 12.20 LAT. 34.26 N. LONG. 15.47 W. MET SAILINGBOAT MDPV STOP REQUESTED TO REPORT TO YOU THEIR POSITION GOOD HEALTH AND GOOD CONDITION ENDS.

Two flies had flown aboard. Presumably Turkish, and very energetic. They led us a pretty dance before they were swatted. By that time the ship was a small grey square on the horizon.

The mention of the word 'photograph' in connection with this trip makes me want to say 'Oof!' I had already taken ten or fifteen shots of Otilia, thinking that I might as well capitalise out of the business if possible. I had taken:

Stowaway at helm.
Stowaway on foredeck.
Stowaway peeling potatoes.
Stowaway sunbathing… and so on ad nauseam.

The whole thing was a pitiful failure.
The film had not turned in the camera.

35

LAND

For some time we had been giving each other lessons in languages.
I would teach her English and she would teach me Portuguese,
although it must be confessed right away that it was not an unqual-
ified success; when we finally got to port we both spoke French together.

As a matter of fact her English was improving far more than my
Portuguese, but she could never understand the difference between 'to
have' and 'to be', and she once came out with the extraordinary statement: 'I was a pair of trousers,' and things even more startling to my
innocent ears.

We had become good friends and her companionship made such
a winter voyage great fun, whilst by myself it would have been too
cold and my spells at the helm too long, to make it anything but a
necessary duty.

Otilia would remain cheerful and bright all day; it was only when
the shades of night were drawing in that she would show signs of
sadness and misgiving. We would normally be together in the cockpit then; she would go silent, her lips drooping at the corners, and
her lovely eyes would widen with apprehension of the unknown.
This was probably due to a psychological fear of darkness itself,
caused by terrifying experiences she had suffered as a child.

She told me that once she was in a dark room at home, reading by
a guttering light of a candle, when she received a call that it was time
for her to go up to bed. She opened the door. A fearful black-robed
figure wearing a tall witch's hat was standing outside.

With a scream, Otilia rushed to the other door, wrenched it open and nearly fainted with fright on seeing a tiny black figure, a miniature edition of the witch. She was not to know that one was her grandmother and the other her younger brother dressed up for the occasion—a grim practical joke.

Evidently it is common practice in the Azores to frighten children with stories of evil black figures, which is supposed to make them more obedient—a fear with which to threaten them if they were not good. One can well imagine the effect this could have on a child's mind. It seems that the Azoreans are better at fancy dress than child psychology.

After sailing well for half the night under the light of a silvery moon, the wind fell away; were we in for another calm? I turned-in two hours before the dawn, but awoke to find the vessel lying well over on her side with the wind thrumming through the rigging.

Peering through the lee port, which was nearly level with the surface of the sea, I saw the water racing past. A quick look out showed that this was no mere squall but a new and energetic wind. After hesitating ten minutes I rolled back into my bunk. *Temptress* seemed safe enough.

At dawn the yawl was still going like a rater; the sea was making up every moment. With difficulty on the steeply inclined deck, my oilskins were donned (their stickiness had been overcome with cement at Horta). After rolling down two more turns of the main boom, reducing canvas to the equivalent of close-reef, I lashed the helm farther down. The boat crashed on. I continued my interrupted slumbers. One hundred more miles had been ironed out astern.

By late afternoon I wrote:

Moderate Gale Force with no signs of improvement.

After an exceptionally big breaking sea had crashed over the foredeck and poured green over the top of the dinghy, the time had certainly come to heave to. I played the old game, rolling up the jib and backing the staysail. The boat lay stopped, safe from the breaking seas.

After the turmoil on deck it was miraculously quiet below. The difference was almost unbelievable. During all my hectic activities on deck Otilia had been reading, while reclining gracefully on the lee settee.

The moon rose that night, big and orange, flooding the swiftly moving surface with an uncanny light.

(Otilia writes: *We are now well beyond Madeira and Porto Santo. The moon rose shyly.* Temptress *leaves a silver furrow in her wake. Very decorative these* luca nocti.

Then the morning starts for her, and she finds that we are still hove to. *Waiting, waiting and more waiting—a good exercise for impatient children.*

I am longing to see a tree. Every day I look up at the highest tree on our ship, but there is something very essential missing about it.

After nearly twenty-four hours hove to, we picked up course again.

Otilia continues: *27th January. Eduardo spent the day at the helm. Rough sea. Huge waves, impregnated with wind, falling on* Temptress.

A ship passes us in the distance, about 6,000 tons, I should say. When it is in the bottom of a wave, we cannot see it: not even the top of the masts. Some curtains of rain.

I feel genuinely, overwhelmingly happy. It is so lovely to watch the wind lightly drawing vague paths across the sea.

How I would like a piece of bread and island cheese! Even stale bread would do.)

*   *   *

In bad weather, the fo'c'sle was always dripping wet, owing to the poor design of forehatch and sundry other leaks past deck fittings. But one could not avoid going in there, because that is where the pump lavatory is situated.

Otilia gradually conceived a dread of this 'black hole of Calcutta', which was summed up as, 'Oof! Very bad. I don't want,' while eyeing askance the nightmare door leading to this place; on one side, in the saloon, it was comparatively warm and comfortable, but on the other side it was cold, dark (the light rarely worked) and very wet, apart from the fact that in a head sea the movement forward is intolerable.

Also, by misplaced humour, someone had installed a leaky ventilator immediately above the seat of operations, so positioned that when a wave flooded on to the foredeck, a stream of icy water was shot down one's neck. Discouraging to say the least.

Anyway, it was bad weather now, and *Temptress*, although hove to, was acting like a New York elevator. The exceptional giddy lurches and rolling made Otilia sea-sick again, and caused her intense pain across her eyes and the back of her head. She took this moment to inform me that she was sometimes subject to attacks of appendicitis. After taking two aspirins, she retired and lay as an inert mass with a blanket pulled right over her. Perhaps our stringent food rationing was taking effect.

By now stores were very low. The extra mouth and the unexpectedly long time at sea had caused havoc among our supplies. We would have been in an awkward position if it had not been for the bunch of bananas, all of which ripened at the same time. We still, however, had plenty of rice.

I wondered how long Otilia was going to be sick, and thought that at least we were saving some food by her indisposition. However, she recovered the next day, when the wind abated and the sea went down. In fact, she was in exceptional spirits, possibly brought on by the bracing north-east wind, which, now we were approaching the continent, was cooled by sweeping across the winter snows of Spain.

(Otilia was moved sufficiently to write: *30th January. What a wonderful day, and what a wonderful life! Less than a month ago I was living quietly in Fayal without the remotest chance of travelling. Today here I am in mid-Atlantic, with so many choices for our next port of call that it has become a joke. First of all we decided on Gibraltar, then Tangier and now we are contemplating Casablanca. Eduardo says we are 116 miles from Casablanca. If the wind does not behave naughty we could be there tomorrow.*

31st. January The wind did not change. We are heading for Casablanca. Eduardo makes himself ridiculous: up and down all day with the sextant: and doing sums in the saloon. We expect to sight land at any moment, but the sky is laden with heavy clouds. There is an occasional shower and a steady breeze.

Afternoon. The smell of land, African land, is in the air. Africa! It seems a dream.)

*   *   *

We were visited by six solan geese*, and three small ships passed through our range of vision. Coasters!

Just before sunset, having strained my eyes the whole day, I saw an indistinct mauve strip over the eastern horizon.

'Land,' I shouted. 'Come up quickly and see Africa,' but it was impossible for anybody without experience of sighting land among clouds to see it.

Landsmen and seamen treat the sighting of land in very different fashions. A landsman will look up while a seaman always looks down low on the horizon.

Nightfall swiftly came and before it was properly dark there was a faint and regular flash of light reflected in the clouds. The lighthouse on Cape Dar el Beida. Half an hour later there was a great glow in the sky— the lights of fabulous Casablanca.

By midnight many lights were in sight all along the shore, and the beams of the lighthouse swept extravagantly through the night— three sharp flashes every fifteen seconds.

We sailed in to about eight miles offshore. The great wind that had borne us on became hushed. We were finished with the breezes of the ocean and it was the land which now had control. Switching on the masthead light and pinning in the mainsheet we left *Temptress* rolling to the incessant north-west swell, waiting for the daylight.

In the bright morning sun, the land was visible stretching for many miles in either direction, and the white houses of Casablanca could be clearly seen.

It was the first day of February. We had been twenty-four days at sea, but the sighting of land and the imminent entry to such a port completely swamped our minds, and in a flash the whole

---

*   Gannets—Ed.

voyage was forgotten. The change overnight had been more than abrupt. On the yesterday the great blue rollers of the ocean were being driven before a strong wind, and now *Temptress* was rolling in swells of unnatural pale green.

By the time we had finished breakfast and the engine had been started, fog blotted out the land, but I had already taken bearings and headed confidently for the end of the long breakwater.

An hour later the lighthouse came into view, and dimly through the haze one could see splashes of white —huge breakers murdering themselves on the jagged rocks. It seemed calm enough for our little boat, but there was a steamer lying off with engines stopped, beam on to the seas, and she gave a series of hair-raising rolls which must have perturbed the Captain, for the propeller boiled up water by the stern, and she swung round to point into the rollers.

Our engine behaved well and, passing several ships, we headed to round the end of the breakwater, giving it a good berth.

We had actually passed the end of the mole and altered course ninety degrees to starboard to enter the harbour, when a mighty roar sounded to seaward and a giant breaker rearing up into the sky, bore down on our beam. By the time I had altered course to take it stern on it was upon us and *Temptress* was lifted up in a mass of foam, and sucked down into the trough; she was thrown up again, on four consecutive waves before we could alter course again. By this time the breakers had swept on and cast themselves in a turmoil of foam upon the opposite shore.

A few minutes later we had the breakwater between us and the ocean, and were warbling our quiet way up the long harbour, past ship after ship, past small fishing boats manned by rough Arabs wearing the fez, past two French destroyers. We saw some yachts at moorings. I gave Otilia, who was steering, a sign to head into the light wind, and dropped all canvas.

Seeing a man rowing out to us in a dinghy, I threw the engine into neutral and hailed him in my best French. He answered in perfect English, then proceeded to pilot us to a little basin, where several other boats could be seen.

This sudden meeting with other people had a curious effect on

Otilia; one never knows how she is going to react; she bolted below, even before we had moored, and nothing would induce her to come out on deck.

Max Tourniquet, of the Société Nautique, who had come out to meet us, helped me lay out an anchor ahead and astern, then went off to see about formalities.

A motor-boat arrived alongside—harbour officials and police: details, passports, embarrassing questions, ship's papers, signing forms. But all was in order. We gave sighs of relief as the Frenchmen queued up to ascend our ladder to the deck. They went—we were free.

Otilia recovered her poise instantly. She jumped up and impulsively threw her arms round my neck.

I kissed her, and said, 'Come on! Let's visit Africa.'

36

CASABLANCA

Horta of Fayal with its cobbled main street, to Casablanca of Morocco with its avenues and boulevards; from a sleepy island port to one of the biggest and busiest of the world. Could a more sensational contrast have been chosen for Otilia Frayao of the Azores? It was an impact enough for me; how was it going to affect her, I wondered.

The first two days were spent sight-seeing. We would row the few yards to the Société Nautique, then walk along the white and dusty shore-road which would reflect the dazzling glare of the sun, on past the Old Medina and up the Boulevard des XIVe Zouaves with its many palm trees dividing it down the centre. Arabs, confused as to our nationality, would call out to us in different languages, from their colourful shops, offering receptacles of beaten brass, silky carpets, carved ivory and gay leather goods of all descriptions.

Reaching one of the big squares, perhaps La Place de la France, we would sit down at one of the little round tables which always line the pavements off the cafes. The *garçon* would see to our thirsty needs. Then while Otilia quaffed her long drink and I sipped a Martini, we would watch the diverse cosmopolitan crowd filtering by, rich men, poor men, beggar men and thieves, and women, from an emaciated Arab to a fat French Jewess, and plenty of good-looking girls as well, although I pretended not to look at them.

Otilia was especially interested in the book stores and one of her first purchases was some poetry of Jean Cocteau and Rilke. I pointed out other items of interest—motor-coaches, cinemas, theatres, multi-storied buildings, great shops, and last but not least, a railway station!

But it was too much for one time. It was like the story of the
small boy who had been naughty and, in a family of twelve, was not
allowed to eat mushrooms for dinner. In short, they were not mushrooms and everyone died except the one boy. But he could not grieve;
his loss was so big that it was beyond grief.

It was the same sort of thing for Otilia. She had seen so many
things for the first time that, finally, she was no more impressed by
the many than the few. But, just the same, Casablanca was pretty
fantastic for the both of us. Occasionally, having seen something
especially odd, we would look at each other and laugh—sharing a
secret, and thinking of our magic carpet, *Temptress*, lying patiently
to her anchors.

After these two fairly peaceful days, there came the increasing
shock of publicity. An alarming stream of reporters and cameramen
descended on us from the Société Nautique from early morning
until late at night, demanding, demanding, demanding. One thing
would have been fatal: for us to refuse them aboard.

I had discovered by now that with regard to the publicity game,
if one wants peace, it is essential to keep on good terms with all the
newspapermen possible, at any rate to begin with, providing them
equally with all accurate information and facts of the voyage. Otherwise one not only gets harassed for weeks, but ridiculous and inaccurate news is published. Now that there were two of us aboard, it was
even more important that they should be given the true facts, and
not allowed to invent and romance.

I had expected and indeed was accustomed to publicity after my
American experience, but I had thought it best not to upset Otilia
by telling her what must be expected, and what we might have to
endure. I most certainly did not want publicity, and she doubly did
not, but anybody who achieves any sort of fame or notoriety must
not fight but accept, with resignation, the resultant publicity.

Although I had mentally bowed to the inevitable, Otilia most
certainly had not, and each day she became more and more nervous
and distraught, until she hardly thought life worth living. Our tem-
po of sea life on board was violently disrupted by this coming into
port, and the transitory period of mental adjustment to land life was

a very difficult one. It is easier for the phlegmatic Anglo-Saxon to regain mental equilibrium than for the temperamental Latin. However, with courage one gets used to anything in the end, and finally Otilia learned to wear the cloak of publicity with indifference.

Otilia had certainly caused an unholy commotion; it even came to the notice of the Foreign Office, and I received a stilted letter, through the British Consul, informing me of some regulation or other about repatriation. Overboard it went.

After about ten days I decided that the time had come to refer late arrivals from the journalistic world to newspapers of the previous week for information. All we wanted was to be left in peace to form our own plans for the future.

This change in our attitude, far from having the desired effect, produced an outburst of sensational rumours which, however, we did not hear at the time, as neither of us read the newspapers. Some papers ran a story that we had parted company, others said we were about to marry, and one went so far as to say that we *were* married, even stating where—the town of Marrakesh. (I do not think, anyway, that I could ever marry a girl who could not put on the toothpaste cap properly!) The whole thing to us was very futile and unnecessary.

*   *   *

The cruiser H.M.S. *Liverpool* steamed in for an official visit one day. Otilia and I were invited to the inevitable quarter-deck party. The Captain was somewhat horrified at my alarmist stories about the 'swell' at Casablanca, given more impetus by the fact that there was a 'swell warning' out at that moment. I was not far wrong, as it happened. The following morning the First Lieutenant told me that during the night they were snapping their massive mooring lines like bits of string, and that for the first time in his life he had seen wire hawsers wringing out drops of water.

In the ship's cinema one morning I gave a lecture on my double crossing of the Atlantic. I had rowed to the cruiser in my dinghy, which seemed much heavier to pull on the way back. By a strange coincidence *Temptress* had much stronger moorings after the cruiser left, and the topsides were painted in a colour very similar to Navy Grey.

The next 'boat' to arrive from the ocean was a Jeep, an amphibious Jeep owned by Ben Carlin and his wife Eleanor. Very few believed that they had crossed the Atlantic (Halifax, Fayal, San Miguel, Madeira, Canary Islands and Morocco). But it is true. Ben's ambition is to drive this thing right round the world. It taints rather of stunt; and they have been rescued several times, once when the fuel tank they were towing broke adrift. However, it shows great courage and endurance. I was to meet them again in London.

There was one thing we disproved, and that was the indigestible myth that two can live as cheaply as one, even on a boat. This is just an invention by women to trap unwary men (quoth the hardened bachelor). As a matter of fact, it is about four times as expensive. Two tend to go out more, and generally in terms of food, warmth and dress the standard set is much higher—and so is the cost!

Within a week of our arrival a tremendous storm had come roaring out of the south-west. Great seas flooded over the long breakwater; spray even spattered *Temptress* in her safe little basin in the inner port; one of the sixty-ton iron and cement blocks, of which the breakwater was constructed, was shifted several feet. It was scaring enough our side of the wall. What it must have been like at sea I could well imagine.

I somehow felt convinced that I would have been lost if out in that gale, and wondered whether the girl coming aboard at Horta had been indeed an act of Providence.

Also, had I left Horta alone and gone to San Miguel, there would have been that south-easterly gale to combat moored at Ponta Delgada instead of at sea, which would in this case have been safer, as that wind direction leaves the harbour wide open to the Atlantic.

Thirdly, had I gone to Gibraltar, as planned, I might have been caught by the ammunition ship *Debenham*, which blew up, causing death and destruction.

Shoals of letters came from all over the globe; Otilia received several proposals of marriage from total strangers. In fact, all that could be expected from this comic world, and much more, came to pass.

One letter came from a lady in London, a Bee-venom specialist. This seemed a little more sensible than the others, and not only offered to pay Otilia's fare to England, but also accommodation for one year.

After many letters the girl decided to fly to London, and at four o'clock one sorry morning she stepped on board a coach belonging to Air France and headed for the airport. Two hours later I stood in my hatch and gazed towards the east; roaring through the dawn mists was the four-engined air-liner taking my Otilia away to new adventures. I prayed that the new world to which she was flying would not prove a disappointment to her island dreams.

Until she had gone I had not realised how much I would miss her on board. Together we had weathered the storms at sea and weathered even greater difficulties on shore, and finally we had become a good team on board; while I had worked on deck, painting and refitting, she had worked below and managed all the chores. She had indeed, after a somewhat inauspicious start, developed into an excellent cook, and I had lived on board more comfortably, and eaten better than anywhere else before (or since, to date!).

She did me good too; it is bad for someone always to live alone, as one is apt to acquire habits, and 'habits are first cobwebs, then cables'.

The first day after Otilia's departure I could not bear to be on board and I stayed ashore for all my meals.

As one is naturally mistrustful of any offer to a young girl, I had made an arrangement with Otilia that if she found the invitation to London had not been genuine, or should she become suspicious of some ulterior motive she was to send me a telegram stating: 'Things much better than expected.' On receipt of this I would have immediately contacted Scotland Yard. However, no such telegram arrived; I did get a long letter from Otilia saying that she had taken matters into her own hands and left her hostess, as there was not mutual accord.

From what she had earned from her story to a Sunday newspaper she paid back the cost of the fare and rid herself of any financial obligation.

37

ALONE AGAIN

Once again on my own I threw myself into activity, working on the boat, hardly ever going ashore except at the week-ends. In fact, although *Temptress* was moored only sixty feet or so from the shore I remained alone aboard almost as much as if in mid-ocean.

Casablanca is an expensive place to live in, compared with England, but prices of food are similar to those in America. Some things were much cheaper. For instance, my big night binoculars had grown some sort of fungus inside the lenses, and these were cleaned by Erard Freres et Deforges for only £1. The New York people had quoted me twelve times this for the same job.

The rotator log was also completely renovated and new ball-bearings fitted. It came back looking brand new, glistening with shiny grey paint. As a matter of fact, it proved to be utterly useless as, although it did not seem to be stiff, it would not rotate under two and a half knots, and over five knots it would jam.

The greatest snag about the berth in Casablanca, safe though it may have been from the elements, was that there were still the Arabs with which to contend. They may have been good at some things; but they are certainly not good seamen.

Over and over again would a vessel smash against my already stained topsides, and even a small rowing boat would come so close that the oars would scrape along the bottom of *Temptress*, causing me to jump out in anger and wave the intruder away. It does not take much to remove anti-fouling paint and allow the deadly gribble or teredo ship-worm to penetrate the planking.

Of course one of the chief amusements of any port is to watch

the various types of local craft. The greatest fault I noticed with nearly all the boats in Casablanca was that the rudders, when hard over,
could be turned well past the theoretical efficiency angle of thirty-seven degrees.

I saw one big fishing-boat backing and filling for over a quarter
of an hour trying to turn round in what should have been plenty of
space. There was no wind at the time to upset the manoeuvre and
the failure was due entirely to the rudder being put over to ninety
degrees, rendering it inoperative.

Another time, a fishing boat of forty feet or so was being towed
into my basin by a heavy rowing boat. A landlubber at the helm had
the iron tiller so far over that the rudder was at one hundred degrees,
giving an effect completely opposite to the one desired. This heavy
boat charged down on *Temptress*. There followed much running
about with fenders, pushing off with boat-hooks and slackening
away my mooring lines. All this was enlivened by furious shouting.

Apart from the rowing-boats, which seemed to delight in hitting
any yacht, fishing-boats under power would pass with perhaps only
an inch to spare. I soon found that politeness or requests were quite
useless— only loudness of voice and hard swearing kept the Arab at
a distance. They probably came close to see whether there was any
loose gear on deck worth stealing.

However, it must be said in all fairness that I never lost anything
there. A guardian on the pontoon of the Société Nautique, a picturesque Arab in flowing white robes, kept a very good eye on any yacht
moored off the pontoon.

There were, in fact, three yachts. There was a Swiss called *Ascona*,
which had the interesting rig of a wishbone ketch, surely in theory the
best rig that could possibly be designed, for it is the only rig that completely fills in all available space with canvas. The snag with this rig is,
of course, the wishbone which has to be light yet impossibly strong.
The snatching of the wishbone in both calm and rough seas transmits
heavy shocks to the mizzen mast, to which it has to be attached by a
vang. If and when these difficulties are overcome this will be the rig of
the future.

This particular ketch had been built in Switzerland and had

made its first voyage by rail to the Mediterranean. She was bound
for the West Indies and America. The hull was strong but her gear
and equipment were inadequate for the ocean crossing. Every time it
came on to blow she dragged dangerously about the basin to her far
too light anchor. When they beached her for painting it was found
that the propeller shaft had corroded almost completely away; undoubtedly the propeller would have fallen off at sea. Of course any
salt-water seaman knows that one just does not attach a bronze propeller to a mild steel shaft as the steel soon gets eaten away by elec-
trolytic action.

I walked out to the end of the breakwater to see her go; she
looked a beautiful picture as she headed south-west for the Canaries.

The other boat was a little twenty-five-foot Bermudian sloop
called *Les 4 Vents*, belonging to a Frenchman, Marcel Bardiaux.
He was another of these round-the-world-single-handed cranks,
but he had made the mistake of publishing his route, with dates,
prior to departure—1950 said Cape Horn and the Pacific; anyway,
he had reached Casablanca. The boat was strongly built but it was
obvious to me that he would have to endure much greater hardships as the design was not suitable for the job. She had a short
rockered keel which made it impossible to beach with any safety
for repairs and painting and, like most racing boats, she could only
be made to steer herself with difficulty.

The cockpit was self-draining but as there was no sliding hatch
in the coachroof he had a door with a sill only four inches high. In a
very rough sea he would be unable to open this door without letting
volumes of water down below. There was not even a coaming round
the cockpit, and no life-lines whatsoever. He will learn, I thought,
hoping it would be before he got to the Cape Horn area. He, too,
had come in originally for only a few days, but left after a stay of
five or six months. Nine months later I saw that he had reached Rio
de Janeiro, after making a record passage from Dakar, averaging no
less than 118 miles a day, not having experienced one calm day when
crossing the doldrums, but gone right through this zone in squally
weather.

It was on 14th May, the great fête day when I was on my way

to see the French Exposition, with two friends, Andre and Pierre, that I saw another yacht come in, the *Frisia*, flying the Swedish flag, but with a single-handed crew—a mysterious Russian. The boat was built of steel and very rusty. He was bound for Buenos Aires and had put into Casablanca because the bottom was foul and he had lost his anchor. He was told to get out of the port as soon as possible.

He was unfortunate, that Russian. He could not speak French or English, and the one man who could speak his language was the Chief of Police.

Six months later, sitting in my rooms in Chelsea, I picked up a newspaper and was interested to read that the *Frisia* had reached Buenos Aires. So he got there in the end.

38

THE PORT

One thing that struck me was the intense activity that prevailed in Casablanca, above all in the port itself. The harbour, absolutely artificial, is an all-time tribute to the engineering skill of the French. It was a simply magnificent achievement to build out that great breakwater. Earlier this century the town had been nothing but a tiny fishing village open to the mighty rollers of the Atlantic, now it is one of the largest ports of the African coast and still increasing. One day I was there, no less than twenty-five steamers were waiting to enter the port. But the big ships had little interest for me; it was the sailing vessels that gladdened my eyes.

Apart from the French tunnymen (yawls and ketches), there were various trading schooners. One graceful green schooner came in from Portugal; she was called *Flora de Setubal*, but what a descent from the glorious sailing schooners of old. Looking at the thin wavy spars that formed the mast, and the general state of the equipment, I wondered just what was the condition of the gardens in Setubal to give the vessel such a name.

Perhaps the cheap wine—one could buy a bottle for elevenpence—generally caused the seamanship to fall below the highest standards. For instance, one of the big modern motor trawlers left the quay opposite, and promptly rammed a house at the entrance to my tiny port, giving me an excuse to stop work (I was scraping the rail) to watch a tug pull her off.

My stay had extended to several weeks when a visitor to tea was horrified because I had not burnt the bread. With all the flies and the heat, one should always put a flame round the bread to kill off the worst of the bugs. Once I had asked an Arab in a shop to cut a long loaf in half. 'The knife is not clean,' he said, and then proceeded to break the loaf in two with his dirty hands.

While lying in the port the boat's bottom had become very foul indeed; in fact, from the water-line some sort of weed was sprouting up to two feet long. One night a peculiar scratching noise disturbed me. I leaped up on deck thinking that an Arab was trying to get away with the mainmast, or some more easily removed gear, but there was nothing in sight. Several times that night that performance was repeated; when daylight came, I found that all the weed round the water-line had vanished. Later the mystery was solved when I found an eel vigorously attacking this weed. It is not many ports which provide cleaning free of charge. However, the eels are not yet sufficiently trained to work below the water-line, and the paint which had been applied in the Azores had encouraged rather than prevented the weed. Even during the sea passage from the Azores the bottom had become foul, which no doubt was a cause of some of our poor day's runs.

At high-tide springs, on Saturday, 21st April, I weighed the two anchors and took *Temptress* alongside the wall. Casablanca is an ideal place for scraping and painting the bottom. There is ample tide, a good hard, and this convenient wall. As the tide left her, long weeds and thousands of jelly-like pendulums were exposed to view. Even with the help of an enthusiastic Frenchman, it was hard work cleaning all this off, but underneath the paint was in good condition. At one place forward on the stem the worms had started their deadly work. I lit my blow-lamp and for a moment, a very brief moment, they realised they had committed an error of judgment.

On Sunday we were at work at six-thirty with sandpaper, wire brush and plenty of elbow-grease, all ready for the paint on Monday. Such is the perversity of weather that, after brilliant sunshine for a month or more, down came the rain in solid sheets, turning the dust on the decks into mud. 'Ah! good for the crops,' I supposed, 'one man's meat… '; but still there were anxious moments at each side. Although a mile or two from the entrance to the harbour, there was always a surge there and when the tide was up the keel would pound on the concrete, making the whole boat shudder and the equipment rattle in protest.

The following morning was perfect and as fair as one could wish. *Temptress*, well and truly protected against the worm and weed, proceeded back to her berth off the Société Nautique.

On the following Sunday I was invited to a baptism of a new Club boat. In England if someone bought a small open boat to add to the Club fleet, perhaps one or two friends would deign to go and look at it, but not so with the French. Ceremonies and champagne parties are the order of the day.

The new little boat, all spick and span, dressed overall with flags fluttering in the breeze, was moved to the pontoon. The boy scouts stiffened to attention. The parson in his white robes nervously fingered his prayer book. We were ready.

The idea was a shot, to seal the event, from one of the two starting cannon. Max Tourniquet was in charge of the two cannon and had himself converted the twelve-bore cartridges into blanks. There was some slight hitch in the proceedings. Max pulled the lanyard for the first time. Everybody held their breath. Nothing happened. A second pull merely resulted in an anaemic 'pouf' from the gun.

'*Comme d'habitude,*' someone said.

There was the second gun in reserve though, and there was no nonsense about that one. It gave a tremendous explosion and the cheers of the multitude were mingled with the cries of the wounded, as an unfortunate scout, who had received the wad in his arm, was led away into the background.

Later, in the Club Room, itching fingers were held back from the cool inviting champagne laid out, row upon row, upon the long table, while a lengthy speech ran its interminable course. All things come to an end, however, and, with unbecoming alacrity, hands rushed forward to seize the sparkling liquid, and a good time was had by all—except perhaps the hapless scout.

The gunner of this episode, and also the starter of most of the sailing races, Max Tourniquet de Brandt (to give him his full name), is the Vice-President of the Société Nautique; he was the first person I met coming into the port, and, on leaving, almost the last. He is a tremendous help and a mine of information to any bona fide yachtsman.

Anyone contemplating an ocean voyage cannot but benefit from Max's dealings with the ocean-going fraternity, from Captain Bernicot and M. Marin-Marie to the number of budding navigators who call in at Casablanca.

He does not seem to be able to find the time to sail himself, however; his *Jeanette* is hauled up on the concrete slipway, and is used as a non-floating home. This beautiful little boat, a schooner, is, nevertheless, slowly but surely being fitted with every known labour-saving gadget. When, if ever, he launches her, she will be able to do anything but talk. This is amply made up for by her owner. *Quel bavard!*

I mentioned above Captain Bernicot, who at the moment seems almost unknown outside France. Yet he is one of the great five who have sailed round the world single-handed, choosing the route taken by Captain Slocum, by the Magellan Straits. Only a limited number of copies of his journal were published in French, but I have now had some correspondence with him regarding the translation of his book into English.

One evening when having dinner with Max aboard his schooner we were discussing coastal navigation, and Max, talking in French, said that a compass and lead were very useful, but even more so was to have a good 'pifomètre' aboard.

'*Qu'est-ce que c'est qu' un pifomètre?*' I asked, which caused roars of laughter. I suppose the best translation in English for this word would be 'a good nose', or sixth sense. I was not the only one to put my foot in it with regard to this important instrument. The Frenchman who was teaching the native cadets navigation, hearing this expression, had gone up to the Captain and asked if there was a 'pifomètre' on board. The poor fellow has never lived this down.

Between the basin where *Temptress* was lying and the French part of the town lay the famous Medina, the Arab quarter, and I used this as a short cut, fascinated by the narrow crude streets and the colourful vendors. All the Arab women wore the yashmak, above which dancing and beautiful eyes would flash mischievously, hinting at an exciting loveliness beneath; but imagination betters reality, and the thick lips and rounded tattooed chin do not conform to the European sense of beauty.

One would think it would not involve much skill to wear a veil tied across one's nose and mouth, but I observed two feats which probably need considerable practice. The first was in the local bus where a girl was eating an orange without exposing her face to view, somehow passing the pieces underneath, while another in the street reversed the procedure by expectorating strongly and accurately from under her yashmak. This garment must be popular with ill-favoured women; the better looking girls sometimes cheat by using transparent nylon.

Generally, I found the narrow streets quite friendly. No one seemed to take any notice of me. I was not touted as one is apt to be in passing the Arab shops in the European part of the town. Most of my shopping was done in the Arab quarter; it was less expensive and more interesting.

Leather goods were exceptionally cheap but of bad quality. A handsome leather suit-case, looking rather like pigskin, cost a mere twenty-five shillings, but lasted only ten minutes of travelling before the handle broke. This made me glad that I had not paid the three pounds originally asked.

This bargaining business is rather a bore if you are hurried, although sometimes quite amusing. As buyer one is in an exceedingly strong position, and one's final ace is merely to say that one will return tomorrow, and start to make preparation to leave the store. The voluble Arab, waving his arms, immediately halves the price. Just how Moroccan leather has become so famous I cannot imagine because nearly all of it is very inferior; perhaps it is because there is such a vast quantity.

On arrival I had been warned it was dangerous to pass through the Arab quarter at night, so, to begin with, I would only do so in daylight; but after a time, as it was such a good short cut, I would pass right across the so-called worst quarter, without meeting any very alarming incidents.

However, one night things might have developed a little awkwardly. I had already wandered through the lighted part of the shops on the way back to the boat, and had just reached the unlighted stretch when two typical Arab toughs suddenly appeared, one on each side of me.

'You want beer? Nice woman? Yes?'

I answered loudly: '*No quiero nada,*' which took them aback.

'You know English, yes?' one said.

'*Oui, un peu,*' I replied, adding: 'Zee speek Engleesh?'

A stunned silence followed my remark. They were baffled. In any case, they had lost the initiative; I pressed my advantage, pretending to be very angry, shouting wildly in French.

Heads began to appear in windows which were being rattled up. My trump card was, '*Vous êtes fous, hein? j'habite là,*' gesticulating wildly in the direction I was going. At this final parry they muttered something to themselves and disappeared as quickly as they had come.

I could imagine well enough what would happen if one was not strong enough to refuse their persuasive offers. They would either lead you to a dark corner, give you a crippling punch and steal everything you had, including your clothing, or if they were genuine they would give you some half-doped beer before you were robbed by the 'nice woman'.

*   *   *

Originally we had come in for a couple of days merely to buy stores, but, as usually happens with visitors to Casablanca, I was still there after three months. In fact, I felt like one of the inhabitants, and looked with scorn upon a new-comer.

Of the greatest interest, of course, were the little things that happened in the port. Fishing out the odd corpse was not an unusual form of entertainment.

One day there was an ear-splitting crash in the shipyard, followed by the inevitable gathering of a crowd. The engineers, who had been trying to instal a motor in one of the local fishing boats, had distinguished themselves by dropping it clean through the bottom of the boat, fracturing the keel (this does not say much for the strength of construction).

Why on earth don't these wretched little bath-tubs of fishing-boats carry SOME SAIL? I wondered. Rows and rows of boats were laid up out of service, waiting for engine parts. One would think that even a riding sail would be carried to ease the strain on the engine, especially when running; after all, there are good winds off the port which would at least be fair one way. I reached the conclusion that the fishermen were just lazy and not true sailors.

However, the local boys certainly go in for colour. There was one boat ready for launching after the periodic overhaul. The bottom was red, and (reading upwards) the rubbing strake was green, boot-top black, white bulwarks, grey aft, green rail, wheelhouse white, deck fittings brilliant blue and grey, and masts yellow with white tops—and this was nothing unusual. However, the paint is of poor quality and the vivid colours soon tone down.

The visiting Spaniards show no such display, but paint their hulls a ghastly yellow all over.

Nearly all the big fishing-boats were powered by huge single- or twin-cylinder diesel engines with terrific vibration, which shook the hulls, of inferior timber, cruelly. It was waggishly said that the bump, bump, bump so plainly heard was the sound of the planks snapping together again. The exhausts were led out of a funnel and, on a quiet day, could be clearly heard although the boat might be below the horizon.

Temptress was so near the pontoon of the Société Nautique, where the bathers congregated and the racing shells (twos, fours and eights) were launched, that although I was too busy working on board to meet them, I soon got to know most of the members by sight, both men and girls. Incidently the French girls made me wonder whether the rowing forms their shapely legs, or do they take up rowing (and the opportunity to show them off) because they have shapely legs?

On Sundays everybody seemed to gravitate to the harbour, sailing, rowing, bathing or merely idly looking at others sailing, rowing, bathing...

Heavy row-boats full of colourful Arabs would progress slowly by. The women looked a bit queer, to European eyes, completely covered as they were in voluminous white garments, with just a slit to see through. They looked quite ghostly sitting in rows, motionless. Just what did they think about the French girls in front of the Club, dressed in abbreviated (and very attractive) two-piece bathing suits? Were they shocked? It is difficult to imagine Arab women being shocked. Maybe they were envious. As regards the men, however, there was no doubt at all about what they were thinking.

39

ARABIAN INTERLUDE

One friend who used to visit me quite often was a Frenchman, named Van Geem. He was one of those electric maniacs. Most usefully he managed to repair my large wireless set which had not worked for many months. But he did not stop at that; he had the most awful ideas of plastering poor *Temptress* with all sorts of electrical gadgets powered by air-screws and the Lord knows what else.

I am deeply indebted to him, however, for his kind hospitality, and also for introducing me to an Arab who invited us to visit him in one of his houses way back in the interior of Morocco. It turned out to be a most interesting experience.

Leaving Casablanca soon after dawn, we were driven by an Arab in flowing robes which frequently got mixed up with the gear lever of the ancient and protesting automobile. After a couple of hours the road dwindled into a mere track. Camels, oxen and donkeys (usually supporting a colossal Arab) would surrender only at the last moment. Our driver would never slacken speed, but would just hold his hand on the horn. Accidents were avoided by the Grace of Allah.

We arrived at the farm with a flourish, hens and children scattering in all directions. The white house and walls of the courtyard were set amidst green plains rolling away into the misty blue distance.

Owing to the early start and the fresh keen air it was not long before I began looking forward to a good 'blow-out', my first Arab feast, though it was tinged with a certain amount of anxiety whether I would remember all the correct etiquette.

Our host appeared. He was short and stout. Kindly eyes shone out of a lined but handsome face. His small beard was grey. He mustered a quiet dignity which many Europeans fail to attain. I liked him at once.

When our numbers had swollen to twelve we were shown to a doorway and, leaving our shoes outside, entered what was the 'guest room'. This was built out from, but had no access to, the rest of the house, where lived the chief and his wives. On the stone floor and along the whitewashed walls thin mattresses lay end to end. A very low table completed the furnishings. There was no window.

We sat down, round the table, cross-legged on the mattresses and waited hopefully for food.

Ben Larbi was the one who spoke French and acted as interpreter. Up to his arrival I had been somewhat of a mystery figure, and I had had several quizzical glances shot in my direction. All that was now changed, and they all heard about my voyages. They treated the whole thing as a great joke. The more horrific the story the louder their laughter. By the time I had told them how *Temptress* had been rolled upside-down and lost a mast they were nearly biting the mattresses, and tears were rolling down their cheeks. Even after sailing a distance equivalent to one-third round the world, it will not get you very far if you hope to be treated seriously by the Arabs.

At last, after some altercation and scuffling outside which we all pretended not to notice, the doorway darkened and two men came staggering in with an enormous copper bowl several feet across—food—and in quantity. There remained enough room round the edge of the table to park our individual chunks of bread, ready to be broken up by our left hand and use for mopping up liquid.

Some prayer was murmured and right hands were plunged into the steaming mess, which, by the smell and the shape of the odd bone, appeared to be chicken.

I was a bit slow in starting. My host made signs for me to commence. Restraining an impulse to say 'Bob's your uncle', I supplicated 'For what we are about to receive...' and dug in with my first two fingers and thumb, managing to withdraw a piece of meat without scalding my fingers too much. Gradually I became more expert and with the meat a more reasonable temperature I succeeded in stowing an adequate quantity.

At a sign the dish was carried away. However, a few minutes later it reappeared filled to the brim with lumps of mutton swimming in fat—hot fat. Every now and again someone would give a stifled exclamation and plunge his burning fingers into his mouth to cool. I struggled gamely on. Whenever I looked away, playing for time, a large piece of meat would be thrown into my excavation. I would smile, nod and point to the food with my dripping greasy hand. It became obvious why the others had rolled up their sleeves to the elbow.

Eating went slower. The level dropped more gradually, but once again the bowl was whisked away only to be returned filled with cous-cous, the national dish. 'How many more?' I groaned inwardly, making an effort to continue my smiling, nodding and pointing. My stomach had reached the full stage. This latest dish was the most difficult to eat. One had to form a cement-like ball with rice, fat and meat, if possible without getting the resultant mess all over the palm. By an awkward flicking motion of my bent thumb I managed to get a considerable percentage in my mouth. Incidentally it does not help allowing it to cool, for the congealing fat makes it reluctant to leave the hand…

A harmless dish of junket followed. By then the heat and the superabundance of food had forced us into a sort of coma. Eating had almost stopped. Our host gave a meaning cough. The meal was over. The more delicate of us then used napkins we had brought. A slave brought round a wooden bowl of water to sprinkle on our hands. We tottered, completely distended, to a standing posture, thanking our host loudly.

The others went to sleep it off, but my only desire was to try and recover by some exercise. After a ramble over the hill to watch men and women filling their jars at the water-hole, I had sufficiently revived to take advantage of the loan of a magnificent horse, a white thoroughbred Arab. Before I had the time to get both my feet into the stirrups, it was off like the wind across the plains. After a mile or two I succeeded in getting the helm hard over. A sharp turn nearly had me off, then off we went like a rocket again, luckily in the direction of home. I was highly complimented on my horsemanship, but in reality the steed had done just what it liked, ignored all my English type of commands, and was not in any way under my control.

A week later much comment was caused in the Société Nautique when a colourful Arab in full dress visited *Temptress*; it was my friend Ben Larbi, the one who spoke French—luckily, or the visit might have been a bit of a strain. I was secretly glad that the Chief had not come. To begin with, he would have had great difficulty in getting his bulk down the hatch, then all we could have done would have been to sit in the saloon nodding and smiling at each other.

It is an odd fact that the uneducated Arab, although he cannot write a word of any tongue, seems to be able to pick up French or English with remarkable ease, while the educated Arabs appear to have great difficulty in learning foreign languages.

It was not before the 2nd June that my last job on board was finished—a new watertight hatch for the after cockpit locker. She was almost ready for sea, and about time too. The bottom had become very weedy again and, contemplating the hundreds of miles of beating to windward which lay before me, I decided to repaint her.

It was an exhausting labour. There was no one to help me this time, and it had to be done single-handed. I moved her against the wall and, as the tide receded, scraped off the weed with a brush, myself waist deep in the oily water. After sandpapering, both sides of her ample bottom were painted, and I motored back to the anchorage at midnight. It was quite enough work for one day. My back aches to think of it still.

I did a final round of shopping, followed by a dinner with Max aboard his *Jeannette*.

Arriving back on *Temptress* after midnight I started to write my final letters. No sleep for me that night. The dock police had been told I was leaving at six o'clock in the morning, and leave at six I would.

40

HOMEWARD BOUND

At three o'clock in the morning I started preparations for getting under way for England.

By the time the two anchors had been raised and *Temptress* moved over to the pontoon, with all warps coiled and stowed, it was exactly six o'clock.

Hoping the Authorities were impressed by my punctuality, I put the engine in 'ahead' and moved slowly out of the little basin.

Of course, half-way down the harbour one plug had to oil up, and we drifted haphazardly about amid the shipping while another was installed.

Clearing the end of the breakwater *Temptress* lifted to the low swell. The clangour of the City had been changed once again for the splendour of the Sea.

The log recorded my 'departure' thus:

> *5th June.*
> 06.50:   *The whistle buoy abeam: streamed log 0: course N.*
> *by W. slight N.W. swell. Sunny and clear. Wind*
> *E.N.E.—0 to 1. Hoist mainsail.*

As the massive breakwater gradually faded away into the haze astern, the cold thin wind of early dawn steadied from the north-east. Full sail was promptly set. When the log showed 19, land was a faint grey smudge on the horizon, and at 20 it had disappeared.

What would be the next land sight, I mused, Portugal? Spain? France? or England? ¿Quién sabe?

At noon the batteries were fully charged and a gap of twenty-five miles stretched between me and the coast. Turning off the engine I let *Temptress* sail herself close-hauled on the starboard tack, and as there were only two other vessels in sight, left her to it and dropped into my bunk for a rest...

I was awakened by the vibrating note of a diesel engine, and assumed that a boat was passing near to look at me. Just in case, I rolled quickly out of the bunk and put my head up through the hatch. Christopher Columbus! There was a yellow Spanish fishing boat only a few yards ahead, crossing my bow. Danger of collision was imminent. I leapt out of the hatch, naked as I was (no time to stand on ceremony) and dived for the tiller, tore off the lashing and rammed it hard down. The stemhead of the fishing-boat was only three feet away. *Temptress* spun round like a rater, the bowsprit just shaving his hull. My bow swung ahead of him and the flare of his bow was actually overlapping the cockpit; I had to straighten up to avoid smashing the bumpkin.

Luckily there was no sea to stop our way and *Temptress*, after going straight into the wind's eye for some feet, paid off on the opposite tack—safe. All this had been done in complete silence aboard both boats. I was silent no longer, letting fly in a broadside of French, telling him what was my opinion of his boat, his seamanship and his parents. Then realising that he was Spanish, I repeated the whole thing in his language. The Captain, looking very pink in the face, shouted in reply but got no support from his crew lining the rails. Climbing out of the shelter of the cockpit, with as much dignity as could be mustered in my unclothed state, I disappeared down the hatch.

It was a disgraceful bit of seamanship on his part; *Temptress* must have been in sight for over an hour and was doing only a steady two knots on the starboard tack, having complete right of way.

This dangerous incident put me in a vile temper for the rest of the day.

The first day at sea is never very pleasant, and a near misfortune like this, right at the start, seemed a bad omen for the voyage.

Shortly after this episode, the wind freshened; with ill grace I noticed that it had backed to the north. There were hundreds of miles of beating to windward ahead of me.

My first noon to noon run was sixty-five miles, but the fresh wind had died away leaving *Temptress* rolling in a flat calm, occasionally creeping forward before a vagrant air. Once we glided slowly past a fleet of tiny Portuguese men-of-war, not much bigger than half-crowns.

I thought of Otilia and how much she would have liked to be there in those fine conditions. She would have improved the hours, but nevertheless I was glad to be in my single-handed state. One tends to wish more for company when it is calm. I smiled to think how I had searched the boat for stowaways before leaving Casablanca.

I dived overboard into the blue water, swimming right round the yawl as she heaved and sighed in the bosom of the ocean, and completely regained my normally buoyant spirits.

A pocket storm followed, from the west, making *Temptress* roar through the whole night over a breaking sea. She seemed to fly before the squalls. The wind suddenly veered to the north-west, and, using the first light of dawn, I rolled down four turns in the mainsail and hove to. The cross seas pummelled the hull as I slept below.

The following night the loom of the flash of Cape St. Vincent was bearing 333 degrees.

At the first green light of daybreak I was gazing northwards trying to sight land which was, as I knew perfectly well, below the horizon.

The short nights were a great joy after the winter darkness that had always seemed so unending during my previous passage.

Many ships were in sight on the great steamship lane leading to and from the Straits of Gibraltar. A large tanker, *Lord Canning*, sped past, lifting and sinking to the ocean swell.

Although we were thirty miles off shore, the land gave me a lee from the wind which I knew would be howling down the Portuguese coast. There was a tempting bay offering perfect shelter to the north-east, but we pressed on westwards, driving against the Atlantic seas. As darkness fell the loom of the lighthouse could still be seen, but bearing more easterly.

There was a rare and beautiful sight in the sky that night. As the sickle of the new moon altered its position in relation to the stars, it crossed near Venus giving the impression that this planet was hanging suspended from its lowest point.

On the fourth day out of Casablanca, at noon, *Temptress* was jammed close-hauled to a fresh wind, in big seas. The position was fifty miles west of Cape St. Vincent. The first stage of my journey was over. My general chart was folded up and put away; my position was plotted on the bottom of the chart of Portuguese West Coast.

To Finisterre was the next step. Only 350 miles, but to windward and against the current.

The evening was more peaceful. I sighted my only steamer of the day, obviously bound out from Lisbon and heading for Madeira. She crossed my bow half a mile off; silhouetted black against the falling sun, she looked like a child's toy cut out of paper and stuck on the horizon. They probably thought I was bound for the Azores, considering my course.

Taking cat-naps below, I risked allowing *Temptress* to continue through the night under full sail. This would be a very dangerous practice further south owing to the squalls.

How conditions change from day to day at sea. How different was the next morning, to the jabble of the day before, and what delight it was gliding along close-hauled to a gentle current of air instead of bashing into head seas. How much better it was to be a hundred miles from land in the brilliant sunlight, with few steamers, than in the foggy congested vicinity of the coast.

At one o'clock in the afternoon I performed a masterly nautical manoeuvre by going about on a port tack, having been on the starboard tack for 135 miles. One could imagine this manoeuvre hailed as an act of genius to combat the head winds. Alas, the secret is that I had come to the edge of the chart and had to tack to stop falling off the edge altogether.

Dusk was beautiful with the clear green sky succeeding a fine-weather sunset; the lovely night breeze whispered softly, caressing the canvas, as *Temptress* clove her way through phosphorescent waters. The light of the growing moon flooded the north-west swell which rolls unendingly down to the Portuguese coast.

Early the following morning I missed the chance of a wonderful photograph as well as an opportunity to report my position. While I was washing-up after breakfast, the throb of an engine fell on my ears, followed immediately by a 'toot-toot'. It was the *Gorgola*, or some similar name, of Lisbon, a small coaster, dashing by. The crew waved and cheered, making frantic signals for me to hoist my national colours, which I promptly did, but she was well on her way. Taking a careful bearing of her course and laying it off on the chart I could see that she was bound to Lisbon from Madeira. It would have caused quite a stir had they realised that it was *Temptress* that had crossed her path—she was a very well-known boat in Portugal by now, on account of my stowaway.

My enemy, the northerly wind, came back again with renewed force. As *Temptress* drove into the head sea I did my best to take a sight while soused in spray.

Thus ended the first week at sea.

41

FALSE HOPES

The start of the second week was promising; the stiff wind had eased for one thing, and the sea gone down sufficiently to allow me good progress. I had finished hauling on the halyards to increase the area to full sail, and was back at the helm muffling myself up with pullover, jersey, windbreaker and oilskin—for it was cloudy and cold—when I sighted a smart motorship coming straight for me from the north-east. Immediately my signal letters were hoisted from the yardarm and my ensign from the mizzenmast head.

She came closer. Through my levelled binoculars the letters HUBERT PROM were visible. As she crossed my stern I hoisted M-I-K and the code pennant. This was acknowledged smartly. I took a photograph. She rushed by smoothly without altering course or speed—just as signalling should be. It is not right for yachts to stop ships which are engaged in commerce. Again levelling my glasses I read BORDEAUX on the stern. It was pleasing to think that my parents would know my exact position; less pleasing, so would the newspapers. At least so I thought. Actually their show of efficiency must have left them exhausted, because the report was never made to Lloyd's, after all.

The sun set as an orb of gold. Crouched at the helm against the cold north-east wind, I watched it slowly sink into the wastes of the Atlantic. Lord! What space there is!

Gradually twilight gave place to night, and the tracery of rigging and angles of sails were black and clear-cut against the horizon sky. On the beam, the silvery light of the first quarter of the moon shone steadfastly, and one by one the stars pin-pointed the heavens. Even the wind was hushed as in reverence. There was only the rhythm of silence—silence that at sea is full of small sounds, in no way disturbing.

Those swells, awe-inspiring in the moonlight, would be frightening in their magnitude to anyone unaccustomed to the way of the sea. *Temptress* knew them well and picked her way delicately with the confidence born of long practice.

Mildews were beginning to sprout on the bread by this time—only eight days out. It was not wholly unexpected. But mildews were growing even more lustily on the bacon and I was a little vague what to do about that. Before frying it for lunch, I brushed it with a nail brush, comforting myself, for what it was worth, with the thought that in Spain there had been rows of hams hanging in the shops, completely enveloped in mildew, having presumably been there for months.

The day's run of seventy miles was quite enough to satisfy me. It gave me a position a little north of Lisbon, and 160 miles off shore, an excellent strategic position for meeting the north-westerlies which I hoped to pick up any day.

Cape Finisterre was then bearing N.E. and 295 miles off.

By the early hours of the morning the wind fell right away, leaving a complete calm. My hopes were raised at once. Was this the precursor of the westerlies? It was a chance anyway to gain northing and, with the engine going, *Temptress* ploughed through the mirror-like surface of the water, lifting and swaying to the silent oily swells.

Later, shining through the overcast sky came a glimpse of the moon, and I saw with interest and satisfaction that the clouds passing across its face came from the north-west. This was followed by faint cats-paws from this quarter. Then again calm. I stopped engine after a five-hour run.

Peeling potatoes usually is tackled unenthusiastically, but on that day it was such a pleasant chore, with my bare legs dangling over the bulwarks, that I was sorry when it was completed. Such simple moments are good for the soul.

While lunch was cooking I plunged again and again into the invigorating water. Swimming on my back ahead of the boat, I noticed she was catching me up, and, twisting round in the water, swam at my greatest speed until it was only just possible to hold my own. I hesitated a moment; she caught me up; grabbing the bobstay I swung myself aboard via the bowsprit shrouds like an acrobat. Five minutes later we were doing three knots under full sail. Towards England. The north-westerly had arrived.

A school of leaping dolphins made a great commotion rushing towards, then pretending to flee away, from *Temptress*. Leaving me waiting hopefully with the camera, they splashed off joyously to the distant horizon.

Had it not been for the steady barometer I would have supposed, by all the black clouds, that we were in for some bad weather. The atmosphere became very muggy and fog banks loomed ahead. Towards sunset we sailed into the gloomiest part of the area, with queer light and dark paths of water.

Rain started slowly, drop by drop, then came a few short puffs of wind. I lowered the mizzen and watched out for more, but nothing happened. Gradually it became clear and the whole box of tricks muttered away to the east leaving a steady wind.

By dusk it was blowing fresh with the wind veering sharply. The old norther after all. Thus were my hopes for a north-westerly swept away.

42

CLOSE SHAVE

Eight days had passed since I doubled Cape St. Vincent, and yet we were only half-way to Finisterre. Two days of fair wind would have taken me clear of the inhospitable Portuguese coast.

It had blown hard from the north for two days, and that night it worsened. After several heavy seas had crashed on top of us, stopping dead fourteen tons of boat in a few feet, I feared that some damage might result; going on deck I ran her off before the waves, rolled up the jib and finally left her hove to under backed staysail and reduced main. Now the way was off her she lay-to, dry and comfortable. With every hour we were losing ground with wind, sea and current pushing us southwards.

With this gradual edging in towards the shore, navigation had to be watched, but the noon sight was pretty hectic for me, one arm round the mizzenmast and the other holding the sextant.

No more fresh bread. The last loaf was toasted over the primus. Whiskers were beginning to grow inside. For the first time in my life I had actually bought the right amount of bread, consuming every single loaf. One usually buys too much bread; it goes bad before it can be eaten, and has to be dumped over the side.

The wind backed a little, blowing across the old sea, and immense waves surrounded me, pinnacled with jagged spurs. The sea became even more irregular and a heavy one burst green right over the boom, sending *Temptress* smashing down with a paralysing blow.

Black cylindrical clouds pointed in a great 'V' to windward, as they had for the last forty-eight hours. It was the end of another unpleasant and unenjoyable day. *Temptress* just fought, fought, fought.

The best we could do was to hang on to our position.

The following dawn broke absolutely clear without a cloud in the sky, but it was blowing gale force nevertheless. After periods in my bunk I would look out of the windward porthole, but found no sign of lessening. Once a tanker, pointing south, came near to look at me. We were then only about forty miles off shore. As the coast bent slightly westward to the south of me, it would leave a very small margin in a shift of wind. A north-westerly wind would put me on a direct lee shore.

Various plans ran through my brain. Cape Roca at the entrance to the River Tagus was only one hundred miles to the south, and the Berlingers, with a good lighthouse, only sixty miles away. It might be prudent to run southward. The blow could last a week and was increasing every day. In sixteen hours shelter could be reached. It was a gamble. Should I run for it and lose one hundred miles so painfully gained? or hang on and hope a change of wind would put an end to the fourth day of gale?

Whilst this problem occupied my mind the boat was completely buried under a great sea. There was no damage, although water was pouring out of the mainsail. But I decided to hold on.

Through the lee port could be seen a permanent rainbow born of the stream of spindrift blowing over the bow. Gusts of Force 8 were logged.

At night a careful watch was kept for steamers, but *Temptress* had manoeuvred nicely in this matter, drifting across the shipping track during the day.

On Tuesday, 19th June, the gale was over and the wind eased to Force 4 to 5. Through a veil of mist towards the east, could be seen the loom of land. A definite bump. I guessed that it was Cape Mondego, which is the only bump shown on the chart.

After wearing the ship round, I lay to on the other tack until noon, when a shot of the sun confirmed my estimated position. It was strange, this glimpse of land after a fortnight at sea, a hill just popping up where it should be, before disappearing in the haze.

The forced inactivity below during the gale made me eager to get moving, and in spite of the heavy confused sea I drove *Temptress* to windward all the afternoon and evening, re-crossing the steamer track. I had never driven her so hard before. In spite of the chaotic conditions and well-reefed mainsail she knocked up twenty-four miles by sunset.

In the saloon some books had jumped out of the shelves, but everything else was in good order and dry considering the frequent lumps of water which had dolloped aboard.

One little coaster, evidently bound for Vigo, came ploughing up to windward. To those seamen *Temptress* must have looked a stirring sight driving and leaping right out of the water, and at times enveloped in heavy spray.

After sunset came the rare sight of a huge moon, pink and oval, rising out of the seas in the east. The deck was black, like wet and polished onyx, in the tranquil light of this full moon.

On the 20th June my voyage was nearly brought to a sudden close by a joker on a steamer; the weather was crystal clear; in broad daylight I could see the masts and bridge of the ship coming up on the beam. My colours were made ready to hoist. She mounted over the horizon and converged rapidly upon me.

Temptress was doing four knots, close-hauled in a choppy sea. She headed across my bow. I thought: 'By Jingo! He is cutting it a bit fine.'

She came tearing through the water at about twenty knots; it was too late for me to bear away. Her bow cut across my bowsprit, and 600 feet more to come. I luffed up to take off way. The bridge passed almost overhead and above my cross-trees. The wash from her bow wave knocked the yawl almost out of control.

For agonising moments it looked as if we would collide but her beam narrowed aft, and *Temptress* was sucked in under her stern. I looked up and saw the huge letters of LOIDE-HAITI—RIO DE JANEI-RO. A man was hoisting the national colours, and gazed with blank astonishment at his sudden view of a sailing boat beneath him, with an outraged Englishman on deck shaking his fist and shouting expletives.

The stern of the ship was wrenched out of sight as *Temptress* went mad in the whirlpool of her wash. The helm was useless. She gybed, backed and gybed again with the spars smashing violently from side to side. Struggling to regain mastery, I passed across the far edge of the steamer's wake; she was already a mile away. 'That,' I said quietly, 'is a fine bit of steamercaptain seamanship.'

I seized my log book and composed the following letter:

The Captain of the *Loide-Haiti*.

Dear Sir,

With reference to the meeting between *Loide-Haiti* and my ten-metre boat *Temptress*, off the Portuguese coast on 20th June, 1951, should we have the pleasure of renewing our acquaintance at sea, I would be much obliged if you would kindly issue orders to your helmsman to leave a gap of at least ten metres between our respective vessels, as I have no wish to cause any damage to your ship.

I am, yours faithfully...

43

SPANISH ISLAND

The 21st June sent me a light north-north-westerly breeze prompting me to put the boat about and wrest some miles to the north with the help of the engine. The fix at noon put us 120 miles from land and 175 miles to Cape Finisterre.

I stopped the engine at lunch-time, and started to prepare some dried cod which had been soaking for twenty-four hours. Dried cod is not everybody's dream dish, nor is it mine, but it is infinitely superior to tinned fish, as smoked bacon (however mildewy) is to tinned meat.

Otilia had told me that this cod was the Portuguese national dish, and is such a treat that they ask their friends in to the feast; they prepare it soused in olive oil and with a kind of cabbage. In Casablanca, Otilia used to buy dried cod, and I always managed to put on the required show of enthusiasm. The Portuguese call it Bacalhau; there is a book called *A Hundred Ways How to Cook Bacalhau*; perhaps the hundred and first way will be more universally appreciated.

Lunch over, I busied myself setting up the rigging which was, as usual, hanging in bights, and oiling the engine. It seemed a pity on this wonderful evening of light breeze, to disturb the peace with the noise of the engine, but it was wise to grab every chance to make northing.

However, just as I was about to go below to tackle the machinery, the wind backed to the north-west and hardened. After easing the sheets, I dashed to the fo'c'sle to drag out the huge reaching staysail. It slid up the stay and bellied out. Bubbles frothed past.

Temptress had spread her wings and soared over the blue sea like a homing bird. Better still, the wind backed more to the west. Once again I thought I had picked up the westerlies and all that was ahead of me now was a lovely June sail across the Bay of Biscay.

It was the start of a glorious sail on Midsummer Night!

Black clouds to windward prompted me to change the reaching staysail to the working sail, and gradually the sky became overcast. But *Temptress* slipped along hour after hour at four to five knots. Then rain sprinkled and spattered; the wind freshened.

For over an hour I had the lights of a steamer to steer by, but the rest of the night there was only the glowing bowl of the compass ahead of me, on which my eyes were levelled. The usual expression is eyes 'riveted' or 'glued' to the compass, but reading this I can never help visualising the unpleasant inconvenience of the literal interpretation.

The rain fell more heavily and struck cold, but it kept the water as smooth as velvet. *Temptress* rushed along with little noise, only the boiling of water under her forefoot. The rain stopped, then came again. The wind strengthened and started to veer in the early hours of the morning; squalls became more frequent and it was necessary to run off before them to kill their force. *Temptress* was still under full sail.

All night the speed never dropped below four knots and was often up to seven knots; I swear she did eight once or twice.

At dawn the wind was back in the hated north. Four turns were rolled down in the mainsail and the yawl was hove to, but the fair wind had been used to the maximum and the chance had been grabbed. Over sixty miles to the north had been knocked up—well worth the loss of a night's sleep.

In spite of the earlier calm and only twelve and a half hours of actual sailing, the noon to noon run was seventy miles, so I had averaged six knots right through the night.

Once again the wind was blowing directly in my face. A head wind and a cross sea. Immediately a wind shifts, the new sea runs across the old, churning up great lumps and ridges. *Temptress* staggered one way and the other as if uncertain what was expected of her.

The wind eased next morning, leaving a tumbling sea, but taking great care I obtained a good observed altitude of the sun. In fact it was a remarkable sight, the position line was only half a mile off from the dead reckoning.

At noon we were sixty miles off and converging on the land; ahead lay the broken coast and chain of islands south of Finisterre. All the coast passed during the previous week or two had been inhospitable, only a few artificial harbours.

By the afternoon I was on the edge of the shipping track. The ships looked so steady and safe riding evenly on the waves, compared to my own rough and tumble progress. I decided to make for the coast by Vigo Bay—out of that accursed wind.

After dark it was rougher; as *Temptress* crashed through the seas she would occasionally plunge in her bow and a wall of water would come driving over the fo'c'sle, right over the top of the dinghy, and land in my lap.

Several ships passed very close, making me glad of my full display of lights. One of these ships stopped dead astern and spotted a searchlight on me for about five minutes. Suddenly the light went out and the ship drew away on her course to the south. Naturally these tramps were not used to seeing such a small boat at sea. The lights must have confused them as they were continually winking on and off as they got hidden by the crest of a steep sea.

At nine-thirty that night I sighted ahead the loom from the flash of a lighthouse—the entrance to Vigo Bay. It had been another perfect landfall.

By midnight we were in smoother water but it was very cold. Gradually as we converged with the coast the wind fell away owing to the wind-lapse over the peninsular to the north. The gap in the coast which was my goal was only just north of the border between Spain and Portugal.

The Portuguese coast had been the enemy. It was odd that directly the Spanish coast was opposite, the wind and sea eased right away.

Having a different wind just because it was a different country reminded me of the man who had to choose whether to have his farm in Russia or Poland, as the line drawn on the map ran right through the centre of his land. In the end he had chosen Poland for his country, explaining that he could not stand another Russian winter.

It was exciting, approaching land in the early hours of the morning. I suddenly turned my face into the wind. There it was—Land; a strong perfume, grass scented, dust scented, rose to my nostrils—the smell of Spain.

The lights of Spain were stabbing their message through the cold night. I clambered stiffly out of the cockpit, with the handbearing compass. Cross bearings of Monte D'Or light and Silleiro, plotted on the chart, told me that we were sixteen miles off shore.

Being clear of the steamer track, I dived below out of the cold, and started the stove. The kettle was soon singing, and a few minutes later I was sipping hot cocoa, my chilled hands clasped round the welcome cup. I threw myself on to the bunk for a short nap.

Broad daylight awakened me. The sun had not yet risen, but, right ahead, only nine miles away, were the great mountains of Spain, while farther to the north could be seen humps of numerous islands, silhouetted against the pink sky of dawn.

Temptress was cutting through the smooth water, close hauled on the port tack. A slight swell would occasionally set in from the north-west, making the mainsheet snatch at the blocks. Soon there was not a breath of wind, so, under engine the boat was headed towards Vigo Bay.

Feasting my tired eyes on the colourful land to the south and a small rocky island close to the north, I swung round a point, and, spread out before me, was an enchanting bay with golden sands.

Running in to three and a half fathoms, I thankfully dropped anchor, and stowed the sails. A heavenly feeling of relaxation filled my being. I glanced about me, hugely satisfied with my deserted anchorage. One could see right up the bay to the houses of Vigo; but there was no desire in me yet to meet civilisation.

Off that uninhabited and beautiful island of my choice, there would be perfect peace for a while, sheltered from that tearing, excited northerly wind. Before me was the pleasurable anticipation of a long night of undisturbed sleep—the first good sleep for twenty days.

44

CAPE FINISTERRE

The yellow sun had scarcely risen when my mainsail, already hoisted, was flapping noisily to a squally wind from the north, as I plied the lever of the windlass to and fro. A final tug, and the anchor was broken out—we were under way.

We rapidly overhauled two lovely trading ketches, which were also beating up towards Finisterre. These two had been a mile up to windward when I weighed anchor, yet I drew level with them, took several coloured photographs, passed and left them two miles astern before the morning was out.

The wind blew harder and harder; two turns were taken in the main. Under the lee of Islaona, we were smitten by a succession of heavy squalls; our speed was terrific through the smooth water. As soon as we rounded the point, the wind hit *Temptress* like a slap in the face, as it increased to half a gale. It would have been eleven hours against that wind before I could have hoped to reach the shelter of Muros Bay, so, sailing swiftly into an indentation of the mainland I anchored, and proceeded to have lunch.

It was over two hours before the second trading ketch arrived. She too, sought temporary haven and brought up near by.

Under the point of land towards the ocean, Punta Morro de la Sabosa, a veritable fleet of open fishing-boats were anchored, the tiny masts raking about forty-five degrees. Their rig has not altered for a century or more.

When the wind lost vehemence in the evening, the little fishing-boats hoisted sail and spun off downwind for home. There were first five, then ten, then twenty, then forty sails all bobbing and dancing amongst the waves in the evening sun.

The next day I beat up towards Finisterre, but once again after midday the wind blew furiously, and we joined the fishing boats, running for shelter into Muros Bay. This was another paradise anchorage. Still having no desire to go ashore, I launched the dinghy to record *Temptress* in colour.

There were some boats anchored close by, and I rowed over to ask them if they had any fresh fish. They said they had very little, *poco poco*. However, I gave them two tins of Heinz beans and prepared to row away. They then understood that I was 'solitario', and this password goaded them into action; thereon it was very difficult to refuse handful after handful of sardines.

In the evening the wind eased and veered; the fishing-boats grew masts and enormous sails, as if by magic, and scudded off downwind. What wonderful sailors these men are! They cannot reef the lateen sail, nor can they go about without lowering the whole works and hoisting it up on the other side. It is the most unhandy rig one can imagine, but they certainly waste no time on passage.

It was a wonderful beat in the fresh wind and sun up to Cape Finisterre. On approaching the Cape, as soon as the dazzling white horses on the ocean side of it could be seen, I put the ship about, leaving her hove to with the headsails aback.

I determined not to make a fool of myself signalling with flags as I had at this very spot on my outward voyage. The signal letters were hoisted smoothly, then 'Please report me by telegraph to Lloyd's, London.' After acknowledging my signals they hoisted 'Bon Voyage!' as they had done previously, but this time I was ready, and 'Thanks' shot up on my halyards.

With three turns in the mainsail *Temptress* drifted slowly across the bay hove to, while I enjoyed a leisurely lunch.

I took coloured photographs of the Cape (1/200 of a second, F/3.2), and wondered whether they would reproduce the faint blue-green which hazed the whole atmosphere.

Once again the afternoon wind tore out of the north until it was blowing moderate gale force, with gusts so strong that it was necessary to lower the staysail and beat up past the little port of Finisterre with jib and close-reefed mainsail only.

It was blowing gale force when I ran off to furl the jib, and, under mainsail alone, tacked close in to the sandy beach, and anchored.

What an energetic wind it was! Every day it seemed to pipe up about midday, reaching Force 6 or 7 between two and three in the afternoon, and beginning to die away again in the evening. Starting off at north-east in the morning, it would slowly back to north-north-west.

Before turning in I stared at my chart of the Bay of Biscay. We were just on it. The last lap of my journey was about to begin.

The following morning *Temptress* was skipping down the rocky coast in the bare half-light of dawn, doubling Cape Finisterre. She plunged out into the open sea, driving westwards for a time to clear the disturbance of land, then hauled up to the north-west. More head winds, straight from Ushant.

Several days of stiff head seas followed; as the wind varied one side or the other of north, I would go about to lay on the best tack.

It was on the 1st July, while *Temptress* was slamming into a mass of exploding whitecaps driven by a strong north-easterly wind, that I sighted some French tunnymen. The first one caught me up and came foaming by, rigged with foresail, trisail and mizzen. She was a picturesque sight with light brown sails, blue topsides and red bottom, setting off the greeny blue of the seas—seas which were all the time gashed with white. Enormous rods, one on either side and about ninety feet long, sprouted out like great antennae. This colourful foreground contrasted sharply with the grey horizon haze beneath the pale and cloudless sky.

Rolling heavily, she passed me on the windward side, too far off for a coloured photograph, although the camera was in readiness.

The seas were up to fifteen feet high, but visibility was good.

Temptress plunged on unattended. While reading below, I suddenly heard a shout of voices and saw a huge tunnyman close to the porthole. Grasping my camera and hastily guessing the setting, I opened the hatch and took a shot in the poor light. Later Kodak made a grand reproduction.

A couple of days later we were far out into the Atlantic, still 425 miles off the Lizard, and still that confounded head wind. No proper sleep was possible now either by day or night, owing to the number of fishing-boats in the area. Almost every time I went below to try and snatch a little rest, I was awakened by whistling and shouting and would rush to the hatch to find vessels alongside, some so close that their rods ran the risk of fouling my rigging.

There was no let-up in the head wind. The wind, waves and current had set me 130 miles off course in a longitude even west of Ireland, and still no sign of a change.

Seeing a fish by the stern, I prepared to throw out my spinner, and before the line was disentangled the fish was on—a stone bass eighteen inches long, caught in ten seconds.

> 3rd July.
>
> 11.30: *It is cold with fog, the erratic wind not enough to drive* Temptress *through the short head sea. Progress is virtually nil. This is a trip of no pleasure at all. The accumulative effect of thirty days' strong head winds is beginning to tell on my nerves. It was exasperating enough off Portugal but it was at least expected there, but not in the Bay of Biscay! and all the time I creep north the wind slowly changes so as to come always from my destination. Even the current which should be running to S.E. has been turned to S.W. by the benighted wind.*
>
> 12.55: *Noon to noon run 51 miles: not in the right direction. Correct course… E.N.E. Wind direction… E.N.E. Santa Maria!!!*

45

SICKNESS

Came the calm.

There were many signs though that I had left behind me the sapphires and diamonds of the tropical South, and had reached the gloomy weather of the British Isles; for instance, it was much colder, there were flocks of petrels, there was more phosphorescence in the water, the wind tended to drop at night instead of increasing, and last but not least, it remained overclouded in settled weather and high barometer.

The grey cloud sailing above was uncanny and rather depressing after the incessant blue skies and glorious sun of the south. One expects cloud in bad weather, not in fine weather—it somehow hardly seems fair.

The sea became so smooth that one could even stand on deck without holding on—rare enough on the restless ocean.

During the night of the 5th July it was very calm and, as *Temptress* motored through the still water, with phosphorescence smoking out astern, we passed five tunnymen resting motionless in sleep. At dawn, there was the wonderful sight of no less than two dozen tunnymen under full sail. When their crews came on deck they must have been very surprised to find a little yawl in their midst, as if drawn up from the ocean overnight.

We all drifted about in the quiet airs. The *Marianne* of Concarneau gybed round to pass close, a magnificent sight with blue topsail, white mainsail and gigantic brown jib. Across the water came the strains of an accordion. We had a brief conversation: 'Are you alone?' 'Yes. I'm from Casablanca.' This pronouncement caused a stir of interest aboard. I took several photographs and promised to send them a copy.

After a month of strong head winds and rough seas, the joy of that settled, fine weather and the delight of cruising amongst sailing vessels was almost too good to be true. I felt light-hearted and eager.

A light easterly breeze rose and fell. The *EL 5170* came gliding up astern, trying to overhaul me. *Temptress* drew away from him in the light airs, but on the hardening of the wind he came pushing up close, with a soft ripple on his bluff bows; the sawing of the gear sounded like a B.B.C. sound effect of 'a sailing vessel at sea. The skipper shouted:

'What have you for noon?'

I gave him my latitude, which differed only three miles from his.

By evening the calm was absolutely glassy. The overcast sky, and the white water stretching from horizon to horizon, gave a most curious effect to the tunnymen. They had all lowered their headsails, and lay pointing towards the east like weather vanes to an almost imperceptible air; motionless, they looked unreal, like a fleet of toy boats on a painted sea.

With chin resting on arms folded over the side of the hatch, I watched the darkness slowly gather, and was left with the impression of looking backwards through time; these still and silent vessels were the relics of an age already passed, of which *Temptress*, and possibly myself, were a part.

Footprints of an advancing breeze spread over the sea from the east, and pressed out the folds in our sails. We were soon doing five knots, fast enough for me to catch a tunny myself. Generally these fish do not bite under this speed, and it is this which makes the great fishing yawls such a pathetic sight in a calm, while the less aesthetic motor-boats dash about, raking in one fish after another.

After two hours of this fair breeze, there came a faint rattle of rain which completely killed the wind, leaving the boat rolling and gear jolting in the short swell.

I had felt cold at the helm throughout the breeze, but now found myself shivering violently, unaccountably, alarmingly. I could not understand quite what was wrong and went below to get between some blankets. I fell into a sort of half-sleep, experiéncing terrible night-mares, and awoke with a sharp headache. I felt hot and cold alter-nately, and had difficulty, on occasions, in remembering where I was.

The following day found me as bad as ever, and weak. There was a good breeze from the west in the afternoon, just what was wanted, but I decided to lower the mainsail in case my malady became worse. Leaving the boat to sail slowly downwind, under headsails alone, I dosed myself with aspirin and lay in my bunk where I lay shivering and occasionally delirious, not knowing half the time where I was, and imagining myself to be amongst many people whom I would ha-rangue at some length, presumably out loud.

I once opened my eyes and found that it was night; a series of frightful nightmares followed.

I felt well enough on the next day to go up on deck, although nauseated and weak. The breeze was north-westerly. Illness or no illness, the show must go on; a second day of fair wind could not be wasted, and I prepared to hoist the mainsail. This was no mean task, and was done in stages, with frequent stops for cups of water. The halyards too, swollen in the rain, tended to stick in the blocks. Had the boat been rigged as a Bermudian ketch, the mainsail and mizzen would have been easy to hoist, even in my poor condition.

The wind backed and freshened from aft, and we stepped out at five to six knots, passing through another tunny fleet, a different type of boat and coming from Ile d'Yeu. One of them ran very close; a man held up a tunny fish as if to throw it across, but I waved a 'No thanks' with my right hand, then tipped up my saucepan to show that they were not the only fishermen on the ocean. His offer might have been very welcome though. As it was, I tried but could not eat.

After eight hours at the tiller I had sailed over thirty miles, but could not stand any more. My throat was terribly dry and I was pe-riodically vomiting. Cramps gripped my stomach. I assumed that food-poisoning had laid me low. A rest of half an hour helped, then back to the helm; a fair wind could not be wasted, and at the end of every hour another five and a half miles showed on the face of the (still erratic) log. But this trial was too much for me to bear; the boat was hove to for the night, in a rising wind, and rain.

An hour later, a brilliant light shining on my face awakened me in my bunk. Was it a dream or not? I wondered, but was up quickly; a steamer loomed right above us with a searchlight bathing the whole boat in light, revealing at the same time how rough the sea had become. Sheets of silvery rain streamed across the brilliance and vanished into the dark beyond.

It had been a triumph, though, for *my* masthead light to have been seen in such weather; the regulation lights, red and green, which a sailing vessel should carry, would never have been seen. I gave a casual wave of the arm, facing the light, and then went quickly below out of the driving wet.

My stomach still felt very weak, and I had another nightmare. I dreamed that there was a bombing raid in the town where I was—a strange town—and felt the presence of a 'Thing' which was radio controlled by the enemy. It could cut swathes through house and buildings in any direction—a proceeding which to my terror was in full operation. The 'Thing' was invisible, but it made a tearing, whining noise which was neither a moan nor a cry but a mixture of both, and which rose and fell sickeningly. The buildings crashed, sometimes with the noise of explosion, and sometimes with the slow rumble of falling masonry, dominated always with that terrifying moan-shriek of the 'Thing'.

I awoke sweating, to realise that the noises so alarmingly distorted in my dream were in reality occasioned by the heavy weather outside.

*   *   *

At daybreak it was blowing half a gale over a big regular sea. It would have been ideal for running downwind, but I felt physically too weak to attempt it; nearly all day was spent doubled up in my bunk.

While endeavouring to remain on my feet to tune in on the radio, I had to lie down on the lee settee several times to prevent blacking out. Nevertheless, afraid that the wind would blow up to gale force again during the night, I struggled out on deck to reduce sail. Crawling on all fours, still doubled up with pain and sickness, I managed to roll down four more turns in the boom.

Hearing what I thought was a breaking sea making an odd noise, I looked round to windward and there right alongside, so close that I could have hit it with a boat-hook, was the back of a blue whale, approximately 100 feet long and completely dwarfing *Temptress*. It sank below the surface for a moment, only to reappear half its length farther forward before again submerging. At any moment I expected to feel the shuddering shock as it came up underneath the boat, but the next time it blew just ahead of us. Had we been moving, the situation would have been eventful.

The first shock was followed by a second one—I seized the windward shroud to steady myself, and found it slack—broken. Sitting weakly on the dinghy, I rolled the boom round and round until the gaff jaws were on the gooseneck, and then, after lashing the boom on to the gallows, it was a comparatively simple matter to capture the gaff and lash it to the boom. The mainsail stowed, I rigged the gantline as a temporary shroud.

I crept below shivering and vomiting violently.

All next day it blew and a great pulsing sea and falling barometer indicated worse things to come. The motion, with only a staysail set, was awful.

During the afternoon, two tunnymen passed close and gave a hail. I went on deck and, pointing to the furled mainsail, made an expressive gesture meaning it could not be hoisted, then waved them away: 'No assistance required.'

Before the night was over, it was blowing full gale force, and four seas broke right over the top of us.

Eating was impossible, and I continued to be terribly sick all day.

11th July.

8.00:   *No question of eating. Stomach is a dull ache. God! what nursing I have had since I became ill. Barometer 29.77 in. rising at last. Feel as if my guts are being dredged up.*

46

PLYMOUTH, ENGLAND

At last the wind relented. The sun came out, allowing me to take a sight—an intercept of only half a mile—not bad after two days' guesswork of dead reckoning.

The log was still useless. I stripped it down once more, and threw overboard a little brass washer which had been inserted at Casablanca. After it was assembled and lubricated with gun oil it completely recovered, recording at two knots.

I hoisted the jib to make some progress, then managed a cup of thick soup. Visions of champagne and thick slices of ripe, iced cantaloupe melon, haunted me…

It was just as well that eating was impossible, for there was almost nothing left on board, nothing at all with which to build up my strength; the sea was now too shallow for catching tunny.

The Lizard was 125 miles off, when the wind first headed me, then dropped to a calm. In the morning I made a wonderful discovery on looking through some supposedly empty tins—a whole packet of porridge oats! They looked to me what nuggets of gold must look like to a prospector.

While trying to take photographs of two humpbacked whales, I was stung to action by the sight of a steamer from the south-east coming directly towards me. She was a merchant-ship of about 2000 tons, heavily laden. She lumbered by, taking not the slightest notice of my signals requesting her to report me to Lloyd's. However, one man did have the decency—unprofitable it's true—to leave the wheelhouse for a moment to look at me through binoculars, before retiring again.

It was very hot on deck and *Temptress* wallowed for a while on the blue-and-white quilt of the sea.

Eventually a northerly wind sprang up so I hoisted the mainsail and 'to hell with the broken shroud', driving harder and harder to windward. Thirty miles on course were quickly grabbed.

My spinners were jumping astern at dusk, and several mackerel fell for the shining lure and were hauled, wriggling impotently, over the bulwark.

We were closing the land, but visibility was probably not more than fifteen to twenty miles or it would have been in sight. Bishop's Rock lighthouse was estimated to be on the port beam, only forty-two miles off, whilst Plymouth was under the 100 miles. It seemed scarcely credible.

By dawn the Lizard was thirty miles to the north, but still no sign of land.

The wind continued but backed during the day, evidently eddying round Land's End, giving a tearing breeze just forward of the beam and gathering more and more strength. 'Let it blow and be damned to it,' I muttered. 'Let the sails take themselves in.'

Full sail—even the huge reaching staysail, stretched to breaking point—spurred the yawl to a gallop. Steering became wild, so overpressed was *Temptress*, but I was sick in mind and body and found sadistic satisfaction in being callous to her needs. 'Drive,' I shouted. And drive it was—six, seven knots and more as we staggered through a welter of foam. I leant forward, feeling in the locker for my log book, then wrote: 'No signs of the windlass coming aft yet.' I thought this a great joke, and kept repeating to some imaginary passer-by: 'It's all right, there's no sign of the windlass coming aft yet.'

It was about eight o'clock in the evening when I shouted 'LAND O!' at the top of my voice. In the fog to the north there were two little brown humps of land. I almost forgot my illness at the exciting moment of seeing my country after an absence of three years. I still could not fix my position and was impatient for the darkness, for we were in the range of the Eddystone light. It was exactly eight forty-five when a single bright flash stabbed the evening mist on the port bow. I was five miles out of estimated position, to the east.

My sails held and the wind died away at the start of a cold, clear, moonlit night. This was the second night of no sleep, as the course lay through the dense coastal traffic. To try and keep myself warm I sat below drinking innumerable cups of coffee while *Temptress* slipped along quietly, under full sail.

It never got quite dark to the north all night. What a pleasant thought, to be rid of the ocean swell for good, with the resultant rattle and crash of gear.

The sea was as smooth as a billiard table. At two-thirty in the chill morning a reddish tinge could be seen in the sky. Land was invisible at dawn but, gripped by the familiar excitement, I knew it was there, through the fog, a bare eight miles away.

Soon a fog bank enveloped me in thick swathes. Many a time did I go to the foredeck, ears straining for the wash of breakers on the shore, until suddenly the fog thinned and the land of Devon burst into sight. There it was, close by, rearing above me in beautiful colours—green, a glorious green! I had not realised before what a wonderful colour green could be, after the monotonous blues and greys of the sea.

I still felt sick but it was only a dull aching sickness. My whole body was yellow, even to the eyeballs. Obviously it was not food-poisoning, but jaundice which had attacked me—jaundice and dysentery.

After idling around in the calm for several hours a lovely draught blew in from the south-west, and I tacked up to the Mewstone, then dodged out to sea again to avoid a target-towing launch astern of which rocket shells were falling.

Sailing swiftly past the west end of the breakwater I busied myself with preparations for berthing under sail—mooring lines handy, anchor ready to drop, fenders lying on deck.

As the bowsprit swung round to point at the entrance of Millbay Dock, I thought: 'Thank goodness, there will be no reception.' Nobody could know that I was coming in that morning. But who were all those people at the end of the quay?

A voice hailed me:

'Do you want a berth?'

'Yes.'

'Where are you from?'

'Casablanca.'

'Go alongside the pontoon, please.'

'OK.'

I ran along the deck and hurriedly cast off the staysail halyard. Back to the helm. Leaning forward to roll up the jib, I heard a voice shout: 'Look up, please. Look up!'

Surprised, I did so. A battery of cameras faced me. (Yet purposely I had refrained from reporting to a ship the last two days. They must have had a man stationed on the breakwater or the lighthouse.)

I bore away, hardened in the mainsheet and jammed the helm down to round up alongside the pontoon. Two lines ashore, and the long voyage was over.

Somebody passed me an apple, and I rested on the boom, chewing it. I felt listless and weak, after forty-eight hours tending the helm, and was, I'm afraid, very curt with the reporters, giving them the bare minimum of information.

Thank Heavens—the fact that I had jaundice escaped their notice. However, I was mildly amused to read in the next day's papers that I 'looked 'bronzed' and fit!'.

I was too weary to meet visitors and, after moving the boat alongside the topsail schooner *Nellie Bywater* in the inner basin, managed to hide myself ashore in a small hotel. The staff could not have been more kind to me and I shall always remember that wonderful breakfast Mr. Gregory sent up to my bedroom at nine-thirty next morning.

One of the first things I did was to telephone Otilia. It seemed queer to hear her talking in English—it was nearly four months since she had left me in Casablanca. She informed me that a newspaper had offered her a free plane trip to Plymouth, and twenty pounds, if she agreed to have her photograph taken on board *Temptress* with me. She had refused. We had a lot to talk about, but would prefer to meet in our own time.

The doctor advised me not to do any work, but I could not rest until *Temptress* was again at St. Germans Quay from whence she had set off on her 14,000 mile jaunt. So, three days after my arrival, with my old friend Bill Voisey as crew, I left Millbay Dock under power (there was still eighty miles' worth of fuel left), and phut-phutted, helped with the last of the flood, up the tortuous and beautiful river of St. Germans.

The tide was full as we slipped alongside the quay wall. There they were—all my old friends, the local inhabitants, lined up. The sturdy Cornishman, Len Craddock, was in the vanguard.

I felt embarrassed and killed the silence by calling out: 'It's great to be back.' Then, unexpectedly, a steady clapping from the whole throng beat the still air, so still that even the sea-birds had been silent. I felt a lump in my throat and could not reply.

I had received all sorts of receptions during the voyage, the roar of ship's sirens and cheers of thousands of people even, but this was somehow entirely different. It was intimate and personal in a special way.

No, I will never forget that quiet insistent clapping that welcomed me to St. Germans Quay.

MORE DETAILS ABOUT TEMPTRESS

Temptress has two headsails: jib and staysail. The jib is set flying on the bowsprit and, being a working sail, is permanently set—except in untoward conditions when it can be furled from the cockpit by pulling on a line leading to the Wykeham Martin gear which rolls it up round its luff wire rope, made of three-eighths of an inch diameter stainless steel rigging wire.

The working staysail is permanently hanked to the forestay, which is attached to the stemhead. A large reaching staysail of light canvas can be clipped on to this stay and hoisted in place of the working sail in reasonable weather.

The mizzen, although having an area of only 50 square feet, is a useful sail. It helps the boat sail herself and often improves the speed; for instance, under headsails alone the yawl would carry lee helm with a beam wind; but with mizzen set, she needs no helm and sails maybe a knot faster.

All the sails are of hand-sewn flax. Cloths run parallel to the leach, so that the strain comes on the canvas and not on the stitching in the seams.

Her accommodation below is split up into three compartments. Forward is the fo'c'sle, with a folding cot to port, lockers to starboard and a partitioned-off toilet. Amidships is the saloon, with a settee either side, under which are situated the two twenty-five-gallon fresh-water tanks; above are shelves holding my library of seventy books—mostly on small boat voyages. The after compartment has my bunk to port and the galley to starboard, with the engine in between. This engine is of 7 h.p. and can run on gasoline or kerosene, giving the boat four knots. The galley equipment includes two Primus stoves slung in gimbals and a stainless steel sink fed by both fresh and salt water pumps, and emptied by a special non-choke pump.

Apart from the water tanks mentioned above, there are loose emergency containers holding twelve more gallons. Enough fuel is carried to give a range of two hundred and fifty miles. The propeller positioned on the quarter is of a patent feathering type giving almost no resistance when sailing.

MORE ADVICE TO DREAMERS

It is remarkable how ocean sailing in small boats has developed over the last twenty years or so. When Alain Gerbault crossed the Atlantic single-handed in the 'twenties, it caused a great stir and his book was translated into seventeen languages. Nowadays it is commonplace for small yachts to cross oceans; the news, say, of a thirty-footer with a crew of two sailing the Atlantic passes almost unnoticed—and quite right too; but it has all sprung from the daring of the original navigators who proved that, even in a severe gale, a small boat can be safe at sea provided certain rules are obeyed.

In *Single-handed Passage*, after my first crossing of the Atlantic (I have sailed it three times now), in an endeavour to help those who wish to engage in similar enterprises, I included a list of requirements to which, in my opinion, the ideal ocean-sailing yacht should conform. Some of the more alarming incidents recorded in this book appear to confirm the advice as sound, and I cannot do better than repeat and enlarge on it. This Appendix is therefore directed to those who dream of far-off lands, and who wish to reach them by their own efforts—and under sail.

CREW PROBLEMS

The whole success of the project hangs on this knotty question. It is not natural for a small number of men to be cooped up in a small place together, and in adversity tempers are apt to get ragged. Maybe a crew of three is best, then the third can patch up any 'moods' which develop between the other two. On one cruise, one of the two crew locked himself in the fo'c'sle, and they corresponded by pushing notes under the door. It is all a question of temperament. To be single-handed is my choice.

Of course one can marry a crew, but this is somewhat drastic; or one can hopefully wait for a charming stowaway—but you must not expect to be as fortunate as I was.

In any case, it would obviously be prudent to have a boat which can be managed short-handed—one can at least get home if the crew melts away, a not uncommon occurrence.

THE BOAT

It would be easy to specify the 'ideal' ocean cruising boat, but it would cost a fabulous amount of money. The money available governs the type of boat one buys. It must be sound and strongly built—avoid long overhangs, narrow beam and short keels. Experience has led me to believe that the ketch is the best rig for off-sounding work, and I favour two headsails, for easy handling. The length of the boat is governed by the accommodation required. Seaworthiness has nothing to do with size.

ADVICE FOR DEEP SEA

Beware of a large cockpit. One might sail the oceans for a long time before meeting winds of hurricane force—but one should fit one's vessel to be safe in all weathers. The importance of having a small watertight cockpit cannot be stressed too much.

Assume that one day the boat will be totally submerged by a sea.

See that hatches and deck superstructure are such that a submersion would not be permanent. Many dog-houses one sees could be pushed off by one heavy sea breaking aboard.

Hatches can be made watertight by the double-coaming principle.

Have your working sails of stout canvas, but keep the light-weather sails light.

Have your sails cut vertically, the cloths running parallel to the leach, so that the strain will come on the canvas and not on the stitching.

If Bermudian rigged, avoid tracks, which often jam in moments of stress; use mast hoops up to the spreaders, and hank the upper part of the sail to a jackstay stretched from the masthead to the boom gooseneck.

Fit roller reefing. The commercial type with a large diameter gear-wheel is best.

Treat all sails with anti-mildew solution. I always use a preparation which also seems to prevent chafe; Kanvo, made by David Weston Co., 61 Dunlop Street, Glasgow, Scotland.

Don't use continuous lacing on sails, use separate stops.

Have at least sixty fathoms of anchor chain, and mark it.

If equipped with patent anchors, have also at least one heavy fisherman type—best in bad holding ground.

Beware of 'yachty' fittings.

Examine the rudder stock carefully. If it is of wood, have a steel tube slid over it, with steel flats welded to it and extending right across the blade each side. The after side of the tube can be cut away to take the forward edge of the rudder blade.

The rudder should never fail. Nor should the mast.

Have extra stout rigging screws on the shrouds.

Be sure that the auxiliary engine is very reliable and will run in any sea. Pay special attention to the exhaust-pipe layout. A good engine is the best insurance.

Use blocks of ample size. Halyards should not jam if swollen by wet.

Use stainless steel wire rope. It is cheaper in the long run. Use wire rope for halyards wherever possible.

If halyards are of line, splice in a short length of chain at the 'nip.'

Use metal to metal connections. Lashings part.

Fit two non-choke bilge-pumps. One to be worked from the helm, the other from below.

Twin deep sinks are the best for the galley, but install non-choke waste-pumps. Gravity outlets are no use at sea, as the heeling of the vessel can put the sink below water level.

Have at least one stove slung in gimbals, and have the galley aft where the motion is less.

Fit a sea-water pump to the sink, and use it.

The galley should be arranged so that the cook can sit, chocked in, and administer with both hands.

Regular hot food, properly prepared, is a must. Upset stomachs mean upset tempers.

One half-gallon of fresh water per day per man is sufficient at sea. Many soap powders and liquids work well with sea water.

Have a swing table in the saloon.

Have no equipment that cannot be used both at sea and in port.

Wherever the ballast is, see that it stays there.

Assume that one day the boat will turn upside down, so bolt things down.

Don't have electric plugs and sockets on deck; they corrode.

All deck fittings should be bolted down, not screwed.

Have two radios for checking G.M.T.

Have at least one reliable chronometer watch.

Have batteries of ample capacity.

Have an all-round white light on top of the mast, and have it connected to a morse tapper.

For a long trade-wind run, some type of athwartships rig is worth fitting. It saves the mainsail, and many hours at the helm. Twin stay-sails with the sheets led to the tiller appear to be the most popular. But allow for plenty of sail area.

Fit ratlines.

Fit adequate lifelines.

Fit anti-chafing gear.

Keep the deck tight. Canvas is the easiest method. All laid decks seem to leak in the tropics.

If the boat has a bowsprit, use a chain or stainless steel wire-rope bobstay, attached to a fitting secured by fore and aft bolts passing right through the stem.

Don't catch gadgetitis—it is expensive. Strive for simplicity.

Don't buy a boat without a professional survey.

Do all the work on the boat yourself, if possible; if not, ask for a written estimate.

Don't run up bills—they have an alarming tendency to swell if left alone. This has been the end of many a cruise.

Check the compass for deviation; carry a spare, and a hand bearing compass as well.

Fit wide, permanent boom gallows, not the usual flimsy crutch. Worse still are those abominable 'scissors.' A firm gallows is a safety measure, useful to cling on to when taking sights or doing other operations.

Arrange for good dinghy stowage. It is better to lose twelve inches off the bottom of the mainsail than to have a dinghy in the way on the side deck.

Burgees or flags last no time at sea. Fit a wind-sock on the masthead—it can be floodlit at night by the truck light.

Beware of stove gas—it is a danger. So is gasoline.

Design a proper fire prevention system.

Arrange stowage for everything—not forgetting the galley gash bucket, and the bread board, and the flashlight…

A ship is not complete without a vice clamped to a work-bench, a sharp axe handy to the deck, and (outside the tropics) a coal stove below.

Have your water supply divided up into several tanks, in case of leakage.

A boat is never finished. When the hull and gear can be called 'sound' do not delay. Go!

BEAUFORT SCALE OF WIND FORCE

A knot is a speed not a distance
1 knot = 1 nautical mile per hour = 1.152 statute miles per hour

BEAUFORT WIND FORCE	MEAN WIND SPEED IN KNOTS	LIMITS OF WIND SPEED IN KNOTS	DESCRIPTIVE TERMS	SEA CRITERIA
0	0	Less than 1	Calm	Sea like a mirror
1	2	1–3	Light air	Ripples
2	5	4–6	Light breeze	Small wavelets
3	9	7–10	Gentle breeze	Large wavelets Crests begin to break
4	13	11–16	Moderate breeze	Small waves Fairly frequent white horses
5	18	17–21	Fresh breeze	Moderate waves Many white horses
6	24	22–27	Strong breeze	Large waves begin to form
7	30	28–33	Moderate gale	Spindrift begins to lift
8	37	34–40	Fresh gale	Moderately high waves Extensive spindrift
9	44	41–47	Strong gale	High waves Sea begins to roll
10	52	48–55	Whole gale	Very high waves Visibility affected
11	60	56–63	Storm	Storm
12	68	64–71	Hurricane	Difficult to differentiate between wind and sea. Visibility very seriously affected

GLOSSARY

(This is not a technical book. This short glossary may explain some nautical terms unfamiliar to the general reader*.)

Aweather	To windward; one pulls the staysail aweather to heave to
Back	Shift of wind anti-clockwise; to haul a sail to weather
Beam	Vessel's width
Bend on	To fit a sail to a boat
Bermudian	A rig with triangular sails, i.e., no gaff
Bobstay	The stay under the bowsprit
Boom	Spar along the foot of a sail
Bowsprit	Spar outboard of stem
Bumpkin	Spar outboard of stern
Close-hauled	Sailing as close the the wind as possible
Cutter	Fore-and-aft rigged vessel with one mast and two or more foresails
Draft	Depth of vessel under water, measured from waterline to lowest point of keel
Freeboard	Height of topsides
Gaff	Spar along the head of a sail
Gaff jaws or saddle	Fitting at end of gaff which slides up and down mast
Gallows	Raised rest to take boom when sail is lowered
Grains	Barbed and spiked weapon for spearing fish

---

*   With minor clarifications since the first edition—Ed

Gybe	To bring the wind on the other side when running before the wind
Halyard	Rope which hoists a sail
Heave to	Take way off the vessel, usually by backing staysail
Horse	Fitting across deck to take mainsheet block
Jib	Forward headsail, set on bowsprit on *Temptress*
Jury rig	Improvised rig, after damage
Kedge	A second anchor, lighter than the main
Ketch	Two-masted rig with the (shorter) mizzen forward of the steering position
Log	Instrument for measuring mileage run, worked by a rotator towed astern on a line; the ship's log book
Mizzen	Aft mast in a ketch or yawl
Reef	To reduce sail area
Sheet	Line attached to aft corner of a sail, for trimming it
Schooner	Two-masted vessel with (taller) mainmast aft
Shroud	Wire rigging supporting mast
Staysail	Sail set between mainmast and stem
Tack	To bring the wind on the other side by steering through the eye of the wind
Topping lift	Rigging to hold boom up when unsupported by the sail
Topsides	Outside of hull between waterline and deck
Veer	To let out line; shift of wind clockwise
Warp	Heavy mooring line
Yawl	Two-masted vessel with (shorter) mizzen mast abaft the steering position

EDWARD ALLCARD was born in 1914, learned to sail when six years old, and had a lifelong passion for boats and the sea. Following apprenticeship with Clydeside shipbuilders he qualified as a naval architect before World War II. At the time of the *Temptress* voyages he was in his early thirties. In later years he conducted a leisurely circumnavigation, and made a year-long cruise around Patagonia, Tierra del Fuego and Cape Horn, all in *Sea Wanderer*, a boat he restored from a derelict hull acquired in New York for $250. In 1967 Allcard met his future wife Clare, 31 years his junior, and the following year they drove from the UK to Singapore in a Land Rover. In the early 1970s the Allcards, now with young daughter Kate, acquired the 69ft ex-Baltic Trader *Johanne Regina*, built in 1929. Over some thirty years they restored her while sailing between the Caribbean, Europe, the Seychelles and the Far East. In 2006, aged 91, Edward Allcard finally forsook the sea and moved with Clare to a house in the mountains of Andorra, where he died in 2017, aged 102.